SOUPS

SOUPS

Create the perfect start to a meal with
over 400 recipes for fabulous first courses

edited by Felicity Forster

BARNES & NOBLE BOOKS

NEW YORK

This edition published by Barnes & Noble, Inc.,
by arrangement with Anness Publishing Limited

2004 Barnes & Noble Books

M 10 9 8 7 6 5 4 3 2 1

ISBN 0-7607-6245-7

A CIP catalogue record for this book is available from the British Library.

Publisher: Joanna Lorenz; *Managing Editor:* Judith Simons;
Project Editor: Felicity Forster; *Editor:* Linda Doeser.

Recipes: Catherine Atkinson, Alex Barker, Steve Baxter, Michelle Berriedale-Johnson, Angela Boggiano, Janet Brinkworth,
Carla Capalbo, Kit Chan, Jacqueline Clarke, Maxine Clarke, Frances Cleary, Carole Clements, Andi Cleveley, Trish Davies,
Roz Denny, Patrizia Diemling, Matthew Drennan, Sarah Edmonds, Joanne Farrow, Rafi Fernandez, Silvano Franco, Christine France,
Uasako Fukuoka, Sarah Gates, Shirley Gill, Brian Glover, Nicola Graimes, Rosamund Grant, Carole Handslip, Rebekah Hassan,
Deh-Ta Hsiung, Shehzad Husain, Judy Jackson, Peter Jordan, Emi Kasuko, Sheila Kimberley, Lucy Knox, Masaki Ko, Elisabeth Lambert Ortiz,
Ruby Le Bois, Clare Lewis, Sara Lewis, Gilly Love, Leslie Mackley, Norma MacMillan, Kathy Man, Sally Mansfield, Sue Maggs,
Sallie Morris, Annie Nichols, Maggie Pannell, Katherine Richmond, Kieth Richmond, Anne Sheasby, Marlena Spieler, Jenny Stacey,
Liz Trigg, Hilaire Walden, Laura Washburn, Steven Wheeler, Kate Whiteman, Elizabeth Wolf-Cohen, Jenni Wright.
Photographers: Karl Adamson, Edward Allwright, David Armstrong, Steve Baxter, James Duncan, John Freeman, Ian Garlick,
Michelle Garrett, Peter Henley, John Hesseltine, Amanda Heywood, Janine Hosegood, David Jordan, Maria Kelly, Dave King,
Don Last, William Lingwood, Patrick McLeary, Michael Michaels, Thomas Odulate, Juliet Piddington, Peter Reilly, Sam Stowell.
Designer: Michael Morey; *Editorial Reader:* Jonathan Marshall; *Production Controller:* Ben Worley.

Previously published in separate volumes, *Appetizers, Starters and Hors d'Oeuvres, Best-Ever Salads* and *The Soup Bible*.

Printed in China

CONTENTS

INTRODUCTION

Careful thought often goes into planning a main course, especially when we are entertaining, but often less consideration is given to what to serve first. Yet, in some ways, the first course makes or breaks a dinner party or informal supper because it sets the mood, stimulates the appetite and promises that exciting things are to come.

There are a number of aspects to consider. If you are planning a substantial main course, then a light appetizer, such as a mousse or consommé, might be the best choice. On a cold winter's evening, on the other hand, a steaming bowl of chunky vegetable soup or a hot soufflé would fit the bill. Some element of contrast between the different courses makes for an interesting meal, but obviously it would be unsuitable to serve a fiery hot starter that will drown the subtlety of a delicate main course.

You could create a theme for your meal, based on the main ingredients: following a lobster soup or shrimp cocktail with a fish dish, for example, or centered on a specific cuisine, such as French, Thai or Indian.

Also, think about practicalities. If the main course will require last-minute attention, a chilled soup or cold hors d'oeuvre that can be prepared in advance is ideal. Nibbles, canapés and dips that can be served with drinks may make catering for a large number of guests easier.

If you have only an hour between rushing in from work and your guests arriving, choose from the Instant Salads.

There are hundreds of recipes for soups, appetizers and salads in this book, grouped to make these choices as simple as possible. Whatever the occasion, from a sophisticated dinner party (try Warm Salads) to an *al*

fresco lunch (try Chilled Soups), and whatever your tastes, from a family gathering (try Pasta, Noodle and Legume Salads) to a night in with the girls

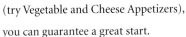

(try Vegetable and Cheese Appetizers), you can guarantee a great start.

Each of the three main sections begins with a guide to ingredients and their preparation. SOUPS includes recipes for those all-important stocks, plus some easy-to-make garnishes. APPETIZERS also offers some decorative flourishes, as well as advice on how to make marinades, oils and dressings. SALADS will guide you through the large variety of vegetables, fruit, herbs, spices, oils and vinegars available.

With all this information and this huge collection of mouthwatering recipes, the world's best soups, appetizers and salads are at your fingertips.

SOUPS

Homemade soup is always a treat and turns any
meal into a special occasion. It is not difficult to
make, and success is guaranteed if you use one of the
fresh stock recipes that begins this section. It is
immensely versatile, and this huge collection of recipes
includes something perfect for all occasions and every
season – hearty winter soups, luxurious seafood bisques,
creamy chowders, filling vegetarian broths and chilled
soups for *al fresco* dining.

Making your own stocks

Fresh stocks are indispensable for creating good homemade soups. They add a depth of flavor that plain water just cannot achieve.

Although many supermarkets now sell tubs of fresh stock, these can work out to be expensive, especially if you need large quantities for your cooking. Making your own is surprisingly easy and much more economical, particularly if you can use leftovers – the chicken carcass from Sunday lunch, for example, or the shells you're left with once you've peeled

shrimp. But homemade stocks aren't just cheaper, they're also tastier and much more nutritious, precisely because they're made with fresh, natural ingredients.

You can, of course, use bouillon cubes or granules, but be sure to check the seasoning, as these tend to be high in salt.

One good idea for keen and regular soup-makers is to freeze homemade stock in plastic freezer bags, or ice-cube trays, so you always have a supply at your disposal whenever you need some.

Frozen stock can be stored in the freezer for up to six months. Make sure that you label each stock carefully for easy identification.

Use the appropriate stock for the soup you are making. Onion soup, for example, is improved with a good beef stock. Be particularly careful to use a vegetable stock if you are catering for vegetarians.

Recipes are given on the following pages for vegetable stock, chicken stock, meat stock, fish stock and basic stocks for Chinese and Japanese soups.

Vegetable Stock

Use this versatile stock as the basis for all vegetarian soups.

INGREDIENTS

Makes 4½ pints/11 cups

2 leeks, coarsely chopped
3 celery sticks, coarsely chopped
1 large onion, unpeeled, chopped
2 pieces fresh root ginger, chopped
1 yellow bell pepper, seeded
    and chopped
1 parsnip, chopped
mushroom stalks
tomato peelings
3 tablespoons light soy sauce
3 bay leaves
bunch of parsley stalks
3 fresh thyme sprigs
1 fresh rosemary sprig
2 teaspoons salt
freshly ground black pepper
6 pints/15 cups water

1 Put all the ingredients into a very large pan. Gradually bring to the boil, then lower the heat and simmer for 30 minutes, stirring occasionally.

2 Leave to cool. Strain, then discard the vegetables. The stock is ready to use. Alternatively, chill or freeze the stock and keep it to use as required.

Fish Stock

*Fish stock is much quicker to make
than poultry or meat stock. Ask your
supermarket for heads, bones and
trimmings from white fish.*

INGREDIENTS

Makes about 1³/4 pints/4 cups

1¹/2 pounds heads, bones and trimmings
  from white fish

1 onion, sliced

2 celery sticks with leaves, chopped

1 carrot, sliced

¹/2 lemon, sliced (optional)

1 bay leaf

a few fresh parsley sprigs

6 black peppercorns

2¹/4 pints/6 cups cold water

¹/4 pint/²/3 cup dry white wine

1 Rinse the fish heads, bones
and trimmings well under
cold running water. Put in a
stockpot with the vegetables and
lemon, if using, the herbs,
peppercorns, water and wine.
Bring to the boil, skimming the
surface frequently, then reduce the
heat and simmer for 25 minutes.

2 Strain the stock without
pressing down on the
ingredients in the sieve. If not
using immediately, leave to cool
and then store in the refrigerator.
Fish stock should be used within
2 days, or it can be frozen for up to
3 months.

Chicken Stock

A good homemade poultry stock is invaluable in the kitchen. If poultry giblets are available, add them (except the livers) with the wings. Once made, chicken stock can be kept in an airtight container in the refrigerator for 3–4 days, or frozen for up to 6 months.

INGREDIENTS

Makes about 4 ½ pints/11 cups

2½–3 pounds chicken or turkey (wings, backs and necks)
2 onions, unpeeled, quartered
1 tablespoon olive oil
7 pints/17½ cups cold water
2 carrots, coarsely chopped
2 celery sticks, with leaves if possible, coarsely chopped
small handful of fresh parsley
few fresh thyme sprigs or
    ¾ teaspoon dried thyme
1 or 2 bay leaves
10 black peppercorns, lightly crushed

1 Combine the poultry wings, backs and necks in a stockpot with the onion quarters and the oil. Cook over a moderate heat, stirring occasionally, until the poultry and onions are lightly and evenly browned.

2 Add the water and stir well to mix in the sediment on the base of the pan. Bring to the boil and skim off the impurities as they rise to the surface of the stock.

3 Add the chopped carrots and celery, fresh parsley, thyme, bay leaf and black peppercorns. Partly cover the stockpot and gently simmer the stock for about 3 hours.

4 Strain the stock through a sieve into a bowl and leave to cool, then chill in the refrigerator for an hour.

5 When cold, carefully remove the layer of fat that will have set on the surface. Store in the refrigerator for 3–4 days or freeze until required.

Meat Stock

The most delicious meat soups rely on a good homemade stock for success. Once it is made, meat stock can be kept in the refrigerator for 4–5 days, or frozen for longer storage (up to 6 months).

Makes about 3¹/₂ pints/9 cups

4 pounds beef bones, such as shank,
    leg, neck and chuck, or veal or
    lamb bones, cut into
    2¹/₂ inch pieces
2 onions, unpeeled, quartered
2 carrots, coarsely chopped
2 celery sticks, with leaves if possible,
    coarsely chopped
2 tomatoes, coarsely chopped
7¹/₂ pints/20 cups water
handful of parsley stalks
a few fresh thyme sprigs or
    ³/₄ teaspoon dried thyme
2 bay leaves
10 black peppercorns, lightly crushed

1 Preheat the oven to 450°F. Put the bones in a roasting pan and roast, turning occasionally, for 30 minutes, until they start to brown.

2 Add the onions, carrots, celery and tomatoes and baste with the fat in the roasting pan. Return the pan to the oven and roast for a further 20–30 minutes, until the bones are well browned. Stir and baste occasionally.

3 Transfer the bones and roasted vegetables to a stockpot. Spoon off the fat from the roasting pan. Add a little of the water to the roasting pan and bring to the boil on the stovetop, stirring well to scrape up any browned sediment. Pour this liquid into the stockpot.

4 Add the remaining water to the pot. Bring just to the boil, skimming frequently to remove all the foam from the surface. Add the parsley, thyme, bay leaves and black peppercorns.

5 Partly cover the stockpot and gently simmer the stock for 4–6 hours. All the bones and vegetables should always be covered with liquid, so top up with a little boiling water from time to time if necessary.

6 Strain the stock through a colander into a bowl, then skim as much fat as possible from the surface. If possible, cool the stock and then chill it in the refrigerator; the fat will rise to the top and set in a layer that can be removed easily.

Stock for Chinese Soups

This stock is an excellent basis for delicate Chinese soups.

Makes 4¹/₂ pints/11 cups

1¹/₂ pounds chicken portions

1¹/₂ pounds pork spareribs

6 pints/16 cups water

3–4 pieces fresh root ginger, unpeeled
   and crushed

3–4 scallions, each tied into a knot

3–4 tablespoons Chinese rice wine

1 Trim off any excess fat from the chicken and spareribs and chop them into large pieces.

2 Place the chicken and sparerib pieces in a large stockpot with the water. Add the ginger and scallion knots.

3 Bring to the boil and, using a sieve, skim off the froth. Reduce the heat and simmer, uncovered, for 2–3 hours.

4 Strain the stock, discarding the chicken, pork, ginger and scallions. Add the rice wine and return to the boil. Simmer for 2–3 minutes. Store the stock in the refrigerator when it has cooled. It will keep for up to 4–5 days. Alternatively, it can be frozen in small containers and thawed when it is required.

Stock for Japanese Soups

Dashi *is the stock that gives the characteristically Japanese flavor to many dishes. Known as* Ichiban-dashi, *it is used for delicately flavored dishes, including soups. Of course instant stock is available in all Japanese supermarkets, either in granule form, in concentrate or even in a tea-bag style. Follow the instructions on the packet.*

INGREDIENTS

Makes about 1¹⁄₃ pints/3¹⁄₂ cups
¹⁄₄ **ounce dried kombu seaweed**
¹⁄₄–¹⁄₂ **ounce katsuobushi**
    (**dried bonito tuna**)

VARIATION
∿

For vegetarian dashi, just omit the katsuobushi and follow the same method.

1 Wipe the kombu seaweed with a damp cloth and cut two slits in it with scissors, so that it flavors the stock effectively.

2 Soak the kombu in 3³⁄₄ cups cold water for 30–60 minutes.

3 Heat the kombu in its soaking water over a moderate heat. Just before the water boils, remove the seaweed. Then add the katsuobushi and bring to the boil over a high heat, then remove the pan from the heat.

4 Leave the stock until all the katsuobushi has sunk to the base of the pan. Line a strainer with paper towels or cheesecloth and place it over a large bowl, then gently strain.

Garnishes

Sometimes, a soup needs something to lift it out of the ordinary, and garnishes are the answer. They are an important finishing touch; they not only look good, but also add an extra dimension to the flavor.
A garnish can be as simple as a sprinkling of chopped parsley, a swirl of cream or some freshly grated cheese. Alternatively, it can be something that requires a little more attention, such as homemade croûtons or sippets. All the garnishes featured here are suitable for vegetarian soups.

DUMPLINGS

These dumplings are easy to make and add an attractive and tasty finishing touch to country soups.

INGREDIENTS

3 ounces/¹⁄₂ cup semolina or flour
1 egg, beaten
3 tablespoons milk or water
generous pinch of salt
1 tablespoon chopped fresh parsley

1 Combine all the ingredients into a soft, elastic dough. Leave to stand, covered with plastic wrap, for 10 minutes.

2 Drop small rounded spoonfuls of this mixture into the soup and cook for 10 minutes, until firm.

CRISPY CROÛTONS

Croûtons add a lovely crunchy texture to creamy soups and are a good way of using up stale bread. Use thinly sliced ciabatta or French bread for delicious results.

INGREDIENTS

bread
good quality, flavorless oil, such as
   sunflower or peanut or, for a fuller
   flavor, extra-virgin olive oil or
   a flavored oil, such as one with
   garlic and herbs or chili

1 Preheat the oven to 400°F. Cut the bread into small cubes and place on a cookie sheet.

2 Brush with your chosen oil, then bake for 15 minutes, until golden and crisp. Leave to cool slightly: they crisp up further as they cool down.

3 Store them in an airtight container for up to a week. Reheat in a warm oven, if you like, before serving.

RIVELS

Rivels are pea-size pieces of dough that swell when cooked in a soup.

INGREDIENTS

1 egg
3–4 ounces/³⁄₄–1 cup flour
¹⁄₂ teaspoon salt
freshly ground black pepper

1 Beat the egg in a bowl. Add the flour, salt and pepper to taste and mix with a wooden spoon. Finish mixing with your fingers, rubbing to blend the egg and flour together to form pea-size pieces.

2 Bring the soup back to the boil. Sprinkle in the pieces of dough, stirring gently.

3 Reduce the heat and simmer for about 6 minutes, until the rivels are slightly swollen and cooked through. Serve the garnished soup immediately.

SWIRLED CREAM

An attractive swirl of cream is the classic finish for many soups, such as a smooth tomato soup and chilled asparagus soup. The garnish gives a delightfully professional finish to your soup, although the technique is simplicity itself.

INGREDIENTS
light cream

1 Transfer the cream into a pitcher. Pour a swirl onto the surface of each bowl of soup.

2 Draw the tip of a fine skewer quickly backward and forward through the cream to create a delicate pattern. Serve the soup immediately.

SIPPETS

Another good way of using up slightly stale bread, sippets are larger than croûtons and have a more intense flavor because of the addition of fresh herbs. Experiment with the herbs according to the flavor of the soup.

INGREDIENTS
3 slices day-old bread
2 ounces/4 tablespoons butter
3 tablespoons finely chopped fresh
    parsley, or cilantro or basil

1 Cut the bread into fingers about 1 inch long.

2 Melt the butter in a large frying pan, toss in the small fingers of bread and cook gently until golden brown.

3 Add the fresh herbs and stir well to combine. Cook for a further minute, stirring constantly. Sprinkle the sippets on top of the soup and serve.

LEEK HAYSTACKS

Stacks of golden leek look good served on a creamy soup, and the crunchy texture contrasts well with the smoothness of the soup.

INGREDIENTS
1 large leek
2 tablespoons all-purpose flour
oil, for deep-frying

1 Slice the leek in half lengthwise and then cut into quarters. Cut into 2-inch lengths and then into very fine strips. Place in a bowl, sprinkle the flour over and toss to coat.

2 Heat the oil to 325°F. Drop small spoonfuls of the floured leeks into the oil and cook for 30–45 seconds, until golden. Drain on paper towels. Repeat with the remaining leeks.

3 Serve the soup with a small stack of leeks piled on top of each bowl.

CHILLED
SOUPS

There can hardly be a more delightful way to start a summer
lunch or *al fresco* dinner than with a refreshing chilled soup.
Make the most of seasonal vegetables, such as tomatoes and
asparagus, or surprise your guests with a chilled fruit soup.
Choose from classic recipes, such as Gazpacho with Avocado
Salsa, or Vichyssoise, or try a more adventurous dish, such as
Sorrel and Spinach Soup or Miami Avocado Soup. All are easy
to make, look fabulous and taste of pure sunshine.

Almond Soup

Unless you are prepared to spend time pounding all the ingredients for this soup by hand, a food processor is essential. Then you'll find that this Spanish soup is simple to make and refreshing to eat on a hot summer's day.

INGREDIENTS

Serves 6

4 ounces fresh white bread

1¼ pints/3 cups water

4 ounces/1 cup blanched almonds

2 garlic cloves, sliced

5 tablespoons olive oil

1½ tablespoons sherry vinegar

salt and ground black pepper

For the garnish

toasted sliced almonds

seedless green and black grapes, halved
    and skinned

1 Break the bread into a bowl and pour ⅔ cup of the water on top. Leave for 5 minutes.

2 Put the almonds and garlic in a blender or food processor and process until finely ground. Blend in the soaked bread.

3 Gradually add the oil until the mixture forms a smooth paste. Add the sherry vinegar, then the remaining cold water and process until smooth.

4 Transfer to a bowl and season with salt and pepper, adding a little more water if the soup is too thick. Chill for at least 2–3 hours. Serve sprinkled with the toasted almonds and grapes.

Tomato and Sweet Pepper Soup

V

This recipe was inspired by the Spanish gazpacho, the difference being that this soup is cooked first, and then chilled.

INGREDIENTS

Serves 4

2 red bell peppers, halved and seeded

3 tablespoons olive oil

1 onion, finely chopped

2 garlic cloves, crushed

1½ pounds ripe well-flavored tomatoes

¼ pint/⅔ cup red wine

1 pint/2½ cups Chicken Stock

salt and ground black pepper

chopped fresh chives, to garnish

For the croûtons

2 slices white bread, crusts removed

4 tablespoons olive oil

1 Cut each red bell pepper half into quarters. Place them skin-side up on a broiler rack and cook until the skins are charred. Transfer to a bowl and cover with a plate or pop into a plastic bag and seal.

2 Heat the oil in a large pan. Add the onion and garlic and cook gently until soft. Meanwhile, remove the skin from the peppers and coarsely chop the flesh. Cut the tomatoes into chunks.

3 Add the peppers and tomatoes to the pan, then cover and cook gently for 10 minutes. Add the wine and cook for a further 5 minutes, then add the stock and salt and pepper and continue to simmer for 20 minutes.

4 To make the croûtons, cut the bread into cubes. Heat the oil in a small frying pan, add the bread and cook until golden. Drain on paper towels and store in an airtight box.

5 Process the soup in a blender or food processor until smooth. Pour into a clean glass or ceramic bowl and leave to cool thoroughly before chilling in the refrigerator for at least 3 hours. When the soup is cold, season to taste with salt and pepper.

6 Serve the soup in bowls, topped with the croûtons and garnished with chopped chives.

Gazpacho with Avocado Salsa

V

Tomatoes, cucumber and peppers form the basis of this classic, chilled soup. Add a spoonful of chunky, fresh avocado salsa and a small sprinkling of croûtons for a delicious summer appetizer. This is quite a substantial soup, so follow with a light main course, such as broiled fish or chicken.

INGREDIENTS

Serves 4–6

2 slices day-old bread

1 pint/2½ cups chilled water

2¼ pounds tomatoes

1 cucumber

1 red bell pepper, seeded and chopped

1 green chile, seeded and chopped

2 garlic cloves, chopped

2 tablespoons extra virgin olive oil

juice of 1 lime and 1 lemon

few drops of Tabasco sauce

salt and ground black pepper

handful of fresh basil, to garnish

8–12 ice cubes, to serve

For the croûtons

2–3 slices day-old bread, crusts removed

1 garlic clove, halved

1–2 tablespoons olive oil

For the avocado salsa

1 ripe avocado

1 teaspoon lemon juice

1 inch piece cucumber, diced

½ red chile, seeded and finely chopped

1 Make the soup first. In a shallow bowl, soak the day-old bread in ⅔ cup water for 5 minutes.

COOK'S TIP

For a superior flavour choose Haas avocados with the rough-textured, almost black skins.

2 Meanwhile, place the tomatoes in a heatproof bowl; cover with boiling water. Leave for 30 seconds, then peel, seed and chop the flesh.

3 Thinly peel the cucumber, cut in half lengthwise and scoop out the seeds with a teaspoon. Discard the seeds and chop the flesh.

4 Place the bread, tomatoes, cucumber, red bell pepper, chile, garlic, oil, citrus juices, Tabasco and scant 2 cups chilled water in a food processor or blender. Blend until mixed but still chunky. Season and chill well.

5 To make the croûtons, rub the slices of bread with the cut surface of the garlic clove. Cut the bread into cubes and place in a plastic bag with the olive oil. Seal the bag and shake until the bread cubes are coated with the oil. Heat a large non-stick frying pan and cook the croûtons over a medium heat until crisp and golden.

6 Just before serving make the avocado salsa. Halve the avocado, remove the pit, then peel and dice the flesh. Toss the avocado in the lemon juice to prevent it from browning, then mix with the cucumber and chile.

7 Ladle the soup into bowls, add the ice cubes and top with a spoonful of avocado salsa. Garnish with the basil and hand around the croûtons separately.

Cucumber and Yogurt Soup with Walnuts

V

This is a particularly refreshing cold soup, using a classic combination of cucumber and yogurt.

INGREDIENTS

Serves 5–6

1 cucumber

4 garlic cloves

½ teaspoon salt

3 ounces/¾ cup walnut pieces

1½ ounces day-old bread, torn
   into pieces

2 tablespoons walnut or sunflower oil

14 fluid ounces/1⅔ cups plain yogurt

4 fluid ounces/½ cup cold water

1–2 teaspoons lemon juice

For the garnish

1½ ounces/scant ½ cup walnuts,
   coarsely chopped

1½ tablespoons olive oil

fresh dill sprigs

3 When the mixture is smooth, gradually add the walnut or sunflower oil and combine well.

COOK'S TIP

If you prefer your soup smooth, process it in a food processor or blender before serving.

4 Transfer the mixture to a large bowl and beat in the yogurt and diced cucumber. Add the cold water and then stir in lemon juice to taste.

5 Pour the soup into chilled soup bowls to serve. Garnish with the chopped walnuts and drizzle with the olive oil. Finally, arrange the sprigs of dill on top and serve immediately.

1 Cut the cucumber in half and peel one half of it. Dice the cucumber flesh and set aside.

2 Using a large mortar and pestle, crush together the garlic and salt well, then add the walnuts and bread.

V

Green Pea and Mint Soup

Perfect partners, peas and mint really capture the flavors of summer.

INGREDIENTS

Serves 4

2 ounces/4 tablespoons butter
4 scallions, chopped
1 pound fresh or frozen peas
1 pint/2½ cups Vegetable Stock
2 large fresh mint sprigs
1 pint/2½ cups milk
pinch of sugar (optional)
salt and ground black pepper
small fresh mint sprigs, to garnish
light cream, to serve

1 Heat the butter in a large pan, add the chopped scallions and cook gently on a low heat until they are softened, but not browned.

2 Stir the peas into the pan, add the stock and mint and bring to the boil. Cover and simmer gently for about 30 minutes if you are using fresh peas (15 minutes if you are using frozen peas), until they are tender. Remove about 3 tablespoons of the peas, and set aside to use for a garnish.

3 Pour the soup into a food processor or blender, add the milk and process until smooth. Season to taste, adding a pinch of sugar, if you like. Leave to cool, then chill lightly in the refrigerator.

4 Pour the soup into bowls. Swirl a little cream into each, then garnish with the mint and the reserved peas.

Watercress and Orange Soup

*This is a healthy and refreshing
soup, which is just as good served
either hot or chilled.*

INGREDIENTS

Serves 4

1 large onion, chopped

1 tablespoon olive oil

2 bunches or bags of watercress

grated rind and juice of 1 large orange

1 pint/2½ cups Vegetable Stock

¼ pint/⅔ cup light cream

2 teaspoons cornstarch

salt and ground black pepper

a little thick cream or plain yogurt,
    to garnish

4 orange wedges, to serve

1 Soften the onion in the oil in a
large pan. Add the watercress,
unchopped, to the onion. Cover
and cook for about 5 minutes,
until the watercress is wilted.

2 Add the orange rind and juice
and the stock to the watercress
mixture. Bring to the boil, then
lower the heat, cover and simmer
for 10–15 minutes.

3 Process the soup thoroughly
in a blender or food processor
and sieve if you want to increase
the smoothness of the finished
soup. Blend the cream with the
cornstarch until no lumps remain,
then add to the soup. Season to
taste with salt and pepper.

4 Bring the soup gently back
to the boil, stirring constantly
until just slightly thickened. Check
the seasoning.

5 Leave the soup to cool, then
chill in the refrigerator. Serve
the soup with a swirl of cream or
yogurt, and a wedge of orange to
squeeze in at the last moment.

6 If serving the soup hot, garnish
with a swirl of cream or yogurt
and orange wedges, as above, and
serve immediately.

V

Hungarian Sour Cherry Soup

Particularly popular in summer, this fruit soup is typical of Hungarian cooking. The recipe makes good use of plump, sour cherries. Fruit soups are thickened with flour, and a touch of salt is added to help bring out the flavor of the cold soup.

INGREDIENTS

Serves 4

1 tablespoon all-purpose flour

4 fluid ounces/½ cup sour cream

a generous pinch of salt

1 teaspoon superfine sugar

8 ounces/1½ cups fresh sour or morello
  cherries, pitted

1½ pints/3¾ cups water

2 ounces/¼ cup granulated sugar

1 In a bowl, blend the flour with the sour cream until completely smooth, then add the salt and superfine sugar.

2 Put the cherries in a pan with the water and granulated sugar. Gently poach for about 10 minutes.

3 Remove from the heat and set aside 2 tablespoons of the cooking liquid as a garnish. Stir another 2 tablespoons of the cherry liquid into the flour and sour cream mixture, then pour this onto the cherries.

4 Return to the heat. Bring to the boil, then simmer gently for 5–6 minutes.

5 Remove from the heat, cover with plastic wrap and leave to cool. Add extra salt if necessary. Serve with the reserved cooking liquid swirled in.

Sorrel and Spinach Soup

This is an excellent Russian summer soup. If sorrel is unavailable, use double the amount of spinach instead and add a dash of lemon juice to the soup just before serving.

INGREDIENTS

Serves 4

1 ounce/2 tablespoons butter
8 ounces sorrel, washed and
    stalks removed
8 ounces young spinach, washed and
    stalks removed
1 ounce fresh horseradish, grated
1¼ pints/3 cups *kvas* or hard cider
1 pickled cucumber, finely chopped
2 tablespoons chopped fresh dill
8 ounces cooked fish, such as pike,
    perch or salmon, skinned
    and boned
salt and ground black pepper
fresh dill sprig, to garnish

1 Melt the butter in a large pan. Add the sorrel and spinach leaves and fresh horseradish. Cover and cook gently for 3–4 minutes, or until the leaves are wilted.

2 Spoon into a food processor and process to a fine purée. Ladle into a tureen or bowl and stir in the *kvas* or hard cider, cucumber and dill.

3 Chop the fish into bitesize pieces. Add to the soup, then season with plenty of salt and pepper. Chill for at least 3 hours before serving, garnished with a sprig of dill.

Melon and Basil Soup

This is a deliciously refreshing, fruit soup, just right for a hot day.

INGREDIENTS

Serves 4–6

2 Charentais or canteloupe melons
3 ounces/scant ½ cup superfine sugar
6 fluid ounces/¾ cup water
finely grated rind and juice of 1 lime
3 tablespoons shredded fresh basil, plus
    whole leaves, to garnish

2 Place the sugar, water and lime rind in a small pan over a low heat. Stir until dissolved, bring to the boil and simmer gently for 2–3 minutes. Remove from the heat and leave to cool slightly. Pour half the mixture into the blender or food processor with the melon flesh. Blend until smooth, adding the remaining syrup and lime juice to taste.

3 Pour the mixture into a bowl, stir in the shredded basil and chill in the refrigerator. Serve garnished with whole basil leaves and the reserved melon balls.

1 Cut the melons in half across the middle. Scrape out the seeds and discard. Using a melon baller, scoop out 20–24 balls and set aside for the garnish. Scoop out the remaining flesh and place in a blender or food processor.

COOK'S TIP

Add the syrup in two stages, as the amount of sugar needed will depend on the sweetness of the melon.

Asparagus Soup

*This delicate, pale green soup,
garnished with a swirl of cream or
yogurt, is as pretty as it is delicious.*

INGREDIENTS

Serves 6

2 pounds fresh asparagus

4 tablespoons butter or olive oil

6 ounces/1½ cups sliced leeks
   or scallions

3 tablespoons all-purpose flour

2½ pints/6¼ cups Chicken Stock or water

120ml/4 fluid ounces/½ cup light cream
   or plain yogurt

1 tablespoon chopped fresh tarragon
   or chervil

salt and ground black pepper

3 Heat the butter or oil in a
heavy pan. Add the sliced leeks
or scallions and cook over a low
heat, stirring occasionally, for
5–8 minutes, until softened, but
not browned. Stir in the chopped
asparagus stalks, cover and cook
for a further 6–8 minutes, until the
stalks are tender.

4 Add the flour and stir well to
blend. Cook for 3–4 minutes,
uncovered, stirring occasionally.

5 Add the stock or water. Bring
to the boil, stirring frequently,
then reduce the heat and simmer
for 30 minutes. Season to taste
with salt and pepper.

6 Process the soup in a food
processor or food mill. If
necessary, strain it to remove any
coarse fibers. Stir in the asparagus
tips, most of the cream or yogurt,
and the herbs. Cool, then chill
well. Stir before serving and check
the seasoning. Garnish each bowl
with a swirl of cream or yogurt.

1 Cut the top 2½ inches off the
asparagus spears and blanch
in boiling water for 5–6 minutes,
until just tender. Drain thoroughly.
Cut each tip into two or three
pieces and set aside.

2 Trim the ends of the stalks,
removing any brown or
woody parts. Chop the stalks into
½-inch pieces.

Shrimp and Cucumber Soup

If you've never served a chilled soup before, this is the one to try first. Delicious and light, it's the perfect way to celebrate summer.

INGREDIENTS

Serves 4

1 ounce/2 tablespoons butter

2 shallots, finely chopped

2 garlic cloves, crushed

1 cucumber, peeled, seeded and diced

½ pint/1¼ cups milk

8 ounces cooked peeled shrimp

1 tablespoon each finely chopped fresh
   mint, dill, chives and chervil

½ pint/1¼ cups whipping cream

salt and ground white pepper

For the garnish

2 tablespoons crème fraîche or sour
   cream (optional)

4 large, cooked shrimp, peeled with
   tails intact

fresh chives and dill

1 Melt the butter in a pan and cook the shallots and garlic over a low heat until soft but not colored. Add the cucumber and cook the vegetables gently, stirring frequently, until tender.

2 Stir in the milk, bring almost to the boil, then lower the heat and simmer for 5 minutes. Tip the soup into a blender or food processor and process until very smooth. Season to taste with salt and ground white pepper.

3 Pour the soup into a bowl and set aside to cool. When cool, stir in the shrimp, chopped herbs and the whipping cream. Cover, transfer to the refrigerator and chill for at least 2 hours.

4 To serve, ladle the soup into four chilled individual bowls and top each portion with a spoonful of crème fraîche or sour cream, if using. Place a large shrimp over the edge of each soup bowl. Garnish with the chives and dill.

COOK'S TIP

For a change try fresh or canned crab meat, or cooked, flaked salmon fillet.

Vichyssoise

This classic leek and potato soup was created by a French chef who named it after his home town.

INGREDIENTS

Serves four

1 ounce/2 tablespoons butter
1 tablespoon vegetable oil
1 small onion, chopped
3 leeks, sliced
2 medium floury potatoes, diced
1 pint/2½ cups Vegetable Stock
½ pint/1¼ cups milk
3 tablespoons light cream
a little extra milk (optional)
salt and ground black pepper
4 tablespoons plain yogurt and
    fried chopped leeks, to serve

1 Heat the butter and oil in a large, heavy pan and add the onion, leeks and potatoes. Cover and cook over a medium heat for 15 minutes, stirring occasionally.

2 Stir in the stock and milk. Bring to the boil, reduce the heat, cover the pan again and simmer for 10 minutes.

3 Ladle the vegetables and liquid into a blender or a food processor, in batches, and process to a smooth purée. Return to the pan, stir in the cream and season to taste with salt and pepper.

4 Leave the soup to cool, and then chill for 3–4 hours. You may need to add a little extra milk to thin down the soup, as it will thicken slightly as it cools.

5 Ladle the soup into soup bowls and serve topped with a spoonful of natural yogurt and a sprinkling of fried leeks.

Summer Tomato Soup

The success of this soup depends on having ripe, full-flavored tomatoes, such as the oval plum variety, so make it when the tomato season is at its peak.

INGREDIENTS

Serves 4

1 tablespoon olive oil

1 large onion, chopped

1 carrot, chopped

2¼ pounds ripe tomatoes, quartered

2 garlic cloves, chopped

5 fresh thyme sprigs, or
    ¼ teaspoon dried thyme

4–5 fresh marjoram sprigs, or
    ¼ teaspoon dried marjoram

1 bay leaf

3 tablespoons crème fraîche, sour cream
    or plain yogurt, plus a little extra
    to garnish

salt and ground black pepper

1 Heat the olive oil in a large, preferably stainless-steel pan or flameproof casserole.

2 Add the onion and carrot and cook for 3–4 minutes.

3 Add the quartered tomatoes, chopped garlic and herbs. Reduce the heat and simmer, covered, for 30 minutes.

4 Discard the bay leaf and pass the soup through a food mill or press through a sieve. Leave to cool, then chill in the refrigerator.

VARIATION
∼

If you like, you can use oregano instead of marjoram, and parsley instead of thyme.

Miami Avocado Soup

Avocados are combined with lemon juice, dry sherry and an optional dash of hot pepper sauce, to make this subtle chilled soup.

INGREDIENTS

Serves 4

2 large or 3 medium-ripe avocados

1 tablespoon fresh lemon juice

3 ounces/³⁄₄ cup coarsely chopped
    peeled cucumber

2 tablespoons dry sherry

1 ounce/¹⁄₄ cup coarsely chopped
    scallions, with some of the
    green stems

16 fluid ounces/2 cups Chicken Stock

1 teaspoon salt

hot pepper sauce (optional)

plain yogurt, to garnish

1 Cut the avocados in half, remove the pits and peel. Coarsely chop the flesh and place in a food processor or blender. Add the lemon juice and process until very smooth.

2 Add the cucumber, sherry and most of the scallions, reserving a few for the garnish. Process again until smooth.

3 In a large bowl, combine the avocado mixture with the chicken stock. Whisk until well blended. Season with the salt and a few drops of hot pepper sauce, if you like. Cover the bowl with plastic wrap and place in the refrigerator to chill thoroughly.

4 To serve, fill four individual bowls with the soup. Place a spoonful of yogurt in the centre of each bowl and swirl with a spoon. Finally, sprinkle with the reserved chopped scallions.

CREAMED VEGETABLE SOUPS

~

Whether family favorites, such as Cream of Tomato Soup,
luxurious dinner-party dishes, such as Wild Mushroom Soup,
or international classics, such as Fresh Pea Soup St Germain,
there is something wonderfully comforting and welcoming
about creamy soups. Some are warming and filling, others
are delicate and elegant, still more are rich and colorful.
Whatever the season or occasion, a creamed vegetable
soup is the perfect choice for whetting the appetite and
stimulating the taste buds.

Italian Tomato Soup

This is the perfect soup for late summer when fresh tomatoes are at their most flavorsome.

Serves 4–6

1 tablespoon olive oil

1 ounce/2 tablespoons butter

1 onion, finely chopped

2 pounds ripe Italian plum tomatoes, coarsely chopped

1 garlic clove, coarsely chopped

1¼ pints/3 cups Chicken Stock

4 fluid ounces/½ cup dry white wine

2 tablespoons sun-dried tomato paste

2 tablespoons shredded fresh basil, plus a few whole leaves to garnish

¼ pint/⅔ cup heavy cream

salt and ground black pepper

1 Heat the oil and butter in a large pan until foaming. Add the onion and cook gently, stirring frequently, for about 5 minutes, until softened, but not brown.

2 Stir in the chopped tomatoes and garlic, then add the stock, white wine and sun-dried tomato paste and season with salt and pepper to taste.

3 Bring to the boil, then lower the heat, half-cover the pan and simmer gently for 20 minutes, stirring occasionally to stop the tomatoes from sticking to the base of the pan.

4 Process the soup with the shredded basil in a food processor or blender, then press through a sieve into a clean pan.

5 Add the heavy cream and heat through, stirring. Do not allow the soup to approach boiling point. Check the consistency and add more stock, if necessary. Adjust the seasoning to taste, pour the soup into heated bowls and garnish with whole basil leaves. Serve immediately.

Wild Mushroom Soup

*Wild mushrooms are expensive.
Dried porcini have an intense flavor,
so only a small quantity is needed.
Meat stock may seem odd in a
vegetable soup, but it helps to
strengthen the earthy flavor.*

INGREDIENTS

Serves 4

1 ounce/2 cups dried porcini
   mushrooms
8 fluid ounces/1 cup warm water
2 tablespoons olive oil
¹/₂ ounces/1 tablespoons butter
2 leeks, thinly sliced
2 shallots, coarsely chopped
1 garlic clove, coarsely chopped
8 ounces fresh wild mushrooms
2 pints/5 cups Meat Stock
¹/₂ teaspoon dried thyme
¹/₄ pint/²/₃ cup heavy cream
salt and ground black pepper
fresh thyme sprigs, to garnish

3 Chop or thinly slice the fresh
mushrooms and add to the
pan. Stir over a medium heat for
a few minutes until they begin
to soften. Pour in the meat stock
and bring to the boil. Add the
porcini, soaking liquid, dried
thyme and salt and pepper. Lower
the heat, half-cover the pan and
simmer gently for 30 minutes,
stirring occasionally.

4 Pour about three-quarters
of the soup into a blender or
food processor and process until
smooth. Return to the soup
remaining in the pan, stir in the
heavy cream and heat through.
Check the consistency, adding
more stock or water if the soup
is too thick. Taste and adjust the
seasoning. Serve hot, garnished
with sprigs of fresh thyme.

1 Put the dried porcini in a
bowl, add the warm water and
leave to soak for 20–30 minutes.
Lift out of the liquid and squeeze
to remove as much of the soaking
liquid as possible. Strain all the
liquid and reserve to use later.
Finely chop the porcini.

2 Heat the oil and butter in a
large pan until foaming. Add
the leeks, shallots and garlic and
cook gently for about 5 minutes,
stirring frequently, until softened
but not colored.

Cream of Tomato Soup

Tomato soup is an old favorite. This version is made special by the addition of fresh herbs and cream.

Serves 4

1 ounce/2 tablespoons butter or margarine

1 onion, chopped

2 pounds tomatoes, peeled and quartered

2 carrots, chopped

³/₄ pint/scant 2 cups Chicken Stock

2 tablespoons chopped fresh parsley

¹/₂ teaspoon fresh thyme leaves, plus extra
    to garnish

5 tablespoons whipping cream

salt and ground black pepper

1 Melt the butter or margarine in a large, heavy pan. Add the onion and cook for 5 minutes, until softened.

2 Stir in the tomato quarters, carrots, chicken stock, parsley and thyme. Bring to the boil, then reduce the heat to low, cover the pan and simmer gently for about 15–20 minutes, until all the vegetables are tender.

3 Purée the soup in a vegetable mill until it is smooth. Alternatively, process the soup in a blender or food processor, then press through a sieve. Return the puréed soup to the pan.

4 Stir in the cream and reheat gently. Season the soup to taste with salt and ground black pepper. Ladle into warmed soup bowls and serve immediately while piping hot, garnished with fresh thyme leaves.

COOK'S TIP

Meaty and flavorful, Italian plum tomatoes are the best choice for this soup.

Cream of Scallion Soup

The oniony flavor of this soup is
surprisingly delicate.

INGREDIENTS

Serves 4–6

1 ounce/2 tablespoons butter

1 small onion, chopped

bunch of scallions, chopped

8 ounces potatoes, chopped

1 pint/2½ cups Vegetable Stock

12 fluid ounces/1½ cups
    light cream

2 tablespoons lemon juice

salt and freshly ground white pepper

chopped fresh chives, to garnish

1 Melt the butter in a pan and
add the onion and scallions.
Cover and cook over very low heat
for about 10 minutes or until soft.

2 Add the potatoes and the
stock. Bring to the boil, then
cover again and simmer over a
moderately low heat for about
30 minutes. Cool slightly.

3 Process the soup in a blender
or food processor.

4 If serving the soup hot, pour
it back into the pan. Add the
cream and season to taste with salt
and pepper. Reheat the soup
gently, stirring occasionally. Add
the lemon juice.

5 If serving the soup cold, pour
it into a bowl. Stir in the
cream and lemon juice and season
with salt and pepper. Cover the
bowl and chill for at least 1 hour.

6 Sprinkle with the chopped
fresh chives before serving,
whether hot or chilled.

Butternut Squash Bisque

This is a fragrant, creamy and delicately flavored soup.

INGREDIENTS

Serves 4

1 ounce/2 tablespoons butter
   or margarine
2 small onions, finely chopped
1 pound butternut squash, peeled, seeded
   and cubed
2 pints/5 cups Chicken Stock
8 ounces potatoes, cubed
1 teaspoon paprika
4 fluid ounces/½ cup whipping
   cream (optional)
1½ tablespoons chopped fresh chives,
   plus a few whole chives to garnish
salt and ground black pepper

1 Melt the butter or margarine in a large pan. Add the onions and cook over a medium heat for about 5 minutes, until soft.

2 Add the squash, chicken stock, potatoes and paprika. Bring to the boil. Reduce the heat to low, cover the pan and simmer gently for about 35 minutes until all the vegetables are soft.

3 Pour the soup into a food processor or blender and process until smooth. Return the soup to the pan and stir in the cream, if using. Season with salt and pepper. Reheat gently.

4 Stir in the chopped chives just before serving. Garnish each serving with a few whole chives and serve hot.

Cream of Red Pepper Soup

Broiling bell peppers gives them a sweet, smoky flavor, which is delicious in salads or, as here, in a velvety soup with a secret flavoring of rosemary to add aromatic depth. The soup is equally good served hot or chilled, as you prefer.

INGREDIENTS

Serves 4

4 red bell peppers
1 ounce/2 tablespoons butter
1 onion, finely chopped
1 fresh rosemary sprig
2 pints/5 cups Chicken or
    Vegetable Stock
3 tablespoons tomato paste
4 fluid ounces/¹/₂ cup heavy cream
paprika
salt and ground black pepper

1 Preheat the broiler. Put the peppers in the broiler pan under the broiler and turn them regularly until the skins have blackened all around. Put them into plastic bags, sealing them closed. Leave them for 20 minutes.

2 Peel the blackened skin off the peppers. If possible, avoid rinsing them under running water, as they will lose some of their natural oil and hence their flavor.

3 Halve the peppers, removing the seeds, stalks and pith, then coarsely chop the flesh.

4 Melt the butter in a deep pan. Add the onion and rosemary and cook gently over a low heat for about 5 minutes. Remove the rosemary and discard.

5 Add the peppers and stock to the onion, bring to the boil and simmer for 15 minutes. Stir in the tomato paste, then process or sieve the soup to a smooth purée.

6 Stir in half the cream and season with paprika, salt, if necessary, and pepper.

7 Serve the soup hot or chilled, with the remaining cream swirled delicately on top. Speckle the cream very lightly with a pinch of paprika.

Corn Soup

This is a simple to make, yet very flavorsome soup. It is sometimes made with sour cream and cream cheese. Poblano chiles may be added, but these are rather difficult to locate outside Mexico. However, you may be able to find them canned in some of the larger supermarkets and delicatessens.

INGREDIENTS

Serves 4

2 tablespoons corn oil

1 onion, finely chopped

1 red bell pepper, seeded and chopped

1 pound corn kernels, thawed
    if frozen

1¼ pints/3 cups Chicken Stock

8 fluid ounces/1 cup light cream

salt and ground black pepper

½ red bell pepper, seeded and finely
    diced, to garnish

1 Heat the oil in a frying pan and sauté the onion and red bell pepper for about 5 minutes, until soft. Add the corn and sauté for 2 minutes.

2 Carefully tip the contents of the pan into a food processor or blender. Process until the mixture is smooth, scraping down the sides and adding a little of the stock, if necessary.

3 Put the mixture into a clean pan and stir in the stock. Season to taste with salt and pepper, bring to a simmer and cook for 5 minutes.

4 Gently stir in the cream. Serve the soup hot or chilled, with the diced red bell pepper sprinkled over. If serving hot, reheat gently after adding the cream, but do not allow the soup to boil.

Zucchini Soup

This soup is so simple – in terms of ingredients and preparation. It would provide an elegant start to a dinner party.

INGREDIENTS

Serves 4

1 ounce/2 tablespoons butter

1 onion, finely chopped

1 pound young zucchini, trimmed
    and chopped

1¼ pints/3 cups Chicken Stock

4 fluid ounces/½ cup light cream, plus
    extra to serve

salt and ground black pepper

1 Melt the butter in a pan and sauté the onion until it is soft. Add the zucchini and cook, stirring, for 1–2 minutes.

2 Add the chicken stock. Bring to the boil over a moderate heat and then simmer for about 5 minutes, or until the zucchini are just tender.

COOK'S TIP

Always use the smallest zucchini available, as these have the best flavor.

3 Strain the stock into a clean pan, saving the vegetable solids in the sieve. Purée the solids in the food processor and add to the pan. Season the soup to taste with salt and pepper.

4 Stir the cream into the soup and heat through very gently without allowing it to boil. Ladle into bowls and serve hot with a little extra cream swirled in.

V

Yogurt Soup

Some communities in India add sugar to this soup.

INGREDIENTS

Serves 4–6

¾ pint/scant 2 cups plain
    yogurt, beaten
1 ounce/¼ cup besan
½ teaspoon chili powder
½ teaspoon turmeric salt, to taste
2–3 fresh green chiles, finely chopped
4 tablespoons vegetable oil
1 dried red chile
1 teaspoon cumin seeds
3–4 curry leaves
3 garlic cloves, crushed
2-inch piece fresh root
    ginger, crushed
2 tablespoons chopped fresh cilantro

1 Mix together the yogurt, flour, chili powder and turmeric salt and pass through a strainer into a pan. Add the fresh green chiles and cook gently for about 10 minutes, stirring occasionally. Be careful not to let the soup boil over.

2 Heat the oil in a frying pan and fry the dried chile, cumin seeds, curry leaves, garlic and ginger until the dried chile turns black. Stir in 1 tablespoon of the chopped fresh cilantro.

3 Pour the spices over the yogurt soup, cover the pan and leave to rest for 5 minutes. Mix well and gently reheat for 5 minutes more. Serve hot, garnished with the remaining chopped cilantro.

Broccoli and Stilton Soup

*This is a really easy, but rich soup –
choose something simple to follow,
such as plainly roasted or broiled
meat, poultry or fish.*

INGREDIENTS

Serves 4

12 ounces broccoli

1 ounce/2 tablespoons butter

1 onion, chopped

1 leek, white part only, chopped

1 small potato, cut into chunks

1 pint/2½ cups hot Chicken Stock

½ pint/1¼ cups milk

3 tablespoons heavy cream

4 ounces Stilton cheese, rind
    removed, crumbled

salt and ground black pepper

1 Break the broccoli into florets,
discarding any tough stems.
Set aside two small florets to
garnish the finished dish.

2 Melt the butter in a large pan
and cook the onion and leek
until soft, but not colored. Add the
broccoli and potato, then pour in
the stock. Cover and simmer for
15–20 minutes, until the vegetables
are tender.

3 Cool slightly then pour into a
blender or food processor and
process until smooth. Strain the
mixture through a sieve back into
the rinsed pan.

4 Add the milk and heavy cream
to the pan. Season to taste
with salt and ground black pepper.
Reheat gently. At the last minute,
add the cheese, stirring until it just
melts. Do not boil.

5 Meanwhile, blanch the
reserved broccoli florets and
cut them vertically into thin slices.
Ladle the soup into warmed bowls
and garnish with the sliced
broccoli and a generous grinding
of black pepper.

Fresh Pea Soup St Germain

This soup takes its name from a suburb of Paris where peas used to be cultivated in market gardens.

INGREDIENTS

Serves 2–3

small pat of butter

2–3 shallots, finely chopped

14 ounces/3 cups shelled fresh peas
   (from about 3 pounds garden peas)

16 fluid ounces/2¼ cups water

3–4 tablespoons whipping
   cream (optional)

salt and ground black pepper

Crispy Croûtons, to garnish

3 When the peas are tender, ladle them into a blender or food processor with a little of the cooking liquid and process until completely smooth.

4 Strain the soup into the pan or casserole, stir in the cream, if using, and heat through without boiling. Add the seasoning and serve hot, garnished with croûtons.

COOK'S TIP

If fresh peas are not available, use frozen peas, but thaw and rinse them before use.

1 Melt the butter in a heavy pan or flameproof casserole. Add the shallots and cook over a medium heat for about 3 minutes, stirring occasionally.

2 Add the peas and water and season with salt and a little pepper. Cover and simmer for about 12 minutes for young peas and up to 18 minutes for large or older peas, stirring occasionally.

Green Bean and Parmesan Soup

V

Fresh green beans and Parmesan cheese make a simple, but delicious combination of flavors.

INGREDIENTS

Serves 4

1 ounce/2 tablespoons butter or
   margarine
8 ounces green beans, trimmed
1 garlic clove, crushed
³/₄ pint/scant 2 cups Vegetable Stock
1¹/₂ ounces/¹/₂ cup grated
   Parmesan cheese
2 fluid ounces/¹/₄ cup light cream
salt and ground black pepper
2 tablespoons chopped fresh parsley,
   to garnish

1 Melt the butter or margarine in a medium pan. Add the green beans and garlic and cook for 2–3 minutes over a medium heat, stirring frequently.

2 Stir in the stock and season with salt and pepper. Bring to the boil, then simmer, uncovered, for 10–15 minutes, until the beans are tender.

3 Pour the soup into a blender or food processor and process until smooth. Alternatively, purée the soup in a food mill. Return to the pan and reheat gently.

4 Stir in the Parmesan and cream. Sprinkle with the parsley and serve immediately.

Cream of Spinach Soup

*This is a deliciously creamy soup
that you will make again and again.*

INGREDIENTS

Serves 4

1 ounce/2 tablespoons butter
1 small onion, chopped
1½ pounds fresh spinach, chopped
2 pints/5 cups Vegetable Stock
8 fluid ounces/1 cup coconut cream
freshly grated nutmeg
½ pint/1¼ cups whipping cream
salt and ground black pepper
long strips of fresh chives,
  to garnish

3 Return the mixture to the pan and add the remaining stock and the coconut cream, with salt, pepper and nutmeg to taste. Simmer for 15 minutes to thicken.

4 Add the whipping cream to the pan, stir well and heat through, but do not allow the soup to boil. Serve immediately, garnished with long strips of chives.

1 Melt the butter in a pan over a moderate heat and sauté the onion, stirring occasionally, for a few minutes until soft. Add the spinach, cover the pan and cook gently for 10 minutes, until the spinach has wilted and reduced.

2 Pour the spinach mixture into a blender or food processor and add a little of the stock. Blend until smooth.

Cream of Leek and Potato Soup

Serve this flavorful soup with a spoonful of crème fraîche or sour cream and sprinkle with a few chopped fresh chives – or, for special occasions, with a spoonful of caviar.

INGREDIENTS

Serves 6–8

1 pound potatoes, peeled and cubed

2½ pints/6¼ cups Chicken Stock

12 ounces leeks, trimmed

¼ pint/⅔ cup crème fraîche or
    sour cream

salt and ground black pepper

3 tablespoons chopped fresh chives,
    to garnish

1 Put the cubed potatoes and chicken stock in a pan or flameproof casserole and bring to the boil over a medium heat. Reduce the heat and simmer for 15–20 minutes.

2 Make a slit along the length of each leek and rinse well under cold running water to wash away any soil. Slice thinly.

VARIATION

∾

To make a low-fat soup, use low-fat farmer's cheese instead of cream.

---

3 When the potatoes are barely tender, stir in the leeks. Taste, then season with salt and ground black pepper and simmer, stirring occasionally, for 10–15 minutes, until both the vegetables are soft. If the soup is too thick, thin it down with a little more chicken stock or water.

4 Process the soup in a blender or food processor. If you prefer a very smooth soup, pass it through a food mill or press through a coarse sieve. Stir in most of the cream and reheat gently, but do not boil. Ladle into warmed bowls and garnish with a swirl of cream and the chopped chives.

V

Cauliflower Cream Soup

This delicately flavored, thick winter soup is enriched at the last minute with chopped hard-boiled eggs and crème fraîche.

INGREDIENTS

Serves 4

1 cauliflower, cut into large pieces
1 large onion, coarsely chopped
1 large garlic clove, chopped
bouquet garni
1 teaspoon ground coriander
pinch of mustard powder
1½ pints/3¾ cups Vegetable Stock
1–2 teaspoons cornstarch
¼ pint/⅔ cup milk
3 tablespoons crème fraîche
2 eggs, hard-boiled and coarsely
    chopped
1 tablespoon chopped fresh cilantro
salt and ground black pepper

1 Place the cauliflower in a large pan with the onion, garlic, bouquet garni, coriander, mustard, salt and pepper and stock. Simmer for 10–15 minutes. Cool slightly.

2 Remove and discard the garlic and the bouquet garni. Process the cauliflower and onion with some of the cooking liquid in a food processor. Return to the pan along with the rest of the liquid.

3 Blend the cornstarch with a little of the milk to make a smooth paste, then add to the soup with the rest of the milk.

4 Return to the heat and cook until thickened, stirring constantly. Season to taste and, just before serving, turn off the heat and blend in the crème fraîche. Stir in the chopped egg and cilantro and serve immediately.

Creamy Zucchini and Dolcelatte Soup

The beauty of this soup is its delicate color, its creamy texture and its subtle taste. If you prefer a more pronounced cheese flavor, use Gorgonzola instead of Dolcelatte.

INGREDIENTS

Serves 4–6

2 tablespoons olive oil

¹/₂ ounce/1 tablespoon butter

1 onion, coarsely chopped

2 pounds zucchini, sliced

1 teaspoon dried oregano

about 1 pint/2¹/₂ cups Vegetable Stock

4 ounces Dolcelatte cheese, diced

¹/₂ pint/1¹/₄ cups light cream

salt and ground black pepper

To garnish

fresh oregano sprigs

extra Dolcelatte cheese

1 Heat the olive oil and butter in a large, heavy pan until foaming. Add the onion and cook over a medium heat for about 5 minutes, stirring frequently, until softened, but not brown.

2 Add the zucchini and oregano and season with salt and pepper to taste. Cook over a medium heat for 10 minutes, stirring frequently.

3 Pour in the stock and bring to the boil, stirring frequently. Lower the heat, half-cover the pan and simmer gently, stirring occasionally, for about 30 minutes. Stir in the diced Dolcelatte until it is melted.

4 Process the soup in a blender or food processor until smooth, then press through a sieve into a clean pan.

5 Add two-thirds of the cream and stir over a low heat until hot, but not boiling. Check the consistency and add more stock if the soup is too thick. Taste and adjust the seasoning if necessary.

6 Pour into heated bowls. Swirl in the remaining cream, garnish with fresh oregano and extra Dolcelatte cheese, crumbled, and serve immediately.

Tomato and Blue Cheese Soup

The concentrated flavor of roasted tomatoes strikes a great balance with strong blue cheese.

INGREDIENTS

Serves 4

3 pounds ripe tomatoes, peeled, quartered
   and seeded
2 garlic cloves, crushed
2 tablespoons vegetable oil or butter
1 leek, chopped
1 carrot, chopped
2 pints/5 cups Chicken Stock
4 ounces blue cheese, crumbled
3 tablespoons whipping cream
several large fresh basil leaves or 1–2 fresh
   parsley sprigs, plus extra to garnish
salt and ground black pepper
6 ounces bacon, cooked and crumbled,
   to garnish

1 Preheat the oven to 400°F. Spread the tomatoes in a shallow ovenproof dish. Sprinkle with the garlic and some salt and pepper. Place in the oven and bake for 35 minutes.

2 Heat the oil or butter in a large pan. Add the leek and carrot and season lightly with salt and pepper. Cook over a low heat, stirring frequently, for about 10 minutes, until softened.

3 Stir in the stock and baked tomatoes. Bring to the boil, then lower the heat, cover and simmer for about 20 minutes.

4 Add the blue cheese, cream and basil or parsley. Transfer to a food processor or blender and process until smooth (work in batches if necessary). Taste and adjust the seasoning.

5 Reheat the soup, but do not boil. Serve garnished with bacon and a sprig of fresh herbs.

Cream of Mushroom Soup

V

A good mushroom soup makes the most of the subtle and sometimes rather elusive flavor of mushrooms. White mushrooms are used here for their pale color; cremini or, better still, portabello mushrooms give a fuller flavour, but turn the soup brown.

INGREDIENTS

Serves 4

10 ounces white mushrooms

1 tablespoon sunflower oil

1½ ounces/3 tablespoons butter

1 small onion, finely chopped

1 tablespoon all-purpose flour

¾ pint/scant 2 cups Vegetable Stock

¾ pint/scant 2 cups milk

pinch of dried basil

2–3 tablespoons light cream

salt and ground black pepper

fresh basil leaves, to garnish

1 Separate the mushroom caps from the stalks. Finely slice the caps and finely chop the stalks.

2 Heat the oil and half the butter in a large, heavy pan and add the onion, mushroom stalks and about three-quarters of the sliced mushroom caps. Cook for about 1–2 minutes, stirring frequently, then cover and sweat over a gentle heat for 6–7 minutes, stirring occasionally.

3 Stir in the flour and cook for about 1 minute. Gradually add the stock and milk, stirring to make a smooth, thin sauce. Add the dried basil, and season to taste. Bring to the boil and simmer, partly covered, for 15 minutes.

4 Cool the soup slightly and then pour into a blender or food processor and process until smooth. Melt the remaining butter in a frying pan, add the remaining mushroom caps and cook gently for 3–4 minutes, until they are just tender.

5 Pour the soup into a clean pan and stir in the fried mushrooms. Heat until very hot. Taste and adjust the seasoning if necessary. Stir in the cream and heat briefly, but do not boil. Serve sprinkled with fresh basil leaves.

Cream of Avocado Soup

*Avocados make wonderful soup –
pretty, delicious and refreshing.*

INGREDIENTS

Serves 4

2 large ripe avocados

1¾ pints/4 cups Chicken Stock

8 fluid ounces/1 cup light cream

fresh cilantro leaves

salt and freshly ground white pepper

1 Cut the avocados in half,
remove the pits and scoop out
the flesh. Mash the flesh, then put
it into a sieve and press it through
the sieve with a wooden spoon
into a warm soup tureen.

2 Heat the chicken stock with
the cream in a pan. When the
mixture is hot, but not boiling,
whisk it into the puréed avocado in
the tureen.

3 Season to taste with salt and
pepper. Serve immediately,
sprinkled with the fresh cilantro.
The soup may be served chilled,
if you like.

Carrot Soup with Ginger

The zing of fresh ginger is an ideal complement to the sweetness of cooked carrots.

INGREDIENTS

Serves 6

1 ounces2 tablespoons butter
   or margarine
1 onion, chopped
1 celery stick, chopped
1 potato, chopped
1½ pounds carrots, chopped
2 teaspoons crushed fresh root ginger
2 pints/5 cups Chicken Stock
7 tablespoons whipping cream
good pinch of freshly grated nutmeg
salt and ground black pepper

1 Put the butter or margarine, onion and celery into a large pan and cook for about 5 minutes, until softened.

2 Stir in the potato, carrots, ginger and stock. Bring to the boil. Reduce the heat to low, cover and simmer for about 20 minutes.

3 Pour the soup into a blender or food processor and process until it is smooth. Alternatively, use a vegetable mill to purée the soup. Return the soup to the pan. Stir in the cream and nutmeg and season with salt and pepper to taste. Reheat gently, but do not allow the soup to boil. Serve hot.

Pear and Watercress Soup

The sweetness of the pears in the soup is complemented beautifully by Stilton croûtons. Their flavors make them natural partners.

INGREDIENTS

Serves 6

1 bunch of watercress
4 pears, peeled, cored
    and sliced
1½ pints/3¾ cups Chicken Stock
4 fluid ounces/½ cup heavy cream
juice of 1 lime
salt and ground black pepper

For the croûtons
1 ounce/2 tablespoons butter
1 tablespoon olive oil
7 ounces/3 cups cubed stale bread
5 ounces/1 cup chopped Stilton cheese

1 Reserve about a third of the watercress leaves. Place the rest of the leaves and stalks in a pan with the pears, stock and a little seasoning. Simmer for about 15–20 minutes. Reserving some watercress leaves for garnishing, add the rest of the leaves and then process in a blender or food processor until smooth.

2 Put the mixture into a bowl and stir in the cream and the lime juice to mix the flavors thoroughly. Taste and adjust the seasoning if necessary. Pour all the soup back into a clean pan and reheat, stirring gently until warmed through.

3 To make the croûtons, melt the butter with the olive oil in a frying pan and cook the bread cubes until golden brown. Drain on paper towels. Put the cheese on top and heat under a hot broiler until bubbling. Reheat the soup and pour into bowls. Divide the croûtons and the reserved watercress leaves among the bowls and serve immediately.

Spiced Parsnip Soup

This pale, creamy textured soup is given a special touch with an aromatic, spiced garlic and coriander garnish.

INGREDIENTS

Serves 4–6

1½ ounces/3 tablespoons butter
1 onion, chopped
1½ pounds parsnips, diced
1 teaspoon ground coriander
½ teaspoon ground cumin
½ teaspoon ground turmeric
¼ teaspoon chili powder
2 pints/5 cups Chicken Stock
¼ pint/⅔ cup light cream
1 tablespoon sunflower oil
1 garlic clove, cut into julienne strips
2 teaspoons yellow mustard seeds
salt and ground black pepper

1 Melt the butter in a large pan, add the onion and parsnips and cook gently for 3 minutes.

2 Stir in the spices and cook for 1 minute more. Add the stock, season with salt and pepper to taste and bring to the boil.

3 Reduce the heat, cover and simmer for about 45 minutes, until the parsnips are tender. Cool slightly, then process the soup in a blender or food processor until smooth. Return the soup to the pan, add the cream and heat through gently over a low heat, but do not allow to boil.

4 Heat the oil in a small pan, add the julienne strips of garlic and the yellow mustard seeds and fry quickly until the garlic is beginning to brown and the mustard seeds start to pop and splutter. Remove from the heat.

5 Ladle the soup into warmed soup bowls and pour a little of the hot spice mixture over each one. Serve immediately.

Mushroom and Bread Soup with Parsley

Thickened with bread, this rich mushroom soup will warm you up on cold winter days.

INGREDIENTS

Serves 8

3 ounces/6 tablespoons sweet butter
2 pounds portabello mushrooms, sliced
2 onions, coarsely chopped
1 pint/2½ cups milk
8 slices white bread
4 tablespoons chopped fresh parsley
½ pint/1¼ cups heavy cream
salt and ground black pepper

1 Melt the butter in a large pan, add the sliced mushrooms and chopped onions and cook over a low heat, stirring occasionally, for about 10 minutes, until soft but not browned. Add the milk.

2 Tear the bread into pieces, drop them into the soup and leave to soak for 15 minutes. Purée the soup and return it to the pan. Add 3 tablespoons of the parsley, the cream and seasoning. Reheat, without boiling. Serve garnished with the remaining parsley.

Baby Carrot and Fennel Soup

Sweet tender carrots find their moment of glory in this delicately spiced soup. Fennel provides a very subtle aniseed flavor that does not overpower the carrots.

INGREDIENTS

Serves 4

2 ounces/4 tablespoons butter

1 small bunch of scallions, chopped

5 ounces fennel bulb, chopped

1 celery stick, chopped

1 pound baby carrots, grated

½ teaspoon ground cumin

5 ounces new potatoes, diced

2 pints/5 cups Chicken Stock

4 tablespoons heavy cream

salt and ground black pepper

4 tablespoons chopped fresh parsley, to garnish

1 Melt the butter in a large pan and add the scallions, fennel, celery, carrots and cumin. Cover and cook over a low heat, stirring occasionally, for about 5 minutes, or until soft.

2 Add the diced potatoes and chicken stock, and gently simmer the mixture for a further 10 minutes.

3 Purée the soup in the pan with a hand-held blender. Stir in the cream and season to taste. Serve in individual soup bowls and garnish with chopped parsley.

COOK'S TIP

For convenience, you can freeze the soup in portions before adding the cream, seasoning and parsley.

Squash Soup with Horseradish Cream

The combination of cream, curry powder and horseradish makes a wonderful topping for this beautiful golden soup.

INGREDIENTS

Serves 6

1 butternut squash
1 cooking apple
1 ounce/2 tablespoons butter
1 onion, finely chopped
1–2 teaspoons curry powder, plus extra to garnish
1½ pints/3¾ cups Vegetable Stock
1 teaspoon chopped fresh sage
¼ pint/⅔ cup apple juice
salt and ground black pepper
lime shreds, to garnish (optional)

For the horseradish cream
4 tablespoons heavy cream
2 teaspoons horseradish sauce
½ teaspoon curry powder

1 Peel the squash, remove the seeds and chop the flesh. Peel, core and chop the apple.

2 Melt the butter in a large pan. Add the onion and cook over a medium heat, stirring frequently, for 5 minutes, until soft. Stir in the curry powder. Cook to bring out the flavor, stirring constantly, for 2 minutes.

3 Add the stock, squash, apple and sage. Bring to the boil, lower the heat, cover and simmer for 20 minutes, until the squash and apple are soft.

4 Meanwhile, make the horseradish cream. Whip the cream in a bowl until stiff, then stir in the horseradish sauce and curry powder. Cover and chill until required.

5 Process the soup in a blender or food processor. Return to the clean pan and add the apple juice, with salt and pepper to taste. Reheat gently, without boiling.

6 Serve the soup in warm bowls, topped with a spoonful of horseradish cream and a dusting of curry powder. Garnish with a few lime shreds, if you like.

Simple Cream of Onion Soup

This wonderfully soothing soup has a deep, buttery flavor that is complemented by crisp croûtons or chopped chives, sprinkled over just before serving.

Serves 4

4 ounces/½ cup sweet butter
2¼ pounds yellow onions, sliced
1 fresh bay leaf
7 tablespoons dry white vermouth
1¼ pints/4 cups Chicken or
    Vegetable stock
¼ pint/⅔ cup heavy cream
a little lemon juice (optional)
salt and ground black pepper
croûtons or chopped fresh chives,
    to garnish

1 Melt 3 ounces/6 tablespoons of the butter in a large, heavy pan. Set about 7 ounces of the onions aside and add the rest to the pan with the bay leaf. Stir to coat in the butter, then cover and cook very gently for about 30 minutes. The onions should be very soft and tender, but not browned.

2 Add the vermouth, increase the heat and boil rapidly until the liquid has evaporated. Add the stock, 1 teaspoon salt and pepper to taste. Bring to the boil, lower the heat and simmer for 5 minutes, then remove from the heat.

3 Leave the soup to cool, then remove and discard the bay leaf. Process the soup in a blender or food processor. Return the soup to the rinsed pan.

4 Meanwhile, melt the rest of the butter in another pan and add the remaining onions, cover and cook gently until soft but not browned. Uncover and continue to cook gently until the onions are golden yellow.

5 Add the cream to the soup and reheat it gently until hot, but do not allow it to boil. Taste and adjust the seasoning, adding a little lemon juice if you like. Add the buttery onions and stir for 1–2 minutes, then ladle the soup into bowls. Sprinkle with croûtons or chopped chives and serve.

COOK'S TIP
〜

Adding the second batch of onions gives texture and a lovely buttery flavor to this soup. Make sure the onions do not brown.

Jerusalem Artichoke Soup

Topped with saffron cream, this soup is wonderful on a chilly day.

INGREDIENTS

Serves 4

2 ounces/4 tablespoons butter
1 onion, chopped
1 pound Jerusalem artichokes, peeled and
    cut into chunks
1½ pints/3¾ cups Chicken Stock
¼ pint/⅔ cup milk
¼ pint/⅔ cup heavy cream
good pinch of saffron powder
salt and ground black pepper
chopped fresh chives, to garnish

1 Melt the butter in a large, heavy pan and cook the onion for 5–8 minutes, until soft but not browned, stirring occasionally.

2 Add the Jerusalem artichokes to the pan and stir until coated in the butter. Cover and cook gently for 10–15 minutes, but do not allow the artichokes to brown.

3 Pour in the chicken stock and milk, then cover and simmer for 15 minutes. Cool slightly, then process in a blender or food processor until smooth.

4 Strain the soup back into the pan. Add half the cream, season to taste with salt and pepper and reheat gently. Lightly whip the remaining cream and the saffron powder. Ladle the soup into warmed soup bowls and put a spoonful of saffron cream in the centre of each. Sprinkle the chopped chives over the top and serve immediately.

Watercress Soup

A delicious and nutritious soup, which should be served with crusty bread.

INGREDIENTS

Serves 4

1 tablespoon sunflower oil
½ ounce/1 tablespoons butter
1 onion, finely chopped
1 potato, diced
about 6 ounces watercress
14 fluid ounces/1⅔ cups Vegetable Stock
14 fluid ounces/1⅔ cups milk
lemon juice, to taste
salt and ground black pepper
sour cream, to serve

1 Heat the oil and butter in a large, heavy pan and cook the onion over a gentle heat for about 5 minutes, until soft but not browned. Add the potato, cook gently for 2–3 minutes and then cover and sweat for 5 minutes over a gentle heat, stirring occasionally.

2 Strip the watercress leaves from the stalks and coarsely chop the stalks.

COOK'S TIP

Provided you leave out the sour cream, this is a low-calorie soup.

---

3 Add the stock and milk to the pan, stir in the chopped watercress stalks and season to taste with salt and pepper. Bring to the boil, lower the heat and simmer gently, partially covered, for 10–12 minutes, until the potatoes are tender. Add all but a few of the watercress leaves and simmer for 2 minutes more.

4 Process the soup in a blender or food processor, then pour into a clean pan and heat gently with the reserved watercress leaves.

5 Taste the soup when hot, add a little lemon juice and adjust the seasoning.

6 Pour the soup into warmed soup bowls and garnish with a little sour cream in the center just before serving.

SMOOTH
VEGETABLE
SOUPS

~

What better way to persuade fussy children – or awkward
adults – to eat a healthy portion of vegetables than to make
any of these superb soups? Their deliciously smooth texture
makes them very moreish and there are recipes to suit all
tastes, from hot and spicy to rich and warming and from
exotic and sweet to substantial and earthy. All you need is this
marvelous collection of recipes and a blender, food processor
or food mill and you will truly be a "whizz" in the kitchen.

Fresh Mushroom Soup with Tarragon

This is a light mushroom soup,
subtly flavored with tarragon.

INGREDIENTS

Serves 6

½ ounce/1 tablespoons butter
  or margarine
4 shallots, finely chopped
1 pound/6 cups cremini mushrooms,
  finely chopped
½ pint/1¼ cups Vegetable Stock
½ pint/ 1¼ cups low-fat milk
1–2 tablespoons chopped fresh tarragon
2 tablespoons dry sherry (optional)
salt and ground black pepper
fresh tarragon sprigs, to garnish

1 Melt the butter or margarine in a large pan, add the shallots and cook over a low heat, stirring occasionally, for 5 minutes. Add the mushrooms and cook gently for 3 minutes, stirring. Add the stock and milk.

2 Bring to the boil, then cover and simmer gently for about 20 minutes, until the vegetables are soft. Stir in the chopped tarragon and season to taste with salt and pepper.

3 Leave the soup to cool slightly, then process in a blender or food processor, in batches if necessary, until smooth. Return the soup to the rinsed pan and reheat gently.

4 Stir in the sherry, if using, then ladle into soup bowls and serve garnished with tarragon.

VARIATION

If you like, use a mixture
of wild and white
mushrooms instead.

Italian Pea and Basil Soup

V

*Plenty of crusty country bread is
a must with this fresh-tasting soup.*

INGREDIENTS

Serves 4

5 tablespoons olive oil

2 large onions, chopped

1 celery stick, chopped

1 carrot, chopped

1 garlic clove, finely chopped

14 ounces/3½ cups frozen baby peas

1½ pints/3¾ cups Vegetable Stock

1 ounce/1 cup fresh basil leaves, coarsely
   torn, plus extra to garnish

salt and ground black pepper

freshly grated Parmesan cheese,
   to serve

1 Heat the oil in a large pan and
add the onions, celery, carrot
and garlic. Cover the pan and
cook over a low heat, stirring
occasionally, for 45 minutes, or
until the vegetables are soft.

2 Add the baby peas and stock
to the pan and bring to the
boil. Reduce the heat, add the basil
and season to taste, then simmer
gently for 10 minutes.

3 Spoon the soup into a food
processor or blender and
process until smooth. Ladle into
warm bowls, sprinkle with grated
Parmesan, garnish with basil and
serve immediately.

COOK'S TIP
~

It is always sensible to leave the
hot soup to cool slightly before
processing to avoid steam being
forced out of the top and, possibly,
scalding you severely.

VARIATION
~

Use mint or a mixture of parsley,
mint and chives in place of the basil.

V

Broccoli and Almond Soup

The creaminess of the toasted almonds combines perfectly with the slightly bitter taste of the broccoli.

INGREDIENTS

Serves 4–6

2 ounces/¹/₂ cup ground almonds

1¹/₂ pounds broccoli

1¹/₂ pints/3³/₄ cups Vegetable Stock
   or water

¹/₂ pint/1¹/₄ cups skimmed milk

salt and ground black pepper

1 Preheat the oven to 350°F. Spread the ground almonds evenly on a baking sheet and toast in the oven for about 10 minutes, until golden. Reserve one quarter of the toasted almonds and set aside to garnish the finished dish.

2 Cut the broccoli into small florets and steam for about 6–7 minutes, until tender.

3 Place the remaining toasted almonds, broccoli, vegetable stock or water and milk in a blender or food processor and process until smooth. Season with salt and pepper to taste.

4 Pour the soup into a pan and heat gently. Ladle into warm bowls and serve sprinkled with the reserved toasted almonds.

Fresh Tomato Soup

Intensely flavored sun-ripened tomatoes need little embellishment in this fresh-tasting soup. If you shop at the supermarket, choose the juiciest looking ones and add the amount of sugar and vinegar necessary, depending on their natural sweetness. On a hot day, this Italian soup is also delicious chilled.

INGREDIENTS

Serves 6

3–3½ pounds ripe tomatoes

14 fluid ounces/1⅔ cups Chicken or
    Vegetable Stock

3 tablespoons sun-dried tomato paste

2–3 tablespoons balsamic vinegar

2–3 teaspoons superfine sugar

small handful of basil leaves

salt and ground black pepper

basil leaves, to garnish

toasted cheese croûtes and crème fraîche,
    to serve

1 Plunge the tomatoes into boiling water for 30 seconds, then refresh in cold water. Peel off the skins and quarter the tomatoes

2 Put the tomatoes in a large pan and pour over the chicken or vegetable stock. Bring just to the boil, reduce the heat, cover and simmer the mixture gently for about 10 minutes, until the tomatoes are pulpy.

3 Stir in the sun-dried tomato paste, vinegar, sugar and basil. Season with salt and pepper, then cook gently, stirring, for 2 minutes. Process the soup in a blender or food processor, then return to the pan and reheat gently. Serve in warm bowls topped with one or two toasted cheese croûtes and a spoonful of crème fraîche and garnished with basil leaves.

Nettle Soup

This country-style soup is a tasty variation of the classic Irish potato soup. Use wild nettles if you can find them, or a washed head of butterhead lettuce if you prefer.

INGREDIENTS

Serves 4

4 ounces/½ cup butter
1 pound onions, sliced
1 pound potatoes, cut into chunks
1¼ pints/3 cups Chicken Stock
1 ounce/1 cup nettle leaves
small bunch of fresh chives, chopped
salt and ground black pepper
heavy cream, to serve

2 Wearing latex gloves, remove the nettle leaves from their stalks. Wash the leaves under cold running water, then dry on paper towels. Add to the pan and cook for a further 5 minutes.

3 Ladle the soup into a blender or food processor and process until smooth. Return to a clean pan and season well. Stir in the chives and serve with a swirl of cream and a sprinkling of pepper.

1 Melt the butter in a large pan and add the sliced onions. Cover and cook over a low heat for about 5 minutes, until softened. Add the potatoes to the pan with the chicken stock. Cover and cook for 25 minutes.

COOK'S TIP

If you like, cut the vegetables finely and leave the cooked soup chunky rather than puréeing it.

Mushroom, Celery and Garlic Soup

This is a robust soup in which the dominant flavor of mushrooms is enhanced with garlic, while celery introduces a contrasting note.

INGREDIENTS

Serves 4

12 ounces/4½ cups chopped mushrooms

4 celery sticks, chopped

3 garlic cloves

3 tablespoons dry sherry or white wine

1¼ pints/3 cups Chicken Stock

2 tablespoons Worcestershire sauce

1 teaspoon freshly grated nutmeg

salt and ground black pepper

celery leaves, to garnish

1 Place the mushrooms, celery and garlic in a pan and stir in the sherry or wine. Cover and cook over a low heat for 30–40 minutes, until the vegetables are tender.

2 Add half the stock and process in a food processor or blender until smooth. Return to the pan and add the remaining stock, the Worcestershire sauce and nutmeg.

3 Bring to the boil and season to taste with salt and pepper. Ladle the soup into warm bowls and serve immediately, garnished with celery leaves.

Cauliflower and Walnut Soup

This classic combination works well in a number of dishes – especially this richly flavored soup.

INGREDIENTS

Serves 4

1 cauliflower

1 onion, coarsely chopped

¾ pint/scant 2 cups Chicken or
Vegetable Stock

¾ pint/scant 2 cups skimmed milk

3 tablespoons walnut pieces

salt and ground black pepper

paprika and chopped walnuts, to garnish

1 Trim the cauliflower of outer leaves and break into small florets. Place the cauliflower, onion and stock in a large pan.

2 Bring to the boil, cover and simmer for about 15 minutes, until soft. Add the milk and walnut pieces, then process in a blender or food processor until smooth.

3 Season the soup to taste with salt and pepper, then reheat and bring to the boil. Serve hot sprinkled with a dusting of paprika and chopped walnuts.

VARIATION
◡
If you like, you can make this soup using broccoli instead of cauliflower.

Pumpkin Soup

V

The sweet flavor of pumpkin is excellent in soups, teaming well with other savory ingredients, such as onions and potatoes, to make a warm and comforting dish. For added flavor, try roasting the pumpkin chunks instead before adding to the soup with the stock.

INGREDIENTS

Serves 4–6

1 tablespoon sunflower oil

1 ounce/2 tablespoons butter

1 large onion, sliced

1½ pounds pumpkin, cut into
    large chunks

1 pound potatoes, sliced

1 pint/2½ cups Vegetable Stock

good pinch of freshly grated nutmeg

1 teaspoon chopped fresh tarragon

1 pint/2½ cups milk

1–2 teaspoons lemon juice

salt and ground black pepper

1 Heat the oil and butter in a heavy pan, add the onion and cook for 4–5 minutes over a gentle heat until soft but not browned, stirring frequently.

2 Add the pumpkin and sliced potatoes, stir well, then cover and sweat over a low heat for about 10 minutes, until the vegetables are almost tender, stirring occasionally to stop them sticking to the pan.

3 Stir in the vegetable stock, grated nutmeg and tarragon and season to taste with salt and pepper. Bring to the boil, then lower the heat and simmer for about 10 minutes, until the vegetables are completely tender.

4 Leave the soup to cool slightly, then pour into a blender or food processor and process until smooth. Pour back into a clean pan and add the milk. Heat gently and then taste, adding lemon juice to taste and extra seasoning, if necessary. Serve piping hot.

Moroccan Vegetable Soup

*Creamy parsnip and pumpkin give
this soup a wonderfully rich texture.*

INGREDIENTS

Serves 4

1 tablespoon olive or sunflower oil

½ ounce/1 tablespoons butter

1 onion, chopped

8 ounces carrots, chopped

8 ounces parsnips, chopped

8 ounces pumpkin

about 1½ pints/3¾ cups Vegetable or
  Chicken Stock

lemon juice, to taste

salt and ground black pepper

For the garnish

1½ teaspoons olive oil

½ garlic clove, finely chopped

3 tablespoons chopped fresh parsley and
  cilantro, mixed

good pinch of paprika

1 Heat the oil and butter in a
large pan and cook the onion,
stirring occasionally, for about
3 minutes, until softened. Add the
carrots and parsnips, stir well,
cover and cook over a gentle heat
for a further 5 minutes.

2 Cut the pumpkin into chunks,
discarding the skin and pith,
and stir into the pan. Cover and
cook for a further 5 minutes, then
add the stock and seasoning and
gradually bring to the boil. Cover
and simmer for 35–40 minutes,
until the vegetables are tender.

3 Leave the soup to cool slightly,
then pour in to a blender or
food processor and process until
smooth, adding a little extra water
or stock if the soup seems too
thick. Pour back into a clean pan
and reheat gently.

4 To make the garnish, heat the
oil in a small pan and cook the
garlic and herbs for 1–2 minutes.
Add the paprika and stir well.

5 Taste and adjust the seasoning
of the soup and stir in lemon
juice to taste. Pour into bowls and
spoon a little of the prepared
garnish on top, which should then
be swirled carefully into the soup.

Sweet Potato and Parsnip Soup

V

The natural sweetness of these two popular root vegetables comes through very strongly in this delicious soup.

INGREDIENTS

Serves 6

1 tablespoon sunflower oil

1 large leek, sliced

2 celery sticks, chopped

1 pound sweet potatoes, diced

8 ounces parsnips, diced

1½ pints/3¾ cups Vegetable Stock

salt and ground black pepper

For the garnish

1 tablespoon chopped fresh parsley

roasted strips of sweet potatoes
   and parsnips

1 Heat the oil in a large pan and add the leek, celery, sweet potatoes and parsnips. Cook gently for about 5 minutes, stirring to prevent them from browning or sticking to the pan.

2 Stir in the vegetable stock and bring to the boil, then cover and simmer over a low heat for about 25 minutes, or until the vegetables are tender, stirring occasionally. Season to taste with salt and pepper . Remove the pan from the heat and leave the soup to cool slightly.

3 Process the soup in a blender or food processor until smooth, then return it to the pan and reheat gently. Ladle into warmed soup bowls to serve and sprinkle over the chopped fresh parsley and roasted strips of sweet potatoes and parsnips.

Sweet Potato and Red Pepper Soup

As colorful as it is good to eat, this soup is a sure winner, whether for a midweek family supper or a dinner-party first course.

INGREDIENTS

Serves 6

2 red bell peppers (about 8 ounces) seeded and cubed

1¼ pounds sweet potatoes, cubed

1 onion, coarsely chopped

2 large garlic cloves, coarsely chopped

½ pint/1¼ cups dry white wine

2 pints/5 cups Vegetable Stock

Tabasco sauce, to taste

salt and ground black pepper

fresh country bread, to serve

1 Dice a small quantity of red pepper for the garnish and set aside. Put the rest into a pan with the sweet potato, onion, garlic, wine and vegetable stock. Bring to the boil, lower the heat and simmer for 30 minutes, or until all the vegetables are quite soft. Leave to cool slightly.

2 Transfer the mixture to a blender or food processor and process until smooth. Season to taste with salt, pepper and a generous dash of Tabasco.

3 Leave to cool to serve warm or at room temperature. Garnish with the reserved diced red pepper.

Roasted Garlic and Butternut Squash Soup

This is a wonderful, richly flavored dish. A spoonful of the hot and spicy tomato salsa gives bite to the sweet-tasting squash and garlic soup.

INGREDIENTS

Serves 4–5

2 garlic bulbs, outer papery skin removed
5 tablespoons olive oil
a few fresh thyme sprigs
1 large butternut squash, halved and seeded
2 onions, chopped
1 teaspoon ground coriander
2 pints/5 cups Vegetable or
    Chicken Stock
30–45ml/2–3 tbsp chopped fresh oregano
salt and ground black pepper

For the salsa

4 large ripe tomatoes, halved and seeded
1 red bell pepper, halved and seeded
1 large fresh red chile, halved and seeded
2–3 tablespoons extra virgin olive oil
1 tablespoon balsamic vinegar
pinch of superfine sugar

1 Preheat the oven to 425°F. Place the garlic bulbs on a piece of foil and pour over half the olive oil. Add the thyme sprigs, then fold the foil around the garlic bulbs to enclose them completely. Place the foil parcel on a baking sheet with the butternut squash and brush the squash with 1 tablespoon of the remaining olive oil. Add the tomatoes, red bell pepper and fresh chile for the salsa.

2 Roast the vegetables for 25 minutes, then remove the tomatoes, pepper and chile. Reduce the temperature to 375°F and cook the squash and garlic for 20–25 minutes more, or until the squash is tender.

3 Heat the remaining oil in a large, heavy pan and cook the onions and ground coriander gently for about 10 minutes, or until softened.

4 Peel the pepper and chile and process in a food processor or blender with the tomatoes and 30ml/2 tbsp olive oil. Stir in the vinegar and seasoning to taste, adding a pinch of superfine sugar, if necessary. Add the remaining oil if you think the salsa needs it.

5 Squeeze the roasted garlic out of its papery skin into the onions and scoop the squash out of its skin, adding it to the pan. Add the stock, 1 teaspoon salt and plenty of black pepper. Bring to the boil and simmer gently for 10 minutes.

6 Stir in half the oregano and cool the soup slightly, then process it in a blender or food processor. Alternatively, press the soup through a fine sieve.

7 Reheat the soup without allowing it to boil, then taste for seasoning before ladling it into warmed bowls. Top each with a spoonful of salsa and sprinkle over the remaining chopped oregano. Serve immediately.

Cauliflower, Cannellini and Fennel Seed Soup

The sweet, anise-liquorice flavor of the fennel seeds gives a delicious edge to this hearty soup.

INGREDIENTS

Serves 4–6

1 tablespoon olive oil

1 garlic clove, crushed

1 onion, chopped

2 teaspoons fennel seeds

1 cauliflower, cut into small florets

2 x 14-ounce cans small cannellini beans, drained and rinsed

2 pints/5 cups Vegetable Stock or water

salt and ground black pepper

chopped fresh parsley, to garnish

toasted slices of French bread, to serve

3 Bring the mixture to the boil. Reduce the heat and simmer for about 10 minutes, or until the cauliflower is tender. Leave to cool slightly, then pour the soup into a blender or food processor and process until smooth.

4 Stir in the remaining beans and season to taste with salt and pepper. Reheat the soup and pour into warmed bowls. Sprinkle with chopped parsley and serve immediately with toasted slices of French bread.

1 Heat the olive oil. Add the garlic, onion and fennel seeds and cook gently for 5 minutes, or until the onion is softened.

2 Add the cauliflower florets, half the beans and the vegetable stock or water.

Root Vegetable Soup

V

Simmer a selection of popular and inexpensive winter root vegetables together for a wonderfully warming and satisfying soup.

INGREDIENTS

Serves 6

3 carrots, chopped

1 large potato, chopped

1 large parsnip, chopped

1 large turnip or small rutabaga, chopped

1 onion, chopped

2 tablespoons sunflower oil

1 ounce/2 tablespoons butter

2¹/₂ pints/6¹/₄ cups Vegetable Stock
   or water

1 piece fresh root ginger, grated

¹/₂ pint/1¹/₄ cups milk

3 tablespoons crème fraîche
   or mascarpone

2 tablespoons chopped fresh dill

1 tablespoon lemon juice

salt and ground black pepper

fresh dill sprigs, to garnish

1 Put the carrots, potato, parsnip, turnip or rutabaga and onion into a large pan with the oil and butter. Cook lightly, then cover and sweat the vegetables over a low heat for 15 minutes, shaking the pan occasionally.

2 Pour in the stock or water, bring to the boil and season to taste with salt and pepper. Cover and simmer for 20 minutes until the vegetables are soft.

3 Strain the vegetables, reserving the cooking liquid, add the ginger and vegetables to a food processor or blender and process until smooth. Return the puréed mixture and cooking liquid to the pan. Add the milk and stir while the soup gently reheats.

4 Remove the pan from the heat and stir in the crème fraîche or mascarpone, plus the dill and lemon juice. Taste and adjust the seasoning if necessary. Reheat the soup, but do not allow it to boil or it may curdle. Serve garnished with sprigs of dill.

Celeriac and Spinach Soup

Celeriac has a wonderful flavor that is reminiscent of celery, but also adds a slightly nutty taste. Here, it is combined with spinach to make a delicious soup.

INGREDIENTS

Serves 6

1¾ pints/4 cups water
8 fluid ounces/1 cup dry white wine
1 leek, thickly sliced
1¼ pounds celeriac, diced
7 ounces fresh spinach leaves
freshly grated nutmeg
salt and ground black pepper
1 ounce/¼ cup pine nuts, to garnish

1 Mix the water and wine in a pitcher. Place the leek, celeriac and spinach in a deep pan and pour the liquid over the top. Bring to the boil, lower the heat and simmer for 10–15 minutes, until the vegetables are soft.

2 Pour the celeriac mixture into a blender or food processor and process until smooth, in batches if necessary. Return to the clean pan and season to taste with salt, pepper and grated nutmeg. Reheat gently.

3 Heat a non-stick frying pan (do not add any oil) and add the pine nuts. Dry-fry until golden brown, stirring occasionally so that they do not stick. Sprinkle them over the soup and serve.

COOK'S TIP

If the soup is too thick, thin with a little water or low-fat milk when processing.

Spicy Carrot Soup with Garlic Croûtons

V

Carrot soup is given a touch of spice with coriander, cumin and chili powder.

INGREDIENTS

Serves 6

1 tablespoon olive oil
1 large onion, chopped
1½ pounds carrots, sliced
1 teaspoon ground coriander
1 teaspoon ground cumin
1 teaspoon hot chili powder
1½ pints/3¾ cups Vegetable Stock
salt and ground black pepper
fresh cilantro sprigs, to garnish

For the garlic croûtons
4 slices bread, crusts removed
a little olive oil
2 garlic cloves, crushed

1 To make the soup, heat the oil in a large pan, add the onion and carrots and cook over a low heat for 5 minutes, stirring occasionally. Add the ground spices and cook gently for 1 minute, stirring constantly.

2 Stir in the stock, bring to the boil, then cover and simmer gently for about 45 minutes, until the carrots are tender.

3 Meanwhile, make the garlic croûtons. Cut the bread into ½-inch cubes. Heat the oil in a frying pan, add the garlic and cook gently for 30 seconds, stirring constantly. Add the bread cubes, turn them over in the oil and fry over a medium heat for a few minutes, until they are crisp and golden brown all over, turning frequently. Drain on paper towels and keep warm.

4 Process the soup in a blender or food processor until smooth, then season to taste with salt and pepper. Return the soup to the rinsed pan and reheat gently. Serve hot, sprinkled with garlic croûtons and garnished with fresh cilantro sprigs.

Curried Carrot and Apple Soup

The combination of carrot, curry and apple is a highly successful one. Curried fruit is delicious.

INGREDIENTS

Serves 4

2 teaspoond sunflower oil

1 tablespoon mild korma curry powder

1¼ pounds carrots, chopped

1 large onion, chopped

1 large cooking apple, chopped

1¼ pints/3 cups Chicken Stock

salt and ground black pepper

plain yogurt and carrot curls,
      to garnish

1 Heat the oil in a large, heavy pan and gently cook the curry powder for 2–3 minutes.

2 Add the chopped carrots and onion and the cooking apple, stir well until coated with the curry powder, then cover the pan.

3 Cook over a low heat for about 15 minutes, shaking the pan occasionally, until the vegetables are softened. Spoon the vegetable mixture into a food processor or blender, add half the stock and process until smooth.

4 Return the mixture to the pan and pour in the remaining chicken stock. Bring the soup to the boil, then taste and adjust the seasoning. Ladle into warm bowls and serve, garnished with a swirl of yogurt and curls of raw carrot.

Leek, Parsnip and Ginger Soup

V

A flavorsome winter warmer, with the added spiciness of fresh ginger, this unusual soup is destined to become a family favorite.

INGREDIENTS

Serves 4–6

2 tablespoons olive oil

8 ounces leeks, sliced

1 ounce fresh root ginger, finely chopped

1½ pounds parsnips, coarsely chopped

½ pint/1¼ cups dry white wine

2 pints/5 cups Vegetable Stock
    or water

salt and ground black pepper

fromage blanc and paprika,
    to garnish

1 Heat the oil in a large pan and add the leeks and ginger. Cook gently for 2–3 minutes, until the leeks start to soften.

2 Add the parsnips and cook for a further 7–8 minutes, until they are beginning to soften.

3 Pour in the wine and stock or water and bring to the boil. Reduce the heat and simmer gently for 20–30 minutes, or until the parsnips are tender. Leave the soup to cool slightly.

4 Process the soup in a blender or food processor until smooth. Season to taste with salt and pepper. Reheat and garnish with a swirl of fromage blanc and a light dusting of paprika.

Curried Celery Soup

V

An unusual, but stimulating
combination of flavors, this
warming soup is an excellent way
to transform celery. Serve with
warm whole-wheat bread rolls.

INGREDIENTS

Serves 4–6

2 teaspoons olive oil

1 onion, chopped

1 leek, sliced

1½ pounds celery, chopped

1 tablespoon medium or hot
   curry powder

8 ounces unpeeled potatoes, washed
   and diced

1½ pints/3¾ cups Vegetable Stock

1 bouquet garni

2 tablespoons chopped fresh mixed herbs

salt

celery seeds and leaves, to garnish

COOK'S TIP

For a change, use celeriac and
sweet potatoes in place of celery
and standard potatoes.

1 Heat the oil in a large pan. Add
the onion, leek and celery, cover
and cook over a low heat for about
10 minutes, stirring occasionally.

2 Sprinkle in the curry powder
and cook gently, stirring
occasionally, for 2 minutes.

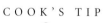

3 Add the potatoes, vegetable
stock and bouquet garni, cover
and bring to the boil. Reduce the
heat and simmer gently for about
20 minutes, until the vegetables
are tender, but not too soft.

4 Remove and discard the
bouquet garni and set the
soup aside to cool slightly before
processing it.

5 Transfer the soup to a blender
or food processor and process,
in batches, until smooth.

6 Add the mixed herbs, season
to taste with salt and process
briefly again. Return to the pan
and reheat gently until piping hot.
Ladle into warm bowls and
garnish each one with a sprinkling
of celery seeds and a few celery
leaves before serving.

CHUNKY VEGETABLE SOUPS

It isn't really surprising that many of the world's best-known and best-loved soups are based on vegetables, for few other ingredients can offer so much versatility and variety. Some, such as the classic French Onion Soup with Gruyère Croûtes, feature a single vegetable in a starring role, while others, such as Genoese Minestrone, glory in a veritable cornucopia. Take a culinary trip around the world with mouth-watering recipes from places as diverse as Japan, Russia, Spain, North Africa, Italy, China and the Caribbean.

French Onion Soup with Gruyère Croûtes

This is perhaps the most famous of all onion soups. Traditionally, it was served as a sustaining early-morning meal to the porters and workers of Les Halles market in Paris.

INGREDIENTS

Serves 6

2 ounces/¼ cup butter
1 tablespoon olive oil
4½ pounds yellow onions, peeled
    and sliced
1 teaspoon chopped fresh thyme
1 teaspoon superfine sugar
1 tablespoon sherry vinegar
2½ pints/6¼ cups Meat or Chicken Stock
1½ tablespoons all-purpose flour
¼ pint/⅔ cup dry white wine
3 tablespoons brandy
salt and ground black pepper

For the croûtes
6–12 thick slices day-old French bread,
    about 1-inch thick
1 garlic clove, halved
1 tablespoon French mustard
4 ounces/1 cup coarsely grated
    Gruyère cheese

1   Melt the butter with the oil in a large pan. Add the onions and stir to coat them in the fat. Cook over a medium heat for 5–8 minutes, stirring once or twice, until the onions begin to soften. Stir in the thyme.

2   Reduce the heat to very low, cover the pan and cook the onions for 20–30 minutes, stirring frequently, until they are very soft and golden yellow.

3   Uncover the pan and increase the heat slightly. Stir in the sugar and cook for 5–10 minutes, until the onions start to brown. Add the sherry vinegar and increase the heat again, then continue cooking, stirring frequently, until the onions turn a deep, golden brown – this could take up to 20 minutes.

4   Meanwhile, bring the stock to the boil in another pan. Stir the flour into the onions and cook, stirring constantly, for about 2 minutes, then gradually pour in the hot stock. Add the wine and brandy and season the soup to taste with salt and pepper. Simmer for 10–15 minutes.

5   For the croûtes, preheat the oven to 300°F. Place the slices of bread on a greased baking tray and bake for 15–20 minutes, until dry and lightly browned. Rub the bread with the cut surface of the garlic and spread with the mustard, then sprinkle the grated Gruyère cheese over the slices.

6   Preheat the broiler on the hottest setting. Ladle the soup into a large flameproof tureen or six flameproof bowls. Float the croûtes on the soup, then broil until the cheese melts, bubbles and turns golden brown. Serve immediately.

COOK'S TIP

The long, slow cooking of the onions is the key to success with this soup. If the onions brown too quickly the soup will be bitter.

Green Pea Soup with Spinach

This lovely green soup was invented by the wife of a 17th-century British Member of Parliament, and it has stood the test of time.

INGREDIENTS

Serves 6

1 pound/generous 3 cups podded fresh or
    frozen peas
1 leek, finely sliced
2 garlic cloves, crushed
2 rindless lean bacon rashers,
    finely diced
2 pints/5 cups Chicken Stock
2 tablespoons olive oil
2 ounces fresh spinach, shredded
1½ ounces/⅓ cup white cabbage,
    finely shredded
½ small lettuce, finely shredded
1 celery stick, finely chopped
large handful of parsley, finely chopped
½ carton cress
4 teaspoons chopped fresh mint
pinch of ground mace
salt and ground black pepper

1 Put the peas, leek, garlic and bacon in a large pan. Add the chicken stock, bring to the boil, then lower the heat and simmer for 20 minutes.

2 About 5 minutes before the pea mixture is ready, heat the oil in a deep frying pan.

3 Add the spinach, cabbage, lettuce, celery and herbs to the frying pan. Cover and sweat the mixture over a low heat until soft.

4 Transfer the pea mixture to a blender or food processor and process until smooth. Return to the clean pan, add the sweated vegetables and herbs and heat through. Season with mace, salt and pepper and serve.

Leek and Thyme Soup

V

*This heart-warming soup can be
processed to a smooth purée or
served in its original peasant style.*

INGREDIENTS

Serves 4

2 pounds leeks

1 pound potatoes

4 ounces/½ cup butter

1 large fresh thyme sprig, plus extra to
garnish (optional)

½ pint/1¼ cups milk

salt and ground black pepper

4 tablespoons heavy cream,
to serve

3 Melt the butter in a large pan
and add the leeks and 1 sprig
of thyme. Cover and cook for
4–5 minutes, until softened. Add
the potato pieces and just enough
cold water to cover the vegetables.
Re-cover and cook over a low heat
for 30 minutes.

4 Pour in the milk and season to
taste with salt and pepper.
Cover and simmer for a further
30 minutes. You will find that
some of the potato breaks up,
leaving you with a semi-puréed
and rather lumpy soup.

5 Remove the sprig of thyme
(the leaves will have fallen
into the soup) and serve, adding
1 tablespoon cream and a garnish
of thyme to each portion, if using.

1 Trim the leeks. If you are using
large winter leeks, strip away
all the coarse outer leaves, then cut
the leeks into thick slices. Wash
thoroughly under cold running
water to remove any traces of soil.

2 Cut the potatoes into coarse
dice, about 1 inch, and dry on
paper towels.

Borscht

Beet is the main ingredient of borscht, and its flavor and color dominate this well-known soup. It is a classic of both Russia and Poland.

INGREDIENTS

Serves 4–6

2 pounds uncooked beets, peeled
2 carrots, peeled
2 celery sticks
1½ ounces/3 tbsp butter
2 onions, sliced
2 garlic cloves, crushed
4 tomatoes, peeled, seeded
    and chopped
1 bay leaf
1 large fresh parsley sprig
2 cloves
4 whole peppercorns
2 pints/5 cups Meat or Chicken Stock
¼ pint/⅔ cup beet *kvas* (see *Cook's Tip*)
    or the liquid from pickled beet
salt and ground black pepper
sour cream, garnished with chopped
    fresh chives or fresh dill sprigs,
    to serve

1 Cut the beets, carrots and celery into fairly thick strips. Melt the butter in a large pan and cook the onions over a low heat for 5 minutes, stirring occasionally.

COOK'S TIP

Beet *kvas*, fermented beet juice, adds an intense color and a slight tartness. If unavailable, peel and grate 1 beet, add ¼ pint/⅔ cup stock and ½ tsp lemon juice. Bring to the boil, cover and leave for 30 minutes. Strain before using.

2 Add the beets, carrots and celery and cook for a further 5 minutes, stirring occasionally.

3 Add the garlic and chopped tomatoes to the pan and cook, stirring, for 2 more minutes.

4 Place the bay leaf, parsley, cloves and peppercorns in a piece of cheesecloth and tie with string.

5 Add the muslin bag to the pan with the stock. Bring to the boil, reduce the heat, cover and simmer for 1¼ hours, or until the vegetables are very tender. Discard the bag. Stir in the beet *kvas* and season. Bring to the boil. Ladle into bowls and serve with sour cream garnished with chives or dill.

Leek and Potato Soup

These two vegetables make a very tasty and substantial, simple soup, and are readily available and inexpensive throughout the year.

INGREDIENTS

Serves 4

2 ounces/4 tablespoons butter
2 leeks, chopped
1 small onion, finely chopped
12 ounces floury potatoes, chopped
1½ pints/3¾ cups Vegetable Stock
salt and ground black pepper
rustic bread, to serve

1 Heat 1 ounce/2 tablespoons of the butter in a large, heavy pan, add the chopped leeks and onion and cook over a low heat, stirring occasionally so that they do not stick to the base of the pan, for about 7 minutes, until softened but not browned.

2 Add the potatoes to the pan and cook, stirring occasionally, for 2–3 minutes.

3 Add the stock and bring to the boil, then reduce the heat to very low, cover and simmer gently for 30–35 minutes, until the vegetables are very tender.

4 Season to taste with salt and pepper, remove the pan from the heat and stir in the remaining butter in small pieces at a time. Ladle the soup into warm bowls and serve immediately with slices of thick rustic bread.

v

Spinach and Rice Soup

Use very fresh, young spinach leaves and risotto rice to prepare this surprisingly light, refreshing soup.

INGREDIENTS

Serves 4

1½ pounds fresh spinach, washed
3 tablespoons extra virgin olive oil
1 small onion, finely chopped
2 garlic cloves, finely chopped
1 small fresh red chile, seeded and
   finely chopped
4 ounces/generous ½ cup risotto rice
2 pints/5 cups Vegetable Stock
salt and ground black pepper
4 tablespoons grated Pecorino cheese,
   to serve

1 Place the spinach in a large pan with just the water that clings to its leaves after washing. Add a large pinch of salt. Heat gently until the spinach has wilted, then remove from the heat and drain, reserving any liquid. Use a knife to chop finely.

2 Heat the oil in a large pan and cook the onion, garlic and chile over a medium heat, stirring occasionally, for 4–5 minutes, until softened. Stir in the rice until well coated, then pour in the stock and reserved spinach liquid.

3 Bring to the boil, lower the heat and simmer gently for 10 minutes. Add the spinach and cook for 5–7 minutes more, until the rice is tender. Season with salt and freshly ground pepper to taste and serve immediately with the Pecorino cheese.

Apple Soup

A delicious soup that makes the most of freshly picked apples.

INGREDIENTS

Serves 6

3 tablespoons oil
1 kohlrabi, diced
3 carrots, diced
2 celery sticks, diced
1 green bell pepper, seeded and diced
2 tomatoes, diced
3½ pints/9 cups Chicken Stock
6 large green apples
3 tablespoons all-purpose flour
¼ pint/⅔ cup heavy cream
1 tablespoon granulated sugar
2–3 tablespoons lemon juice
salt and ground black pepper
lemon wedges and rustic bread, to serve

1 Heat the oil in a large pan. Add the kohlrabi, carrots, celery, bell pepper and tomatoes and cook, stirring occasionally, for 5–6 minutes, until just softened.

2 Pour in the chicken stock, bring to the boil, then reduce the heat and simmer for about 45 minutes.

3 Meanwhile, peel and core the apples, then chop into small cubes. Add to the pan and simmer for a further 15 minutes.

4 In a bowl, mix together the flour and cream, then pour slowly into the soup, stirring well, and bring to the boil. Add the sugar and lemon juice before seasoning. Serve immediately with lemon wedges and rustic bread.

Pistou

Serve this delicious vegetable soup from Nice, in the south of France, with a sun-dried tomato pesto and fresh Parmesan cheese.

INGREDIENTS

Serves 4

1 zucchini, diced
1 small potato, diced
1 shallot, chopped
1 carrot, diced
8 ounces can chopped tomatoes
2 pints/5 cups Vegetable Stock
2 ounces green beans, cut into
    ½-inch lengths
2 ounces/½ cup baby peas
2 ounces/½ cup small pasta shapes
4–6 tablespoons pesto, either home-ade
    or ready-made
1 tablespoon sun-dried tomato paste
salt and ground black pepper
grated Parmesan cheese, to serve

1 Place the zucchini, potato, shallot, carrot and tomatoes in a large pan. Add the vegetable stock and season with salt and pepper. Bring to the boil, then cover and simmer for 20 minutes.

2 Add the green beans, baby peas and pasta shapes. Cook for a further 10 minutes, until the pasta is tender.

3 Taste the soup and adjust the seasoning as necessary. Ladle the soup into individual bowls. Mix together the pesto and sun-dried tomato paste, and stir a spoonful into each serving.

4 Hand around a bowl of grated Parmesan cheese for sprinkling into each bowl.

Garlic and Cilantro Soup

This recipe is based on the wonderful bread soups or açordas *of Portugal. Being a simple soup it should be made with the best ingredients – plump garlic, fresh cilantro, high-quality rustic country bread and, of course, extra virgin olive oil.*

INGREDIENTS

Serves 6

1 ounce fresh cilantro, leaves and stalks
    chopped separately

2½ pints/6¼ cups Vegetable or Chicken
    Stock, or water

5–6 plump garlic cloves, peeled

6 eggs

10 ounces day-old bread, most of
    the crust removed and torn into
    bitesize pieces

salt and ground black pepper

6 tablespoons extra virgin olive oil, plus
    extra to serve

1 Place the cilantro stalks in a pan. Add the stock or water and bring to the boil. Lower the heat and simmer for 10 minutes. Cool slightly, then process in a blender or food processor and sieve back into the pan.

2 Crush the garlic with 1 teaspoon salt, then stir in 4 fluid ounces/½ cup hot soup. Return the mixture to the pan.

3 Meanwhile, poach the eggs separately in a small frying pan of gently simmering water for about 3–4 minutes, until just set.

4 Use a slotted spoon to remove them from the pan and transfer to a warm plate. Trim off any untidy bits of white.

5 Bring the soup back to the boil and add seasoning. Stir in the chopped cilantro leaves and remove from the heat.

6 Place the bread in six soup plates or bowls and drizzle the oil over it. Ladle in the soup and stir. Add a poached egg to each bowl and serve immediately, offering olive oil at the table so that it can be drizzled over the soup to taste.

V | # Spanish Potato and Garlic Soup

Traditionally served in earthenware dishes, this classic Spanish soup should be savored.

INGREDIENTS

Serves 6

2 tablespoons olive oil

1 large onion, thinly sliced

4 garlic cloves, crushed

1 large potato, halved and thinly sliced

1 teaspoon paprika

14-ounce can chopped tomatoes, drained

1 teaspoon fresh thyme leaves

1½ pints/3¾ cups Vegetable Stock

1 teaspoon cornstarch

salt and ground black pepper

chopped fresh thyme leaves, to garnish

1 Heat the oil in a large pan and cook the onions, garlic, potato and paprika, stirring frequently, for 5 minutes, until the onions have softened, but not browned.

2 Add the tomatoes, thyme and vegetable stock and simmer for 15–20 minutes, until the potatoes have cooked through.

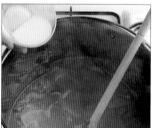

3 Mix the cornstarch with a little water to form a paste and stir into the soup, then simmer for 5 minutes, until thickened.

4 Using a wooden spoon break the potatoes up slightly. Season to taste with salt and pepper. Serve hot, garnished with the chopped thyme leaves.

Summer Vegetable Soup

This brightly colored, fresh-tasting soup makes the most of summer's vegetable crop.

INGREDIENTS

Serves 4

3 tablespoons olive oil

1 large onion, finely chopped

1 tablespoon sun-dried tomato paste

1 pound ripe Italian plum tomatoes, peeled and finely chopped

8 ounces green zucchini, trimmed and coarsely chopped

8 ounces yellow zucchini, trimmed and coarsely chopped

3 waxy new potatoes, diced

2 garlic cloves, crushed

about 2 pints/5 cups Vegetable Stock or water

4 tablespoons shredded fresh basil

2 ounces/²/₃ cup grated Parmesan cheese

salt and ground black pepper

1 Heat the oil in a large pan, add the onion and cook over a low heat for about 5 minutes, stirring constantly, until softened.

2 Stir in the sun-dried tomato paste, chopped tomatoes, zucchini, diced potatoes and garlic. Mix well and cook gently for 10 minutes, uncovered, shaking the pan frequently to stop the vegetables sticking to the base.

3 Pour in the stock or water. Bring to the boil, lower the heat, half-cover the pan and simmer gently for 15 minutes, or until the vegetables are just tender. Add more stock if necessary.

4 Remove the pan from the heat and stir in the basil and half the cheese. Taste and adjust the seasoning. Serve hot, sprinkled with the remaining cheese.

Corn and Sweet Potato Soup

The combination of corn and sweet potato gives this soup a real depth of flavor, as well as making it look very colorful.

INGREDIENTS

Serves 6

1 tablespoon olive oil

1 onion, finely chopped

2 garlic cloves, crushed

1 small fresh red chile, seeded and
    finely chopped

3 pints/7½ cups Vegetable Stock

2 teaspoons ground cumin

1 medium sweet potato, diced

½ red bell pepper, finely chopped

1 pound corn kernels

salt and ground black pepper

lime wedges, to serve

1 Heat the oil in a pan and cook the onion for 5 minutes, until softened. Add the garlic and chile and cook for a further 2 minutes.

2 Add ½ pint/1¼ cups of the stock, and simmer gently for 10 minutes.

3 Mix the cumin with a little of the stock to form a smooth paste and then stir into the soup. Add the diced sweet potato, stir and simmer for 10 minutes. Season and stir again.

4 Add the bell pepper, corn and remaining stock and simmer for 10 minutes. Process half of the soup until smooth and then stir into the chunky soup. Adjust the seasoning and serve with lime wedges for squeezing over.

Genoese Minestrone

The variations on this soup are almost endless. This pasta-free version is packed with heaps of vegetables to make a substantial start to any meal.

INGREDIENTS

Serves 6

3 pints/7½ cups Vegetable Stock

1 large onion, chopped

3 celery sticks, chopped

2 carrots, finely diced

2 large floury potatoes, finely diced

½ head of cabbage, very finely diced

8 ounces green beans, diagonally sliced

2 x 14-ounce cans cannellini beans,
    drained and rinsed

4 tablespoons ready-made pesto sauce

salt and ground black pepper

rustic bread and freshly grated Parmesan
    cheese, to serve

1 Pour the stock into a large pan. Add the onion, celery and carrots. Simmer for 10 minutes.

2 Add the potatoes, cabbage, and beans and simmer gently for 10–12 minutes, or until the potatoes are tender.

3 Stir in the cannellini beans and pesto, and gradually bring the mixture to the boil. Season to taste with salt and pepper. Ladle into warm bowls or soup plates and serve the soup hot with rustic bread and plenty of freshly grated Parmesan cheese.

V | # Italian Arugula and Potato Soup

This filling and hearty soup is based on a traditional Italian peasant recipe. If arugula is unavailable, watercress or baby spinach leaves make an equally delicious alternative.

INGREDIENTS

Serves 4

2 pounds new potatoes

1½ pints/3¾ cups Vegetable Stock

1 carrot

4 ounces arugula

½ teaspoon cayenne pepper

½ loaf stale ciabatta bread, torn into chunks

4 garlic cloves, thinly sliced

4 tablespoons olive oil

salt and ground black pepper

3 Add the cayenne pepper, plus salt and black pepper to taste, then add the chunks of bread. Remove the pan from the heat, cover and leave to stand for about 10 minutes.

4 Meanwhile, sauté the garlic in the olive oil until golden brown. Pour the soup into bowls, add a little of the sautéed garlic to each bowl and serve.

1 Dice the potatoes, then place them in a pan with the stock and a little salt. Bring to the boil and simmer for 10 minutes.

2 Finely dice the carrot and add to the potatoes and stock, then tear the arugula leaves and drop into the pan. Simmer for a further 15 minutes, until the vegetables are tender.

Corn and Potato Chowder

*This creamy yet chunky soup is rich
with the sweet taste of corn. It's
excellent served with thick rustic
bread and topped with some melted
Cheddar cheese.*

INGREDIENTS

Serves 4

1 onion, chopped

1 garlic clove, crushed

1 medium baking potato, chopped

2 celery sticks, sliced

1 small bell pepper, seeded, halved
    and sliced

2 tablespoons sunflower oil

1 ounce/2 tablespoons butter

1 pint/2½ cups stock or water

½ pint/1¼ cups milk

7-ounce can cannellini beans

11-ounce can corn kernels

good pinch of dried sage

salt and ground black pepper

grated Cheddar cheese, to serve

1 Put the onion, garlic, potato,
celery and green bell pepper
into a large, heavy pan with the oil
and butter.

2 Heat until sizzling, then
reduce the heat to low. Cover
and cook gently for 10 minutes,
shaking the pan occasionally.

3 Pour in the stock or water,
season with salt and pepper to
taste and bring to the boil. Reduce
the heat, cover again and simmer
gently for about 15 minutes, until
the vegetables are tender.

4 Add the milk, beans and corn
– including their can juices –
and the sage. Simmer, uncovered,
for 5 minutes. Check the seasoning
and serve hot, sprinkled with
grated cheese.

Plantain and Corn Soup

Here the sweetness of the corn and plantains is offset by a little chile to create an unusual soup.

INGREDIENTS

Serves 4

1 ounce/2 tablespoons butter or margarine
1 onion, finely chopped
1 garlic clove, crushed
10 ounces yellow plantains, peeled
    and sliced
1 large tomato, peeled and chopped
6 ounces/1 cup corn kernels
1 teaspoon dried tarragon, crushed
1½ pints/3¾ cups Vegetable or
    Chicken Stock
1 fresh green chile, seeded and chopped
pinch of freshly grated nutmeg
salt and ground black pepper

1 Melt the butter or margarine in a pan over a moderate heat, add the onion and garlic and cook, stirring occasionally, for a few minutes until the onion is soft.

2 Add the plantains, tomato and corn kernels, and cook for a further 5 minutes.

3 Add the tarragon, stock, chile and salt and pepper, then simmer for 10 minutes. or until the plantain is tender. Stir in the grated nutmeg and serve.

V

Groundnut Soup

Groundnuts, or peanuts, are widely used in sauces in African cooking. You'll find peanut paste in health food stores – it makes a wonderfully rich soup – but you could use peanut butter instead if you like.

INGREDIENTS

Serves 4

3 tablespoons peanut paste or
    peanut butter
2½ pints/6¼ cups Vegetable Stock
    or water
2 tablespoons tomato paste
1 onion, chopped
2 slices fresh root ginger
¼ teaspoon dried thyme
1 bay leaf
chili powder
8 ounces white yam, diced
10 small okra, trimmed (optional)
salt

1 Place the peanut paste or peanut butter in a bowl, add ½ pint/1¼ cups of the stock or water and the tomato purée and blend together to make a smooth paste.

2 Spoon the nut mixture into a pan and add the onion, ginger, thyme, bay leaf, chili powder and salt to taste and the remaining vegetable stock or water.

3 Heat gently until simmering, then cook for 1 hour, whisking occasionally to prevent the nut mixture from sticking.

4 Add the white yam, cook for a further 10 minutes, and then add the okra, if using, and simmer until both vegetables are tender. Ladle the soup into warm bowls and serve immediately.

Spicy Peanut Soup

A thick and warming vegetable soup, flavored with mild chili and roasted peanuts.

INGREDIENTS

Serves 6

2 tablespoons oil

1 large onion, finely chopped

2 garlic cloves, crushed

1 teaspoon mild chili powder

2 red bell peppers, seeded and chopped

8 ounces carrots, finely chopped

8 ounces potatoes, finely chopped

3 celery sticks, sliced

1½ pints/3¾ cups Vegetable Stock

6 tablespoons crunchy peanut butter

4 ounces/⅔ cup corn kernels

salt and ground black pepper

coarsely chopped unsalted roasted
  peanuts, to garnish

1 Heat the oil in a large pan and cook the onion and garlic for about 3 minutes. Add the chili powder and cook for a further 1 minute.

2 Add the red bell peppers, carrots, potatoes and celery. Stir well, then cook for a further 4 minutes, stirring occasionally.

3 Add the vegetable stock, followed by the peanut butter and corn kernels. Stir well until thoroughly combined.

4 Season to taste with salt and pepper. Bring to the boil, cover and simmer for about 20 minutes, until all the vegetables are tender. Taste and adjust the seasoning if necessary before serving, sprinkled with the chopped peanuts.

Caribbean Vegetable Soup

V

*This unusual vegetable soup is
refreshing and filling.*

INGREDIENTS

Serves 4

1 ounce/2 tablespoons butter
    or margarine
1 onion, chopped
1 garlic clove, crushed
2 carrots, sliced
2½ pints/6¼ cups Vegetable Stock
2 bay leaves
2 fresh thyme sprigs
1 celery stick, finely chopped
2 green bananas, peeled and cut into
    4 pieces
6 ounces white yam or eddoe, peeled
    and cubed
1 ounce/2 tablespoons red lentils
1 chayote, peeled and chopped
2 ounce/2 tablespoons macaroni
    (optional)
salt and ground black pepper
chopped sscallions, to garnish

COOK'S TIP

Use other root vegetables or
potatoes if yam or eddoes are
not available. Add more stock if
you want a thinner soup.

1 Melt the butter or margarine
and cook the onion, garlic and
carrots for a few minutes, stirring
occasionally, until beginning to
soften. Add the stock, bay leaves
and thyme and bring to the boil.

2 Add the celery, green bananas,
white yam or eddoe, lentils,
chayote and macaroni, if using.
Season to taste with salt and
pepper and simmer for 25 minutes,
until all the vegetables are cooked.
Serve garnished with chopped
scallions.

North African Spiced Soup

This soup is often served in the evening during Ramadan, the Muslim festival when followers fast during the daytime for a month.

INGREDIENTS

Serves 6

1 large onion, chopped
2 pints/5 cups Vegetable Stock
1 teaspoon ground cinnamon
1 teaspoon ground turmeric
1 tablespoon grated fresh root ginger
pinch of cayenne pepper
2 carrots, diced
2 celery sticks, diced
14-ounce can chopped tomatoes
1 pound floury potatoes, diced
5 saffron threads
14-ounce can chickpeas, drained
2 tablespoons chopped fresh cilantro
1 tablespoon lemon juice
salt and ground black pepper
fried wedges of lemon, to serve

1 Place the onion in a large pan with ½ pint/1¼ cups of the vegetable stock. Simmer gently for about 10 minutes.

2 Meanwhile, mix together the cinnamon, turmeric, ginger, cayenne pepper and 2 tablespoons of stock to form a paste. Stir into the onion mixture with the carrots, celery and remaining stock.

3 Bring the mixture to the boil, reduce the heat, then cover and simmer gently for 5 minutes.

4 Add the tomatoes and potatoes, cover again and simmer gently for 20 minutes. Add the saffron, chickpeas, cilantro and lemon juice. Season to taste with salt and pepper, and when piping hot, serve with fried wedges of lemon.

Tamarind Soup with Peanuts and Vegetables

Known in Indonesia as Sayur Asam, *this is a colorful and refreshing soup from Jakarta with more than a hint of sharpness.*

INGREDIENTS

Serves 4

5 shallots or 1 red onion, sliced

3 garlic cloves, crushed

1 inch galangal, peeled and sliced

1–2 fresh red chiles, seeded and sliced

2 ounce/¼ cup raw peanuts

½ inch cube shrimp paste, prepared

2 pints/5 cups Vegetable Stock

2–3 ounces/½–¾ cup salted peanuts,
　　lightly crushed

1–2 tablespoons dark brown sugar

1 teaspoon tamarind pulp, soaked in
　　5 tablespoons warm water for
　　15 minutes

salt

For the vegetables

1 chayote, thinly peeled, seeds removed,
　　flesh finely sliced

4 ounces green beans, thinly sliced

2 ounces corn kernels (optional)

a handful of green leaves, such as
　　watercress, arugula or Chinese cabbage,
　　finely shredded

1 fresh green chile, seeded and sliced,
　　to garnish

2 Pour in some of the stock to moisten and then pour this mixture into a pan or wok, adding the rest of the stock. Cook for 15 minutes with the crushed salted peanuts and sugar.

4 About 5 minutes before serving, add the chayote slices, beans and corn, if using, to the soup and cook fairly rapidly. At the last minute, add the green leaves and salt to taste.

3 Strain the tamarind pulp, discarding the seeds, and reserve the juice.

5 Add the tamarind juice and adjust the seasoning. Serve immediately, garnished with slices of green chile.

1 Grind the shallots or onion, garlic, galangal, chiles, raw peanuts and shrimp paste to a paste in a food processor, or using a mortar and pestle.

Miso Broth with Scallions and Tofu

*The Japanese eat miso broth, a
simple, but highly nutritious soup,
almost every day – it is standard
breakfast fare, and it is eaten with
rice or noodles later in the day.*

INGREDIENTS

Serves 4

1 bunch of scallions or 5 baby leeks

½ oz/½ cup fresh cilantro

3 thin slices fresh root ginger

2 star anise

1 small dried red chile

2 pints/5 cups Stock for Japanese Soup
    or Vegetable Stock

8 ounces bok choy or other Asian greens,
    thickly sliced

7 ounces firm tofu, cut into
    1 inch cubes

4 tablespoons red miso

2–3 tablespoons shoyu

1 fresh red chile, seeded and
    shredded (optional)

1 Cut the coarse green tops off
the scallions or baby leeks and
reserve. Slice the rest of the
scallions or leeks finely on the
diagonal. Place the green tops in a
large, heavy pan with the cilantro
stalks, fresh root ginger, star anise,
dried chile and stock.

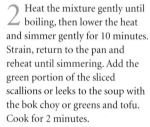

2 Heat the mixture gently until
boiling, then lower the heat
and simmer gently for 10 minutes.
Strain, return to the pan and
reheat until simmering. Add the
green portion of the sliced
scallions or leeks to the soup with
the bok choy or greens and tofu.
Cook for 2 minutes.

3 Mix 3 tablespoons of the miso
with a little of the hot soup in
a bowl, then stir it into the soup.
Taste the soup and add more miso
with soy sauce to taste.

4 Coarsely chop the cilantro
leaves and stir most of them
into the soup with the white part
of the scallions or leeks. Cook for
1 minute, then ladle the soup into
warmed serving bowls. Sprinkle
with the remaining cilantro and
the fresh red chile, if using, and
serve immediately.

Japanese Crushed Tofu Soup

*The main ingredient for this soup
is crushed tofu, which is both
nutritious and satisfying.*

INGREDIENTS

Serves 4

5 ounces fresh tofu, weighed
   without water
2 dried shiitake mushrooms
2 ounces gobo
1 teaspoon rice vinegar
½ black or white konnyaku (about
   4 ounces)
2 tablespoons sesame oil
4 ounces daikon, thinly sliced
2 ounces carrot, thinly sliced
1¼ pints/3 cups Stock for Japanese Soups
   or instant dashi
pinch of salt
2 tablespoons sake or dry white wine
1½ teaspoon mirin
3 tablespoons white or red miso paste
dash of soy sauce
6 snow peas, trimmed, boiled and finely
   sliced, to garnish

1 Crush the tofu coarsely by
hand until it resembles lumpy
scrambled egg in texture – do not
crush it too finely.

2 Wrap the tofu in a clean dish
towel and put it in a sieve,
then pour over plenty of boiling
water. Leave the tofu to drain
thoroughly for 10 minutes.

3 Soak the dried shiitake
mushrooms in lukewarm
water for 20 minutes, then drain
them. Remove their stems and cut
the caps into 4–6 pieces.

4 Use a vegetable brush to scrub
the skin off the gobo and slice
it into thin shavings. Soak the
shavings for 5 minutes in plenty
of cold water to which the rice
vinegar has been added to remove
any bitter taste. Drain.

5 Put the konnyaku in a small
pan and cover with water.
Bring to the boil, then drain and
cool. Tear the konnyaku into
¾ inch lumps: do not use a knife,
as smooth cuts will prevent it from
absorbing flavor.

6 Heat the sesame oil in a deep
pan. Add all the shiitake
mushrooms, gobo, daikon, carrot
and konnyaku. Stir-fry for
1 minute, then add the tofu and
stir well.

7 Pour in the stock/dashi and
add the salt, sake or wine and
mirin. Bring to the boil. Skim the
broth and simmer it for 5 minutes.

8 In a small bowl, dissolve the
miso paste in a little of the
soup, then return it to the pan.
Simmer the soup gently for
10 minutes, until the vegetables
are soft. Add the soy sauce, then
remove from the heat. Serve
immediately in four bowls,
garnished with the snow peas.

V

Hot-and-sour Soup

A classic Chinese soup, this is a warming and flavorsome start to a meal.

INGREDIENTS

Serves 4

¼ ounce dried wood ears

8 fresh shiitake mushrooms

3 ounces tofu

2 ounces/½ cup sliced, drained, canned
    bamboo shoots

1½ pints/3¾ cups Vegetable Stock

1 tablespoon superfine sugar

3 tablespoons rice vinegar

1 tablespoon light soy sauce

¼ teaspoon chili oil

½ teaspoon salt

large pinch of ground white pepper

1 tablespoon cornstarch

1 tablespoons cold water

1 egg white

1 teaspoon sesame oil

2 scallions, cut into fine rings,
    to garnish

COOK'S TIP

Wood ears are a kind of Chinese
mushroom, valued for
their texture more than
for their flavor.

1 Soak the wood ears in hot
water for 30 minutes, or until
soft. Drain, trim off and discard
the hard base from each, and chop
the cloud ears coarsely.

2 Remove and discard the stalks
from the shiitake mushrooms.
Cut the caps into thin strips. Cut
the tofu into ½ inch cubes and
shred the bamboo shoots finely.

3 Place the stock, shiitake
mushrooms, tofu, bamboo
shoots and wood ears in a large
pan. Bring the stock to the boil,
lower the heat and simmer for
about 5 minutes.

4 Stir in the sugar, rice vinegar,
soy sauce, chili oil, salt and
pepper. Mix the cornstarch to a
smooth paste with the water. Add
the mixture to the soup, stirring
until it thickens slightly.

5 Lightly beat the egg white,
then pour it slowly into the
soup in a steady stream, stirring
constantly. Cook, stirring, until the
egg white changes color.

6 Add the sesame oil just before
serving. Ladle the soup into
four heated bowls and garnish
each portion with a sprinkling of
scallion rings.

PASTA AND NOODLE SOUPS

~

The pasta and noodles in these soups are not mere
afterthoughts, but an essential part of the recipes, adding
texture, substance and an attractive appearance. In
some of the dishes, especially the classic Italian pasta
in brodo – literally pasta in broth – and in both Chinese
and Japanese soups, the pasta and noodles play a leading role,
while the soupy component, whether clear, chunky or thick,
is almost subservient. Even when pasta and noodles are only
one of many ingredients, they are no less important.

Broccoli, Anchovy and Pasta Soup

This soup is from Apulia in the south of Italy, where anchovies and broccoli are often used together.

INGREDIENTS

Serves 4

2 tablespoons olive oil
1 small onion, finely chopped
1 garlic clove, finely chopped
1/4–1/3 fresh red chile, seeded and
    finely chopped
2 canned anchovy fillets, drained
7 fluid ounces/scant 1 cup bottled
    strained tomatoes
3 tablespoons dry white wine
2 pints/5 cups Vegetable Stock
11 ounces/2 cups broccoli florets
7 ounces/1¾ cups dried orecchiette
salt and ground black pepper
grated Pecorino cheese, to serve

1 Heat the oil in a large pan. Add the onion, garlic, chile and anchovies and cook over a low heat, stirring constantly, for 5–6 minutes.

2 Add the passata and white wine and season with salt and pepper to taste. Bring to the boil, cover the pan, then cook over a low heat, stirring occasionally, for 12–15 minutes.

3 Pour in the vegetable stock. Bring to the boil, then add the broccoli and simmer for about 5 minutes. Add the pasta and bring back to the boil, stirring constantly. Simmer for 7–8 minutes, or according to the instructions on the packet, stirring frequently, until the pasta is *al dente*.

4 Taste and adjust the seasoning. Serve hot, in individual warmed bowls. Hand around the grated Pecorino cheese separately.

Clam and Pasta Soup

This soup is a variation of the pasta dish spaghetti alle vongole, *using pantry ingredients. Serve it with hot focaccia or ciabatta for a filling first course.*

Serves 4

2 tablespoons olive oil

1 large onion, finely chopped

2 garlic cloves, crushed

14-ounce can chopped tomatoes

1 tablespoon sun-dried tomato paste

1 teaspoon granulated sugar

1 teaspoon dried mixed herbs

about 1¼ pints/3 cups Fish or
    Vegetable Stock

¼ pint/⅔ cup red wine

2 ounces/½ cup small dried pasta shapes

5-ounce jar or can clams in natural juice

2 tablespoons finely chopped fresh flat
    leaf parsley, plus a few whole leaves
    to garnish

salt and ground black pepper

1 Heat the oil in a large, heavy pan. Add the onion and cook gently for 5 minutes, stirring frequently, until softened.

2 Add the garlic, tomatoes, sun-dried tomato paste, sugar, herbs, stock and wine and season with salt and pepper to taste. Bring to the boil. Lower the heat, half-cover the pan and simmer, stirring occasionally, for 10 minutes.

3 Add the pasta and continue simmering, uncovered, for about 10 minutes, or until the pasta is *al dente*. Stir occasionally to prevent the pasta shapes from sticking together.

4 Add the clams and their juice to the soup and heat through for 3–4 minutes, adding more stock if required. Do not allow it to boil, or the clams will become tough. Remove from the heat, stir in the chopped parsley and adjust the seasoning. Serve hot, sprinkled with coarsely ground black pepper and parsley leaves.

Consommé with Agnolotti

Shrimp, crab and chicken jostle for the upper hand in this rich and satisfying consommé.

INGREDIENTS

Serves 4–6

3 ounces cooked, peeled shrimp
3 ounces canned crab meat, drained
1 teaspoon finely grated fresh root ginger
1 tablespoons fresh white bread crumbs
1 teaspoon light soy sauce
1 scallion, finely chopped
1 garlic clove, crushed
1 egg white, beaten
14-ounce can chicken or fish consommé
2 tablespoons sherry or vermouth
salt and ground black pepper

For the pasta dough
7 ounces/1¾ cups all-purpose flour
pinch of salt
2 eggs
2 teaspoons cold water

For the garnish
2 ounces cooked, peeled shrimp
fresh cilantro leaves

1 To make the pasta, sift the flour and salt onto a clean work surface and make a well in the center with your hand.

2 Put the eggs and water into the well. Using a fork, beat the eggs gently together, then gradually draw in the flour from the sides, to make a thick paste.

3 When the mixture becomes too stiff to use a fork, use your hands to mix to a firm dough. Knead the dough for about 5 minutes until smooth. Put in plastic wrap to prevent it from drying out and leave to rest for 20–30 minutes.

4 Meanwhile, put the shrimp, crab meat, fresh ginger, bread crumbs, soy sauce, scallions, garlic and seasoning into a food processor or blender and process until smooth.

5 Roll out the dough into thin sheets. Stamp out 32 rounds 2-inches in diameter, with a fluted cookie cutter.

6 Place 1 teaspoon of the filling in the center of half the pasta rounds. Brush the edges of each round with egg white and top with a second round. Pinch the edges together to seal.

7 Cook the pasta in a large pan of salted, boiling water for 5 minutes (in batches to stop them sticking together). Remove and drop into a bowl of cold water for 5 seconds before placing on a tray. (You can make these pasta shapes a day in advance. Cover with plastic wrap and store in the refrigerator.)

8 Heat the consommé in a pan with the sherry or vermouth. Add the cooked pasta shapes and simmer for 1–2 minutes.

9 Serve the pasta in soup bowls covered with hot consommé. Garnish with peeled shrimp and cilantro leaves.

Meatball and Pasta Soup

This soup, which comes from sunny Sicily, is a substantial primo – a *first course that in Italy is considered as important as the second.*

INGREDIENTS

Serves 4

2 x 11-ounce cans condensed
   beef consommé
3½ ounces/¾ cup very thin dried pasta,
   such as fidelini or spaghettini
chopped fresh flat leaf parsley, to garnish
grated Parmesan cheese, to serve

For the meatballs
1 very thick slice white bread,
   crusts removed
2 tablespoons milk
8 ounces/1 cup ground beef
1 garlic clove, crushed
2 tablespoons grated Parmesan cheese
2–3 tablespoons fresh flat leaf parsley
   leaves, coarsely chopped
1 egg
generous pinch of freshly grated nutmeg
salt and ground black pepper

1 Make the meatballs. Break the bread into a small bowl, add the milk and set aside to soak. Meanwhile, put the ground beef, garlic, Parmesan, parsley and egg in another large bowl. Grate the nutmeg liberally over the top and add salt and pepper to taste.

2 Squeeze the bread with your hands to remove as much milk as possible, then add the bread to the meatball mixture and mix everything together well with your hands. Wash your hands, rinse them under cold water, then form the mixture into tiny balls about the size of small marbles.

3 Tip both cans of consommé into a large pan, add water as directed on the labels, then add an extra can of water. Season to taste with salt and pepper, bring to the boil and add the meatballs.

4 Break the pasta into small pieces and add it to the soup. Bring to the boil, stirring gently. Simmer, stirring frequently, for 7–8 minutes or according to the instructions on the packet, until the pasta is *al dente*. Taste and adjust the seasoning.

5 Ladle into warmed bowls and serve immediately, garnished with chopped parsley and freshly grated Parmesan cheese.

Pasta Soup with Chicken Livers

The fried chicken livers in this dish are so delicious that, even if you do not normally like them, you will find yourself enjoying them in this soup.

INGREDIENTS

Serves 4–6

4 ounces/¹/₂ cup chicken livers, thawed
   if frozen
1 tablespoon olive oil
pat of butter
4 garlic cloves, crushed
3 sprigs each of fresh parsley, marjoram
   and sage, chopped
1 fresh thyme sprig, chopped
5–6 fresh basil leaves, chopped
1–2 tablespoons dry white wine
2 x 11-ounce cans condensed
   chicken consommé
8 ounces/2 cups frozen peas
2 ounces/¹/₂ cup small dried pasta shapes,
   such as farfalle
2–3 scallions, sliced diagonally
salt and ground black pepper

1 Cut the chicken livers into small pieces with scissors. Heat the oil and butter in a frying pan, add the garlic and herbs, with salt and ground black pepper to taste, and cook gently for a few minutes. Add the livers, increase the heat to high and stir-fry for a few minutes until they change color and become dry. Add the wine, cook until it evaporates, then remove from the heat.

2 Tip both cans of chicken consommé into a large pan and add water to the condensed soup as directed on the labels. Add an extra can of water, then stir in a little salt and pepper to taste and bring to the boil.

3 Add the frozen peas to the pan and simmer for about 5 minutes, then add the small pasta shapes and bring the soup back to the boil, stirring constantly. Lower the heat and gently simmer the soup, stirring frequently, for about 5 minutes, or according to the instructions on the packet, until the pasta is *al dente*.

4 Add the fried chicken livers and scallions and heat through for 2–3 minutes. Taste and adjust the seasoning if necessary. Serve hot, in warmed bowls.

Chicken Soup with Vermicelli

In Morocco, the cook – who is almost invariably the most senior woman of the household – would use a whole chicken for this tasty and nourishing soup, to serve to her large extended family.

INGREDIENTS

Serves 4–6

2 tablespoons sunflower oil
¹/₂ ounce/1 tablespoon butter
1 onion, chopped
2 chicken legs or breast portions, halved
   or quartered
all-purpose flour, for dusting
2 carrots, cut into 1¹/₂in pieces
1 parsnip, cut into 1¹/₂in pieces
2¹/₂ pints/6¹/₄ cups Chicken Stock
1 cinnamon stick
good pinch of paprika
pinch of saffron threads
2 egg yolks
juice of ¹/₂ lemon
2 tablespoons chopped fresh cilantro
2 tablespoons chopped fresh parsley
5 ounces dried vermicelli
salt and ground black pepper

1 Heat the oil and butter in a pan and cook the onion for 3–4 minutes, until softened. Dust the chicken pieces in seasoned flour and cook gently until they are evenly browned.

2 Transfer the chicken to a plate and add the carrots and parsnip to the pan. Cook over a low heat for 3–4 minutes, stirring frequently, then return the chicken to the pan. Add the chicken stock, cinnamon stick and paprika and season well with salt and pepper.

3 Bring the soup to the boil, cover and simmer for 1 hour, until the vegetables are very tender.

4 Meanwhile, blend the saffron in 2 tablespoons boiling water. Beat the egg yolks with the lemon juice in a separate bowl and add the cilantro and parsley. When the saffron water has cooled, stir into the egg and lemon mixture.

5 When the vegetables are tender, transfer the chicken to a plate. Spoon away any excess fat from the soup, then increase the heat a little and stir in the vermicelli. Cook for a further 5–6 minutes, until the pasta is *al dente*. Meanwhile, remove the skin and bones from the chicken and chop the flesh into bitesize pieces.

6 When the vermicelli is cooked, stir in the chicken pieces and the egg yolk, lemon and saffron mixture. Cook over a low heat for 1–2 minutes, stirring constantly. Adjust the seasoning and serve.

Pasta Squares and Peas in Broth

This thick soup is from Lazio, the region around Rome, where it is traditionally made with fresh home-made pasta and peas. In this modern version, ready-made pasta is used with frozen peas to save time.

INGREDIENTS

Serves 4–6

1 ounce/2 tablespoons butter
2 ounces/¹⁄₃ cup pancetta or
   rindless smoked fatty bacon,
   coarsely chopped
1 small onion, finely chopped
1 celery stick, finely chopped
14 ounces/3¹⁄₂ cups frozen peas
1 teaspoon tomato paste
1–2 teaspoons finely chopped fresh
   flat leaf parsley
1³⁄₄ pints/4 cups Chicken Stock
11 ounces fresh lasagne sheets
about 2 ounces/¹⁄₃ cup prosciutto, diced
salt and ground black pepper
grated Parmesan cheese, to serve

1 Melt the butter in a large pan and add the pancetta or bacon, with the onion and celery. Cook over a low heat, stirring constantly, for 5 minutes.

COOK'S TIP

Take care when adding salt, because of the saltiness of the pancetta and the prosciutto.

2 Add the peas and cook, stirring, for 3–4 minutes. Stir in the tomato paste and parsley, then add the stock, with salt and pepper to taste. Bring to the boil. Cover the pan, lower the heat and simmer gently for 10 minutes. Meanwhile, cut the lasagne sheets into ³⁄₄ inch squares.

3 Taste the soup and adjust the seasoning if necessary. Drop in the pasta, stir and bring to the boil. Simmer for 2–3 minutes, or until the pasta is *al dente*, then stir in the prosciutto. Ladle the soup into warmed bowls and serve hot, with grated Parmesan cheese handed around separately.

Beet Soup with Ravioli

Beet and pasta make an unusual combination, but this soup is no less good for that.

Serves 4–6

1 quantity of Pasta Dough (see page 118)
1 egg white, beaten, for brushing
all-purpose flour, for dusting
1 small onion or shallot, finely chopped
2 garlic cloves, crushed
1 teaspoon fennel seeds
1 pint/2½ cups Chicken or
   Vegetable Stock
8 ounces cooked beets
2 tablespoons fresh orange juice
fresh fennel or dill leaves, to garnish
crusty bread, to serve

For the filling

4 ounces mushrooms, finely chopped
1 shallot or small onion, finely chopped
1–2 garlic cloves, crushed
1 teaspoon chopped fresh thyme
1 tablespoon chopped fresh parsley
6 tablespoons fresh white bread crumbs
salt and ground black pepper
large pinch of freshly grated nutmeg

1 Put all the filling ingredients in a food processor or blender and process to a paste.

2 Roll the pasta into thin sheets. Lay one piece over a ravioli tray and put 1 teaspoon of the filling into each depression. Brush around the edges of each ravioli with egg white. Cover with another sheet of pasta and press the edges together well to seal. Transfer to a floured dish towel and leave to rest for 1 hour before cooking.

3 Cook the ravioli salted, boiling water for 2 minutes. (Cook in batches to stop them sticking together.) Remove and drop into a bowl of cold water for 5 seconds before placing on a tray. (You can make the ravioli a day in advance and store in the refrigerator.)

4 Put the onion, garlic and fennel seeds into a pan with ¼ pint/⅔ cup of the stock. Bring to the boil, cover and simmer for 5 minutes, until tender. Peel and finely dice the beet, reserving 4 tablespoons for the garnish. Add the rest of it to the soup with the remaining stock, and bring to the boil.

5 Add the orange juice and cooked ravioli and simmer for 2 minutes. Serve in shallow soup bowls, garnished with the reserved diced beets and fresh fennel or dill leaves. Serve hot, with rustic bread.

Avgolemono

The name of this popular Greek soup means "egg and lemon", the two key ingredients. It is a light, nourishing soup made with orzo, a Greek rice-shaped pasta, but you can use any very small pasta shape in its place.

INGREDIENTS

Serves 4–6

3 pints/7½ cups Chicken Stock

4 ounces/½ cup orzo pasta

3 eggs

juice of 1 large lemon

salt and ground black pepper

lemon slices, to garnish

1 Pour the stock into a large pan and bring to the boil over a medium heat. Add the pasta and cook for 5 minutes.

2 Beat the eggs until frothy, then add the lemon juice and 1 tablespoon cold water.

3 Remove the pan from the heat. Stir a ladleful of the hot chicken stock into the egg and lemon mixture, then stir in 1–2 more. Return this mixture to the pan and stir well. Season and serve immediately, garnished with lemon slices.

Tortellini Chanterelle Broth

The savory-sweet quality of chanterelle mushrooms combines well in a simple broth with spinach-and-ricotta-filled tortellini. The addition of a little sherry creates a lovely warming effect.

INGREDIENTS

Serves 4

12 ounces fresh spinach and ricotta
   tortellini, or 6 ounces dried
2 pints/5 cups Chicken Stock
5 tablespoons dry sherry
6 ounces fresh chanterelle mushrooms,
   trimmed and sliced, or ½ ounces/
   ½ cup dried chanterelles
chopped fresh parsley, to garnish

1 Cook the tortellini according to the packet instructions.

2 Bring the chicken stock to the boil, add the dry sherry and fresh or dried mushrooms and simmer for 10 minutes.

3 Strain the tortellini, add to the stock, then ladle the broth into four warmed soup bowls, making sure each contains the same proportions of tortellini and mushrooms. Garnish with the chopped parsley and serve.

Roasted Tomato and Pasta Soup

When the only tomatoes you can buy are not particularly flavorsome, make this soup. The roasting compensates for any lack of flavor in the tomatoes, and the soup has a wonderful, smoky taste.

INGREDIENTS

Serves 4

450g/1lb ripe Italian plum tomatoes, halved lengthwise

1 large red bell pepper, quartered lengthwise and seeded

1 large red onion, quartered lengthwise

2 garlic cloves, unpeeled

1 tablespoon olive oil

2 pints/5 cups Vegetable Stock or water

good pinch of granulated sugar

3½ ounces/scant 1 cup small dried pasta shapes, such as tubetti

salt and ground black pepper

fresh basil leaves, to garnish

1 Preheat the oven to 375°F. Spread out the tomatoes, red bell pepper, onion and garlic in a roasting pan and drizzle with the olive oil. Roast for 30–40 minutes, until the vegetables are soft and charred, stirring and turning them halfway through cooking.

2 Tip the vegetables into a food processor, add about 8 fluid ounces/1 cup of the stock or water, and process to a purée. Scrape into a sieve placed over a large pan and press the purée through with the back of a spoon into the pan.

3 Add the remaining stock or water, the sugar and salt and pepper to taste. Bring to the boil.

4 Add the pasta and simmer for 7–8 minutes (or according to the instructions on the packet), stirring frequently, until *al dente*. Taste and adjust the seasoning with salt and ground black pepper, if necessary. Serve immediately in warmed bowls, garnished with the fresh basil leaves.

COOK'S TIP

You can roast the vegetables in advance, leave them to cool, then store them in a covered bowl in the refrigerator overnight before puréeing.

Tiny Pasta in Broth

In Italy, this filling soup is usually served before a light main course.

INGREDIENTS

Serves 4

2 pints/5 cups Meat Stock

3 ounces/³⁄₄ cup small soup pasta, such as stellette

2 pieces bottled roasted red bell pepper (about 2 ounces)

salt and ground black pepper

grated Parmesan cheese, to serve

1 Bring the stock to the boil in a large pan. Add salt and pepper to taste, then drop in the soup pasta. Stir well and bring the stock back to the boil.

2 Lower the heat to a simmer and cook for 7–8 minutes, or according to the packet instructions, until the pasta is *al dente*. Stir often during cooking to prevent the pasta shapes sticking together.

3 Drain the pieces of bottled roasted pepper and dice them finely. Place them in the bases of four warmed soup plates and set them aside.

4 Taste the soup and adjust the seasoning if necessary. Ladle it into the soup plates and serve immediately, with a bowl of freshly grated Parmesan cheese handed around separately.

Little Stuffed Hats in Broth

This soup is served in northern Italy on Santo Stefano (St Stephen's Day – 26 December) and on New Year's Day. It makes a welcome change from all the special celebration food, the day before. It is traditionally made with the Christmas capon carcass, but chicken stock works equally well.

INGREDIENTS

Serves 4

2 pints/5 cups Chicken Stock

3¹⁄₂–4 ounces/1 cup fresh or dried cappelletti

2 tablespoons dry white wine (optional)

about 1 tablespoon finely chopped fresh flat leaf parsley (optional)

salt and ground black pepper

about 2 tablespoons grated Parmesan cheese, to serve

1 Pour the chicken stock into a large pan and bring to the boil. Add a little salt and pepper to taste, then drop in the pasta.

2 Stir well and bring back to the boil. Lower the heat to a simmer and cook according to the instructions on the packet, until the pasta is *al dente*. Stir frequently during cooking to make sure that the pasta cooks evenly.

3 Swirl in the wine and parsley, if using, then taste and adjust the seasoning if necessary. Ladle into four warmed soup plates, then sprinkle with grated Parmesan. Serve immediately.

COOK'S TIP

Cappelletti is just another name for the pasta tortellini, which comes from the Romagna region of Italy. You can either buy them ready-made or make your own.

Minestrone with Pesto

In Genoa, they often make minestrone like this, with fresh pesto stirred in towards the end of cooking. It is packed full of vegetables and has a strong, heady flavor, making it an excellent vegetarian dish. There is Parmesan cheese in the pesto, so there is no need to serve any extra with the soup.

INGREDIENTS

Serves 4–6

3 tablespoons olive oil
1 onion, finely chopped
2 celery sticks, finely chopped
1 large carrot, finely chopped
5 ounces green beans, cut into
    2 inch pieces
1 zucchini, thinly sliced
1 potato, cut into ½ inch cubes
¼ savoy cabbage, shredded
1 small eggplant, cut into
    ½ inch cubes
7-ounce can cannellini beans, drained
    and rinsed
2 Italian plum tomatoes, chopped
2 pints/5 cups Vegetable Stock
3½ ounces dried spaghetti or vermicelli
salt and ground black pepper

For the pesto
about 20 fresh basil leaves
1 garlic clove
2 teaspoons pine nuts
1 tablespoon freshly grated
    Parmesan cheese
1 tablespoon freshly grated
    Pecorino cheese
2 tablespoons olive oil

1 Heat the oil in a large, heavy pan, add the chopped onion, celery and carrot, and cook over a low heat, stirring frequently, for 5–7 minutes.

2 Mix in the green beans, zucchini, potato and savoy cabbage. Stir-fry over a medium heat for about 3 minutes. Add the eggplant, cannellini beans and plum tomatoes and stir-fry for 2–3 minutes.

3 Pour in the stock and season with salt and pepper to taste. Bring to the boil. Stir well, cover and lower the heat. Simmer for 40 minutes, stirring occasionally.

4 Meanwhile, process all the pesto ingredients in a food processor until the mixture forms a smooth sauce, adding 1–3 tablespoons water through the feeder tube if the sauce seems too thick.

5 Break the pasta into small pieces and add it to the soup. Simmer, stirring frequently, for 5 minutes. Add the pesto sauce and stir it in well, then simmer for 2–3 minutes more, or until the pasta is *al dente*. Check the seasoning and serve hot, in warmed soup plates or bowls.

Star-gazer Vegetable Soup

V

For a different flavor, you could also make this soup with chicken or fish stock. All are equally tasty, and the soup makes an attractive first course for a dinner party.

INGREDIENTS

Serves 4

1 yellow bell pepper

2 large zucchini

2 large carrots

1 kohlrabi

1½ pints/3¾ cups Vegetable Stock

2 ounces rice vermicelli

salt and ground black pepper

1 Cut the bell pepper into quarters, removing the seeds and core. Cut the zucchini and carrots lengthways into ¼ inch slices and slice the kohlrabi into ¼ inch rounds.

2 Using tiny cookie cutters, stamp out shapes from the vegetables or use a very sharp knife to cut the slices into stars and other decorative shapes.

COOK'S TIP

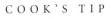

Sauté the leftover vegetable pieces in a little oil and mix with cooked brown rice to make a tasty risotto.

3 Place the vegetables and stock in a pan and simmer for 10 minutes, until the vegetables are tender. Season to taste with salt and pepper.

4 Meanwhile, place the rice vermicelli in a bowl, cover with boiling water and set aside for 4 minutes. Drain, then divide among four warmed soup bowls. Ladle the soup over the rice vermicelli and serve immediately.

Seafood Wonton Soup

This is a variation on the popular wonton soup with pork.

Serves 4

2 ounces raw jumbo shrimp
2 ounces queen scallops
3 ounces cod fillet, skinned and
 coarsely chopped
1 tablespoon finely chopped
 fresh chives
1 teaspoon dry sherry
1 medium egg white, lightly beaten
1/2 teaspoon sesame oil
1/4 teaspoon salt
large pinch of ground white pepper
20 wonton wrappers
2 romaine lettuce leaves, shredded
1 1/2 pints/3 3/4 cups Fish Stock
fresh cilantro leaves and garlic chives,
 to garnish

1 Peel and devein the shrimp. Rinse, pat dry on kitchen paper and cut into small pieces.

2 Rinse and dry the scallops. Chop them into small pieces the same size as the shrimp.

3 Place the cod in a food processor and process until a paste is formed. Scrape into a bowl and stir in the shrimp, scallops, chives, sherry, egg white, sesame oil, salt and pepper. Mix well, cover and leave in a cool place to marinate for 20 minutes.

4 Make the wontons. Place 1 teaspoon of the seafood filling in the center of a wonton wrapper, then bring the corners together to meet at the top. Twist them together to enclose the filling. Fill the remaining wonton wrappers in the same way. Tie with a fresh chive if you like.

COOK'S TIP

The filled wonton wrappers can be made ahead, then frozen for several weeks and cooked straight from the freezer.

5 Bring a large pan of water to the boil. Drop in the wontons. When the water returns to the boil, lower the heat and simmer gently for 5 minutes or until the wontons float to the surface. Drain the wontons and divide them among four heated soup bowls.

6 Add a portion of shredded lettuce to each bowl. Bring the fish stock to the boil in a pan over a medium heat. Ladle it on top of the lettuce and then garnish each portion with fresh cilantro leaves and garlic chives. Serve the wonton soup immediately.

Beef Noodle Soup

Offer your fortunate friends or family a steaming bowl of this soup, packed with delicious and exotic flavors of Asia.

INGREDIENTS

Serves 4

¼ ounce dried porcini mushrooms

¼ pint/⅔ cup boiling water

6 scallions

4 ounces carrots

12 ounces round steak

about 2 tablespoons oil

1 garlic clove, crushed

1-inch piece fresh root ginger, finely chopped

2 pints/5 cups Meat Stock

3 tablespoons light soy sauce

4 tablespoons dry sherry

3 ounces thin egg noodles

3 ounces spinach, shredded

salt and ground black pepper

1 Break the mushrooms into small pieces, place in a bowl and pour over the boiling water. Leave to soak for 15 minutes.

2 Shred the scallions and carrots into 2 inches long, fine strips. Trim any fat off the meat and slice into thin strips.

3 Heat the oil in a large pan and cook the beef, in batches, until browned, adding a little more oil if necessary. Remove the beef with a slotted spoon and drain well on paper towels.

4 Add the garlic, ginger, scallions and carrots to the pan and stir-fry for 3 minutes.

5 Add the meat stock, the pieces of mushroom and their soaking liquid, the soy sauce and sherry. Season generously with salt and ground black pepper. Bring to the boil and simmer, covered, for 10 minutes.

6 Break up the noodles slightly and add them to the pan with the shredded spinach. Simmer gently for 5 minutes, until the beef is tender. Adjust the seasoning to taste if necessary. Ladle into warm bowls and serve immediately.

COOK'S TIP

Dried porcini mushrooms are now widely available in supermarkets. They may seem expensive but are full of flavor, so a small quantity goes a long way and really gives a lift to a soup like this one.

Udon Noodles with Egg Broth and Ginger

In this Japanese dish, called Ankake Udon, *the soup for the udon is thickened with cornstarch and retains its heat for a long time.*

Serves 4

14 ounces dried udon noodles

2 tablespoons cornstarch

4 eggs, beaten

2 ounces cress

2 scallions, finely chopped

1-inch fresh root ginger, finely grated, to garnish

For the soup

1¾ pints/4 cups water

1½ ounces kezuri-bushi

1½ tablespoons mirin

1½ tablespoons shoyu

1½ teaspoons salt

1 To make the soup, place the water and the soup ingredients in a pan and bring to the boil over a medium heat. Remove from the heat when it starts boiling. Stand for 1 minute, then strain through cheesecloth. Check the taste and add more salt if required.

2 Heat at least 3½ pints/9 cups water in a large pan, and cook the udon noodles for 8 minutes, or according to the packet instructions. Drain under cold running water and wash off the starch with your hands. Leave the noodles in the sieve.

3 Pour the soup into a large pan and bring to the boil. Blend the cornstarch with 4 tablespoons water. Reduce the heat to medium and gradually add the cornstarch mixture to the hot soup. Stir constantly. The soup will thicken after a few minutes. Reduce the heat to low.

4 Mix the egg, cress, and scallions in a small bowl. Stir the soup once again to create a whirlpool. Pour the eggs slowly into the soup pan.

5 Reheat the noodles by pouring hot water over them. Divide among four bowls and pour the soup over the top. Garnish with the ginger and serve hot.

Pot-cooked Udon in Miso Soup

Udon is a white wheat noodle, more popular in the south and west of Japan than the north. It is eaten with various hot and cold sauces and soups. Here, in this dish known as Miso Nikomi Udon, *the noodles are cooked in a clay pot with a rich miso soup.*

INGREDIENTS

Serves 4

7 ounces skinless, boneless
   chicken portion

2 teaspoons sake

2 abura-age

1½ pints/3¾ cups water and
   1½ tsp instant dashi

6 large fresh shiitake mushrooms, stalks
   removed, quartered

4 scallions, trimmed and chopped into
   ⅛in lengths

2 tablespoons mirin

about 3½ ounces aka miso or
   hatcho miso

11 ounces dried udon noodles

4 eggs

1 Cut the chicken into bitesize pieces. Sprinkle with sake and leave to marinate for 15 minutes.

2 Put the abura-age in a sieve and thoroughly rinse with hot water to wash off the oil. Drain on paper towels and cut each abura-age into 4 squares.

3 To make the soup, heat the second dashi stock in a large pan. When it has come to the boil, add the chicken pieces, shiitake mushrooms and abura-age and cook for 5 minutes. Remove the pan from the heat and add the scallions.

4 Put the mirin and miso paste into a small bowl. Scoop 2 tablespoons soup from the pan and mix this in well.

5 To cook the noodles, boil at least 3½ pints/9 cups water in a large pan. The water should not come higher than two-thirds of the depth. Cook the noodles for 6 minutes and drain.

6 Put the noodles in one large flameproof clay pot or casserole (or divide among four small pots). Mix the miso paste into the soup and check the taste. Add more miso if required. Ladle in enough soup to cover the udon, and arrange the soup ingredients on top of the udon.

7 Put the soup on a medium heat and break an egg on top. When the soup bubbles, wait for 1 minute, then cover and remove from the heat. Leave to stand for 2 minutes before serving.

Tokyo-style Ramen Noodles in Soup

Ramen is a hybrid Chinese noodle dish presented in a Japanese way, and there are many regional variations, such as this from Tokyo.

INGREDIENTS

Serves 4

9 ounces dried ramen noodles

For the soup stock

4 scallions

3-inch piece of fresh root
    ginger, quartered

raw bones from 2 chickens, washed

1 large onion, quartered

4 garlic cloves, peeled

1 large carrot, coarsely chopped

1 egg shell

4 fluid ounces/½ cup sake

about 4 tablespoons shoyu

½ teaspoon salt

For the cha-shu (pot-roast pork)

1¼ pounds pork shoulder, boned

2 tablespoons vegetable oil

2 scallions, chopped

1-inch piece of fresh root ginger, sliced

1 tablespoon sake

3 tablespoons shoyu

1 tablespoon superfine sugar

For the toppings

2 hard-boiled eggs

5 ounces menma, soaked for 30 minutes
    and drained

½ nori sheet, broken into pieces

2 scallions, chopped

ground white pepper

sesame oil or chili oil

1 To make the soup stock, bruise the scallions and ginger by hitting with the side of a large knife. Pour 2½ pints/6¼ cups water into a wok and bring to the boil. Add the chicken bones and boil until the color of the meat changes. Discard the water and wash the bones under water.

2 In a clean wok, bring 3½ pints/9 cups water to the boil and add the bones and the other stock ingredients, except for the shoyu and salt. Reduce the heat and simmer until the water has reduced by half, skimming off any scum. Strain into a bowl through a sieve lined with cheesecloth.

3 Make the cha-shu. Roll the meat up tightly, 3½ inches in diameter, and tie with string.

4 Heat the oil to smoking point in a clean wok and add the chopped scallions and ginger. Cook briefly, then add the meat. Turn often to brown evenly.

5 Sprinkle with sake and add 14 fluid ounces/1⅔ cups water, the shoyu and sugar. Boil, then reduce the heat and cover. Cook for 25–30 minutes, turning every 5 minutes. Remove from the heat.

6 Slice the pork into 12 thin slices.

7 Shell and halve the boiled eggs, and sprinkle some salt onto the yolks.

8 Pour 1¾ pints/4 cups soup stock from the bowl into a large pan. Boil and add the shoyu and salt. Check the seasoning; add more shoyu if required.

9 Wash the wok again and bring 3½ pints/9 cups water to the boil. Cook the ramen noodles according to the packet instructions until just soft. Stir constantly to prevent them from sticking. If the water bubbles up, pour in 2 fluid ounces/¼ cup cold water. Drain well and divide among four bowls.

10 Pour the soup over the noodles to cover. Arrange half a boiled egg, pork slices, menma and nori on top, and sprinkle with scallions. Serve with pepper and sesame or chili oil. Season to taste with a little salt, if you like.

BEAN,
LENTIL AND
CHICKPEA
SOUPS

Known collectively as legumes, beans, lentils and chickpeas are
nutritional powerhouses, full of flavor and very economical,
so they are perfect for homemade soups. Some of the recipes
are based on fresh beans, while others rely on that useful
pantry standby, dried legumes, or pulses. The choice is
further extended by using canned beans and chickpeas, which,
while a little more expensive than the dried versions, do not
require lengthy soaking before cooking and so are conveniently
quick for busy cooks.

Lamb, Black-eyed Pea and Pumpkin Soup

This is a hearty soup to warm the cockles of the heart.

INGREDIENTS

Serves 4

4 ounces/²⁄₃ cup split black-eyed peas,
   soaked overnight
1¹⁄₂ pounds shoulder or breast of lamb,
   cut into medium-sized chunks
1 teaspoon chopped fresh thyme or
   ¹⁄₂ teaspoon dried thyme
2 bay leaves
2 pints/5 cups Meat Stock
1 onion, sliced
8 ounces pumpkin, diced
2 black cardamom pods
1¹⁄₂ teaspoond ground turmeric
2 tablespoon chopped fresh cilantro
¹⁄₂ teaspoon caraway seeds
1 fresh green chile, seeded and chopped
2 green bananas
1 carrot
salt and ground black pepper

3 Meanwhile, put the lamb in a large pan, add the thyme, bay leaves and stock and bring to the boil. Cover and simmer over a moderate heat for 1 hour, until the meat is tender.

4 Add the onion, pumpkin, cardamoms, turmeric, cilantro, caraway, chile and seasoning and stir. Bring back to a simmer and cook, uncovered, for 15 minutes, stirring occasionally, until the pumpkin is tender.

5 When the beans are cool, spoon into a blender or food processor with their liquid and process to a smooth purée.

6 Peel the bananas and cut into medium slices. Cut the carrot into thin slices. Stir the banana and carrot slices into the soup with the beans and cook for 10–12 minutes, until the carrot is tender. Adjust the seasoning if necessary, ladle into a warm tureen or individual bowls and serve immediately.

1 Drain the black-eyed peas, place them in a pan and cover with fresh cold water.

2 Bring the beans to the boil, boil rapidly for 10 minutes and then reduce the heat and simmer, covered, for about 40–50 minutes, until tender, adding more water if necessary. Remove the pan from the heat and set aside to cool.

Beef Chile Soup

This is a hearty dish based on a traditional chile recipe. It is ideal served with fresh, rustic bread as a warming start to any meal.

INGREDIENTS

Serves 4

1 tablespoon oil

1 onion, chopped

6 ounces/¾ cup ground beef

2 garlic cloves, chopped

1 fresh red chile, sliced

1 ounce/¼ cup all-purpose flour

14-ounce can chopped tomatoes

1 pint/2½ cups Meat Stock

8 ounces/2 cups canned kidney beans, drained and rinsed

2 tablespoons chopped fresh parsley

salt and ground black pepper

rustic bread, to serve

1 Heat the oil in a large pan. Add the onion and ground beef and cook for 5 minutes, until brown and sealed.

2 Add the garlic, chile and flour. Cook for 1 minute. Add the tomatoes and pour in the stock. Bring to the boil.

3 Stir in the kidney beans and season with salt and pepper to taste. Lower the heat and simmer for 20 minutes.

4 Add the chopped parsley, reserving a little to garnish the finished dish. Pour the soup into warm bowls, sprinkle with the reserved parsley and serve with rustic bread.

COOK'S TIP

For a milder flavor, remove the seeds from the chile after slicing.

Fresh Tomato and Bean Soup

This is a rich, chunky tomato soup, with beans and cilantro.

INGREDIENTS

Serves 4

2 pounds ripe plum tomatoes
2 tablespoons olive oil
10 ounces onions, coarsely chopped
2 garlic cloves, crushed
1½ pints/3¾ cups Vegetable Stock
2 tablespoons sun-dried tomato paste
2 teaspoons paprika
1 tablespoon cornstarch
15-ounce can cannellini beans, rinsed
  and drained
2 tablespoons chopped fresh cilantro
salt and ground black pepper
olive ciabatta, to serve

2 Drain the tomatoes and, when they are cool enough to handle, peel off the skins. Quarter them and then cut each piece in half again.

4 Add the tomatoes to the onions and stir in the stock, sun-dried tomato paste and paprika. Season with a little salt and pepper. Bring to the boil and simmer for 10 minutes.

3 Heat the oil in a large pan and cook the onions and garlic for 3 minutes, or until just beginning to soften.

5 Mix the cornstarch to a paste with 2 tablespoons water. Stir the beans into the soup with the cornstarch paste. Cook for a further 5 minutes.

1 First, peel the tomatoes. Using a sharp knife, make a small cross in each one and place in a bowl. Pour over boiling water to cover and leave to stand for 30–60 seconds.

6 Taste and adjust the seasoning if necessary and stir in the chopped cilantro just before serving with olive ciabatta.

V

Tuscan Bean Soup

There are many versions of this wonderful soup. This one uses cannellini beans, leeks, cabbage and good olive oil – and tastes even better when it is reheated.

Serves 4

3 tablespoons extra virgin olive oil
1 onion, coarsely chopped
2 leeks, coarsely chopped
1 large potato, diced
2 garlic cloves, finely chopped
2 pints/5 cups Vegetable Stock
14-ounce can cannellini beans, drained and can juice reserved
6 ounces savoy cabbage, shredded
3 tablespoons chopped fresh flat leaf parsley
2 tablespoons chopped fresh oregano
3 ounces/1 cup shaved Parmesan cheese
salt and ground black pepper

For the garlic toasts
2–3 tablespoons extra virgin olive oil
6 thick slices country bread
1 garlic clove, peeled and bruised

1 Heat the oil in a large, heavy pan, add the onion, leeks, potato and garlic and cook over a low heat, stirring occasionally, for 4–5 minutes, until they are just beginning to soften.

2 Pour on the vegetable stock and the reserved can juice from the beans. Cover and simmer for 15 minutes.

3 Stir in the cabbage, beans and half the herbs, season and cook for a further 10 minutes. Spoon about one-third of the soup into a food processor or blender and process until fairly smooth. Return to the soup in the pan, adjust the seasoning and heat through for 5 minutes.

4 Make the garlic toasts. Drizzle a little oil over the slices of bread, then rub both sides of each slice with the garlic. Toast until browned on both sides. Ladle the soup into bowls. Sprinkle with the remaining herbs and the Parmesan shavings. Add a drizzle of olive oil and serve with the hot garlic toasts.

Ribollita

Ribollita is rather like minestrone, but includes beans instead of pasta. In Italy, it is traditionally served ladled over bread and a rich green vegetable, although you could omit this for a lighter version.

INGREDIENTS

Serves 6–8

3 tablespoons olive oil

2 onions, chopped

2 carrots, sliced

4 garlic cloves, crushed

2 celery sticks, thinly sliced

1 fennel bulb, trimmed and chopped

2 large zucchini, thinly sliced

14-ounce can chopped tomatoes

2 tablespoons pesto, either homemade or
    ready-made

1½ pints/3¾ cups Vegetable Stock

14-ounce can navy or borlotti
    beans, drained

salt and ground black pepper

To serve

1 pound young spinach

1 tablespoon extra virgin olive oil, plus
    extra for drizzling

6–8 slices white bread

Parmesan cheese shavings (optional)

1 Heat the oil in a large, heavy pan. Add the onions, carrots, garlic, celery and fennel and cook over a low heat, stirring frequently, for 10 minutes. Add the zucchini slices and cook, stirring, for a further 2 minutes.

2 Add the chopped tomatoes, pesto, vegetable stock and beans and bring to the boil. Reduce the heat, cover and simmer gently for 25–30 minutes, until all the vegetables are tender. Season with salt and ground black pepper to taste.

3 To serve, cook the spinach in the oil for 2 minutes, or until wilted. Spoon over the bread in soup bowls, then ladle the soup over the spinach. Serve with extra olive oil for drizzling on to the soup and Parmesan cheese to sprinkle on top, if you like.

V

Provençal Vegetable Soup

This satisfying soup captures all the flavors of summer in Provence. The basil and garlic purée, pistou, gives it extra color and a wonderful aroma – so don't leave it out.

INGREDIENTS

Serves 6–8

10 ounces/1½ cups shelled fresh fava
    beans or 6 ounces/¾ cup dried navy
    beans, soaked overnight
½ teaspoon dried herbes de Provence
2 garlic cloves, finely chopped
1 tablespoon olive oil
1 onion, finely chopped
1 large leek, thinly sliced
1 celery stick, thinly sliced
2 carrots, finely diced
2 small potatoes, finely diced
4 ounces green beans
2 pints/5 cups water
2 small zucchini, finely chopped
3 tomatoes, peeled, seeded and
    finely chopped
4 ounces/1 cup shelled garden peas, fresh
    or frozen
handful of spinach leaves, cut into
    thin ribbons
salt and ground black pepper
fresh basil sprigs, to garnish

For the pistou
1 or 2 garlic cloves, finely chopped
½ ounce/½ cup basil leaves
4 tablespoons grated Parmesan cheese
4 tablespoons extra virgin olive oil

1 To make the pistou, put the garlic, basil and Parmesan cheese in a food processor and process until smooth, scraping down the sides once. With the machine running, slowly add the olive oil through the feeder tube. Alternatively, pound the garlic, basil and cheese in a mortar with a pestle and stir in the oil.

2 To make the soup, if using dried navy beans, drain them, place in a pan and cover with water. Boil vigorously for 10 minutes and drain.

3 Place the parboiled beans, or fresh beans, if using, in a pan with the herbes de Provence and one of the garlic cloves. Add cold water to cover by 1 inch. Bring to the boil, reduce the heat and simmer over a medium-low heat until tender, about 10 minutes for fresh beans or 1 hour for dried beans. Remove from the heat and set aside in the cooking liquid.

4 Heat the oil in a large pan or flameproof casserole. Add the onion and leek and cook over a low heat for 5 minutes, stirring occasionally, until they are just beginning to soften.

5 Add the celery, carrots and the remaining garlic clove and cook, covered, for 10 minutes, stirring occasionally.

6 Add the potatoes, green beans and water, then season with salt and pepper. Bring to the boil, skimming any foam that rises to the surface. Cover and simmer gently for 10 minutes.

7 Add the zucchini, tomatoes, peas and the reserved beans with their cooking liquid. Simmer for 25–30 minutes, until tender. Add the spinach and simmer for 5 minutes. Season and swirl a spoonful of pistou into each bowl. Garnish with basil and serve.

· COOK'S TIP ·
~

Both the pistou and the soup can
be made 1–2 days in advance
and chilled. To serve, reheat
gently, stirring occasionally.

Spicy Bean Soup

A filling soup made with two kinds of beans flavored with cumin.

INGREDIENTS

Serves 6–8

6 ounces/1 cup dried black beans, soaked
  overnight and drained
6 ounces/1 cup dried kidney beans,
  soaked overnight and drained
2 bay leaves
6 tablespoons coarse salt
2 tablespoons olive or vegetable oil
3 carrots, chopped
1 onion, chopped
1 celery stick
1 garlic clove, crushed
1 teaspoon ground cumin
1/4–1/2 teaspoon cayenne pepper
1/2 teaspoon dried oregano
2 fluid ounces/1/4 cup red wine
2 pints/5 cups Meat Stock
8 fluid ounces/1 cup water
salt and ground black pepper

For the garnish
sour cream
chopped fresh cilantro

1 Put the black beans and kidney beans in two separate pans with cold water to cover and a bay leaf in each. Boil rapidly for 10 minutes, then cover and simmer for 20 minutes.

2 Add 3 tablespoons coarse salt to each pan and continue simmering for 30 minutes, until the beans are tender. Drain.

3 Heat the oil in a large, heavy flameproof casserole. Add the carrots, onion, celery and garlic and cook over a low heat for 8–10 minutes, stirring, until softened. Stir in the cumin, cayenne, and oregano and season with salt to taste.

4 Add the red wine, meat stock and water and stir to mix all the ingredients together. Remove the bay leaves from the cooked beans and discard, then add the beans to the casserole.

5 Bring to the boil, reduce the heat, then cover and simmer gently for about 20 minutes, stirring occasionally.

6 Transfer half the soup (including most of the solids) to a food processor or blender. Process until smooth. Return to the pan and stir to combine well.

7 Reheat the soup and adjust the seasoning to taste. Serve hot, garnished with sour cream and chopped cilantro.

Beet and Lima Bean Soup

This soup is a simplified version of borscht and is prepared in a fraction of the time. Serve with a spoonful of sour cream and a sprinkling of chopped fresh parsley.

INGREDIENTS

Serves 4

2 tablespoons vegetable oil

1 onion, sliced

1 teaspoon caraway seeds

finely grated rind of ½ orange

9 ounces cooked beet, grated

2 pints/5 cups Meat Stock or rassol
  (see Cook's Tip)

14-ounce can lima beans, drained
  and rinsed

1 tablespoon wine vinegar

4 tablespoons sour cream

4 tablespoons chopped fresh parsley,
  to garnish

1 Heat the oil in a large pan and cook the onion, caraway seeds and orange rind over a low heat until soft, but not colored.

2 Add the beet, stock or rassol, lima beans and vinegar and simmer over a low heat for a further 10 minutes.

3 Divide the soup among four warm bowls, add a spoonful of sour cream to each, sprinkle with chopped parsley and serve.

COOK'S TIP

Rassol is a beet broth, which is used to impart a strong beet color and flavor. You are most likely to find it in kosher food stores.

White Bean Soup

*Use either navy or lima beans for
this velvety soup.*

INGREDIENTS

Serves 4

6 ounces/³⁄₄ cup dried white beans, soaked
   in cold water overnight
2–3 tablespoons oil
2 large onions, chopped
4 celery sticks, chopped
1 parsnip, chopped
1³⁄₄ pints/4 cups Chicken Stock
salt and ground black pepper
chopped fresh cilantro and paprika,
   to garnish

1 Drain the beans and boil
rapidly in fresh water for
10 minutes. Drain, cover with
more fresh water and simmer for
1–2 hours, until soft. Reserve the
liquid and discard any bean skins
on the surface.

2 Heat the oil in a heavy pan
and sauté the onions, celery
and parsnip for 3 minutes.

COOK'S TIP

You can, if you like, use a
14-ounce can cannellini or
lima beans instead of dried
beans. Drain and rinse them
before adding to the dish.

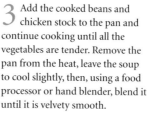

3 Add the cooked beans and
chicken stock to the pan and
continue cooking until all the
vegetables are tender. Remove the
pan from the heat, leave the soup
to cool slightly, then, using a food
processor or hand blender, blend it
until it is velvety smooth.

4 Reheat the soup gently,
gradually adding some of the
bean liquid or a little water if it is
too thick. Season to taste.

5 To serve, transfer the soup
into wide bowls. Garnish
with fresh cilantro and paprika.

Fava Bean and Rice Soup

V

This thick soup makes the most of fresh fava beans while they are in season. It works well with frozen beans for the rest of the year.

INGREDIENTS

Serves 4

2¼ pounds fava beans in their pods,
   or 14 ounces shelled frozen fava
   beans, thawed
6 tablespoons olive oil
1 onion, finely chopped
2 tomatoes, peeled and
   finely chopped
8 ounces/1 cup arborio or other
   non-parboiled rice
1 ounce/2 tablespoons butter
1¾ pints/4 cups boiling water
salt and ground black pepper
grated Parmesan cheese, to
   serve (optional)

1 Shell the beans if they are fresh. Bring a large pan of water to the boil and blanch the beans, fresh or frozen, for 3–4 minutes. Rinse under cold water and peel off the skins.

2 Heat the oil in a large pan. Add the onion and cook over a low to moderate heat until it softens. Stir in the beans and cook for about 5 minutes, stirring to coat them with the oil.

3 Season to taste with salt and pepper. Add the tomatoes and cook for a further 5 minutes, stirring frequently. Add the rice and cook, stirring constantly, for a further 1–2 minutes.

4 Add the butter and stir until it melts. Pour in the water, a little at a time. Adjust the seasoning to taste. Continue cooking until the rice is tender. Serve with grated Parmesan, if you like.

Bean and Pasta Soup

Serve this hearty soup with tasty, pesto-topped French bread croûtons.

INGREDIENTS

Serves 4

4 ounces/½ cup mixed dried beans,
    soaked overnight and drained
1 tablespoon oil
1 onion, chopped
2 celery sticks, thinly sliced
2–3 garlic cloves, crushed
2 leeks, thinly sliced
1 vegetable bouillon cube
14-ounce can or jar pimientos
3–4 tablespoons tomato paste
4 ounces dried pasta shapes
4 slices French bread
1 tablespoon Pesto Sauce (see page 130)
4 ounces/1 cup baby corn cobs, halved
2 ounces broccoli florets
2 ounces cauliflower florets
a few drops of Tabasco sauce
salt and ground black pepper

1 Place the beans in a large pan and cover with water. Bring to the boil and boil rapidly for 15 minutes. Drain and cover with fresh water. Bring to the boil, then simmer for about 45 minutes, or until nearly tender.

2 When the beans are almost ready, heat the oil in a large pan and cook the vegetables for 2 minutes. Add the bouillon cube and the beans with about 1 pint/2½ cups of their liquid. Cover and simmer for 10 minutes.

3 Meanwhile, purée the pimientos with a little of their liquid and add to the pan. Stir in the tomato paste and pasta and cook for 15 minutes. Preheat the oven to 400°F.

4 Meanwhile, make the pesto croûtons. Spread the French bread with the pesto sauce and bake for 10 minutes, or until crisp.

5 When the pasta is just cooked, add the corn cobs, broccoli, cauliflower, Tabasco and seasoning to taste. Heat for 2–3 minutes and serve with the pesto croûtons.

Black and White Bean Soup

V

Although this soup takes time to prepare, the results are so stunning that it is well worth the effort.

Serves 8

12 ounces/2 cups dried black beans,
    soaked overnight and drained
4¼ pints/10½ cups water
6 garlic cloves, crushed
12 ounces/2 cups dried white beans,
    soaked overnight and drained
6 tablespoons balsamic vinegar
4 jalapeño peppers, seeded and chopped
6 scallions, finely chopped
juice of 1 lime
2 fluid ounces/¼ cup olive oil
½ ounce/¼ cup chopped fresh cilantro,
    plus extra to garnish
salt and ground black pepper

1 Place the black beans in a large pan with half the water and garlic. Bring to the boil. Reduce the heat to low, cover the pan, and simmer for about 1½ hours, until the beans are soft.

2 Meanwhile, put the white beans in another pan with the remaining water and garlic. Bring to the boil, cover the pan and simmer for about 1 hour until soft.

3 Process the cooked white beans in a food processor or blender. Stir in the balsamic vinegar, jalapeños, and half the scallions. Return to the pan and reheat gently.

4 Process the cooked black beans in the food processor or blender. Return to the pan and stir in the lime juice, olive oil, cilantro and remaining scallions. Reheat gently.

5 Season both soups with salt and ground black pepper to taste. To serve, place a ladleful of each puréed soup, side by side, in each of eight warmed soup bowls. Swirl the two soups together with a toothpick or skewer. Garnish with chopped fresh cilantro and serve.

Thai Lentil and Coconut Soup

Hot, spicy and richly flavored, this is a substantial soup that is perfect for a cold winter evening. Serve with chunks of warmed naan bread.

INGREDIENTS

Serves 4

2 tablespoons sunflower oil

2 red onions, finely chopped

1 fresh bird's eye chile, seeded and thinly sliced

2 garlic cloves, chopped

1-inch piece of lemon grass, outer layers removed and inside thinly sliced

7 ounces/scant 1 cup red lentils, rinsed

1 teaspoon ground coriander

1 teaspoon paprika

14 fluid ounces/1⅔ cups coconut milk

juice of 1 lime

3 scallions, chopped

¾ ounce/scant 1 cup fresh cilantro, finely chopped

salt and ground black pepper

1 Heat the oil in a large pan and add the onions, chile, garlic and lemon grass. Cook over a low heat for 5 minutes, or until the onions have softened but not browned, stirring occasionally. Add the lentils, ground coriander and paprika.

2 Pour in the coconut milk and 1½ pints/3¾ cups water, and stir well. Bring to the boil, stir, then reduce the heat and simmer for 40–45 minutes.

3 Pour in the lime juice and add the scallions and fresh cilantro, reserving a little of each. Season to taste with salt and pepper, then ladle the soup into warm bowls. Garnish with the reserved scallions and cilantro.

Indian Spiced Lentil Soup

A subtle blend of spices takes this warming soup to new heights. Serve it with rustic bread for a filling start to a winter supper.

INGREDIENTS

Serves 6

2 onions, finely chopped

2 garlic cloves, crushed

4 tomatoes, coarsely chopped

½ teaspoon ground turmeric

1 teaspoon ground cumin

6 cardamom pods

½ cinnamon stick

8 ounces/1 cup red lentils, rinsed
   and drained

1½ pints/3¾ cups water

14-ounce can coconut milk

1 tablespoon lime juice

salt and ground black pepper

cumin seeds, to garnish

1 Put the onions, garlic, tomatoes, turmeric, cumin, cardamom pods, cinnamon, lentils and water into a pan. Bring to the boil, lower the heat, cover and simmer gently for 20 minutes, or until the lentils are soft.

2 Remove the cardamom pods and cinnamon stick, then process the mixture in a blender or food processor. Press the soup through a sieve, then return it to the clean pan.

3 Reserve a little of the coconut milk for the garnish and add the remainder to the pan with the lime juice. Stir well and season with salt and pepper. Reheat the soup without boiling. Swirl in the reserved coconut milk, garnish with cumin seeds and serve.

Lentil and Pasta Soup

Serve this rustic, vegetarian soup before a salad or other light main course. It goes well with whole-wheat or rustic Italian bread.

INGREDIENTS

Serves 4–6

6 ounces/³⁄₄ cup brown lentils
3 garlic cloves
1³⁄₄ pints/4 cups water
3 tablespoons olive oil
1 ounce/2 tablespoons butter
1 onion, finely chopped
2 celery sticks, finely chopped
2 tablespoons sun-dried tomato paste
3 pints/7¹⁄₂ cups Vegetable Stock
few fresh marjoram leaves, plus extra
    to garnish
few fresh basil leaves
leaves from fresh thyme sprig
2 ounces/¹⁄₂ cup small dried
    pasta shapes
salt and ground black pepper

1 Put the lentils in a large pan. Smash one of the garlic cloves (there's no need to peel it first) and add it to the lentils. Pour in the water and bring to the boil. Lower the heat to a gentle simmer and cook for about 20 minutes, stirring occasionally, until the lentils are just tender.

2 Tip the lentils into a sieve, remove the cooked garlic clove and set it aside.

3 Rinse the lentils under cold running water, then leave them to drain. Heat 2 tablespoons of the olive oil with half of the butter in a large pan. Add the onion and celery and cook over a low heat, stirring frequently, for 5–7 minutes, until softened.

COOK'S TIP

Use green lentils instead of brown, if you like, but the orange or red ones are not so good for this soup because they tend to go mushy.

4 Crush the remaining garlic and peel and mash the reserved cooked garlic clove. Add them to the vegetables with the remaining oil, the sun-dried tomato paste and lentils. Stir, then add the stock, herbs and salt and pepper to taste. Bring to the boil, stirring. Simmer for 30 minutes, stirring occasionally.

5 Add the pasta and bring to the boil, stirring. Simmer, stirring frequently, for 7–8 minutes, or according to the instructions on the packet, until the pasta is *al dente*. Add the remaining butter and adjust the seasoning. Serve hot in warmed bowls, garnished with marjoram leaves.

Lentil and Bacon Soup

This is a wonderfully hearty German soup, but a lighter version can be made by omitting the frankfurters, if you like.

INGREDIENTS

Serves 6

8 ounces/1 cup brown lentils

1 tablespoon sunflower oil

1 onion, finely chopped

1 leek, finely chopped

1 carrot, finely diced

2 celery sticks, chopped

4-ounce piece lean bacon

2 bay leaves

2½ pints/6¼ cups water

2 tablespoons chopped fresh parsley, plus extra to garnish

8 ounces frankfurters, sliced

salt and ground black pepper

1 Rinse the lentils thoroughly under cold running water, then drain.

2 Heat the oil in a large pan and gently cook the onion , stirring occasionally, for 5 minutes, until soft. Add the leek, carrot, celery, bacon and bay leaves.

COOK'S TIP

Unlike most pulses, brown lentils do not need to be soaked before cooking.

3 Add the lentils. Pour in the water, then gradually bring to the boil. Skim the surface, then simmer, half-covered, for about 45–50 minutes, or until the lentils are soft.

4 Remove the piece of bacon from the soup and cut into small cubes. Trim off any fat.

5 Return the bacon to the soup with the parsley and sliced frankfurters, and season well with salt and ground black pepper. Simmer for 2–3 minutes, then remove the bay leaves.

6 Transfer to individual soup bowls and serve garnished with chopped parsley.

V

Garlicky Lentil Soup

High in fiber and protein, lentils make a particularly tasty soup, and this recipe just couldn't be simpler or easier.

INGREDIENTS

Serves 6

8 ounces/1 cup red lentils, rinsed
    and drained
2 onions, finely chopped
2 large garlic cloves, finely chopped
1 carrot, finely chopped
2 tablespoons olive oil
2 bay leaves
generous pinch of dried marjoram
    or oregano
2½ pints/6¼ cups Vegetable Stock
2 tablespoons red wine vinegar
salt and ground black pepper
celery leaves, to garnish
rustic bread rolls, to serve

1 Put all the ingredients except for the red wine vinegar, seasoning and garnish in a large, heavy pan. Bring to the boil over a medium heat, then lower the heat and simmer for 1½ hours, stirring the soup occasionally to prevent the lentils from sticking to the base of the pan.

2 Remove the bay leaves and add the red wine vinegar, with salt and pepper to taste. If the soup is too thick, thin it with a little extra vegetable stock or water. Ladle the soup into heated bowls and garnish with celery leaves. Serve immediately with warmed rustic rolls.

COOK'S TIP

If you buy your lentils loose, remember to tip them into a sieve or colander and pick them over, removing any pieces of grit, before rinsing them.

Lentil Soup with Rosemary

A classic rustic Italian soup flavored with rosemary, this is delicious served with garlic bread.

INGREDIENTS

Serves 4

8 ounces/1 cup dried green or
  brown lentils
3 tablespoons extra virgin olive oil
3 rindless fatty bacon rashers, cut into
  small dice
1 onion, finely chopped
2 celery sticks, finely chopped
2 carrots, finely chopped
2 fresh rosemary sprigs, finely chopped
2 bay leaves
14-ounce can plum tomatoes
3 pints/7½ cups Vegetable Stock
salt and ground black pepper
fresh bay leaves and fresh rosemary
  sprigs, to garnish

1 Place the lentils in a bowl and cover with cold water. Leave to soak for 2 hours. Rinse and drain.

2 Heat the olive oil in a large, heavy pan. Add the bacon and cook over a medium heat, stirring occasionally, for about 3 minutes, then add the onion and cook, stirring frequently, for 5 minutes, until softened.

3 Stir in the chopped celery, carrots, herbs and lentils. Toss over the heat for 1 minute, until thoroughly coated in the oil.

4 Tip in the tomatoes and stock, and bring to the boil. Lower the heat, half-cover the pan and simmer for about 1 hour, until the lentils are perfectly tender.

5 Remove and discard the bay leaves and season the soup with salt and pepper to taste. Ladle into warm bowls and serve hot with a garnish of fresh bay leaves and sprigs of rosemary.

COOK'S TIP

Keep an eye open for the small, flat green lentils in Italian groceries or delicatessens, as they have an excellent flavor.

Smoked Turkey and Lentil Soup

Lentils seem to enhance the flavor of smoked turkey, and combined with four tasty vegetables they make a fine appetizer.

INGREDIENTS ·

Serves 4

1 ounce/2 tablespoons butter
1 large carrot, chopped
1 onion, chopped
1 leek, white part only, chopped
1 celery stick, chopped
4 ounces/1½ cups mushrooms, chopped
2 fluid ounces/¼ cup dry white wine
2 pints/5 cups Chicken Stock
2 teaspoons dried thyme
1 bay leaf
4 ounces/½ cup green lentils, rinsed
3 ounces smoked turkey meat, diced
salt and ground black pepper

1 Melt the butter in a large pan. Add the carrot, onion, leek, celery and mushrooms. Cook over a medium heat, stirring frequently, for 3–5 minutes, until softened and golden brown.

2 Stir in the wine and chicken stock. Bring to the boil and skim off any foam that rises to the surface. Add the thyme and bay leaf. Lower the heat, cover and simmer gently for 30 minutes.

3 Add the lentils, re-cover the pan and continue cooking over a low heat for 30–40 minutes more, until they are just tender. Stir the soup occasionally to prevent the lentils from sticking to the base of the pan.

4 Stir in the smoked turkey and season to taste with salt and pepper. Cook until just heated through. Ladle the soup into bowls and serve immediately.

Chickpea and Pasta Soup

This is a simple, country-style, soup, packed with flavor. The shape of the pasta and the beans complement one another beautifully.

INGREDIENTS

Serves 4–6

4 tablespoons olive oil

1 onion, finely chopped

2 carrots, finely chopped

2 celery sticks, finely chopped

14-ounce can chickpeas, drained
   and rinsed

7-ounce can cannellini beans, drained
   and rinsed

1/4 pint/2/3 cup bottled strained tomatoes

4 fluid ounces/1/2 cup water

2 1/2 pints/6 1/4 cups Vegetable or
   Chicken Stock

1 fresh rosemary sprig, extra to garnish

7 ounces/scant 2 cups dried conchiglie

salt and ground black pepper

shavings of Parmesan cheese,
   to serve

1 Heat the olive oil in a large, heavy pan, add the chopped vegetables and cook over a low heat, stirring frequently, for 5–7 minutes.

2 Add the chickpeas and cannellini beans, stir well to mix, then cook for 5 minutes. Stir in the tomatoes and water. Cook, stirring, for 2–3 minutes.

3 Add 16 fluid ounces/2 cups of the stock, the rosemary sprig and salt and ground black pepper to taste. Bring to the boil, cover, then simmer over a low heat, stirring occasionally, for 1 hour.

VARIATIONS

You can use other pasta shapes, but conchiglie are ideal because they scoop up the chickpeas and beans. If you like, crush 1–2 garlic cloves and cook them with the vegetables.

4 Pour in the remaining stock, add the pasta and bring to the boil. Lower the heat and simmer for 7–8 minutes, or according to the instructions on the packet, until the pasta is *al dente*. Remove the rosemary sprig. Serve the soup sprinkled with rosemary leaves and Parmesan shavings.

Moroccan Harira

This tasty soup is traditionally eaten during the month of Ramadan, when the Muslim population fasts between sunrise and sunset.

INGREDIENTS

Serves 4

1 ounce/2 tablespoons butter
8 ounces lamb, cut into ½ inch pieces
1 onion, chopped
1 pound well-flavored tomatoes
4 tablespoons chopped fresh cilantro
2 tablespoons chopped fresh parsley
½ teaspoon ground turmeric
½ teaspoon ground cinnamon
2 ounces/¼ cup red lentils
3 ounces/½ cup chickpeas,
  soaked overnight
1 pint/2½ cups water
4 pearl onions, peeled
1 ounce/¼ cup soup noodles
salt and ground black pepper

For the garnish
chopped fresh cilantro
lemon slices
ground cinnamon

1 Heat the butter in a large pan or flameproof casserole and cook the lamb and chopped onion for 5 minutes, stirring frequently.

2 Peel the tomatoes, if you like, by plunging them into boiling water to loosen the skins. Wait for them to cool a little before peeling off the skins. Then cut them into quarters and add to the lamb with the herbs and spices.

3 Rinse the lentils under cold running water and drain the chickpeas. Add both to the pan with the water. Season with salt and pepper. Bring to the boil, cover and simmer gently for 1½ hours.

4 Add the baby onions and cook for a further 30 minutes. Add the noodles 5 minutes before the end of the cooking time. Serve the soup when the noodles are tender. Ladle into warm bowls, garnish with the cilantro, lemon slices and cinnamon.

Chickpea and Parsley Soup

*Parsley and a hint of lemon bring
freshness to chickpeas.*

INGREDIENTS

Serves 6

8 ounces/1⅓ cups chickpeas,
   soaked overnight
1 small onion
bunch of fresh parsley (about 1½ ounces)
2 tablespoons olive and sunflower
   oils, mixed
2 pints/5 cups Chicken Stock
juice of ½ lemon
salt and ground black pepper
lemon wedges and finely pared strips of
   rind, to garnish

1 Drain the chickpeas and rinse under cold water. Cook them in boiling water for 1–1½ hours. Drain and rub off the skins.

2 Place the onion and parsley in a food processor or blender and process until finely chopped.

3 Heat the olive and sunflower oils in a pan or flameproof casserole and cook the onion mixture over a low heat, stirring frequently, for about 4 minutes until the onion is slightly softened.

4 Add the chickpeas, cook gently for 1–2 minutes, then add the stock. Season with salt and pepper. Bring the soup to the boil, then cover and simmer for 20 minutes, until the chickpeas are tender.

5 Leave the soup to cool a little and then mash the chickpeas with a fork until the soup is thick, but still quite chunky.

6 Reheat the soup gently and stir in the lemon juice. Serve immediately, garnished with lemon wedges and rind.

Chickpea and Spinach Soup with Garlic

This thick and creamy soup is richly flavored – perfect for vegetarians.

INGREDIENTS

Serves 4

2 tablespoons olive oil

4 garlic cloves, crushed

1 onion, coarsely chopped

2 teaspoons ground cumin

2 teaspoons ground coriander

2 pints/5 cups Vegetable Stock

12 ounces potatoes, finely chopped

15-ounce can chickpeas, drained

1 tablespoon cornstarch

¼ pint/⅔ cup heavy cream

2 tablespoons light tahini

7 ounces spinach, shredded

cayenne pepper

salt and ground black pepper

2 Stir in the ground cumin and coriander and cook for 1 minute. Add the vegetable stock and potatoes. Bring to the boil and simmer for 10 minutes.

3 Add the chickpeas and simmer for a further 5 minutes, or until the potatoes are just tender.

4 Blend together the cornstarch, cream, tahini and plenty of seasoning. Stir into the soup with the spinach. Bring to the boil, stirring, and simmer for a further 2 minutes. Adjust the seasoning with salt, pepper and cayenne to taste. Serve sprinkled with a little extra cayenne.

1 Heat the olive oil in a large, heavy pan and cook the garlic and onion over a medium heat, stirring occasionally, for about 5 minutes, or until the onion is softened and golden brown.

COOK'S TIP

Tahini is sesame-seed paste and is available from many health-food stores.

Eastern European Chickpea Soup

Chickpeas form part of the staple diet in the Balkans, where this soup originates. It is economical to make, and is a hearty and satisfying dish.

INGREDIENTS

Serves 4–6

1¼ pounds/5 cups chickpeas,
    soaked overnight

3½ pints/9 cups Vegetable Stock

3 large waxy potatoes, cut into
    bitesize chunks

2 fluid ounces/¼ cup olive oil

8 ounces spinach leaves

salt and ground black pepper

spicy sausage, cooked (optional)

1 Drain the chickpeas and rinse under cold water. Place in a large pan with the vegetable stock. Bring to the boil, then reduce the heat and cook gently for about 1 hour.

2 Add the potatoes and olive oil and season with salt and pepper to taste. Cook for about 20 minutes, until the potatoes are just tender.

3 Add the spinach and sliced, cooked sausage (if using) 5 minutes before the end of the cooking time. Ladle the soup into individual warmed soup bowls and serve immediately.

FISH AND SHELLFISH SOUPS

~

There is something incredibly special about fish soups, even
though many of them originated as inexpensive meals for
fishermen to use up leftovers from the day's catch. Nowadays,
many of these traditional recipes, such as Bouillabaisse, are
luxurious treats reserved for dinner parties and special
occasions. However, not all fish and shellfish soups, bisques
and chowders will strain the family budget, and many are
so quick and easy to make that they will provide the perfect
first course for a midweek supper.

Smoked Haddock and Potato Soup

"Cullen Skink" is a classic Scottish dish using one of the country's tastiest fish.

Serves 6

12 ounces smoked haddock fillet
1 onion, chopped
bouquet garni
1½ pints/3¾ cups water
1¼ pounds floury potatoes, quartered
1 pint/2½ cups milk
1½ ounces/3 tbsp butter
salt and ground black pepper
chopped chives, to garnish
rustic bread, to serve

3 Strain the fish stock and return to the pan, then add the potatoes and simmer for about 25 minutes. Remove the potatoes from the pan. Add the milk to the pan and bring to the boil over a low heat.

4 Mash the potatoes with the butter, then whisk them into the soup. Add the fish to the pan and heat through. Season to taste. Ladle into bowls, sprinkle with chives and serve with rustic bread.

1 Put the first four ingredients into a large pan and bring to the boil. Skim off any scum that rises to the surface, then cover and poach gently for 10–15 minutes.

2 Lift the haddock from the pan and cool slightly, then remove the skin and bones. Flake the flesh and put to one side. Return the skin and bones to the pan and simmer for 30 minutes.

Fish Soup with Dumplings

Use a variety of whatever fish is available in this Czech soup, such as perch, catfish, cod or snapper. The basis of the dumplings is the same, whether you use semolina or flour.

INGREDIENTS

Serves 4–8

3 rindless bacon strips, diced

1¹⁄₂ pounds assorted fresh fish, skinned, boned and diced

1 tablespoon paprika, plus extra to garnish

2¹⁄₂ pints/6¹⁄₄ cups Fish Stock or water

3 firm tomatoes, peeled and chopped

4 waxy potatoes, grated

1–2 teaspoons chopped fresh marjoram, plus extra to garnish

For the dumplings

3 ounces/¹⁄₂ cup semolina or all-purpose flour

1 egg, beaten

3 tablespoons milk or water

generous pinch of salt

1 tablespoon chopped fresh parsley

1 Dry-fry the bacon in a large pan until golden brown, then add the pieces of assorted fish. Cook for 1–2 minutes, taking care not to break up the pieces of fish.

2 Sprinkle in the paprika, pour in the fish stock or water and bring to the boil. Reduce the heat and simmer for 10 minutes.

3 Stir the chopped tomatoes, grated potato and marjoram into the pan. Cook for 10 minutes, stirring occasionally.

4 Combine all the dumpling ingredients, then leave to stand, covered with plastic wrap for 5–10 minutes.

5 Drop spoonfuls of the mixture into the soup and cook for 10 minutes. Serve hot with a little marjoram and paprika.

Seafood Soup

This is a really chunky, aromatic mixed fish soup from France, flavored with plenty of saffron and herbs. Rouille, a fiery hot paste, is served separately for everyone to swirl into their soup to flavor.

INGREDIENTS

Serves 6

3 red mullet or snapper, scaled
   and gutted
12 large shrimp
1½ pounds white fish, such as cod
8 ounces fresh mussels
1 onion, quartered
2 pints/5 cups water
1 teaspoon saffron threads
5 tablespoons olive oil
1 fennel bulb, coarsely chopped
4 garlic cloves, crushed
3 strips pared orange rind
4 fresh thyme sprigs
1½ pounds tomatoes
2 tablespoons sun-dried tomato paste
3 bay leaves
salt and ground black pepper

For the rouille
1 red bell pepper, seeded and
   coarsely chopped
1 fresh red chile, seeded and sliced
2 garlic cloves, chopped
5 tablespoons olive oil
½ ounces/¼ cup fresh bread crumbs

1 To make the *rouille*, process all
the ingredients in a blender or
food processor until smooth.
Transfer to a serving dish and chill.

COOK'S TIP
To save time, order the fish and
ask the supermarket to fillet
the mullet or snapper.

2 Fillet the mullet or snapper by
cutting the flesh from the
backbone. Reserve the heads and
bones. Cut the fillets into small
chunks. Peel half the shrimp and
reserve the trimmings to make the
stock. Skin the white fish,
discarding any bones, and cut into
large chunks. Scrub the mussels,
discarding any open ones.

3 Put the fish trimmings and
shrimp trimmings in a pan
with the onion and water. Bring to
the boil, then reduce the heat and
simmer gently for 30 minutes.
Remove the pan from the heat,
cool slightly, then strain.

4 Place the saffron in a small
bowl and add 1 tablespoon
boiling water. Set aside to soak.

5 Heat 2 tablespoons of the olive
oil in a large sauté pan or
heavy pan. Add the gurnard,
mullet or snapper and the white
fish and cook over a high heat for
1 minute. Drain well.

6 Heat the remaining oil and
cook the fennel, garlic, orange
rind and thyme over a medium
heat until beginning to color.
Measure the strained stock and
make up to about 2 pints/5 cups
with water.

7 Plunge the tomatoes into
boiling water for 30 seconds,
then refresh in cold water. Peel and
chop. Add the stock to the pan with
the saffron, tomatoes, tomato paste
and bay leaves. Season to taste, bring
almost to the boil, then simmer
gently, covered, for 20 minutes.

8 Stir in the mullet or snapper,
the white fish, peeled and
unpeeled shrimp and add the
mussels. Cover the pan and cook
for 3–4 minutes. Discard any
mussels that do not open. Serve
the soup hot with the *rouille*.

Matelote

*Traditionally, this fishermen's chunky
soup is made from freshwater fish,
including eel.*

INGREDIENTS

Serves 6

2¼ pounds mixed fish, including 1 pound
   conger eel if possible

2 ounces/¼ cup butter

1 onion, thickly sliced

2 celery sticks, thickly sliced

2 carrots, thickly sliced

1 bottle dry white or red wine

1 fresh bouquet garni containing parsley,
   bay leaf and chervil

2 cloves

6 black peppercorns

beurre manié (see Cook's Tip)

salt and cayenne pepper

For the garnish

1 ounce/2 tablespoons butter

12 pearl onions, peeled

12 white mushrooms

chopped flat leaf parsley

3 For the garnish, heat the butter
in a pan and sauté the pearl
onions until golden and tender.
Add the mushrooms and cook
until golden. Season and keep hot.

> ### COOK'S TIP
> ∾
> To make the beurre manié, mix
> ½ ounce/1 tablespoon softened
> butter with 1 tablespoon
> all-purpose flour.

4 Strain the soup through a large
sieve placed over a clean pan.
Discard the herbs and spices in the
sieve, then divide the fish among
deep soup plates and keep hot.

5 Reheat the soup until it boils.
Lower the heat and whisk in
the beurre manié, piece by piece,
until the soup thickens. Season it
and pour over the fish. Garnish
each portion with the fried pearl
onions and mushrooms and
sprinkle with chopped parsley.

1 Cut all the fish into thick slices,
removing any bones. Melt the
butter in a large pan, add the fish
and sliced vegetables and stir over
a medium heat until lightly browned.

2 Pour in the wine and enough
cold water to cover. Add the
bouquet garni and spices and
season to taste. Bring to the boil,
lower the heat and simmer gently
for 20–30 minutes, until the fish
is tender.

Fish Soup with Rouille

Making this soup is simplicity itself, yet the flavor suggests it is the product of painstaking preparation and complicated cooking.

INGREDIENTS

Serves 6

2¼ pounds mixed fish
2 tablespoons olive oil
1 onion, chopped
1 carrot, chopped
1 leek, chopped
2 large ripe tomatoes, chopped
1 red bell pepper, seeded and chopped
2 garlic cloves, peeled
5 ounces/⅔ cup tomato paste
1 large fresh bouquet garni, containing 3 parsley sprigs, 3 small celery sticks and 3 bay leaves
½ pint/1¼ cups dry white wine
salt and ground black pepper

For the rouille
2 garlic cloves, coarsely chopped
1 teaspoon coarse salt
1 thick slice of white bread, crust removed, soaked in water and then squeezed dry
1 fresh red chile, seeded and coarsely chopped
3 tablespoons olive oil
pinch of cayenne pepper (optional)
salt

For the garnish
12 slices of baguette, toasted in the oven
2 ounces/½ cup finely grated Gruyère cheese

COOK'S TIP

Any firm fish can be used for this recipe. If you use whole fish, include the heads, which enhance the flavor of the soup.

1 Cut the fish into 3-inch chunks, removing any obvious bones. Heat the olive oil in a large pan, then add the prepared fish and chopped vegetables. Stir gently until the vegetables are beginning to color.

2 Now add all the other soup ingredients, then pour in just enough cold water to cover the mixture. Season well and bring to just below boiling point, then lower the heat so that the soup is barely simmering, cover and cook for 1 hour.

3 Meanwhile, make the rouille. Put the garlic and coarse salt in a mortar and crush to a paste with a pestle. Add the soaked bread and chile and pound until smooth, or process in a food processor. Whisk in the olive oil, a drop at a time, to make a smooth, shiny sauce that resembles mayonnaise. Add a pinch of cayenne, if you like, and season to taste with salt. Set aside.

4 Lift out and discard the bouquet garni. Process the soup, in batches, in a food processor, then strain through a fine sieve into a clean pan, pushing the solids through with a ladle.

5 Reheat the soup, but do not boil. Taste and adjust the seasoning, if necessary, and ladle into individual bowls. Top each with two slices of toasted baguette, a spoonful of rouille and some grated Gruyère, then serve.

Bouillabaisse

Perhaps the most famous of all Mediterranean fish soups, this recipe, originating from Marseilles in the south of France, is a rich and colorful mixture of fish and shellfish, flavored with tomatoes, saffron and orange.

INGREDIENTS

Serves 4–6

3–3½ pounds mixed fish and raw
    shellfish, such as mullet, John Dory,
    monkfish, red snapper, whiting, raw
    jumbo shrimp and clams
8 ounces well-flavored tomatoes
pinch of saffron threads
6 tablespoons olive oil
1 onion, sliced
1 leek, sliced
1 celery stick, sliced
2 garlic cloves, crushed
1 bouquet garni
1 strip orange rind
½ teaspoon fennel seeds
1 tablespoon tomato paste
2 teaspoons Pernod
salt and ground black pepper
4–6 thick slices French bread and
    3 tablespoons chopped fresh parsley,
    to serve

COOK'S TIP

Saffron comes from the orange and red stigmas of a type of crocus, which must be harvested by hand and are therefore extremely expensive – the highest-priced spice in the world. However, its flavor is unique and cannot be replaced by any other spice. It is an essential ingredient in traditional bouillabaisse and should not be omitted.

1 Remove the heads, tails and fins from the fish and set the fish aside. Put the trimmings in a large pan with 2 pints/5 cups water. Bring to the boil and simmer for 15 minutes. Strain and reserve the liquid.

2 Cut the fish into large chunks. Leave the shellfish in their shells. Blanch the tomatoes, then drain and refresh in cold water. Peel them and chop coarsely. Soak the saffron in 1–2 tablespoons hot water.

3 Heat the oil in a large pan, add the onion, leek and celery and cook until softened. Add the garlic, bouquet garni, orange rind, fennel seeds and chopped tomatoes, then stir in the saffron and its soaking liquid and the reserved fish stock. Season with salt and pepper, then bring to the boil and simmer for 30–40 minutes.

4 Add the shellfish and boil for about 6 minutes. Add the fish and cook for 6–8 minutes more, until it flakes easily.

5 Using a slotted spoon, transfer the fish to a warmed serving platter. Keep the liquid boiling, to allow the oil to emulsify with the broth. Add the tomato paste and Pernod, then check the seasoning and adjust if necessary.

6 Ladle the soup into warm bowls, add the fish and sprinkle with chopped parsley. Serve immediately with French bread.

Spiced Mussel Soup

Chunky and colorful, this Turkish fish soup is like a chowder in its consistency. It is flavored with harissa, which is more familiar in North African cooking.

INGREDIENTS

Serves 6

3–3¹/₂ pounds fresh mussels

¹/₄ pint/²/₃ cup white wine

2 tablespoons olive oil

1 onion, finely chopped

2 garlic cloves, crushed

2 celery sticks, thinly sliced

bunch of scallions, thinly sliced

1 potato, diced

1¹/₂ teaspoon harissa

3 tomatoes, peeled and diced

3 tablespoons chopped fresh parsley

ground black pepper

thick plain yogurt, to serve

1 Scrub the mussels, discarding any damaged ones or any that do not close when tapped.

2 Bring the wine to the boil in a large pan. Add the mussels and cover tightly with a lid. Cook, shaking the pan occasionally, for 4–5 minutes, until the mussel shells have opened wide. Discard any mussels that remain closed.

3 Drain the mussels, reserving the cooking liquid. Reserve a few mussels in their shells to use as a garnish and shell the rest.

4 Heat the oil in a pan and cook the onion, garlic, celery and scallions for 5 minutes.

5 Add the shelled mussels, reserved liquid, potato, harissa and tomatoes. Bring to the boil, reduce the heat and cover. Simmer gently for 25 minutes.

6 Stir in the parsley and pepper and add the reserved mussels in their shells. Heat through for 1 minute. Serve immediately with a spoonful of yogurt.

Saffron Mussel Soup

This is one of France's most delicious seafood soups. For everyday eating, the French would normally serve all the mussels in their shells. Serve with plenty of French bread.

INGREDIENTS

Serves 4–6

1¹/₂ ounces/3 tablespoons sweet butter

8 shallots, finely chopped

1 bouquet garni

1 teaspoon black peppercorns

12 fluid ounces/1¹/₂ cups dry white wine

2¹/₄ pounds fresh mussels, scrubbed
    and debearded

2 leeks, trimmed and finely chopped

1 fennel bulb, finely chopped

1 carrot, finely chopped

several saffron threads

1³/₄ pints/4 cups Fish or Chicken Stock

2–3 tablespoons cornstarch, blended
    with 3 tablespoons cold water

4 fluid ounces/¹/₂ cup whipping cream

1 tomato, peeled, seeded and
    finely chopped

2 tablespoons Pernod (optional)

salt and ground black pepper

1 In a large, heavy pan, melt half the butter over a medium-high heat. Add half the shallots and cook, stirring frequently, for 1–2 minutes, until softened but not colored. Add the bouquet garni, peppercorns and white wine and bring to the boil. Add the mussels, cover tightly with a lid and cook over a high heat for 3–5 minutes, shaking the pan occasionally, until the mussel shells have opened.

2 With a slotted spoon, transfer the mussels to a bowl and set aside. Strain the cooking liquid through a sieve lined with cheesecloth to remove any sand or grit and reserve.

3 Pull open the shells and remove most of the mussels. Discard any closed mussels.

4 Melt the remaining butter over a medium heat. Add the remaining shallots and cook for 1–2 minutes. Add the leeks, fennel, carrot and saffron and cook for 3–5 minutes.

5 Stir in the reserved cooking liquid, bring to the boil and cook for 5 minutes, until the vegetables are tender and the liquid is slightly reduced. Add the stock and bring to the boil, skimming any foam that rises to the surface. Season with salt, if needed, and black pepper and cook for a further 5 minutes.

6 Stir the blended cornstarch into the soup. Simmer, stirring constantly, for 2–3 minutes, until the soup is slightly thickened, then stir in the cream, mussels and chopped tomato. Add the Pernod, if using, and cook for 1–2 minutes, until hot, then ladle into warm bowls and serve immediately.

Clam and Basil Soup

Subtly sweet and spicy, this soup is an ideal first course for serving as part of a celebration dinner.

Serves 4–6

2 tablespoons olive oil
1 onion, finely chopped
leaves from 1 fresh or dried sprig of
    thyme, chopped or crumbled
2 garlic cloves, crushed
5–6 fresh basil leaves, plus extra to garnish
¼–½ teaspoon crushed red chili,
    to taste
1¾ pints/4 cups Fish Stock
12 fluid ounces/1½ cups bottled
    strained tomatoes
1 teaspoon granulated sugar
3½ ounces/scant 1 cup frozen peas
2½ ounces/⅔ cup small dried pasta
    shapes, such as chifferini
8 ounces frozen shelled clams
salt and ground black pepper

1 Heat the oil in a large pan, add the onion and cook gently for about 5 minutes, until softened, but not colored. Add the thyme, then stir in the garlic, basil leaves and chili.

2 Add the stock, tomatoes and sugar to the pan and season with salt and pepper to taste. Bring to the boil, then lower the heat and simmer gently for 15 minutes, stirring occasionally. Add the frozen peas and cook for a further 5 minutes.

3 Add the pasta to the stock mixture and bring to the boil, stirring constantly. Lower the heat and simmer for about 5 minutes, or according to the packet instructions, stirring frequently, until the pasta is *al dente*.

4 Turn the heat down to low, add the frozen clams and heat through for 2–3 minutes. Taste and adjust the seasoning if necessary. Serve immediately in warmed bowls, garnished with basil leaves.

COOK'S TIP

Frozen shelled clams are available at good supermarkets and supermarkets. If you can't get them, use bottled or canned clams in natural juice (not vinegar). Italian delicatessens sell jars of clams in their shells. These both look and taste delicious and are not too expensive. For a special occasion, stir some into the soup.

Lobster Bisque

Bisque is a luxurious, velvety soup, which can be made with any crustaceans, but lobster is a classic.

INGREDIENTS

Serves 6

1¼ pounds fresh lobster, cut into pieces

3 ounces/6 tablespoons butter

1 onion, chopped

1 carrot, diced

1 celery stick, diced

3 tablespoons brandy, plus extra for
    serving (optional)

8 fluid ounces/1 cup dry white wine

1¾ pints/4 cups Fish Stock

1 tablespoon tomato paste

3 ounces/scant ½ cup long grain rice

1 fresh bouquet garni

¼ pint/⅔ cup heavy cream, plus extra
    to garnish

salt, ground white pepper and
    cayenne pepper

1 Melt half the butter in a large pan, add the vegetables and cook over a low heat until soft. Add the lobster and stir until the shell on each piece turns red.

COOK'S TIP

It is best to buy a live lobster, chilling it in the freezer until it is comatose and then killing it just before cooking. If you can't face the procedure, use a cooked lobster; take care not to overcook the flesh.

2 Pour over the brandy and set it alight. When the flames die down, add the wine and boil until reduced by half. Pour in the fish stock and simmer for 2–3 minutes. Remove the lobster.

3 Stir in the tomato paste and rice, add the bouquet garni and cook until the rice is tender. Meanwhile, remove the lobster meat from the shell and return the shells to the pan. Dice the lobster meat and set it aside.

4 When the rice is cooked, discard all the larger pieces of shell. Tip the mixture into a blender or food processor and process to a purée. Press the purée through a fine sieve placed over the clean pan. Stir the mixture, then heat until almost boiling. Season to taste with salt, pepper and cayenne, then lower the heat and stir in the cream.

5 Dice the remaining butter and whisk it into the bisque, a piece at a time. Add the diced lobster meat and serve immediately. If you like, pour a small spoonful of brandy into each soup bowl and swirl in a little extra cream.

Scallop and Jerusalem Artichoke Soup

The subtle sweetness of scallops combines well with the flavor of Jerusalem artichokes in this attractive golden soup. For an even more colorful version, substitute pumpkin for the artichokes and use extra stock instead of the milk.

INGREDIENTS

Serves 6

2¼ pounds Jerusalem artichokes

juice of ½lemon

4 ounces/½ cup butter

1 onion, finely chopped

1 pint/2½ cups Fish Stock

½ pint/1¼ cups milk

generous pinch of saffron threads

6 large or 12 small scallops, with
    their corals

¼ pint/⅔ cup whipping cream

salt and ground white pepper

3 tablespoons sliced almonds and
    1 tablespoon finely chopped fresh
    chervil, to garnish

1 Working quickly, scrub and peel the Jerusalem artichokes, then cut them into ¾-inch chunks and drop them into a bowl of cold water, which has been acidulated with the lemon juice. This will prevent the artichokes from discoloring.

2 Melt half the butter in a pan, add the onion and cook over a low heat until softened. Drain the artichokes and add them to the pan. Cook gently for 5 minutes, stirring frequently. Pour in the stock and milk, add the saffron and bring to the boil. Lower the heat and simmer until the artichokes are tender but not mushy.

3 Meanwhile, carefully separate the corals from the scallops. Prick the corals and slice each scallop in half horizontally. Heat half the remaining butter in a frying pan, add the scallops and corals and cook very briefly (for about 1 minute) on each side. Dice the scallops and corals, keeping them separate, and set them aside until needed.

4 When the artichokes are cooked, tip the contents of the pan into a blender or food processor. Add half the white scallop meat and process to very smooth purée. Return the soup to the clean pan, season with salt and white pepper and keep hot over a low heat while you prepare the garnish.

5 Heat the remaining butter in a frying pan, add the almonds and toss over a medium heat until golden brown. Add the diced corals and cook for about 30 seconds. Stir the cream into the soup and add the remaining diced white scallop meat.

6 Ladle the soup into warm individual bowls and garnish each serving with the almonds, scallop corals and a sprinkling of chervil.

Saffron Fish Soup

Filling, yet not too rich, this golden soup will make a delicious start to a meal, served with lots of hot, fresh bread and a glass of dry white wine. When mussels are not available use shrimp in their shells instead.

INGREDIENTS

Serves 4

1 parsnip, quartered

2 carrots, quartered

1 onion, quartered

2 celery sticks, quartered

2 smoked bacon strips

juice of 1 lemon

pinch of saffron threads

1 pound fish heads

1 pound fresh mussels, scrubbed

1 leek, shredded

2 shallots, finely chopped

2 tablespoons chopped fresh dill, plus
    extra sprigs to garnish

1 pound haddock fillet, skinned

3 egg yolks

2 tablespoons heavy cream

salt and ground black pepper

1   Put the parsnip, carrots, onion, celery, bacon, lemon juice, saffron threads and fish heads in a large, heavy pan with 1½ pints/3¾ cups water and bring to the boil. Simmer gently for about 20 minutes, or until reduced by half.

2   Discard any mussels that are open and don't close when tapped sharply. Add the mussels to the pan of stock. Cover and cook for about 4 minutes, until they have opened. Strain the soup and return the liquid to the pan. Discard any unopened mussels, then remove the remaining ones from their shells and set aside.

3   Add the leeks and shallots to the soup, bring to the boil, then lower the heat and simmer gently for 5 minutes. Add the dill and haddock, and simmer for a further 5 minutes, until the fish is tender. Remove the haddock, using a slotted spoon, then flake it into a bowl, using a fork.

4   In another bowl, whisk together the eggs and heavy cream. Whisk in a little of the hot soup, then whisk the mixture back into the hot, but not boiling liquid. Continue to whisk for several minutes, but do not boil.

5   Add the flaked haddock and mussels to the soup and check the seasoning. Garnish with tiny sprigs of dill and serve piping hot.

Corn and Scallop Chowder

Fresh corn is ideal for this chowder, although canned or frozen corn also works well.

INGREDIENTS

Serves 4–6

2 corn cobs or 7 ounces/generous 1 cup
    frozen or canned corn kernels
1 pint/2½ cups milk
½ ounce/1 tablespoon butter
    or margarine
1 small leek or onion, chopped
1½ ounces/¼ cup smoked fatty bacon,
    finely chopped
1 small garlic clove, crushed
1 small green bell pepper, seeded
    and diced
1 celery stick, chopped
1 potato, diced
1 tablespoon all-purpose flour
½ pint/1¼ cups Chicken or
    Vegetable stock
4 scallops
4 ounces cooked fresh mussels
pinch of paprika
¼ pint/⅔ cup light cream (optional)
salt and ground black pepper

1 If using fresh corn cobs, slice down them with a sharp knife to remove the kernels. If using canned corn kernels, drain well. Place half the kernels in a food processor or blender and process with a little of the milk. Set the other half aside.

2 Melt the butter or margarine in a large pan and cook the leek or onion, bacon and garlic over a low heat, stirring frequently, for 4–5 minutes, until the leek is soft, but not browned.

3 Add the green bell pepper, celery and potato and sweat over a gentle heat for 3–4 minutes more, stirring frequently.

4 Stir in the flour and cook for about 1–2 minutes, until golden and frothy. Stir in a little milk and the corn mixture, stock, the remaining milk and corn kernels and seasoning.

5 Bring to the boil, and then simmer, partially covered, for 15–20 minutes, until the vegetables are tender.

6 Pull the corals away from the scallops and slice the white flesh into ¼ inch slices. Stir the scallops into the soup, cook for 4 minutes and then stir in the corals, mussels and paprika. Heat through for a few minutes and then stir in the cream, if using. Check the seasoning and serve.

Creamy Fish Chowder

A traditional soup that never fails to please, whether it is made with milk or more luxuriously, with a generous quantity of cream.

INGREDIENTS

Serves 4

3 thick-cut bacon strips

1 large onion

1½ pounds potatoes

1¾ pints/4 cups Fish Stock

1 pound skinless haddock, cut into
   1-inch cubes

2 tablespoons chopped fresh parsley

1 tablespoon chopped fresh chives

½ pint/1¼ cups whipping cream
   or milk

salt and ground black pepper

1 Remove the rind from the bacon and discard it; cut the bacon into small pieces. Chop the onion and cut the potatoes into ¾-inch cubes.

2 Fry the bacon in a deep pan until the fat is rendered. Add the onion and potatoes and cook over a low heat, without browning, for about 10 minutes. Season to taste with salt and pepper.

3 Pour off the excess bacon fat from the pan. Add the fish stock to the pan and bring to a boil. Lower the heat and simmer for about 15–20 minutes, until the vegetables are tender.

4 Gently stir in the cubes of haddock, the parsley and chives. Simmer for 3–4 minutes, until the fish is just cooked.

5 Stir the cream or milk into the chowder and reheat gently, but do not bring to the boil. Taste and adjust the seasoning if necessary and serve immediately.

VARIATION

Cod fillets would be equally good in this chowder, or try smoked fillets for a stronger taste.

Corn and Crab Bisque

This is a Louisiana classic, which is certainly luxurious enough for a dinner party and is therefore well worth the extra time required to prepare the fresh crab. The crab shells, together with the corn cobs, from which the kernels are stripped, make a fine-flavored stock.

INGREDIENTS

Serves 8

4 large corn cobs

2 bay leaves

1 cooked crab (about 2¼ pounds)

1 ounce/2 tablespoons butter

2 tablespoons all-purpose flour

½ pint/1¼ cups whipping cream

6 scallions, shredded

pinch of cayenne pepper

salt and ground black and white pepper

hot French bread or grissini breadsticks,
    to serve

1 Pull away the husks and silk from the cobs of corn and strip off the kernels.

2 Keep the kernels on one side and put the stripped cobs into a deep pan or flameproof casserole with 5 pints/12½ cups water, the bay leaves and 2 teaspoons salt. Bring to the boil, then lower the heat and simmer while you prepare the crab.

3 Pull away the two flaps between the big claws of the crab, stand it on its "nose", where the flaps were, and bang down firmly with the heel of your hand on the rounded end.

4 Separate the crab from its top shell, keeping the shell.

5 Push out the crab's mouth and its abdominal sac immediately below the mouth, and discard.

6 Pull away the feathery gills surrounding the central chamber and discard. Scrape out all the semi-liquid brown meat from the shell and set aside.

7 Crack the claws in as many places as necessary to extract all the white meat. Pick out the white meat from the fragile cavities in the central body of the crab. Set aside all the crab meat, brown and white. Put the spidery legs, back shell and all the other pieces of shell into the pan with the corn cobs. Simmer for a further 15 minutes, then strain the stock into a clean pan and boil hard to reduce to 3½ pints/9 cups.

8 Meanwhile, melt the butter in a small pan and sprinkle in the flour. Stir constantly over a low heat until the roux is the color of rich cream.

9 Remove the pan from the heat and gradually stir in 8 fluid ounces/1 cup of the stock. Return to the heat and stir until it thickens, then stir this thickened mixture into the pan of strained stock.

10 Add the corn kernels, return to the boil and simmer for 5 minutes.

11 Add the crab meat, cream and scallions and season with cayenne, salt and pepper (preferably a mixture of black and white). Return to the boil and simmer for a further 2 minutes. Serve with hot French bread or grissini breadsticks.

Clam Chowder

If fresh clams are hard to find, use frozen or canned clams for this classic recipe from New England. Large clams should be cut into chunky pieces.

Serves 4

3¾ ounces salt pork or thinly sliced
    unsmoked bacon, diced
1 large onion, chopped
2 potatoes, peeled and cut into
    ½-inch cubes
1 bay leaf
1 fresh thyme sprig
½ pint/1¼ cups milk
14 ounces cooked clams, cooking
    liquid reserved
¼ pint/⅔ cup heavy cream
salt, ground white pepper and
    cayenne pepper
finely chopped fresh parsley, to garnish

1 Put the salt pork or unsmoked bacon in a heavy pan, and heat gently, stirring frequently, until the fat runs and the meat is starting to brown. Add the chopped onion and cook over a low heat until softened but not browned.

2 Add the cubed potatoes, bay leaf and thyme sprig, stir well to coat with fat, then pour in the milk and reserved clam cooking liquid and bring to the boil. Lower the heat and simmer gently for about 10 minutes, until the potatoes are tender but still firm. Lift out the bay leaf and thyme sprig and discard.

3 Remove most of the clams from their shells. Add all the clams to the pan and season to taste with salt, white pepper and cayenne. Simmer over a low heat for 5 minutes more, then stir in the heavy cream. Heat until the soup is very hot, but do not let it boil. Pour into a warm tureen, garnish with the chopped parsley and serve.

Clam, Mushroom and Potato Chowder

The delicate, sweet shellfish taste of clams and the soft earthiness of wild mushrooms combine with potatoes to make this a memorable dish – fit for any occasion.

INGREDIENTS

Serves 4

48 clams, scrubbed

2 ounces/4 tablespoons sweet butter

1 large onion, chopped

1 celery stick, sliced

1 carrot, sliced

8 ounces assorted wild mushrooms,
    such as chanterelles, hen of the woods
    or wood ear, sliced

8 ounces floury potatoes, thickly sliced

2 pints/5 cups Chicken or Vegetable
    Stock, boiling

1 fresh thyme sprig

4 fresh parsley stalks

salt and ground black pepper

fresh thyme sprigs, to garnish

1 Place the clams in a large pan, discarding any that are open. Put ½ inch of water in the pan, cover tightly, bring to the boil and steam over a medium heat for 6–8 minutes, until the clams open. Remove and discard any clams that do not open.

2 Drain the clams over a bowl, remove the shells from each one and chop. Strain the cooking juices into the bowl, add the chopped clams and set aside.

3 Add the butter, onion, celery and carrot to the pan and cook gently for 5 minutes, until softened but not colored. Add the mushrooms and cook for 3–4 minutes. Add the potatoes, the clams and their juices, the stock, thyme and parsley stalks.

4 Bring to the boil, then reduce the heat, cover and simmer for 25 minutes. Season to taste with salt and pepper, ladle into soup bowls and garnish with thyme.

Smoked Cod and Okra Soup

The inspiration for this soup came from a Ghanaian recipe for okra soup. Here it is enhanced by the addition of smoked fish.

INGREDIENTS

Serves 4

2 green bananas

2 ounces/¼ cup butter or margarine

1 onion, finely chopped

2 tomatoes, peeled and finely chopped

4 ounces okra, trimmed

8 ounces smoked cod fillet, cut into
    bitesize pieces

1½ pints/3¾ cups Fish Stock

1 fresh chile, seeded and chopped

salt and ground black pepper

fresh parsley sprigs, to garnish

3 Add the cod, fish stock, chile and seasoning. Bring to the boil, then reduce the heat and simmer for about 20 minutes, or until the cod is cooked through and flakes easily.

4 Peel the cooked bananas and cut into slices. Stir into the soup, heat through for a few minutes and ladle into warm soup bowls. Garnish with parsley and serve immediately.

1 Slit the skins of the green bananas and place in a large pan. Cover with water, bring to the boil and cook over a moderate heat for 25 minutes, until the bananas are tender. Transfer to a plate and leave to cool.

2 Melt the butter or margarine in a large pan and cook the onion for about 5 minutes, until soft. Stir in the chopped tomatoes and okra and cook gently for a further 10 minutes.

Fish and Sweet Potato Soup

The subtle sweetness of the potato, combined with the fish and the aromatic flavor of oregano, makes this an appetizing soup.

INGREDIENTS

Serves 4

½ onion, chopped

6 ounces sweet potato, peeled and diced

6 ounces white fish fillet, skinned

2 ounces carrot, chopped

1 teaspoon chopped fresh oregano or
    ½ teaspoon dried oregano

½ teaspoon ground cinnamon

2½ pints/6¼ cups Fish Stock

5 tablespoons light cream

chopped fresh parsley, to garnish

1 Put the chopped onion, diced sweet potato, white fish, chopped carrot, oregano, cinnamon and half of the fish stock in a pan. Bring to the boil, then lower the heat and simmer for 20 minutes, or until the potato is cooked.

2 Leave to cool, then pour into a blender or food processor and process until smooth.

3 Return the soup to the pan, then add the remaining fish stock and gradually bring to the boil. Reduce the heat to low and add the light cream, then gently heat through, without boiling, stirring occasionally.

4 Serve hot in warmed soup bowls, garnished with the chopped fresh parsley.

VARIATION
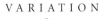
Garnish with chopped fresh tarragon instead of parsley.

Shrimp Creole

Raw shrimp are combined with chopped fresh vegetables and cayenne pepper to make this tasty soup.

Serves 4

1½ pounds raw shrimp in the shell, with
    heads, if available
16 fluid ounces/2 cups water
3 tablespoons olive or vegetable oil
6 ounces/1½ cups very finely
    chopped onions
3 ounces/½ cup very finely chopped celery
3 ounces/½ cup very finely chopped green
    bell pepper
1 ounce/½ cup chopped fresh parsley
1 garlic clove, crushed
1 tablespoon Worcestershire sauce
¼ teaspoon cayenne pepper
4 fluid ounces/½ cup dry white wine
2 ounces/1 cup chopped peeled
    plum tomatoes
1 teaspoon salt
1 bay leaf
1 teaspoon sugar
fresh parsley, to garnish
boiled rice, to serve

1 Peel and devein the shrimp, reserving the heads and shells. Keep the shrimp in a covered bowl in the refrigerator while you make the soup.

2 Put the shrimp heads and shells in a pan with the water. Bring to the boil and simmer for 15 minutes. Strain, then measure 12 fluid ounces/1½ cups of the stock and reserve.

3 Heat the oil in a heavy pan. Add the onions and cook over a low heat for 8–10 minutes, until softened. Add the celery and green pepper and cook for 5 minutes more. Stir in the parsley, garlic, Worcestershire sauce and cayenne. Cook for a further 5 minutes.

4 Raise the heat to medium. Stir in the wine and simmer for 3–4 minutes. Add the tomatoes, reserved shrimp stock, salt, bay leaf and sugar and bring to the boil. Stir well, then reduce the heat to low and simmer for about 30 minutes, until the tomatoes have fallen apart and the sauce has reduced slightly. Remove from the heat and cool slightly.

5 Discard the bay leaf. Pour the sauce into a food processor or blender and process until quite smooth. Taste and adjust the seasoning as necessary.

6 Return the tomato soup to the pan and bring to the boil. Add the shrimp and simmer for 4–5 minutes, until they turn pink. Ladle into warm individual soup bowls, garnish with fresh parsley and serve with rice.

Fish Ball Soup

The Japanese name for this soup is Tsumire-jiru. Tsumire *means, quite literally, sardine balls, and these are added to this delicious soup to impart their robust flavor.*

Serves 4

3¹⁄₂ fluid ounces/generous ¹⁄₃ cup sake or dry white wine

2 pints/5 cups instant dashi

4 tablespoons white miso paste

For the fish balls

³⁄₄ ounce fresh root ginger

1³⁄₄ pounds fresh sardines, gutted and heads removed

2 tablespoons white miso paste

1 tablespoon sake or dry white wine

1¹⁄₂ teaspoon sugar

1 egg

2 tablespoons cornstarch

5 ounces shimeji mushrooms or 6 shiitake mushrooms

1 leek or large scallion

1 First make the fish balls. To do this, grate the ginger and squeeze it well to yield 1 teaspoon ginger juice.

2 Rinse the sardines under cold running water, then cut them in half along the backbones. Remove and discard all the bones. To skin a boned sardine, lay it skin-side down on a board, then run a sharp knife slowly along the skin from tail to head.

3 Coarsely chop the sardines and process with the ginger juice, miso, sake or wine, sugar and egg to a thick paste in a food processor or blender. Transfer to a bowl and mix in the cornstarch until thoroughly blended.

4 Trim the shimeji mushrooms and either separate each stem or remove the stems from the shiitake mushrooms and shred them. Cut the leek or scallion into 1¹⁄₂-inch strips.

5 Bring the ingredients for the soup to the boil. Use 2 wet spoons to shape small portions of the sardine mixture into bitesize balls and drop them into the soup. Add the prepared mushrooms and leek or scallion.

6 Gently simmer the soup until the sardine balls float to the surface. Serve immediately, in individual, deep soup bowls.

Clear Soup with Seafood Sticks

This delicate, Japanese soup, called
O-sumashi, *which is often eaten*
with sushi, is very quick to make
if you prepare the Japanese stock
beforehand or if you use freeze-dried
dashi-no-moto – *instant dashi.*

INGREDIENTS

Serves 4

4 fresh mitsuba sprigs or
   4 fresh chives and a few fresh
   sprigs of cress
4 seafood sticks
14 fluid ounces/1⅔ cups Stock for
   Japanese Soups or the same
   amount of water and 1 teaspoon
   instant dashi
1 tablespoon shoyu
1½ teaspoons salt
grated rind of yuzu or lime (optional),
   to garnish

1 Mitsuba leaves are normally sold with the stems and roots on to retain freshness. Cut off the root, then cut 2 inches from the top, retaining both the long straw-like stem and the leaf.

2 Blanch the stems by pouring over hot water. If you use chives, choose them at least 4 inches in length and blanch, too.

3 Take a seafood stick and carefully tie a mitsuba stem or chive around the middle, holding it in place with a knot. Do not pull too tightly, as the bow will easily break. Repeat the process to make four tied seafood sticks.

4 With your finger, carefully loosen both ends of each seafood stick to make it look like a tassel.

5 Place one seafood stick in each soup bowl, then put the four mitsuba leaves or mustard and cress on top.

6 Heat the stock in a pan and bring to the boil. Add the shoyu and season with salt to taste. Pour the stock gently over the mitsuba and seafood stick. Sprinkle with grated yuzu or lime rind, if using. Serve immediately.

VARIATION

You can use small shrimp
instead of seafood sticks.
Blanch 12 raw shrimp in boiling
water until they curl up and
form a full circle. Drain.
Tie mitsuba stems to make four
bows. Arrange three shrimp, side
by side, in each bowl and put the
mitsuba bows and leaves on top.

New Year's Soup

Japan's elaborate New Year's Day celebration brunch starts with a tiny glass of spiced warm sake, o-toso. Then, this New Year's soup, o-zoni, *and other festive dishes are served.*

INGREDIENTS

Serves 4

4 dried shiitake mushrooms

11 ounces chicken thighs, bones removed
   and reserved

11 ounces salmon fillet, skin on, scaled

2 tablespoons sake

2 ounces satoimo or Jerusalem artichokes

2 ounces daikon, peeled

2 ounces carrots, peeled

4 scallions, white part only, trimmed and
   chopped into 1-inch lengths

4 fresh mitsuba sprigs, root
   part removed

1 yuzu or lime

4 raw jumbo shrimp, peeled, but with
   tails left on

2 tablespoons shoyu

8 mochi slices

salt

1. First, make the soup stock. Soak the dried shiitake overnight in 1¾ pints/4 cups cold water. Remove the softened shiitake and pour the water into a pan. Bring to the boil, add the chicken bones, then reduce the heat to medium. Skim frequently to remove any scum. After about 20 minutes, reduce the heat to low. Simmer for 30 minutes, or until the liquid has reduced by a third. Strain the stock into another pan.

2. Chop the chicken thighs and salmon fillet into small, bitesize cubes. Parboil them both in boiling water with 1 tablespoon sake for 1 minute. Drain and wash off the scum under cold water.

3. Scrub the satoimo or artichokes with a hard brush, and thickly peel. Put in a pan and add enough water to cover. Add a pinch of salt and bring to the boil. Reduce the heat to medium, cook for 15 minutes and drain. Rinse the satoimo or artichokes under running water. Cut the satoimo or artichokes, daikon and carrots into ½-inch cubes.

4. Remove and discard the stalks from the soaked shiitake, and slice the caps thinly.

5. Put the mitsuba sprigs into a sieve and pour hot water over them. Divide the leaf and stalk parts. Take a stalk and fold it into two, then tie it in the middle to make a bow. Make four bows.

6. Cut the yuzu or lime into four ⅛ inch thick round slices. Hollow out the inside to make rings of peel.

7. Add the remaining sake to the soup stock and boil. Add the daikon, carrot and shiitake, reduce the heat and cook for 15 minutes. Put the shrimp, satoimo or artichokes, scallions, chicken and salmon into the pan. Cook for 5 minutes, then add the shoyu. Reduce the heat to low.

8. Cut the mochi in half crosswise. Toast under a medium preheated broiler. Turn every minute until both sides are golden and the pieces have started to swell; this will take about 5 minutes. Place the toasted mochi in individual soup bowls and pour the hot soup over the top. Arrange a mitsuba leaf in the center of each bowl, put a yuzu or lime ring on top, and lay a mitsuba bow across.

Shrimp and Egg-knot Soup

Omelettes and pancakes are often used to add protein to light Asian soups. In this recipe, thin omelettes are twisted into little knots.

Serves 4

1 scallion, thinly shredded

1⅓ pints/3½ cups Stock for Japanese Soups or instant dashi

1 teaspoon soy sauce

dash of sake or dry white wine

pinch of salt

For the shrimp balls

7 ounces/generous 1 cup raw jumbo shrimp, peeled

2½ ounces cod fillet, skinned

1 teaspoon egg white

1 teaspoon sake or dry white wine

4½ teaspoons cornstarch

2–3 drops soy sauce

pinch of salt

For the omelette

1 egg, beaten

dash of mirin

pinch of salt

oil, for cooking

1 To make the shrimp balls, use a pin to remove the black vein running down the back of each shrimp. Place the shrimp, cod, egg white, sake or dry white wine, cornstarch, soy sauce and a pinch of salt in a food processor or blender and process to a thick, sticky paste. Shape the mixture into 4 balls, place in a steaming basket and steam over a pan of vigorously boiling water for about 10 minutes.

2 To make the garnish, soak the scallion in a small bowl of iced water for about 5 minutes, until the shreds have curled, then drain well.

3 To make the omelette, mix the egg with the mirin and salt. Heat a little oil in a frying pan and pour in the egg mixture, coating the pan evenly. When the omelette has set, turn it over and cook for 30 seconds. Leave to cool.

4 Cut the omelette into strips and tie each in a knot. Heat the stock or dashi, then add the soy sauce, sake or wine and salt. Divide the shrimp balls and egg-knots among four bowls and add the soup. Garnish with the scallion curls and serve.

Coconut and Seafood Soup with Garlic Chives

The long list of ingredients in this Thai-inspired recipe could mislead you into thinking that this soup is complicated. In fact, it is very easy to put together.

INGREDIENTS

Serves 4

1 pint/2½ cups Fish Stock
5 thin slices fresh galangal or fresh
　　root ginger
2 lemon grass stalks, chopped
3 kaffir lime leaves, shredded
1 ounce garlic chives (1 bunch)
½ ounce fresh cilantro, stalks and
　　leaves separated
1 tablespoon vegetable oil
4 shallots, chopped
14-fluid ounce can coconut milk
2–3 tablespoons Thai fish sauce
3–4 tablespoons Thai green curry paste
1 pound raw jumbo shrimp, peeled
　　and deveined
1 pound prepared squid
a little lime juice (optional)
salt and ground black pepper
4 tablespoons crisp fried shallot slices,
　　to serve

1 Pour the fish stock into a pan and add the slices of galangal or ginger, the lemon grass and half the shredded kaffir lime leaves.

2 Reserve a few garlic chives for the garnish, then chop the remainder. Add half the chopped garlic chives to the pan with the cilantro stalks. Bring to the boil, reduce the heat and cover the pan, then simmer gently for 20 minutes. Strain the stock.

3 Rinse the pan. Add the oil and shallots. Cook over a medium heat for 5–10 minutes, until the shallots are softened and just beginning to brown.

4 Stir in the strained stock, coconut milk, the remaining kaffir lime leaves and 2 tablespoons of the fish sauce. Heat gently until simmering and cook over a low heat for 5–10 minutes.

5 Stir in the green curry paste and shrimp, then cook for 3 minutes. Add the squid and cook for a further 2 minutes. Add the lime juice, if using, and season, adding more fish sauce to taste.

6 Stir in the remaining chives and the cilantro leaves. Serve immediately in warm bowls sprinkled with fried shallots and whole garlic chives.

Hot-and-Sour Shrimp Soup

*This is a classic Thai seafood soup –
Tom Yam Kung – and it is probably
the most popular and best-known
soup from Thailand.*

INGREDIENTS

Serves 4–6

1 pound raw jumbo shrimp, thawed
   if frozen

1¾ pints/4 cups Chicken Stock
   or water

3 lemon grass stalks, root
   trimmed

10 kaffir lime leaves, torn in half

8 ounces can straw mushrooms

3 tablespoons Thai fish sauce

4 tablespoons lime juice

2 tablespoons chopped scallion

1 tablespoon fresh cilantro leaves

4 fresh red chiles, seeded and
   thinly sliced

salt and ground black pepper

1 Peel the shrimp, putting the
shells in a colander. Devein the
shrimp and set them aside.

2 Rinse the shells under cold
water, then put them in a large
pan with the stock or water. Bring
to the boil.

3 Bruise the lemon grass stalks
and add them to the stock
with half the lime leaves. Simmer
gently for 5–6 minutes, until the
stock is fragrant.

4 Strain the stock, return it to
the clean pan and reheat. Add
the drained mushrooms and the
shrimp, then cook briefly, until
the shrimp turn pink.

5 Stir in the fish sauce, lime
juice, scallion, cilantro, chiles
and the remaining lime leaves.
Taste and adjust the seasoning,
if necessary. The soup should be
sour, salty, spicy and hot. Ladle
into warm soup bowls and
serve immediately.

Malayan Shrimp Laksa

This spicy shrimp and noodle soup tastes just as good when made with fresh crab meat or any flaked cooked fish. If you are short of time or can't find all the spice paste ingredients, buy ready-made laksa paste, which is available from Asian stores.

INGREDIENTS

Serves 3–4

4 ounces rice vermicelli or stir-fry
    rice noodles
1 tablespoon vegetable oil
1 pint/2½ cups Fish Stock
14 fluid ounces/1⅔ cups thin c
    oconut milk
2 tablespoons Thai fish sauce
½ lime
16–24 cooked peeled shrimp
salt and cayenne pepper
4 tablespoons fresh cilantro sprigs and
    leaves, chopped, to garnish

For the spice paste
2 lemon grass stalks, finely chopped
2 fresh red chiles, seeded and chopped
1-inch piece fresh root ginger, sliced
½ teaspoons shrimp paste
2 garlic cloves, chopped
½ teaspoons ground turmeric
2 tablespoons tamarind paste

1 Cook the rice vermicelli or noodles in a large pan of salted, boiling water according to the instructions on the packet. Tip into a large sieve or colander, then rinse under cold water and drain. Set aside on a warm plate.

2 To make the spice paste, place all the ingredients in a mortar and pound with a pestle. Or, if you prefer, put the ingredients in a food processor or blender and then process until a smooth paste is formed.

3 Heat the oil in a large pan, add the spice paste and fry, stirring constantly, for a few moments to release all the flavors, but be careful not to let it burn.

4 Add the fish stock and coconut milk and bring to the boil. Stir in the fish sauce, then simmer for 5 minutes. Season with salt and cayenne to taste, adding a squeeze of lime. Add the shrimp and heat through for a few seconds.

5 Divide the noodles among three or four soup plates. Pour the soup over, making sure that each portion includes an equal number of shrimp. Garnish with cilantro and serve piping hot.

Thai Fish Soup

Thai fish sauce, or nam pla, *is rich in B vitamins and is used extensively in Thai cooking. It is available at Thai or Indonesian stores and good supermarkets.*

INGREDIENTS

Serves 4

12 ounces raw jumbo shrimp
1 tablespoon peanut oil
2 pints/5 cups Chicken or
    Fish Stock
1 lemon grass stalk, bruised and cut into
    1-inch lengths
2 kaffir lime leaves, torn into pieces
juice and finely grated rind of 1 lime
½ fresh green chile, seeded and
    thinly sliced
4 scallops
24 fresh mussels, scrubbed and debearded
4 ounces monkfish fillet, cut into
    ¾-inch chunks
2 teaspoons Thai fish sauce

For the garnish
1 kaffir lime leaf, shredded
½ fresh red chile, thinly sliced

1 Peel the shrimp, reserving the shells, and remove the black vein running along their backs.

2 Heat the oil in a pan and fry the shrimp shells until pink. Add the stock, lemon grass, lime leaves, lime rind and green chile. Bring to the boil, simmer for 20 minutes, then strain through a sieve, reserving the liquid.

3 Cut the scallops in half, leaving the corals attached.

4 Return the stock to a clean pan, add the shrimp, mussels, monkfish and scallops and cook for 3 minutes. Remove from the heat and add the lime juice and fish sauce.

5 Serve immediately, garnished with the shredded lime leaf and thinly sliced red chile.

Chinese Crab and Corn Soup

Thawed frozen white crab meat works as well as fresh in this delicately flavored soup.

INGREDIENTS

Serves 4

1 pint/2½ cups Fish or Chicken Stock
1-inch piece of fresh root ginger, very
    finely sliced
14-ounce can creamed corn
5 ounces cooked white crab meat
1 tablespoon arrowroot or cornstarch
1 tablespoon rice wine or dry sherry
1–2 tablespoons light soy sauce
1 egg white
salt and ground white pepper
shredded scallions, to garnish

1 Put the stock and ginger in a large pan and bring to the boil. Stir in the creamed corn and bring back to the boil.

2 Switch off the heat and add the crab meat. Put the arrowroot or cornstarch in a cup and stir in the rice wine or sherry to make a smooth paste. Stir the paste into the soup. Cook over a low heat for about 3 minutes, until the soup has thickened and is slightly glutinous in consistency. Add light soy sauce, salt and white pepper to taste.

3 In a bowl, whisk the egg white to a stiff foam. Gradually fold it into the soup. Ladle the soup into warm bowls, garnish each portion with scallions and serve immediately.

COOK'S TIP
~

Creamed corn gives a better
texture than whole kernel corn.
If you can't find it in
a can, use thawed frozen
creamed corn instead.

Spinach and Tofu Soup

This is an extremely delicate and mild-flavored soup, which can be used to counterbalance the heat from a hot Thai curry to follow.

Serves 4–6

2 tablespoons dried shrimp

1¾ pints/4 cups Chicken Stock

8 ounces fresh tofu, drained and cut into
   ¾-inch cubes

2 tablespoons Thai fish sauce

12 ounces fresh spinach

ground black pepper

2 scallions, thinly sliced, to garnish

1 Rinse and drain the dried shrimp. Combine the shrimp with the chicken stock in a large pan and bring to the boil. Add the tofu and simmer for about 5 minutes. Season with fish sauce and black pepper to taste.

2 Wash the spinach leaves and tear into bitesize pieces. Add to the soup and cook for another 1–2 minutes.

3 Pour the soup into warmed bowls, sprinkle the chopped scallions on top and serve.

Pumpkin and Coconut Soup

Rich and sweet flavors are married beautifully with sharp and hot in this creamy Southeast Asian-influenced soup.

INGREDIENTS

Serves 4–6

2 garlic cloves, crushed

4 shallots, finely crushed

½ teaspoon shrimp paste

1 tablespoon dried shrimp, soaked
    for 10 minutes and drained

1 lemon grass stalk, chopped

2 fresh green chiles, seeded

1 pint/2½ cups Chicken Stock

1 pound pumpkin, cut into thick chunks

1 pint/2½ cups coconut cream

2 tablespoons Thai fish sauce

1 teaspoon sugar

4 ounces cooked peeled shrimp

salt and ground black pepper

For the garnish

2 fresh red chiles, seeded and
    thinly sliced

10–12 fresh basil leaves

5 Add the shrimp and cook until they are heated through. Serve garnished with the sliced red chiles and basil leaves.

1 Using a mortar and pestle, grind the garlic, shallots, shrimp paste, dried shrimp, lemon grass, green chiles and a pinch of salt into a paste.

2 Bring the chicken stock to the boil in a large pan, add the paste and stir until dissolved.

3 Lower the heat, add the chunks of pumpkin, and simmer for about 10–15 minutes, or until the pumpkin is tender.

4 Stir in the coconut cream, then bring back to a simmer. Add the fish sauce, sugar and ground black pepper to taste.

COOK'S TIP

Shrimp paste, which is made from ground shrimp fermented in brine, is used to give food a savory flavor.

MEAT AND
POULTRY
SOUPS

European and American soups made with beef, lamb,
pork, chicken or duck are often robust, substantial and
warming – just perfect for taking the edge off a hearty appetite
on a cold winter's day. However, Chinese and Asian
soups are usually more delicate and lighter, although no less
flavorsome. This delicious collection of recipes offers the best
of both worlds and even includes an East-meets-West duck
soup based on the French-Vietnamese tradition.

Chicken, Leek and Celery Soup

This is a substantial soup that is ideal for serving before a light, hot or cold main course. Served with plenty of rustic bread, it would make a meal-in-a-bowl lunch.

INGREDIENTS

Serves 4–6

3-pound chicken
1 small head of celery, trimmed
1 onion, coarsely chopped
1 fresh bay leaf
a few fresh parsley stalks
a few fresh tarragon sprigs
4 pints/10 cups cold water
3 large leeks
2½ ounces/5 tablespoons butter
2 potatoes, cut into chunks
¼ pint/⅔ cup dry white wine
2–3 tablespoons light cream
salt and ground black pepper
3½ ounces pancetta, broiled until crisp,
   to garnish

1 Cut the breasts off the chicken and set aside. Chop the remainder of the chicken carcass into 8–10 pieces and place in a large pan.

2 Chop 4–5 of the outer sticks of the celery and add them to the pan with the onion. Tie the bay leaf, parsley and tarragon together and add to the pan. Pour in the cold water to cover the ingredients and bring to the boil. Reduce the heat and cover the pan, then simmer for 1½ hours.

3 Remove the chicken and cut off and reserve the meat. Strain the stock, then return it to the pan and boil rapidly until it has reduced to about 2½ pints/6¼ cups.

4 Meanwhile, set about 5 ounces of the leeks aside. Slice the remaining leeks and the remaining celery, reserving any celery leaves. Chop the celery leaves and set aside to garnish the soup.

5 Melt half the butter in a large, heavy pan. Add the sliced leeks and celery, cover and cook over a low heat for about 10 minutes, or until softened but not browned. Add the potatoes, wine and 2 pints/5 cups of the chicken stock.

6 Season well with salt and pepper, bring to the boil and reduce the heat. Part-cover the pan and simmer the soup for about 15–20 minutes, or until the potatoes are cooked.

7 Meanwhile, skin the reserved chicken breasts and cut the flesh into small pieces. Melt the remaining butter in a frying pan, add the chicken and cook for 5–7 minutes, until tender.

8 Thickly slice the remaining leeks, add to the pan and cook, stirring occasionally, for a further 3–4 minutes, until just cooked.

9 Process the soup with the cooked chicken from the stock in a blender or food processor. Taste and adjust the seasoning, if necessary, and add more stock if the soup is very thick.

10 Stir in the cream and the chicken and leek mixture. Reheat the soup gently. Serve in warmed bowls. Crumble the pancetta over the soup and sprinkle with the chopped celery leaves to garnish.

Split Pea and Ham Soup

The main ingredient for this dish is ham hock, which is the narrow piece of bone cut from a leg of ham. You could use a piece of belly of pork instead, if you prefer, and remove it with the herbs before serving.

INGREDIENTS

Serves 4

1 pound/2½ cups green split peas

4 rindless bacon strips

1 onion, coarsely chopped

2 carrots, sliced

1 celery stick, sliced

4¼ pints/10½ cups water

1 fresh thyme sprig

2 bay leaves

1 large potato, coarsely diced

1 ham hock

ground black pepper

1 Put the split peas into a bowl, cover with cold water and leave to soak overnight.

2 Cut the bacon strips into small pieces. In a large pan, dry-fry the bacon for 4–5 minutes. or until crisp. Remove from the pan with a slotted spoon.

3 Add the chopped onion, carrots and celery to the fat in the pan and cook for 3–4 minutes, until the onion is softened but not brown. Return the diced bacon to the pan with the water.

4 Drain the split peas and add to the pan with the thyme, bay leaves, potato and ham hock. Bring to the boil, reduce the heat, cover and cook gently for 1 hour.

5 Remove the thyme, bay leaves and hock. Process the soup in a blender or food processor until smooth. Return to a clean pan. Cut the meat from the hock and add to the soup and heat through gently. Season with plenty of ground black pepper. Ladle into warm soup bowls and serve immediately.

Chunky Chicken Soup

*This thick chicken and vegetable
soup is served with garlic-flavored
fried croûtons.*

INGREDIENTS

Serves 4

4 skinless, boneless chicken thighs
¹/₂ ounce/1 tablespoon butter
2 small leeks, thinly sliced
2 tablespoons long grain rice
1¹/₂ pints/3³/₄ cups Chicken Stock
1 tablespoon chopped mixed fresh parsley
    and mint
salt and ground black pepper

For the garlic croûtons
2 tablespoons olive oil
1 garlic clove, crushed
4 slices bread, cut into cubes

1 Cut the chicken into ¹/₂-inch
cubes. Melt the butter in a
pan, add the leeks and cook until
tender. Add the rice and chicken
and cook for 2 minutes.

2 Add the stock, then cover the
pan and simmer gently for
15–20 minutes, until tender.

3 To make the garlic croûtons,
heat the oil in a large frying
pan. Add the crushed garlic clove
and bread cubes and cook until the
bread is golden brown, stirring
constantly to prevent burning.
Drain on paper towels and
sprinkle with a pinch of salt.

4 Add the parsley and mint
to the soup and adjust the
seasoning to taste. Serve with
the garlic croûtons.

Bulgarian Sour Lamb Soup

This traditional sour soup uses lamb, although pork and poultry are popular alternatives.

INGREDIENTS

Serves 4–5

2 tablespoons oil

1 pound lean lamb, trimmed and cubed

1 onion, diced

2 tablespoons all-purpose flour

1 tablespoons paprika

1¾ pints/4 cups hot Meat Stock

3 fresh parsley sprigs

4 scallions

4 fresh dill sprigs

2 tablespoons long grain rice

2 eggs, beaten

2–3 tablespoons or more vinegar or lemon juice

salt and ground black pepper

For the garnish

1 ounce/2 tablespoons butter, melted

1 teaspoon paprika

a little fresh parsley or lovage and dill

1 In a large pan heat the oil and cook the meat over a medium heat, stirring frequently, for about 8 minutes, until browned all over. Add the diced onion and cook, stirring frequently, for 5 minutes until it has softened. Sprinkle in the flour and paprika. Stir well, then gradually add the stock and cook for 10 minutes.

2 Tie the parsley, scallions and dill together with kitchen string to make a bouquet garni, then add to the pan with the rice and season to taste with salt and pepper. Bring to the boil, then reduce the heat and simmer for about 30–40 minutes, or until the lamb is tender.

3 Remove the pan from the heat and stir in the eggs. Add the vinegar or lemon juice. Discard the bouquet garni and season to taste.

4 For the garnish, melt the butter in a pan and stir in the paprika. Ladle the soup into warm serving bowls. Garnish with parsley or dill and lovage and a little red paprika butter and serve immediately.

Chicken and Leek Soup with Prunes and Barley

This recipe is based on the famous traditional Scottish soup, Cock-a-leekie. The unconventional combination of leeks and prunes is surprisingly delicious.

INGREDIENTS

Serves 6

1 chicken, weighing about 4¼ pounds

2 pounds leeks

1 fresh bouquet garni containing bay leaf, parsley and thyme

1 large carrot, thickly sliced

4 pints/10 cups Chicken or Meat Stock

4 ounces/generous ½ cup pearl barley

14 ounces ready-to-eat prunes

salt and ground black pepper

chopped fresh parsley, to garnish

1 Cut the breasts off the chicken and set aside. Place the remaining chicken carcass in a large pan. Cut half the leeks into 2-inch lengths and add them to the pan. Add the bouquet garni to the pan with the carrot and the stock. Bring to the boil, then reduce the heat and cover. Simmer gently for 1 hour. Skim off any scum when the water first boils and skim occasionally again during simmering.

2 Add the chicken breasts and cook for a further 30 minutes, until they are just cooked. Leave until cool enough to handle, then strain the stock.

3 Reserve the chicken breasts and meat from the chicken carcass. Discard all the skin, bones, cooked vegetables and herbs. Skim as much fat as you can from the stock, then return it to the pan.

4 Meanwhile, rinse the pearl barley thoroughly in a sieve under cold running water, then cook it in a large pan of boiling water for about 10 minutes. Drain, rinse well and drain thoroughly.

5 Add the pearl barley to the stock. Bring to the boil, then lower the heat and simmer very gently for 15–20 minutes, until the barley is just cooked and tender. Season the soup with 1 teaspoon salt and black pepper to taste.

6 Add the prunes. Slice the remaining leeks and add them to the pan. Bring to the boil, then simmer for 10 minutes.

7 Slice the chicken breasts and add them to the soup with the remaining chicken meat, sliced or cut into neat pieces. Reheat, then ladle into soup bowls and serve with chopped parsley.

Chicken Minestrone

This is a special minestrone made with fresh chicken. Serve with rustic Italian bread.

INGREDIENTS

Serves 4–6

1 tablespoon olive oil
2 chicken thighs
3 rindless fatty bacon strips , chopped
1 onion, finely chopped
few fresh basil leaves, shredded
few fresh rosemary leaves, finely chopped
1 tablespoon chopped fresh flat
    leaf parsley
2 potatoes, cut into ½-inch cubes
1 large carrot, cut into ½-inch cubes
2 small zucchini, cut into ½-in cubes
1–2 celery sticks, cut into ½-in cubes
1¾ pints/4 cups Chicken Stock
7 ounces/1¾ cups frozen peas
3½ ounces/scant 1 cup stellette or other
    small soup pasta
salt and ground black pepper
Parmesan cheese shavings, to serve

1 Heat the oil in a large frying pan, add the chicken thighs and cook over a medium heat for about 5 minutes on each side. Remove with a slotted spoon and set aside.

2 Add the bacon, onion and herbs to the pan and cook gently, stirring constantly, for about 5 minutes. Add the potatoes, carrot, zucchini and celery and cook for 5–7 minutes more.

3 Return the chicken thighs to the pan, add the stock and bring to the boil. Cover and cook over a low heat for 35–40 minutes, stirring the soup occasionally.

4 Remove the chicken thighs with a slotted spoon and place them on a board. Stir the peas and pasta into the soup and bring back to the boil. Simmer, stirring frequently, for 7–8 minutes or according to the instructions on the packet, until the pasta is just *al dente*.

5 Meanwhile, remove and discard the chicken skin, then remove the meat from the chicken bones and cut it into small (½-inch) pieces.

6 Return the meat to the soup, stir well and heat through. Taste and adjust the seasoning as necessary.

7 Ladle the soup into warmed soup plates or bowls, top with Parmesan shavings and serve immediately, while piping hot.

Galician Broth

This delicious Spanish soup is very similar to the warming, chunky meat and potato broths of cooler climates. For extra color, a few onion skins can be added when cooking the gammon, but remember to remove them before serving.

Serves 4

1 pound piece cured ham
2 bay leaves
2 onions, sliced
2¹/₂ pints/6¹/₄ cups water
2 teaspoons paprika
1¹/₂ lb potatoes, cut into large chunks
8 ounces collards
14-ounce can navy or cannellini beans,
 drained and rinsed
salt and ground black pepper

1 Soak the gammon overnight in cold water. Drain and put in a large pan with the bay leaves and onions. Pour the water on top.

2 Bring to the boil, then reduce the heat and simmer gently for about 1¹/₂ hours, until the meat is tender. Keep an eye on the pan to make sure it doesn't boil over.

COOK'S TIP

Ham knuckles can be used instead of the cured ham. The bones will give the juices a delicious flavor.

3 Drain the meat, reserving the cooking liquid, and leave to cool slightly. Discard the skin and any excess fat from the meat and cut into small chunks. Return to the pan with the paprika and potatoes. Cover and simmer gently for 20 minutes.

4 Cut away the cores from the collards. Roll up the leaves and cut into thin shreds. Add to the pan with the beans and simmer for about 10 minutes. Season with salt and ground black pepper to taste. Ladle into warm soup bowls and serve piping hot.

Mediterranean Sausage and Pesto Soup

This hearty soup brings the summery flavor of basil to midwinter meals. Thick slices of warm rustic bread would make the perfect accompaniment.

INGREDIENTS

Serves 4

1 tablespoon olive oil, plus extra
    for frying
1 red onion, chopped
1 pound smoked pork sausages
8 ounces/1 cup red lentils
14-ounce can chopped tomatoes
1¼ pints/4 cups water
vegetable oil, for deep-frying
salt and ground black pepper
4 tablespoons pesto and fresh basil sprigs,
    to garnish
warm, rustic bread, to serve

1 Heat the oil in a large pan and cook the onion until softened. Coarsely chop all but one of the sausages and add them to the pan. Cook, stirring, for 5 minutes.

2 Stir in the lentils, tomatoes and water, and bring to the boil. Reduce the heat, cover and simmer for about 20 minutes. Cool the soup slightly before processing it in a blender.

3 Cook the remaining sausage in a little oil in a small frying pan, turning frequently. Transfer to a chopping board or plate and leave to cool slightly, then slice thinly.

4 Heat the oil for deep-frying to 375°F, or until a cube of day-old bread browns in about 60 seconds. Deep-fry the sausage slices and basil briefly until the sausages are brown and the basil leaves are crisp. Lift them out using a slotted spoon and drain well on paper towels.

5 Reheat the soup, season to taste with salt and pepper, then ladle into warmed individual soup bowls. Sprinkle with the deep-fried sausage slices and basil and swirl a little pesto through each portion. Serve with warm rustic bread.

Onion and Pancetta Soup

This warming winter soup comes from Umbria in Italy, where it is sometimes thickened with beaten eggs and plenty of grated Parmesan cheese. It is then served on top of hot toasted croûtes – rather like savory scrambled eggs.

INGREDIENTS

Serves 4

4 ounces pancetta strips, rinds removed, coarsely chopped
2 tablespoons olive oil
¹/₂ ounce/1 tablespoon butter
1¹/₂ pounds onions, thinly sliced
2 teaspoons granulated sugar
about 2 pints/5 cups Chicken Stock
12 ounces ripe Italian plum tomatoes, peeled and coarsely chopped
few fresh basil leaves, shredded
salt and ground black pepper
grated Parmesan cheese, to serve

1 Put the chopped pancetta in a large pan and heat gently, stirring constantly, until the fat runs. Increase the heat to medium, add the olive oil, butter, sliced onions and granulated sugar and stir well to mix.

2 Half-cover the pan and cook the onions gently for about 20 minutes, until golden. Stir frequently and lower the heat if necessary.

3 Add the stock and tomatoes, season to taste with salt and pepper and bring to the boil, stirring constantly. Lower the heat, half-cover the pan and simmer, stirring occasionally, for about 30 minutes.

4 Check the consistency of the soup and add a little more stock or water if it is too thick.

5 Just before serving, stir in most of the basil and taste and adjust the seasoning, if necessary. Serve immediately, garnished with the remaining shredded basil. Hand around the freshly grated Parmesan separately.

COOK'S TIP

Look for Vidalia onions to make this soup. They are available at large supermarkets, and have a sweet flavor and attractive, yellowish flesh.

Chicken, Tomato and Chayote Soup

Chicken breast portions and smoked haddock take on the flavors of herbs and spices to produce this tasty soup.

INGREDIENTS

Serves 4

8 ounces skinless, boneless chicken breast
    portions, diced
1 garlic clove, crushed
pinch of freshly grated nutmeg
1 ounce/2 tablespoons butter
    or margarine
1/2 onion, finely chopped
1 tablespoon tomato paste
14-ounce can tomatoes, puréed
2 pints/5 cups Chicken Stock
1 fresh chile, seeded and chopped
1 chayote, peeled and diced (about
    12 ounces)
1 teaspoon dried oregano
1/2 teaspoon dried thyme
2 ounces smoked haddock fillet, skinned
    and diced
salt and ground black pepper
chopped fresh chives, to garnish

1 Dice the chicken, place in a bowl and season with salt, pepper, garlic and nutmeg. Mix well to flavor and then set aside for about 30 minutes.

2 Melt the butter or margarine in a large pan, add the chicken and sauté over a moderate heat for 5–6 minutes. Stir in the onion and cook gently, stirring frequently, for a further 5 minutes, or until the onion is slightly softened.

3 Add the tomato paste, puréed tomatoes, chicken stock, chile, chayote, oregano and thyme. Bring to the boil, lower the heat, cover and simmer gently for about 35 minutes, or until the chicken and chayote are tender.

4 Add the smoked haddock and simmer for 5 minutes more, or until the fish is cooked through. Adjust the seasoning and pour into warmed soup bowls. Garnish with a sprinkling of chopped fresh chives and serve piping hot.

Lamb and Lentil Soup

Lamb and red lentils go together so well, they seem to have been made for one another.

INGREDIENTS

Serves 4

about 2½ pints/6¼ cups water

2 pounds shoulder or breast of lamb, cut into chops

½ onion, chopped

1 garlic clove, crushed

1 bay leaf

1 clove

2 fresh thyme sprigs

8 ounces potatoes, cut into 1-inch pieces

6 ounces/¾ cup red lentils

salt and ground black pepper

chopped fresh parsley

1 Put about 2 pints/5 cups of the water and the meat in a large pan with the onion, garlic, bay leaf, clove and sprigs of thyme. Bring to the boil, lower the heat and simmer for about 1 hour, until the lamb is tender.

VARIATION
◒

For a richer, fuller flavor, substitute Meat Stock, made with lamb bones, or Chicken Stock for all or some of the water.

2 Add the pieces of potato and the lentils to the pan and season the soup with a little salt and plenty of black pepper. Add the remaining water to come just above surface of the meat and vegetables; you may need to add more if the soup becomes too thick during cooking.

3 Cover and simmer for about 25 minutes, or until the lentils are cooked and well blended into the soup. Taste the soup and adjust the seasoning as necessary. Stir in the parsley and serve.

Spicy Chicken and Mushroom Soup

This creamy chicken soup makes a wonderful start to a meal.

INGREDIENTS

Serves 4

3 ounces/6 tablespoons sweet butter

¹/₂ teaspoon crushed garlic

1 teaspoon garam masala

1 teaspoon crushed black peppercorns

1 teaspoon salt

¹/₄ teaspoon freshly grated nutmeg

8 ounces skinless, boneless chicken
    breast portions

1 medium leek, sliced

3 ounces/generous 1 cup
    mushrooms, sliced

2 ounces/¹/₃ cup corn kernels

¹/₂ pint/1¹/₄ cups water

8 fluid ounces/1 cup light cream

2 tablespoons chopped fresh cilantro

1 teaspoon crushed dried red chili,
    to garnish (optional)

3 Remove from the heat and leave to cool slightly. Transfer three-quarters of the mixture to a food processor or blender. Add the water and process for about 1 minute.

4 Pour the resulting purée back into the pan with the rest of the mixture and bring to the boil over a medium heat. Lower the heat and stir in the cream.

5 Add the fresh cilantro. Taste and adjust the seasoning. Serve hot, garnished with crushed red chili, if you like.

1 Melt the butter in a pan. Lower the heat slightly and add the garlic and garam masala. Lower the heat further and add the peppercorns, salt and nutmeg.

2 Cut the chicken pieces into very fine strips and add to the pan with the leek, mushrooms and corn. Cook for 5–7 minutes, until the chicken is cooked through, stirring constantly.

Jalapeño-style Soup

Chicken, chile and avocado combine to make this simple but unusual soup.

INGREDIENTS

Serves 6

2¹⁄₂ pints/6¹⁄₄ cups Chicken Stock
2 cooked chicken breast fillets, skinned
    and cut into large strips
1 drained canned chipotle or jalapeño
    chile, rinsed
1 avocado

COOK'S TIP

When using canned chiles,
it is important to rinse them
thoroughly before adding them
to a dish in order to remove the
flavor of any pickling liquid.

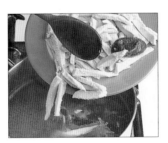

1 Heat the stock in a large pan and add the chicken and chile. Simmer over a very gentle heat for 5 minutes to heat the chicken through and release the flavor from the chile.

2 Cut the avocado in half, remove the pit and peel off the skin. Slice the avocado flesh neatly lengthwise.

3 Using a slotted spoon, remove the chile from the pan and discard it. Pour the soup into heated serving bowls, distributing the chicken evenly among them.

4 Add a few avocado slices to each bowl and serve.

Indian Beef and Berry Soup

The fresh berries give this soup a pleasant kick.

INGREDIENTS

INGREDIENTS

Serves 4

2 tablespoons vegetable oil

1 pound tender beef steak

2 onions, thinly sliced

2 ounce/2 tablespoons butter

1¾ pints/4 cups Meat Stock

½ teaspoon salt

4 ounces/1 cup fresh huckleberries,
   blueberries or blackberries,
   lightly mashed

2 tablespoons clear honey

1 Heat the oil in a heavy pan until almost smoking. Add the steak and cook on both sides over a medium-high heat until well browned. Remove the steak from the pan and set aside.

2 Reduce the heat to low and add the sliced onions and butter to the pan. Stir thoroughly, scraping up the meat juices. Cook over a low heat for 8–10 minutes, until the onions are softened.

3 Add the meat stock and salt and bring to the boil, stirring constantly. Mix in the mashed berries and the honey. Simmer for 20 minutes.

4 Cut the steak into thin slivers. Taste the soup and add more salt or honey if necessary. Add the steak to the pan. Cook gently for 30 seconds, stirring, then serve.

Wonton Soup

In China, wonton soup is served as a snack, or dim sum, but is a popular soup course in the West.

Serves 4

6 ounces pork, coarsely chopped

2 ounces peeled shrimp, finely chopped

1 teaspoon light brown sugar

1 tablespoon Chinese rice wine

1 tablespoon light soy sauce

1 teaspoon finely chopped scallions,
   plus extra to garnish

1 teaspoon finely chopped fresh
   root ginger

24 ready-made wonton skins

about 1¼ pints/3 cups Stock for
   Chinese Soups

1 tablespoon light soy sauce

1 In a bowl, mix the pork and shrimp with the sugar, rice wine, soy sauce, scallions and ginger. Set aside for 25–30 minutes for the flavors to blend.

2 Place about 1 teaspoon of the pork mixture in the center of each wonton skin.

3 Wet the edges of each filled wonton skin with a little water and press them together with your fingers to seal. Fold each wonton parcel over.

4 To cook, bring the stock to a rolling boil in a wok, add the wontons and cook for 4–5 minutes. Season with the soy sauce and add the extra scallions.

5 Transfer to individual soup bowls and serve.

Chinese Chicken and Asparagus Soup

This is a very delicate and delicious soup. When fresh asparagus is not in season, canned white asparagus is an acceptable substitute.

INGREDIENTS

Serves 4

5 ounces skinless, boneless chicken
   breast portion
1 teaspoon egg white
1 teaspoon cornstarch mixed to a paste
   with 1 tablespoon water
4 ounces asparagus
1¼ pints/3 cups Chicken Stock
salt and ground black pepper
fresh cilantro , to garnish

1 Cut the chicken into very thin slices each about 1½ × 1 inch. Mix with a pinch of salt, then add the egg white, and finally the cornstarch paste.

2 Cut off and discard the tough stems of the asparagus, and cut the tender spears diagonally into short, even lengths.

3 In a wok or pan, bring the stock to a rolling boil, add the asparagus, bring back to the boil and cook for 2 minutes. (You do not need to do this if you are using canned asparagus.)

4 Add the chicken, stir to separate and bring back to the boil once more. Taste and adjust the seasoning if necessary. Serve immediately, garnished with fresh cilantro leaves.

Clear Soup with Meatballs

A Chinese-style soup, in which meatballs are combined with lightly cooked vegetables in a tasty stock.

INGREDIENTS

Serves 8

4–6 Chinese mushrooms, soaked in warm
    water for 30 minutes
2 tablespoons peanut oil
1 large onion, finely chopped
2 garlic cloves, finely crushed
½-inch piece fresh root ginger, bruised
3½ pints/9 cups Meat or Chicken stock,
    including the soaking liquid from
    the mushrooms
2 tablespoons soy sauce
4 ounces curly kale, spinach or Chinese
    cabbage, shredded

For the meatballs
6 ounces/¾ cup ground beef
1 small onion, finely chopped
1–2 garlic cloves, crushed
1 tablespoon cornstarch
a little egg white, lightly beaten
salt and ground black pepper

1 First prepare the meatballs. Mix the beef with the onion, garlic, cornstarch and seasoning in a food processor and then bind with sufficient egg white to make a firm mixture. With wet hands, roll into tiny, bitesize balls and set aside.

2 Drain the mushrooms. Reserve the soaking liquid. Trim off and discard the stalks. Slice the caps thinly and set aside.

3 Heat a wok or large pan and add the oil. Cook the onion, garlic and ginger to bring out the flavor, but do not allow to brown.

4 When the onion is soft, pour in the stock. Bring to the boil, then stir in the soy sauce and mushroom slices and simmer for 10 minutes. Add the meatballs and cook for 10 minutes.

5 Just before serving, remove the ginger. Stir in the shredded curly kale, spinach or Chinese cabbage. Heat through for 1 minute only – no longer or the leaves will be overcooked. Ladle the soup into warm bowls and serve.

Duck Consommé

The Vietnamese community in France has had a profound influence on French cooking, as this soup bears witness – it is light and rich at the same time, with intriguing flavors of Southeast Asia.

INGREDIENTS

Serves 4

1 duck carcass (raw or cooked), plus 2 legs or any giblets, trimmed of as much fat as possible
1 large onion, unpeeled, with root end trimmed
2 carrots, cut into 2-inch pieces
1 parsnip, cut into 2-inch pieces
1 leek, cut into 2-inch pieces
2–4 garlic cloves, crushed
1-inch piece fresh root ginger, sliced
1 tablespoon black peppercorns
4–6 fresh thyme sprigs or
   1 teaspoon dried thyme
6–8 fresh cilantro sprigs, leaves and stems separated

For the garnish
1 small carrot
1 small leek, halved lengthwise
4–6 shiitake mushrooms, thinly sliced
soy sauce
2 scallions, thinly sliced
watercress or finely shredded
   Chinese cabbage
ground black pepper

1 Put the duck carcass and legs or giblets, onion, carrots, parsnip, leek and garlic in a large, heavy pan or flameproof casserole. Add the ginger, peppercorns, thyme and cilantro stems, cover with cold water and bring to the boil over a medium-high heat, skimming off any foam that rises to the surface.

2 Reduce the heat and simmer gently for 1½–2 hours, then strain through a sieve lined with cheesecloth into a bowl. Discard the bones and vegetables. Cool the stock and chill for several hours. Skim off any congealed fat and blot the surface with kitchen paper to remove any traces of fat.

3 To make the garnish, cut the carrot and leek into 2-inch pieces. Cut each piece lengthwise into thin slices, then stack and slice into thin julienne strips. Place the carrot and leek strips in a large pan with the sliced mushrooms.

4 Pour over the stock and add a few dashes of soy sauce and some pepper. Bring to the boil over a medium-high heat, skimming any foam that rises to the surface. Adjust the seasoning if necessary. Stir in the scallions and watercress or Chinese cabbage. Ladle the consommé into warmed bowls and sprinkle with the cilantro leaves before serving.

Pork and Pickled Mustard Greens Soup

This highly flavored soup makes an interesting start to a meal.

INGREDIENTS

Serves 4–6

8 ounces pickled mustard greens, soaked

2 ounces cellophane noodles, soaked

1 tablespoon vegetable oil

4 garlic cloves, thinly sliced

1¾ pints/4 cups Chicken Stock

1 pound pork ribs, cut into large chunks

2 tablespoons Thai fish sauce

pinch of sugar

ground black pepper

2 fresh red chiles, seeded and thinly sliced,
  to garnish

1 Cut the pickled mustard greens into bitesize pieces. Taste to check the seasoning. If they are too salty, soak them for a little longer.

2 Drain the cellophane noodles, discarding the soaking water, and cut them into pieces about 2 inches long.

3 Heat the oil in a small frying pan, add the garlic and stir-fry until golden. Transfer to a bowl and set aside.

4 Pour the chicken stock into a large pan, bring to the boil, then add the pork ribs and simmer gently over a low heat for about 10–15 minutes.

5 Add the pickled mustard greens and cellophane noodles. Bring back to the boil. Season to taste with fish sauce, sugar and ground black pepper.

6 Pour the soup into individual serving bowls. Garnish with the fried garlic and the red chiles and serve hot.

Ginger, Chicken and Coconut Soup

This aromatic soup is rich with coconut milk and intensely flavored with galangal, lemon grass and kaffir lime leaves.

INGREDIENTS

Serves 4–6

1¼ pints/3 cups coconut milk
16 fluid ounces/2 cups Chicken Stock
4 lemon grass stalks, bruised and chopped
1-inch piece galangal, thinly sliced
10 black peppercorns, crushed
10 kaffir lime leaves, torn
11 ounces skinless boneless chicken, cut
   into thin strips
4 ounces white mushrooms
2 ounces/½ cup baby corn cobs
4 tablespoons lime juice
3 tablespoons Thai fish sauce

For the garnish
2 red chiles, seeded and chopped
3–4 scallions, chopped
chopped fresh cilantro

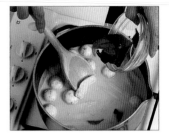

1 Bring the coconut milk and chicken stock to the boil in a large pan. Add the lemon grass, galangal, peppercorns and half the kaffir lime leaves, reduce the heat and simmer gently for 10 minutes.

2 Strain the stock mixture into a clean pan. Return to the heat, then add the chicken strips, mushrooms and baby corn cobs. Cook for about 5–7 minutes, until the chicken is cooked.

3 Stir in the lime juice, fish sauce to taste and the rest of the lime leaves. Ladle the soup into warm bowls, garnish with red chiles, scallions and cilantro and serve.

Miso Soup with Pork and Vegetables

This is quite a rich and filling soup. Its Japanese name, Tanuki Jiru, means raccoon soup for hunters, but as raccoons are not eaten nowadays, pork is used.

INGREDIENTS

Serves 4

7 ounces lean boneless pork

1 parsnip

2 ounces daikon

4 fresh shiitake mushrooms

½ konnyaku or ½ x 8–10¼ ounces
   firm tofu

a little sesame oil, for stir-frying

1 pint/2½ cups water and 2 teaspoons
   instant dashi

4½ tablespoons miso

2 scallions, chopped

1 teaspoon sesame seeds

1 Firmly press the meat down on a chopping board, using the palm of your hand and slice horizontally into very thin, long strips, then cut the strips crosswise into small, neat squares. Set the pork aside.

2 Peel the parsnip with a vegetable peeler, cut it in half lengthwise, then cut it into ½-inch thick half-moon-shaped slices.

3 Peel and slice the daikon into ⅔-inch thick disck. Cut the disck into ⅔-inch cubes. Remove the shiitake stalks and cut the caps into quarters.

4 Place the konnyaku, if using, in a pan of boiling water and cook for 1 minute. Drain and cool. Cut in quarters lengthwise, then crosswise into ⅛-inch thick pieces. If using tofu, cut into ⅛-inch thick pieces.

5 Heat a little sesame oil in a heavy, cast-iron or enamelled pan until purple smoke rises. Stir-fry the pork, then add the konnyaku or tofu and all the vegetables, except for the scallions. When the color of the meat has changed, add the stock.

6 Bring to the boil over a medium heat and skim off the foam until the soup looks fairly clear. Reduce the heat, cover, and simmer for 15 minutes.

7 Put the miso in a small bowl, and mix with 4 tablespoons hot stock to make a smooth paste. Stir one-third of the miso into the soup. Taste and add more miso if required. Add the scallion and remove from the heat. Serve very hot in individual soup bowls and sprinkle with sesame seeds.

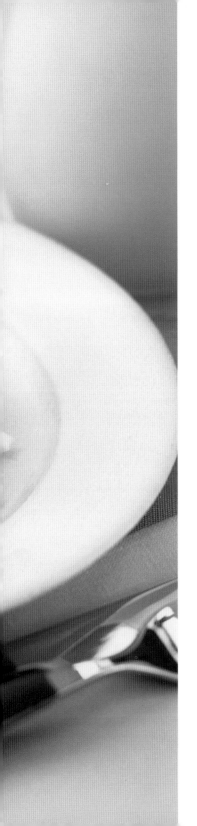

APPETIZERS

While it may be sensible to plan your main course first,
especially when entertaining, it is still important to give
plenty of thought to the appetizer. This section is packed
with inspiring first-course ideas for every occasion,
from informal suppers to sophisticated dinner parties.
You will find clever suggestions for canapés and tasty morsels
to serve with drinks, hot hors d'oeuvres and fabulous
appetizers based on vegetables, cheese, fish, seafood,
meat and poultry, as well as helpful advice and tips
on garnishes, marinades and dressings.

Garnishes

Many garnishes are delicate works of art that seem almost a shame to eat, and others add a dash of texture or a hint of color without which the dish would just not be the same.

CREAM SWIRL

Add a swirl of cream, sour cream or yogurt to make a dip look particularly attractive.

To create a delicate pattern draw the tip of a fine skewer back and forth through the swirl.

CROÛTONS

Croûtons are an easy and effective way to use up stale bread while adding crunch to any dish, and are always served with classic Caesar salads.

Once you have cut your chosen bread into small cubes, either fry them in sunflower oil until they are golden and crisp, or brush them with oil and bake in the oven. They will keep in an airtight container for up to a week.

CUCUMBER FLOWERS

This is a stunning garnish which would grace any dinner party.

1 Cut the cucumber in half lengthwise and remove the seeds. Place each half cut-side down and then cut at an angle into 3-inch lengths. Cut into fine slices stopping ¼-inch short of the far side, so that the slices remain attached.

2 Fan the slices out. Turn in alternate slices to form a loop. Bend the length into a semicircle so the cucumber loops resemble the petals of a flower.

LEMON TWIST

A classic garnish – so simple but very effective.

Cut a lemon into ¼-inch slices. Make a cut in each slice from the center to the skin. Hold the slice either side of the cut and twist to form an "S" shape.

PARMESAN CURLS

Curls of Parmesan add a delicate touch to pasta or risotto.

Holding a swivel-bladed peeler at a 45° angle, draw it steadily across the block of Parmesan cheese to form a curl.

CHILE FLOWERS

Make these chile flowers several hours before needed to allow the "flowers" to open up.

1 Use a small pair of scissors or a slim-bladed knife to cut a chile carefully lengthwise up from the tip to within ½-inch of the stem end. Repeat this at regular intervals around the chile – more cuts will produce more petals. Repeat with the remaining chiles.

2 Rinse the chiles in cold water and remove all the seeds. Place the chiles in a bowl of iced water and chill for at least 4 hours. For very curly flowers leave the chiles overnight.

CHIVE BRAIDS

Try adding a couple of edible braids of chives around your appetizers.

1 Align three chives on a work surface with a bowl on one end to hold them still. Carefully braid the chives together to within 1-inch of the end.

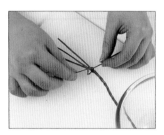

2 Tie a thin chive around the exposed end of the braid. Remove the bowl and tie the other end the same way. Trim both ends with kitchen scissors.

3 Place the braid in a bowl and pour boiling water over it. Leave to stand for 20–30 seconds, then drain and refresh under cold water. Drain again.

SCALLION TASSELS

You can often find this garnish in Chinese restaurants, where looks are almost as important as taste.

Cut the white part of a scallion into a 2½-inch length. Shred one end of each piece, then place in ice water for about 30 minutes until the ends curl.

TOMATO SUNS

Colorful cherry tomato suns look good with pâtés and terrines.

1 Place a tomato stem-side down. Cut lightly into the skin across the top, edging the knife down towards the base on either side. Repeat until the skin has been cut into eight separate segments, joined at the base.

2 Slide the top of the knife under the point of each segment and ease the skin away towards the base. Gently fold the petals back to mimic the sun's rays.

AVOCADO FAN

Avocados are amazingly versatile – they can serve as edible containers, be sliced or diced in a salad, or form the foundation of a delicious sauce. They also make very elegant garnishes for appetizers.

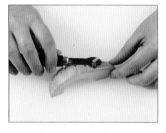

1 Halve, pit and peel an avocado. Slice each half lengthwise into quarters. Gently draw a zester across the quarters at ½-inch intervals, to create regular stripes.

2 Make four cuts lengthwise down each avocado quarter leaving ½-inch intact at the end. Carefully fan out the slices and arrange on a plate.

Marinades, Oils and Dressings

Marinades, flavored oils and dressings can turn a plain piece of fish or a sliced vegetable into a delectable appetizer or hors d'oeuvre. With a few simple ingredients, and in just a few minutes, you can make a fresh herb marinade to tenderize fish or meat, a ginger and garlic oil for fragrant fried dishes, or a sour-cream dressing to bring out the flavor of crisp salad vegetables.

SUMMER HERB MARINADE

Make the best of summer herbs in this marinade. Any combination may be used depending on what you have on hand, and it works well with veal, chicken, pork or lamb.

1 Discard any coarse stalks or damaged leaves from a selection of herb sprigs, such as chervil, thyme, parsley, sage, chives, rosemary and oregano, then chop finely.

2 Mix the herbs with 6 tablespoons olive oil, 3 tablespoons tarragon vinegar, 1 garlic clove, crushed, 2 scallions, chopped, and salt and pepper. Add the meat or poultry, cover and chill for 2–3 hours.

GINGER AND LIME MARINADE

This refreshing marinade is particularly good with chicken.

1 Mix together the rind of one lime and the juice of three limes. Add 1 tablespoon green cardamom seeds, crushed, 1 finely chopped onion, grated fresh root ginger (use a 1-inch piece and peel before grating), 1 large garlic clove, crushed and 3 tablespoons olive oil.

2 Pour over the meat or fish. Stir gently to coat, cover and leave in a cool place for 1 hour.

CHILE AND GARLIC MARINADE

Add extra chiles if you like your food to be very spicy.

Combine 4 small chiles, seeded and finely diced, 2 teaspoons finely grated fresh root ginger, 1 large garlic clove, crushed, and 3 tablespoons light soy sauce in a bowl. Add the meat or fish, cover and chill for 2– 4 hours.

CHINESE MARINADE

This marinade is traditionally used to flavor succulent duck breasts.

Mix 1 tablespoon clear honey, 1¼ teaspoons five-spice powder, 1 garlic clove, finely chopped, 1 tablespoon hoisin sauce and a pinch of salt and pepper. Add the duck breasts or other meat, turning them in the marinade. Cover and leave in a cool place to marinate for 2 hours.

AROMATIC SPICE OIL

As well as tasting delicious, aromatic oils make wonderful gifts. Ginger, Garlic and Shallot Oil is simple and delicious, but you could also try using a combination of other spices and flavorings, such as chiles, cilantro, lemon grass, peppercorns and lime leaves.

Peel and lightly bruise a 2½-inch piece of fresh root ginger and place in a clean bottle. Fill with peanut oil, 2 garlic cloves (left whole) and 3 small peeled shallots. Cover tightly and leave in a cool dark place for 2 weeks, or until the flavor is sufficiently pronounced, before using.

PARSLEY, SAGE AND THYME OIL

Chop a handful each of fresh parsley, sage and thyme. Place in a bottle and fill up with olive oil. Seal and allow to stand at room temperature for about a week, shaking occasionally. Strain the oil into another sterilized, decorative bottle, discard the chopped herbs but add a fresh sprig or two to decorate.

SOUR CREAM AND DILL DRESSING

This unusual dressing can be made in only a couple of minutes.

Blend together 4 fluid ounces/½ cup sour cream, 2 teaspoons creamed horseradish and 1 tablespoon chopped fresh dill in a small bowl and season with a little salt and pepper.

SPICY TOMATO DRESSING

This tangy dressing goes very well with a robust salad, such as bean or potato salad. It can also be used as a marinade.

Mix together 1 teaspoon ground cumin, 1 tablespoon tomato ketchup, 2 tablespoons olive oil, 1 tablespoon white wine vinegar and 1 garlic clove, crushed in a small bowl. Add a little salt and some hot pepper sauce to taste and stir again thoroughly.

HERB GARDEN DRESSING

The dried mixture will keep throughout the winter until your herbs are growing again. It can also be used to sprinkle over vegetables, casseroles and stews.

1 Mix together 4 ounces/1 cup dried oregano, 4 ounces/1 cup dried basil, 2 ounces/½ cup dried marjoram, 2 ounces/½ cup dried dill weed, 2 ounces/½ cup dried mint leaves, 2 ounces/½ cup onion powder, 2 tablespoons dry mustard, 2 teaspoons salt and 1 tablespoon freshly ground black pepper and keep in a sealed jar to use as needed.

2 When making a batch of salad dressing, take 2 tablespoons of the herb mixture and add it to 12 fluid ounces/1½ cups of extra virgin olive oil and 4 fluid ounces/½ cup cider vinegar. Mix thoroughly and allow to stand for 1 hour or so. Mix again before using.

NIBBLES
AND DIPS

This mouth-watering collection of hot and cold morsels is
designed to tempt the appetite. You can serve them as an
hors d'oeuvre, once your guests are seated at the table, or,
in many cases, dispense with formality and serve as canapés
with pre-dinner drinks. Whatever your preference, there is
something to set the taste buds tingling – Tex-Mex dips,
Japanese tempura, Russian blinis, Middle Eastern falafel,
Mediterranean tapenade and a huge array of tempting treats
from around the world.

ⱽ *Marinated Olives*

For the best flavor, marinate the olives for at least 10 days and serve at room temperature.

INGREDIENTS

Serves 4

8 ounces/1⅓ cups unpitted, green olives
3 garlic cloves
1 teaspoon coriander seeds
2 small fresh red chiles
2–3 thick slices of lemon, cut into pieces
1 fresh thyme or rosemary sprig
5 tablespoons white wine vinegar

1 Spread out the olives and garlic on a chopping board. Using a rolling pin, crack and flatten them slightly.

2 Crack the coriander seeds in a mortar with a pestle.

COOK'S TIP
~
For a change, use a mix of caraway and cumin seeds in place of the coriander.

3 Mix the olives and the garlic, coriander seeds, chiles, lemon pieces, thyme or rosemary sprigs and white wine vinegar in a large bowl. Toss well, then transfer the mixture to a clean glass jar. Pour in sufficient cold water to cover. Store in the refrigerator for at least 5 days before serving at room temperature.

ⱽ *Salted Almonds*

These crunchy salted nuts are at their best when fresh so, if you can, cook them on the day you plan to eat them.

INGREDIENTS

Serves 2–4

6 ounces/1½ cups whole almonds in their skins
1 tablespoon egg white, lightly beaten
½ teaspoon coarse sea salt

COOK'S TIP

This traditional method of salt-roasting nuts gives a matt, dry-looking finish; if you want them to shine, turn the roasted nuts into a bowl, add 1 tablespoon of olive oil and shake well to coat.

1 Preheat the oven to 350°F. Spread out the almonds on a baking sheet and roast for about 20 minutes, until cracked and golden.

2 Mix the egg white and salt in a bowl, add the almonds and shake well to coat.

3 Tip the almond and egg mixture onto the baking sheet, give a shake to separate the nuts, then return them to the oven for 5 minutes, until they have dried. Set aside until cold, then store in an airtight container until ready to serve.

Assorted Canapés

These elegant party pieces take a little time to make, but they can be prepared in advance with the final touches added when your guests arrive. Each variation makes 12.

TRUFFLE CANAPÉS

INGREDIENTS

8 ounces rich unsweetened pastry dough,
   thawed if frozen
2 eggs, beaten
½ ounce/1 tablespoons butter
1 teaspoon truffle oil or a few slices or
   shreds of fresh truffle
salt and ground black pepper
chopped fresh chives, to garnish

1 Preheat the oven to 375°F. Roll out the pastry very thinly on a lightly floured work surface and use to line 12 very small muffin pans.

2 Line each pastry shell with baking parchment and bake for 10 minutes. Remove the parchment and bake for a further 5 minutes, until the pastry is crisp and golden.

3 Season the beaten eggs, then melt the butter in a pan, pour in the eggs and stir constantly over a gentle heat. When the eggs are almost set, stir in the truffle oil or fresh truffle. Spoon the mixture into the pastry shells and top with chives.

PRAWN AND TOMATO CANAPÉS

INGREDIENTS

8 ounces rich unsweetened pastry dough,
   thawed if frozen
2 tomatoes, peeled, seeded and chopped
12 large cooked shrimp, peeled but with
   tails left on
4 tablespoons hollandaise sauce
salt and ground black pepper
fresh fennel or chervil sprigs, to garnish

1 Preheat the oven to 375°F. Roll out the pastry very thinly on a lightly floured work surface and use to line 12 very small muffin pans.

2 Line each pastry shell with baking parchment and bake for 10 minutes. Remove the parchment and bake for a further 5 minutes, until the pastry is crisp and golden.

3 Place some chopped tomato in the base of each pastry shell and season with salt and ground black pepper. Top with the shrimp and spoon on some hollandaise sauce. Warm through briefly in the oven and serve garnished with fennel or chervil sprigs.

SALMON AND CILANTRO CANAPÉS

INGREDIENTS

3–4 slices dark rye bread
2 eggs, hard-boiled and
   thinly sliced
4 ounces poached salmon
few fresh cilantro leaves,
   to garnish

For the lime and cilantro mayonnaise

45–60ml/3–4 tablespoons mayonnaise
1 teaspoon chopped fresh cilantro
1 teaspoon lime juice
salt and ground black pepper

1 Cut the slices of rye bread into 12 triangular pieces, using a sharp knife.

2 Make the lime and cilantro mayonnaise. In a small bowl, mix together the mayonnaise, chopped cilantro and lime juice. Season with salt and ground black pepper to taste.

3 Top each bread triangle with a slice of egg, a small portion of salmon and a teaspoon of mayonnaise. Garnish each with a cilantro leaf. Chill the canapés until ready to serve.

WATERCRESS AND
AVOCADO CANAPÉS

INGREDIENTS

3–4 slices dark rye bread

1 small ripe avocado

1 tablespoon lemon juice

3 tablespoons mayonnaise

½ bunch of watercress, chopped, reserving
  a few sprigs to garnish

6 quail eggs, hard-boiled

1 Cut the bread into 12 round
  pieces, using a plain or fluted
cookie cutter.

2 Cut the avocado in half, around
  the pit. Peel one half, then slice
and dip each piece in lemon juice.
Place one piece of avocado on each
bread round.

3 Scoop the remaining avocado
  into a bowl and mash. Mix in
the mayonnaise and watercress.
Spoon a little of the mixture onto
each canapé, top with a shelled,
halved quail egg and garnish with a
sprig of watercress.

Smoked Salmon and Gravadlax Sauce

Gravadlax is cured fresh salmon: it is marinated in dill, salt and sugar and left for 2–3 days with weights on it. It can now be bought in most supermarkets and delicatessens, and you can use it instead of smoked salmon if you like.

INGREDIENTS

Serves 8

1 ounce/2 tablespoons softened butter

1 teaspoon grated lemon rind

4 slices rye or pumpernickel bread

4 ounces smoked salmon

few frisée lettuce leaves

8 lemon slices

8 cucumber slices

4 tablespoons gravadlax sauce

dill sprigs, to garnish

1 Mix the butter and lemon rind together, spread over the bread and cut in half diagonally.

2 Arrange the smoked salmon over the top to cover.

3 Add a little frisée lettuce and a slice each of lemon and cucumber. Spoon over some gravadlax sauce, then garnish with fresh dill sprigs.

Smoked Trout Mousse in Cucumber Cups

*This delicious creamy mousse can be
made in advance and chilled for
2–3 days in the refrigerator. Serve it
in crunchy cucumber cups, or simply
with crudités if you like.*

INGREDIENTS

Makes about 24

4 ounces/½ cup cream cheese, softened

2 scallions, chopped

1–2 tablespoons, chopped fresh dill
  or parsley

1 teaspoon horseradish sauce

8 ounces smoked trout fillets, flaked and
  any fine bones removed

2–4 tablespoons heavy cream

cayenne pepper, to taste

2 cucumbers

salt

fresh dill sprigs, to garnish

1 Put the cream cheese,
scallions, dill or parsley, and
horseradish sauce into a blender or
the bowl of a food processor and
process until well blended. Add the
trout and process until smooth,
scraping down the sides of the
bowl once.

2 With the machine running,
pour in the cream through the
feeder tube until a soft, mousse-
like mixture forms. Season to taste
with salt and cayenne pepper, turn
into a bowl, cover and chill for
15 minutes.

3 Using a zester or vegetable
peeler, score the length of each
cucumber to create a striped effect
on the skin. Cut each cucumber
into ¾-inch thick round shapes.
Using a small spoon or melon
baller, scoop out the seeds from the
center of each cucumber round.

4 Spoon the smoked trout
mousse into a pastry bag fitted
with a medium star nozzle and
pipe swirls of the mixture into the
prepared cucumber rounds. Chill
in the refrigerator until ready to
serve. Garnish the cucumber cups
with small sprigs of dill.

Tapenade and Quail Eggs

Tapenade is a purée made from capers, olives and anchovies. It is popularly used in Mediterranean cooking. It complements the taste of eggs perfectly, especially quail eggs, which look very pretty on open sandwiches.

INGREDIENTS

Serves 8

8 quail eggs
1 small baguette
3 tablespoons tapenade
frisée lettuce leaves
3 small tomatoes, sliced
black olives
4 canned anchovy fillets, drained and
  halved lengthwise
fresh parsley sprigs, to garnish

1 Boil the quail eggs for 3 minutes, then plunge them straight into cold water to cool. Crack the shells and remove them very carefully.

2 Cut the baguette into slices on the diagonal and spread each one with some of the tapenade.

3 Arrange a little frisée lettuce, torn to fit, and the tomato slices on top.

4 Halve the quail eggs and place them on top of the tomato slices.

5 Finish with a little more tapenade, the olives and finally the anchovies. Garnish with small parsley sprigs.

COOK'S TIP

To make ½ pint/1¼ cups of tuna tapenade, put a 3½ ounces canned drained tuna in a food processor with 1 ounce/2 tablespoons capers, 10 canned anchovy fillets and 3 ounces/¾ cup pitted black olives and blend until smooth, scraping down the sides as necessary. Gradually add 4 tablespoons olive oil through the feeder tube. This purée can be used for filling hard-boiled eggs. Blend the tapenade with the egg yolks then pile into the whites.

Eggs Mimosa

*The use of the word mimosa
describes the fine yellow and white
grated egg, which looks not unlike
the flower of the same name. It can
be used to finish any dish, adding a
light summery touch.*

INGREDIENTS

Serves 20

12 hard-boiled eggs, shelled

2 avocados, halved and pitted

1 garlic clove, crushed

Tabasco sauce, to taste

1 tablespoon virgin olive oil

salt and ground black pepper

20 Belgian endive leaves or small crisp
   green lettuce leaves

basil leaves, to garnish

1 Reserve 2 of the eggs, halve the
remainder and put the yolks in
a mixing bowl. Blend or beat the
yolks with the avocados, garlic,
Tabasco sauce, oil and salt and
pepper. Check the seasoning. Pipe
or spoon this mixture back into
the halved egg whites.

2 Sieve the remaining egg whites
and sprinkle over the filled
eggs. Sieve the yolks on top.
Arrange each half egg on a Belgian
endive or lettuce leaf and place
them on a serving platter. Sprinkle
the shredded basil over the filled
egg halves before serving.

Stuffed Deviled Eggs

These eggs are so simple to make, yet guests will always be impressed by them. They have a wonderful flavor and can be given quite a "kick" too by including the cayenne.

INGREDIENTS

Serves 6

6 hard-boiled eggs, shelled

1½ ounces/¼ cup ground
   cooked ham

6 walnut halves, coarsely ground

1 tablespoon very finely chopped scallions

1 tablespoon Dijon mustard

1 tablespoon mayonnaise

2 teaspoons vinegar

¼ teaspoon cayenne pepper (optional)

salt and ground black pepper

paprika and gherkin slices,
   to garnish

1 Cut each hard-boiled egg in half lengthwise. Put the yolks in a bowl and set the whites aside.

2 Mash the yolks well with a fork, or push them through a sieve. Add all the remaining ingredients, except the garnish, and mix well with the yolks. Taste and season with more salt and pepper if necessary.

3 Spoon the filling into the egg white halves, or pipe it in with a pastry bag. Garnish with a little paprika and a small star or other shape cut from the gherkin slices. Serve at room temperature.

Stuffed Celery Sticks

The creamy filling contrasts well with the crunchy celery, and the walnuts add a wonderful flavor.

INGREDIENTS

Serves 4–6

12 crisp, tender celery sticks

1 ounce/¼ cup crumbled blue cheese

4 ounces/½ cup cream cheese

3 tablespoons sour cream

2 ounces/½ cup chopped walnuts

1 Trim the celery sticks. Wash them, if necessary, and dry well on kitchen paper. Cut into 4-inch lengths.

2 In a small bowl, combine the crumbled blue cheese, cream cheese and sour cream. Stir together with a wooden spoon until smoothly blended. Fold in all but 1 tablespoon of the walnuts.

3 Fill the celery pieces with the cheese and nut mixture. Chill before serving, garnished with the reserved walnuts.

COOK'S TIP

Use the same filling to stuff scooped-out cherry tomatoes. Serve together if you like.

Foie Gras Pâté in Filo Cups

This is an extravagantly rich hors d'oeuvre – so save it for a special anniversary or celebration.

Makes 24

3–6 sheets fresh or thawed phyllo pastry

1½ ounces/3 tablespoons butter, melted

8 ounces canned foie gras pâté or other fine liver pâté, at room temperature

2 ounces/4 tablespoons butter, softened

2–3 tablespoons Cognac or other brandy (optional)

chopped pistachio nuts, to garnish

1 Preheat the oven to 400°F. Grease a muffin pan with 24 x 1½-inch cups. Stack the phyllo sheets on a work surface and cut them into 2½-inch squares. Cover with a damp dish towel.

2 Keeping the rest of the phyllo squares covered, place one square on a work surface and brush lightly with melted butter, then turn and brush the other side.

3 Butter a second square and place it over the first at an angle. Butter a third square and place at an angle over the first two sheets to form an uneven edge.

4 Press the layers into a cup of the muffin pan. Continue with the remaining pastry and butter until all the cups in the muffin pan have been filled.

5 Bake the phyllo cups for about 4–6 minutes until crisp and golden, then remove and cool in the tray for 5 minutes. Carefully transfer each phyllo cup to a wire rack and leave to cool completely.

6 In a small bowl, beat the pâté with the softened butter until smooth and well blended. Add the Cognac or brandy to taste, if using. Spoon into a pastry bag fitted with a medium star nozzle and pipe a swirl into each cup. Sprinkle with pistachio nuts. Chill until you are ready to serve, but bring back to room temperature.

COOK'S TIP

The pâté and pastry are best eaten soon after preparation. If preparing ahead of time and then chilling in the refrigerator, be sure to bring back to room temperature before serving.

V | # *Pickled Quail Eggs*

These Chinese eggs are pickled in alcohol and can be stored in a preserving jar in a cool, dark place for several months. They will make delicious bite-size snacks at a drinks party and are sure to delight guests.

INGREDIENTS

Serves 12

12 quail eggs

1 tablespoon salt

1¼ pints/3 cups distilled or previously boiled water

11 teaspoon Sichuan peppercorns

¼ pint/⅔ cup spirit such as Mou-tal (Chinese brandy), brandy, whisky, rum or vodka

dipping sauce (see Cook's Tip) and toasted sesame seeds, to serve

1 Boil the eggs for about 4 minutes, until the yolks are soft but not runny.

2 In a large pan, dissolve the salt in the distilled or previously boiled water. Add the peppercorns, then leave the water to cool and add the spirit.

3 Gently tap the eggs all over but do not peel them. Place in a large, airtight, sterilized jar and fill up with the liquid, totally covering the eggs. Seal the jar and leave the eggs to stand in a cool, dark place for 7–8 days.

4 To serve, remove the eggs from the liquid and peel off the shells carefully. Cut each egg in half or quarters and serve whole with a dipping sauce and a bowl of toasted sesame seeds.

COOK'S TIP
∾

• Although you can buy Chinese dipping sauces in the supermarket, it is very easy to make your own at home. To make a quick dipping sauce, mix equal quantities of soy sauce and hoisin sauce.

• Be sure to use only boiled water or distilled water for the eggs, as the water must be completely free of bacteria or they will enter the porous shells.

Buckwheat Blinis with Mushroom Caviar

These little Russian pancakes are traditionally served with caviar and sour cream. Here is a vegetarian alternative that uses a selection of delicious wild mushrooms in place of the fish roe. The blinis can be made ahead of time and warmed in the oven before topping.

INGREDIENTS

Serves 4

4 ounces/1 cup white bread flour

2 ounces/½ cup buckwheat flour

½ teaspoon salt

½ pint/1¼ cups milk

1 teaspoon dried yeast

2 eggs, separated

7 fluid ounces/scant 1 cup sour cream or
    crème fraîche

For the mushroom caviar

12 ounces mixed wild mushrooms.
    such as portabello mushrooms,
    oyster and wood ear mushrooms,
    cèpes and chanterelles

1 teaspoon celery salt

2 tablespoons walnut oil

1 tablespoon lemon juice

3 tablespoons chopped fresh parsley

ground black pepper

1 To make the caviar, trim and chop the mushrooms, then place them in a glass bowl, toss with the celery salt and cover with a weighted plate.

2 Leave the mushrooms for 2 hours until the juices have run out into the base of the bowl. Rinse the mushrooms thoroughly to remove the salt, drain and press out as much liquid as you can with the back of a spoon. Return them to the bowl and toss gently with the walnut oil, lemon juice and parsley. Season to taste with pepper. Chill in the refrigerator until ready to serve.

3 Sift the two flours together with the salt into a large mixing bowl. Gently warm the milk to lukewarm. Add the yeast, stirring until dissolved, then pour the mixture into the flour, add the egg yolks and stir to make a smooth batter. Cover with a clean damp dish towel and leave in a warm place for 1 hour.

4 Whisk the egg whites in a clean, grease-free bowl until stiff, then fold into the risen batter.

5 Heat an iron pan or griddle to a moderate temperature. Moisten with oil, then drop spoonfuls of the batter onto the surface. When bubbles rise to the top, turn them over and cook briefly on the other side. Spoon on the sour cream or crème fraîche, top with the mushroom caviar and serve immediately.

Potato Blinis

These light-as-air pancakes are luxuriously topped with sour cream and smoked salmon.

INGREDIENTS

Serves 6

4 ounces potatoes, boiled and mashed
1 tablespoon rapid-rise dried yeast
6 ounces/1½ cups all-purpose flour
oil, for greasing
6 tablespoons sour cream
6 slices smoked salmon
salt and ground black pepper
lemon slices, to garnish

1 In a large bowl, mix together the mashed potatoes, dried yeast, flour and ½ pint/1¼ cups lukewarm water.

2 Leave to rise in a warm place for about 30 minutes, until the mixture has doubled in size.

3 Heat a non-stick frying pan and add a little oil. Drop spoonfuls of the mixture onto the preheated pan. Cook the blinis for 2 minutes, until lightly golden on the underside, toss with a spatula and cook on the second side for about 1 minute.

4 Season the blinis with some salt and pepper. Serve with a little sour cream and a small slice of smoked salmon folded on top. Garnish with a final grind of black pepper and a small slice of lemon.

COOK'S TIP

These small pancakes can easily be prepared in advance and stored in the refrigerator until ready for use. Simply warm them through in a low oven.

Eggy Thai Fish Cakes

These tangy little fish cakes, with a kick of Eastern spice, make a really fabulous appetizer and great party food, too.

Makes about 20

8 ounces smoked cod or haddock
　　fillet (undyed)
8 ounces fresh cod or haddock fillet
1 small fresh red chile, seeded and
　　finely chopped
2 garlic cloves, grated
1 lemon grass stalk, very
　　finely chopped
2 large scallions, very finely chopped
2 tablespoons Thai fish sauce
4 tablespoons thick coconut milk
2 extra large eggs, lightly beaten
1 tablespoon chopped fresh cilantro
1 tablespoon cornstarch, plus extra
　　for molding
oil, for frying
soy sauce, rice vinegar or Thai fish sauce,
　　for dipping

2 Add the chile, garlic, lemon grass, scallions, fish sauce and coconut milk and process until well blended. Add the eggs and cilantro and process for a further few seconds. Cover with plastic wrap and chill in the refrigerator for 1 hour.

3 To make the fish cakes, flour your hands with cornstarch and shape large teaspoonfuls into neat balls, coating them with the flour.

4 Heat 2–3 inches oil in a medium pan until a crust of bread turns golden in about 1 minute. Fry the fish cakes, 5–6 at a time, turning them carefully with a slotted spoon, for 2–3 minutes, until they turn golden all over. Remove with a slotted spoon and drain on paper towels. Keep the fish cakes warm in the oven until they are all cooked. Serve them immediately with one or more dipping sauces.

1 Place the smoked fish fillet in a bowl of cold water and set aside to soak for 10 minutes. Dry well on paper towels. Skin the smoked and fresh fish fillets, then chop them coarsely and place in a food processor.

Monti Cristo Triangles

These opulent little sandwiches are stuffed with ham, cheese and turkey, dipped in egg, then fried in butter and oil. They are rich and filling.

Makes 64

16 thin slices firm-textured white bread
4 ounces/$\frac{1}{2}$ cup butter, softened
8 slices oak-smoked ham
3–4 tablespoons whole grain mustard
8 slices Gruyère or Emmenthal cheese
3–4 tablespoons mayonnaise
8 slices cooked turkey or chicken breast
4–5 eggs
2 fluid ounces/$\frac{1}{4}$ cup milk
1 teaspoon Dijon mustard
vegetable oil, for frying
butter, for frying
salt and ground white pepper

For the garnish
pimiento-stuffed green olives
fresh parsley leaves,

1 Arrange 8 of the bread slices on a work surface and spread with half the softened butter. Lay a slice of ham on each slice of bread and spread with a little mustard. Cover with a slice of Gruyère or Emmenthal cheese and spread with a little of the mayonnaise, then cover with a slice of turkey or chicken breast. Butter the rest of the bread slices and use to top the sandwiches. Using a sharp knife, cut off the crusts, trimming to an even square.

2 In a large, shallow, ovenproof dish, beat the eggs with the milk and Dijon mustard until thoroughly combined. Season to taste with salt and pepper. Soak the sandwiches in the egg mixture on both sides until all the egg has been absorbed.

3 Heat about $\frac{1}{2}$-inch of oil with a little butter in a large, heavy frying pan, until hot, but not smoking. Gently fry the sandwiches, in batches, for about 4–5 minutes, until crisp and golden, turning once. Add more oil and butter as necessary. Drain on paper towels.

4 Transfer the sandwiches to a chopping board and cut each into 4 triangles, then cut each in half again. Make 64 triangles in total. Thread an olive and parsley leaf onto a toothpick, then stick into each triangle and serve while warm.

Shrimp Toasts

These crunchy sesame-topped toasts are simple to prepare using a food processor for the shrimp paste.

INGREDIENTS

Makes 64

8 ounces cooked, peeled shrimp, well
   drained and patted dry
1 egg white
2 scallions, chopped
1 teaspoon chopped fresh root ginger
1 garlic clove, chopped
1 teaspoon cornstarch
$\frac{1}{2}$ teaspoon salt
$\frac{1}{2}$ teaspoon sugar
2–3 dashes hot pepper sauce
8 slices firm-textured white bread
4–5 tablespoons sesame seeds
vegetable oil, for frying
scallion tassel, to garnish

1 Put the first 9 ingredients in the bowl of a food processor and process until the mixture forms a smooth paste, scraping down the side of the bowl from time to time.

COOK'S TIP

You can prepare these in advance and heat them through in a hot oven before serving. Make sure they are really crisp and hot though, because they won't be nearly so enjoyable if there's no crunch when you bite them!

2 Spread the shrimp paste evenly over the bread slices, then sprinkle over the sesame seeds, pressing to make them stick. Remove the crusts, then cut each slice diagonally into 4 triangles, and each in half again. Make 64 triangles in total.

3 Heat 2 inches vegetable oil in a heavy pan or wok, until it is hot, but not smoking. Fry the triangles, in batches, for about 30–60 seconds, turning the toasts once. Drain on paper towels and keep hot in the oven while you cook the rest. Serve hot with the garnish.

Parmesan Fish Goujons

Use this batter, with or without the cheese, whenever you feel brave enough to fry fish. This is light and crisp and just melts in the mouth.

INGREDIENTS

Serves 4

13 ounces plaice, flounder or sole fillets,
 or thicker fish such as cod or haddock
a little all-purpose flour
oil, for deep-frying
salt and ground black pepper
fresh dill sprigs, to garnish

For the cream sauce

4 tablespoons sour cream
4 tablespoons mayonnaise
$\frac{1}{2}$ teaspoon grated lemon rind
2 tablespoons chopped gherkins or capers
1 tablespoon chopped mixed fresh herbs,
 or 1 teaspoon dried mixed herbs

For the batter

3 ounces/$\frac{3}{4}$ cup all-purpose flour
1 ounce/$\frac{1}{3}$ cup grated Parmesan cheese
1 teaspoon baking soda
1 egg, separated
$\frac{1}{4}$ pint/$\frac{2}{3}$ cup milk

1 To make the cream sauce, mix the sour cream, mayonnaise, lemon rind, gherkins or capers, herbs and seasoning together, then place in the refrigerator to chill.

2 To make the batter, sift the flour into a bowl. Mix in the other dry ingredients and some salt, and then whisk in the egg yolk and milk to give a thick yet smooth batter. Then gradually whisk in 6 tablespoons water. Season and place in the refrigerator to chill.

3 Skin the fish and cut into thin strips of similar length. Season the flour and then dip the fish lightly in the flour.

4 Heat at least 2 inches oil in a large pan with a lid. Whisk the egg white until stiff and gently fold into the batter until just blended.

5 Dip the floured fish into the batter, drain off any excess and then drop gently into the hot oil.

6 Cook the fish, in batches so that the goujons don't stick to one another, for only 3–4 minutes, turning once. When the batter is golden and crisp, remove the fish with a slotted spoon. Place on paper towels on a plate and keep warm in a low oven while cooking the remaining goujons.

7 Serve hot garnished with sprigs of dill and accompanied by the cream sauce.

Parmesan Thins

These thin, crisp, savory crackers will melt in the mouth, so make plenty for guests. They are a great snack at any time of the day, so don't just keep them for parties.

INGREDIENTS

Makes 16–20

2 ounces/½ cup all-purpose flour

1½ ounces/3 tablespoons butter, softened

1 egg yolk

1½ ounces/⅔ cup freshly grated Parmesan cheese

pinch of salt

pinch of mustard powder

1 Rub together the flour and the butter in a bowl using your fingertips, then work in the egg yolk, Parmesan cheese, salt and mustard. Mix to bring the dough together into a ball. Shape the mixture into a log, wrap in foil or plastic wrap and chill in the refrigerator for 10 minutes.

2 Preheat the oven to 400°F. Cut the Parmesan log into very thin slices, ⅛–¼-inch maximum, and arrange on a baking sheet. Flatten with a fork to give a pretty ridged pattern. Bake for 10 minutes, or until the crackers are crisp, but not changing color.

☑

Celeriac Fritters with Mustard Dip

The combination of the hot, crispy fritters and cold mustard dip is extremely good.

INGREDIENTS

Serves 4

1 egg

4 ounces/1 cup ground almonds

3 tablespoons freshly grated
   Parmesan cheese

3 tablespoons chopped fresh parsley

1 celeriac, about 1 pound

lemon juice

oil, for deep-frying

salt and ground black pepper

sea salt flakes, to garnish

For the dip

¼ pint/⅔ cup sour cream

1–2 tablespoons whole grain mustard

1 Beat the egg well and pour into a shallow dish. Mix together ground the almonds, grated Parmesan and chopped parsley in a separate dish. Season with salt and plenty of ground black pepper. Set aside.

2 Peel the celeriac and cut into batons about ½-inch wide and 2 inches long. Drop them immediately into a bowl of water with a little lemon juice added to prevent discoloration.

3 Heat the oil to 350°F or until a cube of day-old bread browns in 30 seconds. Drain and then pat dry half the celeriac batons. Dip them first into the beaten egg, then into the ground almond mixture, making sure that the pieces are coated completely and evenly.

4 Deep-fry the celeriac fritters, in batches, for 2–3 minutes, until golden. Drain on paper towels. Keep warm while you cook the remaining fritters.

5 Make the dip. Mix the sour cream, mustard and salt to taste. Spoon into a serving bowl. Sprinkle the fritters with sea salt.

Dates Stuffed with Chorizo

This is a delicious combination from Spain, using fresh dates and spicy chorizo sausage.

Serves 4–6

2 ounces chorizo sausage
12 fresh dates, pitted
6 fatty bacon strips
oil, for frying
all-purpose flour, for dusting
1 egg, beaten
2 ounces/1 cup fresh bread crumbs

1 Trim the ends of the chorizo sausage and then peel off the skin. Cut into three ¾-inch slices. Cut these in half lengthwise, then into quarters, giving 12 pieces.

2 Stuff each date with a piece of chorizo, closing the date around it. Stretch the bacon, by running the back of a knife along the rasher. Cut each rasher in half, widthwise. Wrap a piece of bacon around each date and secure with a wooden toothpick.

3 In a deep pan, heat ½-inch of oil. Dust the dates with flour, dip them in the beaten egg, then coat in bread crumbs. Fry the dates in the hot oil, turning them, until golden. Remove the dates with a slotted spoon, and drain on paper towels. Serve immediately.

V

Cheese Aigrettes

Choux pastry is often associated with sweet pastries, such as profiteroles, but these little savory puffs, flavored with Gruyère and dusted with grated Parmesan, are just delicious. They are best made ahead and deep-fried to serve. They make a wonderful party snack.

INGREDIENTS

Makes 30

3½ ounces/scant 1 cup all-purpose flour

½ teaspoon paprika

½ teaspoon salt

3 ounces/6 tablespoons cold
   butter, diced

7 fluid ounces/scant 1 cup water

3 eggs, beaten

3 ounces Gruyère cheese, coarsely grated

corn or vegetable oil, for deep-frying

2 ounces/⅔ cup freshly grated
   Parmesan cheese

ground black pepper

1 Mix the flour, paprika and salt together by sifting them onto a large sheet of waxed paper. Add a generous amount of ground black pepper.

2 Put the diced butter and water into a medium pan and heat gently. As soon as the butter has melted and the liquid starts to boil, quickly tip in all the seasoned flour at once and beat very hard with a wooden spoon until the dough comes away cleanly from the sides of the pan.

3 Remove the pan from the heat and cool the paste for 5 minutes. Gradually beat in enough of the beaten egg to give a stiff, dropping consistency that still holds a shape on the spoon. Mix in the Gruyère.

4 Heat the oil for deep-frying to 350°F. Take a teaspoonful of the choux paste and use a second spoon to slide it into the oil. Make more aigrettes in the same way. Fry for 3–4 minutes, then drain on paper towels and keep warm while you are cooking successive batches. To serve, pile the aigrettes on a warmed serving dish and sprinkle with Parmesan.

COOK'S TIP

Filling these aigrettes gives a delightful surprise as you bite through their crisp shell. Make slightly larger aigrettes by dropping a slightly larger spoonful of dough into the hot oil. Slit them open and scoop out any soft paste. Fill the centers with taramasalata or crumbled Roquefort mixed with a little farmer's cheese.

Pork and Peanut Wontons with Plum Sauce

These crispy filled wontons are delicious served with a sweet plum sauce. The wontons can be filled and set aside for up to 8 hours before they are cooked.

INGREDIENTS

Makes 40–50 wontons

6 ounces/1½ cups ground pork or
  6 ounces pork sausages, skinned
2 scallions, finely chopped
2 tablespoons peanut butter
2 teaspoons oyster sauce (optional)
2 tablespoons cornstarch
40–50 wonton wrappers
vegetable oil, for deep-frying
salt and ground black pepper
lettuces and radishes, to garnish

For the plum sauce
8 ounces/generous ¾ cup dark plum jam
1 tablespoon rice or white wine vinegar
1 tablespoon dark soy sauce
½ teaspoon chili sauce

1 Combine the ground pork or skinned sausages, scallions, peanut butter, oyster sauce, if using, and seasoning, and then set aside.

2 For the plum sauce, combine the plum jam, vinegar, soy and chili sauces in a serving bowl and set aside.

3 Mix the cornstarch with 2–3 tablespoons water to a smooth paste in a small bowl.

4 To make the wontons, place 8 wrappers at a time on a work surface, moisten the edges with the cornstarch paste and place ½ teaspoon of the filling on each. Fold in half, corner to corner, and twist.

5 Fill a wok or deep frying pan one-third full with vegetable oil and heat to 385°F. Have ready a wire strainer or frying basket and a tray lined with paper towels. Drop the wontons, 8 at a time, into the hot oil and deep-fry for 1–2 minutes, until golden all over. Lift out onto the paper-lined tray and sprinkle with fine salt. Serve immediately with the plum sauce garnished with lettuce and radishes.

V

Crispy Spring Rolls

These small and dainty spring rolls are ideal served as appetizers or as cocktail snacks. If you like, you could replace the mushrooms with chicken or pork and the carrots with shrimp.

INGREDIENTS

Makes 40 rolls

8 ounces beansprouts

4 ounces small leeks or scallions

4 ounces carrots

4 ounces bamboo shoots, sliced

4 ounces mushrooms

3–4 tablespoons vegetable oil

1 teaspoon salt

1 teaspoon light brown sugar

1 tablespoon light soy sauce

1 tablespoon Chinese rice wine

20 frozen spring roll wrappers, thawed

1 tablespoon cornstarch paste
   (see Cook's Tip)

all-purpose flour, for dusting

oil, for deep-frying

1 Cut all the vegetables into thin shreds, about the same size and shape as the bean sprouts.

2 Heat the oil in a wok and stir-fry the vegetables for about 1 minute. Add the salt, sugar, soy sauce and Chinese rice wine and continue stirring the vegetables for 1½–2 minutes. Remove and drain away the excess liquid, then leave to cool.

3 To make the spring rolls, cut each spring roll wrapper in half diagonally, then place about a tablespoonful of the vegetable mixture one-third of the way down on the wrapper, with the triangle pointing away from you.

COOK'S TIP

To make cornstarch paste, mix together 4 parts cornstarch with about 5 parts cold water until smooth.

4 Lift the lower edge over the filling and roll once.

5 Fold in both ends and roll once more, then brush the upper pointed edge with a little cornstarch paste, and roll into a neat package. Lightly dust a tray with flour and place the spring rolls in a single layer on the tray with the flapside underneath.

6 To cook, heat the oil in a wok or deep-fryer until hot, then reduce the heat to low. Deep-fry the spring rolls, in batches (about 8–10 at a time), for 2–3 minutes, or until golden and crisp, then remove and drain on paper towels. Serve the spring rolls hot with a dipping sauce, such as soy sauce, or mixed salt and pepper.

Vegetable Tempura

V

Tempura is a Japanese type of savory fritter. Originally shrimp were used, but vegetables can be cooked in the egg batter successfully too. The secret of making the incredibly light batter is to use very cold water, and to have the oil at the right temperature before you start cooking the fritters.

INGREDIENTS

Serves 4

2 zucchini

½ eggplant

1 large carrot

½ small Spanish onion

1 egg

4 fluid ounces/½ cup iced water

4 ounces/1 cup all-purpose flour

vegetable oil, for deep-frying

salt and ground black pepper

sea salt flakes, lemon slices and shoyu,
    to serve

1 Using a potato peeler, pare strips of peel from the zucchini and eggplant to give a striped effect.

2 Using a chef's knife, cut the zucchini, eggplant and carrot into strips measuring about 3–4 inches long and ⅛-inch wide. Place in a colander and sprinkle with salt. Put a small plate over and weight it down. Leave for 30 minutes, then rinse thoroughly. Drain well, then pat dry with paper towels.

3 Thinly slice the onion from top to base, discarding the plump pieces in the middle. Separate the layers so that there are lots of fine, long strips. Mix all the vegetables together and season with salt and pepper.

4 Make the batter immediately before frying. Mix the egg and iced water in a bowl, then sift in the flour. Mix briefly with a fork or chopsticks. Do not overmix: the batter should remain lumpy. Add the vegetables to the batter and mix to combine.

5 Half-fill a wok with oil and heat to 350°F. Scoop up a heaped tablespoonful of the mixture at a time and carefully lower it into the oil. Deep-fry, in batches, for about 3 minutes, until golden brown and crisp. Drain on paper towels.

6 Serve each portion with salt, slices of lemon and a tiny bowl of shoyu for dipping.

COOK'S TIP
Other suitable vegetables for tempura include mushrooms and slices of red, green, yellow or orange bell peppers.

Spicy Peanut Balls

Tasty rice balls, rolled in chopped peanuts and deep-fried, make a delicious appetizer. Serve them simply as they are, or with a chili sauce for dipping.

INGREDIENTS

Makes 16

1 garlic clove, crushed

½-inch piece fresh root ginger, peeled and
    finely chopped

¼ teaspoon turmeric

1 teaspoon granulated sugar

½ teaspoon salt

1 teaspoon chili sauce

2 teaspoons Thai fish sauce or
    soy sauce

2 tablespoons chopped fresh cilantro

juice of ½ lime

8 ounces/2 cups cooked white long
    grain rice

4 ounces/1 cup peanuts, chopped

vegetable oil, for deep-frying

lime wedges and chili dipping sauce,
    to serve (optional)

1 Process the garlic, ginger and turmeric in a food processor or blender until the mixture forms a paste. Add the sugar, salt, chili sauce and fish sauce or soy sauce, with the chopped cilantro and lime juice. Process briefly to mix the ingredients.

2 Add three-quarters of the cooked rice to the paste and process until smooth and sticky. Scrape into a mixing bowl and stir in the remainder of the rice. Wet your hands and shape the mixture into thumb-size balls.

3 Roll the balls in the chopped peanuts, making sure they are evenly coated.

4 Heat the oil in a deep-fryer or wok. Deep-fry the peanut balls until crisp. Drain on paper towels and then pile onto a platter. Serve hot with lime wedges and a chili dipping sauce, if you like.

Guacamole

V

*Avocados discolor quickly, so make
this delicious dip just before serving.
If you do need to keep it for any
length of time, cover the surface of
the sauce with plastic wrap and chill
in the refrigerator.*

INGREDIENTS

Serves 6

2 large ripe avocados

2 red chiles, seeded

1 garlic clove

1 shallot

2 tablespoons olive oil,
    plus extra to serve

juice of 1 lemon or lime

salt and ground black pepper

flat leaf parsley leaves, to garnish

1 Halve the avocados, remove
the pits and scoop out the flesh
into a large bowl.

2 Using a fork or potato
masher, mash the avocado
flesh until fairly smooth.

3 Finely chop the chiles, garlic
and shallot, then stir them into
the mashed avocado with the olive
oil and lemon or lime juice. Season
to taste with salt and pepper.

4 Spoon the mixture into a small
serving bowl. Drizzle over a
little olive oil and sprinkle with a
few flat leaf parsley leaves. Serve
the guacamole immediately.

Basil and Lemon Dip

V

This lovely dip is based on fresh mayonnaise flavored with lemon juice and two types of basil. Serve with crispy potato wedges for a delicious appetizer.

INGREDIENTS

Serves 4

2 extra large egg yolks

1 tablespoon lemon juice

¼ pint/⅔ cup olive oil

¼ pint/⅔ cup sunflower oil

4 garlic cloves

handful of fresh green basil

handful of fresh opal basil

salt and ground black pepper

3 Once half of the oil has been added, the remaining oil can be incorporated more quickly. Continue processing to form a thick, creamy mayonnaise.

5 Tear both types of basil into small pieces and then stir them into the mayonnaise with the crushed garlic.

1 Place the egg yolks and lemon juice in a blender or food processor and process them briefly until lightly blended.

4 Peel and crush the garlic cloves. Alternatively, place them on a chopping board and sprinkle with salt, then flatten them with the heel of a heavy-bladed knife and chop the flesh. Flatten the garlic again to make a coarse purée.

6 Add salt and pepper to taste, then transfer the dip to a serving dish. Cover and chill until ready to serve.

2 Stir the oils together in a pitcher. With the machine running, pour in the oil very slowly, a little at a time.

COOK'S TIP

For potato wedges, bake a large potato until nearly cooked. Slice thickly, brush one side with oil and broil for 7–10 minutes.

Quail Eggs with Herbs and Dips

*For al fresco eating or informal
entertaining, this platter of
contrasting tastes and textures is
delicious and certainly encourages a
relaxed atmosphere. Choose the best
seasonal vegetables and substitute
for what is unavailable.*

INGREDIENTS

Serves 6

1 large Italian focaccia or 2–3 Indian
    parathas or other flatbread
extra virgin olive oil, plus extra to serve
1 large garlic clove, finely chopped
small handful of chopped fresh mixed
    herbs, such as cilantro, mint, parsley
    and oregano
18–24 quail eggs
2 tablespoons mayonnaise
2 tablespoons thick sour cream
1 teaspoon chopped capers
1 teaspoon finely chopped shallot
8 ounces fresh beet, cooked in water or
    hard cider, peeled and sliced
½ bunch of scallions, trimmed and
    coarsely chopped
4 tablespoons red onion or tamarind and
    date chutney
salt and ground black pepper
coarse sea salt and mixed ground
    peppercorns, to serve

1 Preheat the oven to 375°F.
Brush the focaccia or flatbread
liberally with olive oil, sprinkle
with garlic, your choice of herbs
and seasoning and bake for
10–15 minutes, or until golden.
Keep warm.

2 Put the quail eggs into a pan of
cold water, bring to the boil
and boil for 5 minutes. Transfer to
a serving dish. Shell the eggs first if
you like or leave guests to shell
them themselves.

3 To make the dip, combine the
mayonnaise, sour cream,
capers, shallot and seasoning.

4 To serve, cut the bread into
wedges and serve with dishes
of the quail eggs, mayonnaise dip,
beet, scallions and chutney. Serve
with tiny bowls of the coarse salt,
ground peppercorns and olive oil
for dipping.

COOK'S TIP

If you don't have time to make
your own mayonnaise, use the
best store-bought variety
available. You will probably find
that you need to add less
seasoning to it.

Sesame Seed-coated Falafel with Tahini Dip

V

Sesame seeds are used to give a delightfully crunchy coating to these spicy chickpea patties. Serve with the tahini yogurt dip.

INGREDIENTS

Serves 6

9 ounces/1⅓ cups dried chickpeas

2 garlic cloves, crushed

1 fresh red chile, seeded and finely sliced

1 teaspoon ground coriander

1 teaspoon ground cumin

1 tablespoon chopped fresh mint

1 tablespoon chopped fresh parsley

2 scallions, finely chopped

1 extra large egg, beaten

sesame seeds, for coating

sunflower oil, for frying

salt and ground black pepper

For the tahini yogurt dip

2 tablespoons light tahini

7 fluid ounces/scant 1 cup plain yogurt

1 teaspoon cayenne pepper, plus extra
    for sprinkling

1 tablespoon chopped fresh mint

1 scallion, thinly sliced

fresh herbs, to garnish

1 Place the chickpeas in a bowl, cover with cold water and leave to soak overnight. Drain and rinse the chickpeas, then place in a pan and cover with cold water. Bring to the boil and boil rapidly for 10 minutes. Reduce the heat and simmer for about 1½–2 hours, until tender. Drain well.

2 Meanwhile, make the tahini yogurt dip. Mix together the tahini, yogurt, cayenne pepper and mint in a small bowl. Sprinkle the scallions and extra cayenne pepper on top and chill in the refrigerator until required.

3 Combine the chickpeas with the garlic, chile, ground spices, herbs, scallions and salt and pepper, then mix in the egg. Place in a food processor and blend until the mixture forms a coarse paste. If the paste seems too soft, chill it for 30 minutes.

4 Form the chilled chickpea paste into 12 patties with your hands, then roll each one in the sesame seeds to coat thoroughly.

5 Heat enough oil to cover the base of a large frying pan Fry the falafel, in batches if necessary, for 6 minutes, turning once. Serve immediately with the tahini yogurt dip garnished with fresh herbs.

☑

Chili Bean Dip

This deliciously spicy and creamy bean dip is best served warm with triangles of grilled pitta bread or a bowl of crunchy tortilla chips.

INGREDIENTS

Serves 4

2 garlic cloves

1 onion

2 fresh green chiles

2 tablespoons vegetable oil

1–2 teaspoon hot chili powder

14-ounce can kidney beans

3 ounces/¾ cup grated Cheddar cheese

1 fresh red chile, seeded

salt and ground black pepper

1 Finely chop the garlic and onion. Seed and finely chop the green chiles.

2 Heat the vegetable oil in a large sauté pan or deep frying pan and add the garlic, onion, green chiles and chili powder. Cook gently for about 5 minutes, stirring regularly, until the onions are softened and translucent, but not browned.

3 Drain the kidney beans, reserving the can juice. Process all but 2 tablespoons of the beans to a purée in a food processor.

4 Add the puréed beans to the pan with 2–3 tablespoons of the reserved can juice. Heat gently, stirring to mix well.

5 Stir in the whole kidney beans and the Cheddar cheese. Cook over a low heat for 2–3 minutes, stirring until the cheese has melted. Season with salt and pepper to taste.

6 Cut the red chile into tiny strips. Spoon the dip into four individual serving bowls and sprinkle the chile strips over the top. Serve warm.

COOK'S TIP

For a dip with a coarser texture, do not purée the beans; instead mash them with a potato masher.

V

Hummus

Blending chickpeas with garlic and oil creates a surprisingly creamy purée that is delicious as part of a Turkish-style meze, or as a dip with vegetables. Leftovers make a good sandwich filler.

INGREDIENTS

Serves 4–6

5 ounces/¾ cup dried chickpeas

juice of 2 lemons

2 garlic cloves, sliced

2 tablespoons olive oil

pinch of cayenne pepper

¼ pint/⅔ cup tahini

salt and ground black pepper

extra olive oil and cayenne pepper,
   for sprinkling

flat leaf parsley sprigs, to garnish

1 Put the chickpeas in a bowl with plenty of cold water and leave to soak overnight.

2 Drain the chickpeas, place in a pan and cover with fresh cold water. Bring to the boil and boil rapidly for 10 minutes. Reduce the heat and simmer gently for about 1–1½ hours, until soft. Drain in a colander.

3 Process the chickpeas in a food processor to a smooth purée. Add the lemon juice, garlic, olive oil, cayenne pepper and tahini and process until creamy, scraping the mixture down from the sides of the bowl.

4 Season the purée with plenty of salt and ground black pepper and transfer to a serving dish. Sprinkle with a little olive oil and cayenne pepper and serve garnished with a few parsley sprigs.

COOK'S TIP

For convenience, canned chickpeas can be used instead. Allow two 14-ounce cans and drain them thoroughly. Tahini can now be purchased from most good supermarkets or health food stores.

Baba Ganoush

V

Baba ganoush is a delectable eggplant dip from the Middle East. Tahini, a sesame seed paste with cumin, is the main flavoring, giving a subtle hint of spice.

INGREDIENTS

Serves 6

2 small eggplant

1 garlic clove, crushed

4 tablespoons tahini

1 ounce/¼ cup ground almonds

juice of ½ lemon

½ teaspoon ground cumin

2 tablespoons fresh mint leaves

2 tablespoons olive oil

salt and ground black pepper

For the flatbread

4 pitta breads

3 tablespoons sesame seeds

3 tablespoons fresh thyme leaves

3 tablespoons poppy seeds

¼ pint/⅔ cup olive oil

1 Start by making the flatbread. Split the pitta breads through the middle with a sharp knife and carefully open them out. Mix the sesame seeds, chopped thyme and poppy seeds in a mortar. Work them lightly with a pestle to release the flavor.

2 Stir in the olive oil. Spread the mixture over the cut sides of the pitta bread. Broil until golden brown and crisp. When cool, break into pieces.

3 Grill the eggplant, turning them frequently, until the skin is blackened and blistered. Remove the peel, chop the flesh coarsely and leave to drain in a colander.

4 Squeeze out as much liquid from the aubergine as possible. Place the flesh in a blender or food processor, then add the garlic, tahini, ground almonds, lemon juice and cumin, with salt to taste. Process to a smooth paste, then coarsely chop half the mint and stir into the dip.

5 Spoon the paste into a bowl, sprinkle the remaining mint leaves on top and drizzle with the olive oil. Serve at room temperature with the flatbread.

HORS D'OEUVRES

Set the mood with hors d'oeuvres that are delicious enough
to turn any meal into a party. From summery vegetarian
bruschetta to succulent mussels, and from exotic smoked duck
wontons to simple mini baked potatoes with blue cheese,
there is the perfect first course for every meal. Although they
are sure to impress your guests, you may be pleasantly
surprised to discover that many of these tasty appetizers
are astonishingly easy to prepare or can be made in
advance, allowing you to relax with your friends
and a pre-dinner drink.

Marinated Mussels

This is an ideal recipe to prepare and arrange well in advance. Remove from the refrigerator about 15 minutes before serving to allow the flavors to develop fully.

INGREDIENTS

Makes about 48

2¼ pounds fresh mussels, large if possible (about 48)

6 fluid ounces/¾ cup dry white wine

1 garlic clove, finely crushed

4 fluid ounces/½ cup olive oil

2 fluid ounces/¼ cup lemon juice

1 teaspoon hot chili flakes

½ teaspoon mixed spice

1 tablespoon Dijon mustard

2 teaspoons sugar

1 teaspoon salt

1–2 tablespoons chopped fresh dill or cilantro

1 tablespoon capers, drained and chopped if large

ground black pepper

1 Scrub the mussels under cold running water to remove any sand and barnacles; pull out and remove the beards. Discard any open shells that will not shut when they are tapped and any mussels with damaged shells.

2 In a large casserole or pan set over a high heat, bring the white wine to the boil with the garlic and ground black pepper. Add the mussels and cover. Reduce the heat to medium and simmer for 2–4 minutes, until the shells open, stirring occasionally.

3 In a large bowl combine the olive oil, lemon juice, chili flakes, mixed spice, Dijon mustard, sugar, salt, the chopped dill or cilantro and the capers. Stir well, then set aside.

4 Discard any mussels with closed shells. With a small sharp knife, carefully remove the remaining mussels from their shells, reserving the half shells for serving. Add the mussels to the marinade. Toss the mussels to coat well, then cover and chill in the refrigerator for 6–8 hours or overnight, stirring occasionally.

5 With a teaspoon, place one mussel with a little marinade in each shell. Arrange on a platter and cover until ready to serve.

COOK'S TIP

Mussels can be prepared ahead of time and marinated for up to 24 hours. To serve, arrange the mussel shells on a bed of crushed ice, well-washed seaweed or even coarse salt to stop them from wobbling on the plate.

Spinach Empanadillas

These are little pastry turnovers from Spain, filled with ingredients that have a strong Moorish influence – pine nuts and raisins. Empanadillas are also very popular throughout South America.

INGREDIENTS

Makes 20

1 ounce/2 tablespoons raisins

1½ tablespoons olive oil

1 pound fresh spinach, washed
    and chopped

6 drained canned anchovies, chopped

2 garlic cloves, finely chopped

1 ounce/⅓ cup pine nuts, chopped

1 egg, beaten

12 ounces puff pastry, thawed
    if frozen

salt and ground black pepper

1 To make the filling, soak the raisins in a little warm water for 10 minutes. Drain, then chop coarsely. Heat the oil in a large sauté pan or wok, add the spinach, stir, then cover and cook over a low heat for about 2 minutes. Uncover, turn up the heat and let any liquid evaporate. Add the anchovies, garlic and seasoning, then cook, stirring, for a further minute. Remove from the heat, add the raisins and pine nuts, and cool.

2 Preheat the oven to 350°F. Roll out the pastry to an ⅛-inch thickness.

3 Using a 3-inch pastry cutter, cut out 20 round shapes, re-rolling the dough if necessary. Place about two teaspoonfuls of the filling in the middle of each round, then brush the edges with a little water. Bring up the sides of the pastry and seal well.

4 Press the edges of the pastry together with the back of a fork. Brush with beaten egg. Place the turnovers on a lightly greased baking sheet and bake for about 15 minutes, until golden. Serve the empanadillas warm.

Shrimp and Vegetable Crostini

Use bottled carciofini (tiny artichoke hearts preserved in olive oil) for this simple first course, which can be prepared very quickly.

Serves 4

1 pound unpeeled cooked shrimp

4 slices of ciabatta, cut diagonally across

3 garlic cloves, peeled and
   2 halved lengthwise

4 tablespoons olive oil

7 ounces/2 cups small white
   mushrooms, trimmed

12 drained bottled carciofini

4 tablespoons chopped flat leaf parsley

salt and ground black pepper

1   Peel the shrimp and remove the heads. Rub the ciabatta slices on both sides with the cut sides of the halved garlic cloves, drizzle with a little olive oil and broil until lightly browned.

2   Finely chop the remaining garlic. Heat the remaining oil in a frying pan and gently cook the chopped garlic until golden, but do not allow it to burn.

3   Add the mushrooms and stir to coat with oil. Season with salt and pepper and sauté for about 2–3 minutes. Gently stir in the drained carciofini, then add the chopped flat leaf parsley.

4   Season again, then stir in the shrimp and sauté briefly to warm through. Pile the shrimp mixture onto the ciabatta. Pour over any remaining cooking juices and serve immediately.

COOK'S TIP

Don't be tempted to use thawed frozen shrimp, especially those that have been peeled. Freshly cooked shrimp in their shells are infinitely nicer.

Sautéed Mussels with Garlic and Herbs

These mussels are served without their shells, in a delicious paprika-flavored sauce. Eat them with toothpicks.

INGREDIENTS

Serves 4

1 pounds fresh mussels
1 lemon slice
6 tablespoons olive oil
2 shallots, finely chopped
1 garlic clove, finely chopped
1 tablespoon chopped fresh parsley
½ teaspoon sweet paprika
¼ teaspoon dried chili flakes

1 Scrub the mussels, discarding any damaged ones that do not close when tapped with a knife. Put the mussels in a large pan, with 8 fluid ounces/1 cup water and the slice of lemon. Bring to the boil and cook for 3–4 minutes, removing the mussels as they open. Discard any that remain closed. Take the mussels out of the shells and drain on paper towels.

2 Heat the oil in a sauté pan, add the mussels and cook, stirring, for 1 minute. Remove from the pan. Add the shallots and garlic and cook, covered, over a low heat for about 5 minutes, or until soft. Remove the pan from the heat and stir in the parsley, paprika and chili flakes.

3 Return the pan to the heat and stir in the mussels. Cook briefly. Remove from the heat and cover for 1–2 minutes, to let the flavors mingle, before serving.

Cannellini Bean and Rosemary Bruschetta

This variation on a British snack, beans on toast, makes an unusual but sophisticated hors d'oeuvre.

INGREDIENTS

Serves 6

5 ounces/²⁄₃ cup dried cannellini beans

5 tomatoes

3 tablespoons olive oil, plus extra
   for drizzling

2 sun-dried tomatoes in oil, drained and
   finely chopped

1 garlic clove, crushed

2 tablespoons chopped fresh rosemary

12 slices Italian-style bread, such
   as ciabatta

1 large garlic clove

salt and ground black pepper

handful of fresh basil leaves, to garnish

1 Put the beans in a bowl, cover with water and soak overnight. Drain and rinse the beans, then place in a pan and cover with fresh water. Bring to the boil and boil rapidly for 10 minutes. Then lower the heat and simmer for about 1 hour, or until tender. Drain, return to the pan and keep warm.

2 Meanwhile, place the tomatoes in a bowl, cover with boiling water, leave for 30 seconds, then peel, seed and chop the flesh. Heat the oil in a frying pan, add the fresh and sun-dried tomatoes, garlic and rosemary. Cook for 2 minutes, until the tomatoes begin to break down and soften.

3 Add the tomato mixture to the cannellini beans and season to taste. Mix together well. Keep the bean mixture warm.

4 Rub the cut sides of the bread slices with the garlic clove, then toast them lightly. Spoon the cannellini bean mixture on top of the toast. Sprinkle with basil leaves and drizzle with a little extra olive oil before serving.

Mini Baked Potatoes with Blue Cheese

These miniature potatoes can be eaten with the fingers. They provide a great way of starting off an informal supper party.

INGREDIENTS

Makes 20

20 small new or salad potatoes
4 tablespoons vegetable oil
coarse salt
4 fluid ounces/½ cup sour cream
1 ounce blue cheese, crumbled
2 tablespoons chopped fresh chives,
    to garnish

1 Preheat the oven to 350°F. Wash and dry the potatoes. Toss with the oil in a bowl to coat.

2 Dip the potatoes in the coarse salt to coat lightly. Spread the potatoes out on a baking sheet. Bake for 45–50 minutes, until the potatoes are tender.

3 In a small bowl, combine the sour cream and blue cheese, mixing together well.

COOK'S TIP

This dish works just as well as a light snack. If you don't want to be bothered with lots of small potatoes, simply bake an ordinary baking potato.

4 Cut a cross in the top of each potato. Press gently with your fingers to open the potatoes.

5 Top each potato with a spoon of the blue cheese mixture. Place on a serving dish and garnish with the chives. Serve hot or at room temperature.

Potato Skins with Cajun Dip

V

Divinely crisp and naughty, these potato skins are great on their own or served with this piquant dip as a garnish or on the side.

INGREDIENTS

Serves 4
2 large baking potatoes
vegetable oil, for deep-frying

For the dip
4 fluid ounces/½ cup plain yogurt
1 garlic clove, crushed
1 teaspoon tomato paste or
   ½ teaspoon green chili purée
   or ½ small fresh green chile,
   seeded and chopped
¼ teaspoon celery salt
salt and ground black pepper

1 Preheat the oven to 350°F. Bake the potatoes for 45–50 minutes, until tender. Cut them in half and scoop out the flesh, leaving a thin layer on the skins. Keep the flesh for another meal. Cut the potato skins in half once more.

2 To make the dip, mix together all the ingredients and chill.

3 Heat a 1cm/½in layer of oil in a pan or deep-fat fryer. Fry the potato skins until crisp and golden on both sides. Drain on kitchen paper, then sprinkle with salt and black pepper. Serve the potato skins with a bowl of dip or a spoonful of the dip in each skin.

Asparagus with Salt-cured Ham

Serve this tapas when asparagus is plentiful and not too expensive.

Serves 4

6 slices of Serrano ham

12 asparagus spears

1 tablespoon olive oil

sea salt and coarsely ground black pepper

COOK'S TIP

If you can't find Serrano ham, use Italian prosciutto or Portuguese presunto.

1 Preheat the broiler to high. Cut each slice of ham in half lengthwise and then securely wrap one half around each of the asparagus spears.

2 Brush the ham and asparagus lightly with oil and sprinkle with salt and pepper. Place on the broiler rack. Broil, turning frequently, for 5–6 minutes, until the asparagus is tender but still firm. Serve immediately.

Jumbo Shrimp with Spicy Dip

The spicy dip served with this dish is equally good made from peanuts instead of cashew nuts.

INGREDIENTS

Serves 4–6

24 raw jumbo shrimp

juice of ½ lemon

1 teaspoon paprika

1 bay leaf

1 fresh thyme sprig

vegetable oil, for brushing

salt and ground black pepper

For the spicy dip

1 onion, chopped

4 canned plum tomatoes, plus
    4 tablespoons of the juice

½ green bell pepper, seeded
    and chopped

1 garlic clove, crushed

1 tablespoon cashew nuts

1 tablespoon soy sauce

1 tablespoon dry unsweetened
    shredded coconut

1 Peel the shrimp, leaving the tails on. Place in a shallow dish and sprinkle with the lemon juice, paprika and seasoning. Cover and chill in the refrigerator.

2 Put the shells in a pan with the bay leaf and thyme, cover with water, then bring to the boil and simmer for 30 minutes. Strain the stock into a measuring cup. Top up with water, if necessary, to ½ pint/1¼ cups.

3 To make the spicy dip, place all the ingredients in a blender or food processor and process until the mixture is smooth.

4 Pour into a pan with the shrimp stock and simmer over a moderate heat for 30 minutes, until the sauce is fairly thick.

5 Preheat the broiler. Thread the shrimp on to small skewers, then brush the shrimp on both sides with a little oil and broil under a low heat until pink and cooked, turning once. Serve immediately with the dip.

COOK'S TIP

If unpeeled raw shrimp are not available, use cooked jumbo shrimp instead. Just broil them for a short time, until they are completely heated through.

V

Charred Artichokes with Lemon Oil Dip

Here is a lip-smacking change from traditional fare.

INGREDIENTS

Serves 4

1 tablespoon lemon juice or white
  wine vinegar
2 artichokes, trimmed
12 garlic cloves, unpeeled
6 tablespoons olive oil
1 lemon
sea salt
flat leaf parsley sprigs, to garnish

1 Preheat the oven to 400°F. Add the lemon juice or vinegar to a bowl of cold water. Cut each artichoke into wedges. Pull the hairy choke out from the center of each wedge and discard, then drop the wedges into the water.

2 Drain the wedges and place in a roasting pan with the garlic and 3 tablespoons of the oil. Toss well to coat. Sprinkle with salt and roast for 40 minutes, until tender and a little charred.

3 Meanwhile, make the dip. Using a small, sharp knife thinly pare away two strips of rind from the lemon. Lay the strips of rind on a board and carefully scrape away any remaining pith. Place the rind in a small pan with water to cover. Bring to the boil, then lower the heat and simmer for 5 minutes. Drain the rind, refresh in cold water, then chop coarsely. Set aside.

4 Arrange the cooked artichokes on a serving plate and leave to cool for 5 minutes. Using the back of a fork gently flatten the garlic cloves so that the flesh squeezes out of the skins. Transfer the garlic flesh to a bowl, mash to a paste, then add the lemon rind. Squeeze the juice from the lemon, then, using a fork, whisk the remaining olive oil and the lemon juice into the garlic mixture. Garnish with the parsley. Serve the artichokes still warm with the lemon oil dip.

COOK'S TIP

Artichokes are usually boiled, but dry-heat cooking also works very well. If you can get young artichokes, try roasting them over a barbecue.

Rice Triangles

These rice shapes – onigiri *– are very popular in Japan. You can put anything you like in the rice, so you could invent your own* onigiri.

INGREDIENTS

Serves 4

1 salmon steak

1 tablespoon salt

1 pound/4 cups freshly cooked sushi rice

¼ cucumber, seeded and cut into
   thin matchsticks

½ sheet yaki-nori seaweed, cut into four
   equal strips

white and black sesame seeds,
   for sprinkling

1 Broil the salmon steaks on each side, until the flesh flakes easily when tested with the tip of a sharp knife. Set aside to cool while you make other onigiri. When the salmon is cold, flake it, discarding any skin and bones.

2 Put the salt in a bowl. Spoon an eighth of the warm cooked rice into a small rice bowl. Make a hole in the middle of the rice and put in a few cucumber matchsticks. Smooth the rice over to cover.

3 Wet the palms of both hands with cold water, then rub the salt evenly onto your palms.

4 Empty the rice and cucumbers from the bowl onto one hand. Use both hands to shape the rice into a triangular shape, using a firm but not heavy pressure, and making sure that the cucumber is completely encased by the rice. Make three more rice triangles in the same way.

5 Mix the flaked salmon into the remaining rice, then shape it into triangles as before.

6 Wrap a strip of yaki-nori around each of the cucumber triangles. Sprinkle sesame seeds on the salmon triangles.

COOK'S TIP

Always use warm rice to make the triangles. Allow them to cool completely and wrap each in foil or plastic wrap.

Sushi-style Tuna Cubes

These tasty tuna cubes are easier to prepare than classic Japanese sushi, but retain the same fresh taste.

INGREDIENTS

Makes about 24

1½ pounds fresh tuna steak

1 large red bell pepper, seeded and cut into ¾-inch pieces

sesame seeds, for sprinkling

For the marinade

1–2 tablespoons lemon juice

½ teaspoon salt

½ teaspoon sugar

½ teaspoon wasabi paste

4 fluid ounces/½ cup olive or vegetable oil

2 tablespoons chopped fresh cilantro

For the soy dipping sauce

7 tablespoons soy sauce

1 tablespoon rice wine vinegar

1 teaspoon lemon juice

1–2 scallions, finely chopped

1 teaspoon sugar

2–3 dashes hot chili oil

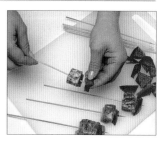

2 Prepare the marinade. In a small bowl, stir the lemon juice with the salt, sugar and wasabi paste. Gradually, whisk in the oil until well blended and slightly creamy. Stir in the cilantro. Pour over the tuna cubes and toss to coat. Cover and marinate for about 40 minutes in a cool place.

4 Preheat the broiler and line a baking sheet with foil. Thread a cube of tuna, then a piece of pepper on to each skewer and arrange on the baking sheet.

3 Meanwhile, prepare the soy dipping sauce. Combine all the ingredients in a small bowl and stir until well blended. Cover until ready to serve.

5 Sprinkle with sesame seeds and broil for about 3–5 minutes, turning once or twice, until just beginning to color, but still pink inside. Serve with the soy dipping sauce.

1 Cut the tuna into 1-inch pieces and then arrange them in a single layer in a large non-metallic ovenproof dish.

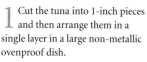

COOK'S TIP

Wasabi is a hot, pungent Japanese horseradish available in powder form (that has to be reconstituted) and as paste in a tube from gourmet and Japanese food stores.

Jumbo Shrimp in Crispy Batter

Serve these delightfully crispy shrimp with an Asian-style dipping sauce, or offer a simple tomato sauce or lemon wedges for squeezing.

Serves 4

4 fluid ounces/½ cup water

1 egg

4 ounces/1 cup all-purpose flour

1 teaspoon cayenne pepper

12 raw jumbo shrimp

vegetable oil, for deep-frying

flat leaf parsley, to garnish

lemon wedges, to serve

For the dipping sauce

2 tablespoons soy sauce

2 tablespoons dry sherry

2 teaspoons clear honey

3 To make the dipping sauce, stir together the soy sauce, dry sherry and honey in a small bowl until well combined.

4 Heat the oil in a large pan or deep-fryer to 350°F, or until a cube of day-old bread browns in 1 minute.

5 Holding the shrimp by their tails, dip them into the batter, one at a time, shaking off any excess. Drop them carefully into the oil and fry for 2–3 minutes, until crisp and golden brown. Drain on paper towels and serve with the dipping sauce and lemon wedges, garnished with parsley.

1 In a large bowl, whisk the water with the egg. Add the flour and cayenne and whisk until smooth.

2 Carefully peel the shrimp, leaving just the tail sections intact. Make a shallow cut down the back of each shrimp n, then pull out and discard the dark intestinal tract.

COOK'S TIP

Use leftover batter to coat thin strips of sweet potato, beet, carrot or bell pepper, then deep-fry until golden.

Tandoori Chicken Sticks

This aromatic chicken dish is traditionally baked in a special clay oven called a tandoor. Here the chicken is broiled.

INGREDIENTS

Makes about 25
1 pound skinless, boneless chicken
    breast portions

For the cilantro yogurt
8 fluid ounces/1 cup plain yogurt
2 tablespoons whipping cream
½ cucumber, peeled, seeded and
    finely chopped
1–2 tablespoons fresh chopped mint
    or cilantro
salt and ground black pepper

For the marinade
6 fluid ounces/¾ cup plain yogurt
1 teaspoon garam masala or curry powder
¼ teaspoon ground cumin
¼ teaspoon ground coriander
¼ teaspoon cayenne pepper (or to taste)
1 teaspoon tomato paste
1–2 garlic cloves, finely chopped
1-inch piece fresh root ginger,
    finely chopped
grated rind and juice of ½ lemon
1–2 tablespoons chopped fresh mint
    or cilantro

1 Prepare the cilantro yogurt. Combine all the ingredients in a bowl and season with salt and ground black pepper. Cover with plastic wrap and chill until you are ready to serve.

2 Prepare the marinade. Place all the ingredients in the bowl of a food processor, and process until the mixture is smooth. Pour into a shallow dish.

3 Freeze the chicken for about 5 minutes to firm, then slice in half horizontally. Cut the slices into ¾-inch strips and add to the marinade. Toss to coat well. Cover and chill in the refrigerator for 6–8 hours or overnight.

4 Preheat the broiler and line a baking sheet with foil. Using a slotted spoon, remove the chicken from the marinade and arrange the pieces in a single layer on the baking sheet. Scrunch up the chicken slightly so it makes wavy shapes. Broil, turning once, for 4–5 minutes until brown and just cooked. When it is cool enough to handle, thread pieces on to short skewers and serve with the cilantro yogurt dip.

Thai Tempeh Cakes with Dipping Sauce

Made from soya beans, tempeh is similar to tofu but has a nuttier taste. Here, it is combined with a fragrant blend of lemon grass, cilantro and ginger and formed into small patties.

INGREDIENTS

Makes 8 cakes

1 lemon grass stalk, outer leaves removed,
    finely chopped
2 garlic cloves, finely chopped
2 scallions, finely chopped
2 shallots, finely chopped
2 fresh chiles, seeded and
    finely chopped
1-inch piece fresh root ginger,
    finely chopped
4 tablespoons chopped fresh cilantro,
    plus extra to garnish
9 ounces/2¼ cups tempeh, thawed if
    frozen, sliced
1 tablespoon lime juice
1 teaspoon superfine sugar
3 tablespoons all-purpose flour
1 extra large egg, lightly beaten
vegetable oil, for frying
salt and ground black pepper

For the dipping sauce
3 tablespoons mirin
3 tablespoons white wine vinegar
2 scallions, thinly sliced
1 tablespoon sugar
2 fresh chiles, seeded and
    finely chopped
2 tablespoons chopped fresh cilantro

1 To make the dipping sauce, mix together the mirin, vinegar, scallions, sugar, chiles, cilantro and a large pinch of salt in a small bowl and set aside.

2 Place the lemon grass, garlic, scallions, shallots, chiles, ginger and cilantro in a food processor or blender, then process to a coarse paste.

3 Add the tempeh, lime juice and sugar, then process until thoroughly combined. Add the flour and egg and season well with salt and pepper. Process again until the mixture forms a fairly coarse, sticky paste.

4 Take a heaped serving spoonful of the tempeh paste mixture at a time and form into rounds with your hands. The mixture will be quite sticky.

5 Heat enough oil to cover the base of a large frying pan. Fry the tempeh cakes for 5–6 minutes, turning once, until golden. Drain on paper towels and serve warm with the dipping sauce, garnished with chopped fresh cilantro.

Aromatic Jumbo Shrimp

There is no elegant way to eat these aromatic shrimp – just hold them by the tails, pull them off the sticks with your fingers and pop them into your mouth.

INGREDIENTS

Serves 4

16 raw jumbo shrimp or extra large
    shrimp tails
½ teaspoon chili powder
1 teaspoon fennel seeds
5 Sichuan or black peppercorns
1 star anise, broken into segments
1 cinnamon stick, broken into pieces
2 tablespoons peanut oil
2 garlic cloves, chopped
¾-inch piece fresh root ginger,
    finely chopped
1 shallot, chopped
2 tablespoons rice vinegar
2 tablespoons soft brown or palm sugar
salt and ground black pepper
lime slices and chopped scallion,
    to garnish

1 Thread the shrimp or extra large shrimp tails in pairs on to 8 wooden toothpicks. Set aside. Heat a frying pan, put in all the chili powder, fennel seeds, Sichuan or black peppercorns, star anise and cinnamon stick and dry-fry for 1–2 minutes to release the flavors. Leave to cool, then grind coarsely in a grinder or tip into a mortar and crush with a pestle.

2 Heat the peanut oil in a shallow pan, add the garlic, ginger and chopped shallot and then cook gently until very lightly colored. Add the crushed spices and seasoning and cook the mixture gently for 2 minutes. Pour in 2 tablespoons water and simmer, stirring constantly, for 5 minutes.

3 Add the rice vinegar and soft brown or palm sugar, stir until dissolved, then add the shrimp or shrimp tails. Cook for about 3–5 minutes, until the seafood has turned pink, but is still very juicy. Serve hot, garnished with lime slices and scallion.

COOK'S TIP

If you buy whole shrimp, remove the heads before cooking them.

Duck Wontons with Spicy Mango Sauce

These Chinese-style wontons are easy to make using ready-cooked smoked duck or chicken, or even leftovers from the Sunday roast.

Makes about 40

1 tablespoon light soy sauce
1 teaspoon sesame oil
2 scallions, finely chopped
grated rind of ½ orange
1 teaspoon brown sugar
10 ounces/1½ cups chopped
    smoked duck
about 40 small wonton wrappers
1 tablespoon vegetable oil
whole fresh chives, to garnish (optional)

For the mango sauce

2 tablespoons vegetable oil
1 teaspoon ground cumin
½ teaspoon ground cardamom
¼ teaspoon ground cinnamon
8 fluid ounces/1 cup mango purée
    (about 1 large mango)
1 tablespoon clear honey
½ teaspoon Chinese chili sauce
    (or to taste)
1 tablespoon cider vinegar
chopped fresh chives, to garnish

2 Stir in the mango purée, clear honey, chili sauce and vinegar. Remove from the heat and leave to cool. Pour into a bowl and cover until ready to serve.

3 Prepare the wonton filling. In a large bowl, mix together the soy sauce, sesame oil, scallions, orange rind and brown sugar until well blended. Add the duck and toss to coat well.

5 Preheat the oven to 375°F. Line a large baking sheet with foil and brush lightly with oil. Arrange the filled wontons in a single layer on the baking sheet and bake for about 10–12 minutes, until crisp and golden. Serve with the mango sauce garnished with chopped fresh chives. If you like, tie each wonton with a fresh chive.

1 First prepare the sauce. In a medium pan, heat the oil over a medium-low heat. Add the ground cumin, cardamom and cinnamon and cook for about 3 minutes, stirring constantly.

4 Place a teaspoonful of the duck mixture in the center of each wonton wrapper. Brush the edges with water and then draw them up to the center, twisting to seal and forming a pouch shape.

COOK'S TIP

Wonton wrappers, available in some large supermarkets and Asian food stores, are sold in 1-pound packets and can be stored in the freezer almost indefinitely. Remove as many as you need, keeping the rest frozen.

VEGETABLE AND CHEESE APPETIZERS

~

You don't have to be a vegetarian to enjoy the recipes here.
In fact, many people prefer to serve a vegetable or cheese dish
as a first course to balance and offer a contrast to the
following meat or fish main course. If you are a vegetarian
or entertaining vegetarian guests, you will be spoiled for
choice with appetizers as diverse as terrines, risottos, tarts,
pies and fritters, all based on delicious fresh produce or
an international selection of cheeses.

Roast Pepper Terrine

[V]

This terrine is perfect for a dinner party because it tastes better if made earlier. Prepare the salsa on the day of serving. Serve with a warmed Italian bread, such as ciabatta or the flavorsome focaccia.

INGREDIENTS

Serves 8

8 bell peppers (red, yellow and orange)

1½ pounds/3 cups mascarpone cheese

3 eggs, separated

2 tablespoons each coarsely chopped fresh
    flat leaf parsley and shredded fresh basil

2 large garlic cloves, coarsely chopped

2 red, yellow or orange bell peppers,
    seeded and coarsely chopped

2 tablespoons extra virgin olive oil

2 teaspoons balsamic vinegar

a few fresh basil sprigs

salt and ground black pepper

1 Place the whole bell peppers under a hot broiler, turning frequently, for 8–10 minutes. Then put them into a plastic bag, tie the top and leave until cold before peeling and seeding them. Chop seven of the peppers lengthwise into thin strips.

2 Put the mascarpone cheese in a bowl with the egg yolks, herbs and half the garlic. Add salt and pepper to taste. Beat well. In a separate bowl, whisk the egg whites to soft peaks, then fold into the cheese mixture until they are evenly incorporated.

3 Preheat the oven to 350°F. Line the base of a lightly oiled 2-pound loaf pan. Put one-third of the cheese mixture in the pan and spread level. Arrange half the pepper strips on top in an even layer. Repeat until all the cheese and peppers are used, ending with a layer of the cheese mixture.

4 Cover the pan with foil and place in a roasting pan. Pour in boiling water to come halfway up the sides of the loaf pan. Bake for 1 hour. Leave to cool in the water bath, then lift out and chill overnight.

5 A few hours before serving, make the salsa. Place the remaining peeled pepper and fresh peppers in a food processor. Add the remaining garlic, oil and vinegar. Set aside a few basil leaves for garnishing and add the rest to the processor. Process until finely chopped. Tip the mixture into a bowl, add salt and pepper to taste and mix well. Cover and chill until ready to serve.

6 Turn out the terrine, peel off the lining paper and slice thickly. Garnish with the reserved basil leaves and serve cold, with the sweet pepper salsa.

Asparagus and Egg Terrine

v

For a special dinner this terrine is a delicious choice, yet it is very light. Make the hollandaise sauce well in advance and warm through gently when required.

INGREDIENTS

Serves 8

¼ pint/⅔ cup milk
¼ pint/⅔ cup heavy cream
1½oz/3 tablespoons butter
1½oz/6 tablespoons all-purpose flour
3 ounces herbed or garlic cream cheese
1½ pounds asparagus spears, cooked
a little oil
2 eggs, separated
1 tablespoon chopped fresh chives
2 tablespoons chopped fresh dill
salt and ground black pepper
fresh dill sprigs, to garnish

For the orange hollandaise sauce
1 tablespoon white wine vinegar
1 tablespoon fresh orange juice
4 black peppercorns
1 bay leaf
2 egg yolks
4 ounces/½ cup butter, melted and
    cooled slightly

1 Put the milk and cream into a small pan and heat to just below boiling point. Melt the butter in a medium pan, stir in the flour and cook to a thick paste. Gradually whisk in the milk and beat to a smooth paste. Stir in the cream cheese, season to taste with salt and ground black pepper and leave to cool slightly.

2 Trim the asparagus to fit the width of a 2 pint/5 cup loaf pan or terrine. Lightly oil the pan and then place a sheet of waxed paper in the base, cut to fit. Preheat the oven to 350°F.

3 Beat the yolks into the sauce mixture. Whisk the whites until stiff and fold in with the chives, dill and seasoning. Layer the asparagus and egg mixture in the pan, starting and finishing with asparagus. Cover the top with foil.

4 Place the terrine in a roasting pan; half-fill with hot water. Cook for 50 minutes, until firm.

5 To make the sauce, put the vinegar, juice, peppercorns and bay leaf in a small pan and heat until reduced by half.

6 Cool the sauce slightly, then whisk in the egg yolks, then the butter, with a balloon whisk over a very gentle heat. Season to taste with salt and pepper and keep whisking until thick.

7 When the terrine is just firm to the touch, remove from the oven and allow to cool, then chill. Carefully invert the terrine onto a serving dish, remove the lining paper and garnish with the dill. Gently reheat the sauce over a pan of hot water. Cut the terrine into slices and pour over the sauce.

Vegetable Terrine

This colorful terrine uses all the vegetables of the Mediterranean.

INGREDIENTS

Serves 6

2 large red bell peppers, quartered
    and seeded
2 large yellow bell peppers, quartered
    and seeded
1 large eggplant, sliced lengthways
2 large zucchini, sliced lengthways
6 tablespoons olive oil
1 large red onion, thinly sliced
3 ounces/½ cup raisins
1 tablespoon tomato paste
1 tablespoon red wine vinegar
14 fluid ounces/1⅔ cups tomato juice
½ ounce/2 tablespoons powdered gelatine
fresh basil leaves, to garnish

For the dressing
6 tablespoons extra virgin olive oil
2 tablespoons red wine vinegar
salt and ground black pepper

1 Place the bell peppers skin-side up under a hot broiler until the skins are blackened. Transfer to a plastic bag and leave to cool.

2 Arrange the eggplant and zucchini slices on separate baking sheets. Brush them with a little oil and cook under the broiler, turning occasionally, until they are tender and golden.

3 Heat the remaining olive oil in a frying pan, and add the sliced onion, raisins, tomato paste and red wine vinegar. Cook gently until the mixture is soft and syrupy. Set aside and leave to cool in the frying pan.

4 Line a 3 pint/7½ cup terrine pan with plastic wrap – it helps if you lightly oil the terrine pan first – leaving a little hanging over the sides.

5 Pour half the tomato juice into a pan, and sprinkle with the gelatine. Dissolve gently over a low heat, stirring to prevent any lumps from forming.

6 Place a layer of red peppers in the base of the terrine, and pour in enough of the tomato juice mixture to cover. Add a layer of yellow peppers, followed by eggplant slices, then zucchini slices and, finally, the onion mixture, pouring a little tomato juice mixture over each layer.

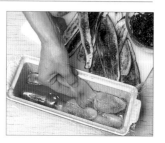

7 Continue layering all the vegetables, adding the tomato juice mixture to each layer and finishing with red peppers. Add the remaining tomato juice to the pan, and pour into the terrine. Give it a sharp tap, to disperse the juice. Cover and chill until set.

8 To make the dressing, whisk together the oil and vinegar, and season. Turn out the terrine and remove the lining. Serve in thick slices, drizzled with dressing and garnished with basil leaves.

COOK'S TIP
∾

Ring the changes and use orange and green bell peppers along with or in place of the red and yellow ones. Green beans, simply boiled first, would make a nice addition, as would a layer of peas or corn kernels.

Risotto Alla Milanese

This classic risotto is often served with the hearty beef stew, osso buco, *but it also makes a delicious first course in its own right.*

INGREDIENTS

Serves 5–6

about 2 pints/5 cups Meat or
    Vegetable Stock
good pinch of saffron threads
3 ounces/6 tablespoons butter
1 onion, finely chopped
10 ounces/1½ cups risotto rice
3 ounces/1 cup freshly grated
    Parmesan cheese
salt and ground black pepper

1 Bring the stock to the boil, then reduce to a low simmer. Ladle a little stock into a small bowl. Add the saffron threads and leave to steep.

2 Melt 2 ounces/4 tablespoons of the butter in a large pan. Add the chopped onion and cook over a low heat for 3–5 minutes, stirring frequently, until softened and translucent, but not browned .

3 Add the rice. Stir until the grains start to swell and burst, then add a few ladlefuls of the stock, with the saffron liquid and salt and pepper to taste. Stir over a low heat until the stock has been absorbed. Add the remaining stock, a few ladlefuls at a time, allowing the rice to absorb all the liquid before adding more, and stirring constantly. After about 20–25 minutes, the rice should be just tender and the risotto golden yellow, moist and creamy.

4 Gently stir in about two-thirds of the grated Parmesan and the remaining butter. Gently heat through until the butter has melted, then taste and adjust the seasoning if necessary. Transfer the risotto to a warmed serving bowl or platter and serve immediately, with the remaining grated Parmesan served separately.

Risotto with Four Cheeses

This is a very rich dish. Serve it for a special dinner-party first course, with a light, dry sparkling white wine to accompany it.

INGREDIENTS

Serves 4–6

1½ ounces/3 tablespoons butter
1 small onion, finely chopped
2 pints/5 cups Vegetable or Chicken Stock
12 ounces/1¾ cups risotto rice
7 fluid ounces/scant 1 cup dry white wine
2 ounces/½ cup grated Gruyère cheese
2 ounces/½ cup diced Taleggio cheese
2 ounces/½ cup diced Gorgonzola cheese
2 ounces/⅔ cup freshly grated
   Parmesan cheese
salt and ground black pepper
chopped fresh flat leaf parsley,
   to garnish

1 Melt the butter in a large, heavy pan or deep frying pan and cook the onion over a gentle heat for about 4–5 minutes, stirring frequently, until softened and lightly browned. Pour the stock into a separate pan and heat it to simmering point.

2 Add the rice to the onion mixture, stir until the grains start to swell and burst, then add the wine. Stir until it stops sizzling and most of it has been absorbed by the rice, then pour in a little of the hot stock. Add salt and ground black pepper to taste. Stir the rice over a low heat until the stock has been absorbed.

3 Gradually add the remaining stock, a little at a time, allowing the rice to absorb the liquid before adding more, and stirring constantly. After about 20–25 minutes the rice will be *al dente* and the risotto will have a creamy consistency.

4 Turn off the heat under the pan, then add the Gruyère, Taleggio, the Gorgonzola and 2 tablespoons of the Parmesan. Stir gently until the cheeses have melted, then taste for seasoning. Spoon into a serving bowl and garnish with parsley. Serve the remaining Parmesan separately.

Baked Mediterranean Vegetables

Crisp and golden crunchy batter surrounds these vegetables, turning them into a substantial appetizer. Use other vegetables instead if you like.

INGREDIENTS

Serves 10–12

1 small eggplant, trimmed, halved and
   thickly sliced
1 egg
4 ounces/1 cup all-purpose flour
½ pint/1¼ cups milk
2 tablespoons fresh thyme leaves,
   or 2 teaspoons dried thyme
1 red onion
2 large zucchini
1 red bell pepper
1 yellow bell pepper
4–5 tablespoons sunflower oil
salt and ground black pepper
2 tablespoons freshly grated
   Parmesan cheese and fresh herbs,
   to garnish

1 Place the eggplant in a colander or sieve, sprinkle generously with salt and leave in the sink for 10 minutes. Drain, rinse and pat dry on paper towels.

2 Meanwhile, to make the batter, beat the egg, then gradually beat in the flour and a little milk to make a smooth thick paste. Blend in the rest of the milk, add the thyme leaves and season to taste with salt and pepper. Blend until completely smooth. Leave in a cool place until required.

3 Quarter the onion, slice the zucchini and seed and quarter the bell peppers. Put the oil in a roasting pan and heat through in the oven at 425°F. Add all the vegetables, turn in the oil to coat them well and return to the oven for 20 minutes, until they start to cook.

4 Whisk the batter again, then pour it over the vegetables and return to the oven for 30 minutes. If well puffed up and golden, then reduce the heat to 375°F and bake for 10–15 minutes more, until crisp around the edges. Sprinkle with Parmesan and herbs and serve immediately.

COOK'S TIP

It is essential to get the oil in the dish very hot before adding the batter, or it will not rise well. Use a dish which is not too deep.

Eggplant and Smoked Mozzarella Rolls

Slices of grilled eggplant are stuffed with smoked mozzarella, tomato and fresh basil to make an attractive hors d'oeuvre. The rolls are also good cooked on a barbecue.

INGREDIENTS

Serves 4

1 large eggplant

3 tablespoons olive oil, plus extra for
    drizzling (optional)

5½ ounces smoked mozzarella cheese, cut
    into 8 slices

2 plum tomatoes, each cut into
    4 even-size slices

8 large basil leaves

balsamic vinegar, for drizzling (optional)

salt and ground black pepper

1 Cut the eggplant lengthwise into 10 thin slices and discard the two outermost slices. Sprinkle the slices with salt and set them aside in a colander or sieve for 20 minutes. Rinse under cold running water, then pat dry with paper towels.

2 Preheat the broiler and line the rack with foil. Place the eggplant slices on the broiler rack and brush liberally with oil. Broil, turning once, for 8–10 minutes, until tender.

3 Remove the eggplant slices from the broiler, then place a slice of mozzarella and tomato and a basil leaf in the center of each eggplant slice, and season to taste. Fold the eggplant over the filling and cook, seam-side down, under the broiler until heated through, when and the mozzarella begins to melt. Serve drizzled with olive oil and a little balsamic vinegar, if using.

Marinated Feta Cheese with Capers

Marinating cubes of feta cheese with herbs and spices gives a marvelous flavor. Serve with toast.

INGREDIENTS

Serves 6

12 ounces feta cheese

2 garlic cloves

$\frac{1}{2}$ teaspoon mixed peppercorns

8 coriander seeds

1 bay leaf

1–2 tablespoons drained capers

fresh oregano or thyme sprigs

olive oil, to cover

hot toast, to serve

1 Cut the feta cheese into cubes. Thickly slice the garlic. Put the mixed peppercorns and coriander seeds in a mortar and crush lightly with a pestle.

2 Pack the feta cubes into a large preserving jar with the bay leaf, interspersing layers of cheese with garlic, crushed peppercorns and coriander, capers and the fresh oregano or thyme sprigs.

3 Pour in enough olive oil to cover the cheese. Close tightly and leave to marinate for 2 weeks in the refrigerator.

4 Lift out the feta cubes and serve on hot toast, with some chopped tomatoes and a little of the flavored oil from the jar drizzled over.

COOK'S TIP
Add pitted black or green olives to the feta cheese in the marinade if you like.

Dolmades

V

If you can't locate fresh grape leaves, use a packet or can of brined leaves. Soak in hot water for 20 minutes, then rinse and pat dry.

Makes 20 to 24

24–28 fresh young grape
   leaves, soaked
2 tablespoons olive oil
1 large onion, finely chopped
1 garlic clove, crushed
8 ounces/2 cups cooked long grain rice,
   or mixed white and wild rice
about 3 tablespoons pine nuts
1 tablespoon sliced almonds
1½ ounces/¼ cup golden raisins
1 tablespoon chopped fresh chives
1 tablespoon finely chopped fresh mint
juice of ½ lemon
¼ pint/⅔ cup white wine
hot Vegetable Stock
salt and ground black pepper
fresh mint sprig, to garnish
garlic yogurt and pitta bread,
   to serve

1 Bring a large pan of water to the boil and cook the vine leaves for about 2–3 minutes. They will darken and go limp after about 1 minute, and simmering for a further minute or so will make sure that they are pliable. If using packet or canned leaves, place in a bowl, cover with boiling water and leave for 20 minutes, until the leaves can be separated easily. Rinse and dry on paper towels.

2 Heat the oil in a small frying pan and cook the onion and garlic for 3–4 minutes over a gentle heat until soft. Spoon the mixture into a large bowl and add the cooked rice. Stir to combine.

3 Stir in 2 tablespoons of the pine nuts, the almonds, golden raisins, chives and mint. Squeeze in the lemon juice. Add salt and pepper to taste and mix well.

4 Set aside four large grape leaves. Lay a grape leaf on a clean work surface, veined side uppermost. Place a spoonful of filling near the stem, fold the lower part of the grape leaf over it and roll up, folding in the sides as you go. Stuff the rest of the grape leaves in the same way.

5 Line the base of a deep frying pan with the reserved grape leaves. Place the dolmades close together in the pan, seam side down, in a single layer. Pour over the wine and enough stock just to cover. Anchor the dolmades by placing a plate on top of them, then cover the pan and simmer gently for 30 minutes.

6 Transfer the dolmades to a plate. Cool, chill, then garnish with the remaining pine nuts and the mint. Serve with a little garlic yogurt and some pitta bread.

Tomato and Zucchini Timbales

Timbales are baked savory custards typical of the South of France, and mainly made with light vegetables. This combination is delicious as an appetizer. It can be served warm or cool. Try other combinations, if you like.

INGREDIENTS

Serves 4

a little butter

2 zucchini, about 6 ounces

2 firm, ripe vine tomatoes, sliced

2 eggs plus 2 egg yolks

3 tablespoons heavy cream

1 tablespoon fresh tomato sauce or bottled strained tomatoes

2 teaspoons chopped fresh basil or oregano or 1 teaspoon dried

salt and ground black pepper

salad leaves, to serve

1 Preheat the oven to 350°F. Lightly butter four large ramekins. Trim the zucchini, then cut them into thin slices. Put them into a steamer and steam over boiling water for 4–5 minutes. Drain well in a colander and, when cool enough to handle, layer the zucchini in the ramekins, alternating with the sliced tomatoes.

2 Whisk together the eggs, cream, tomato sauce or strained tomatoes, herbs and seasoning. Pour the egg mixture into the ramekins. Place them in a roasting pan and half-fill with hot water. Bake the ramekins for 20–30 minutes, until the custard is just firm.

3 Cool slightly, then run a knife around the rims and carefully turn out onto small plates. Serve with salad leaves.

> COOK'S TIP
> ～
> Don't overcook the timbales or the texture of the savory custard will become rubbery.

Wild Mushroom and Fontina Tarts

Italian fontina cheese gives these tarts a creamy, nutty flavor.

INGREDIENTS

Serves 4

1 ounce/$\frac{1}{2}$ cup dried wild mushrooms

2 tablespoons olive oil

1 red onion, chopped

2 garlic cloves, chopped

2 tablespoons medium-dry sherry

1 egg

4 fluid ounces/$\frac{1}{2}$ cup light cream

1 ounce fontina cheese, thinly sliced

salt and ground black pepper

arugula leaves, to serve

For the pastry

4 ounces/1 cup whole-wheat flour

2 ounces/4 tablespoons sweet butter

1 ounce/$\frac{1}{4}$ cup walnuts, roasted
  and ground

1 egg, lightly beaten

1 To make the pastry, rub the flour and butter together until the mixture resembles fine bread crumbs. Add the nuts, then the egg and mix to a soft dough. Wrap, then chill for 30 minutes.

2 Meanwhile, soak the dried wild mushrooms in $\frac{1}{2}$ pint/ $1\frac{1}{4}$ cups boiling water for 30 minutes. Drain and reserve the liquid. Cook the onion in the oil over a low heat for 5 minutes, then add the garlic and cook for about 2 minutes, stirring frequently.

3 Add the soaked mushrooms and cook for 7 minutes over a high heat until the edges become crisp. Add the sherry and the reserved soaking liquid. Cook over a high heat for about 10 minutes, until the liquid evaporates. Season to taste and set aside to cool.

COOK'S TIP

You can prepare the pastry shells in advance, bake them blind for 10 minutes, then store in an airtight container for up to 2 days.

4 Preheat the oven to 400°F. Lightly grease four 4-inch muffin pans. Roll out the pastry on a lightly floured work surface and use to line the muffin pans.

5 Prick the pastry, line with waxed paper and baking beans and bake blind for about 10 minutes. Remove the paper and the beans.

6 Whisk the egg and cream to mix, add to the mushroom mixture, then season to taste. Spoon into the pastry shells, top with cheese slices and bake for 18 minutes, until the filling is set. Serve warm with arugula.

Vegetable Tarte Tatin

This upside-down tart combines Mediterranean vegetables with rice, garlic, onions and olives.

Serves 4

2 tablespoons sunflower oil

about 1½ tablespoons olive oil

1 eggplant, sliced lengthwise

1 large red bell pepper, seeded and cut into long strips

5 tomatoes

2 red shallots, finely chopped

1–2 garlic cloves, crushed

¼ pint/⅔ cup white wine

2 teaspoons chopped fresh basil

8 ounces/2 cups cooked white or brown long grain rice

1½ ounces/⅔ cup pitted black olives, chopped

12 ounces puff pastry, thawed if frozen

ground black pepper

salad leaves, to serve

1 Preheat the oven to 375°F. Heat the sunflower oil with 1 tablespoon of the olive oil and fry the eggplant slices for 4–5 minutes on each side. Drain on paper towels.

COOK'S TIP
〜
Zucchini and mushrooms could be used as well, or use strips of lightly browned chicken.

2 Add the bell pepper strips to the oil remaining in the pan, turning them to coat. Cover the pan with a lid or foil and sweat the peppers over a moderately high heat for 5–6 minutes, stirring occasionally, until the pepper strips are soft and flecked with brown.

3 Slice two of the tomatoes and set them aside. Plunge the remaining tomatoes briefly into boiling water, then peel them, cut them into quarters and remove the core and seeds. Chop the tomato flesh coarsely.

4 Heat the remaining olive oil in the frying pan, add the shallots and garlic and cook over a low heat, stirring occasionally, for 3–4 minutes, until softened. Add the chopped tomatoes and cook for a few minutes, until softened. Stir in the wine and basil and season with black pepper to taste. Bring to the boil, then remove the pan from the heat and stir in the cooked rice and black olives.

5 Arrange the tomato slices, eggplant slices and bell peppers in a single layer on the base of a heavy, 12-inch, shallow ovenproof dish. Spread the rice mixture on top.

6 Roll out the pastry to a round shape slightly larger than the diameter of the dish and place on top of the rice, tucking the overlap down inside the dish.

7 Bake for 25–30 minutes, until the pastry is golden and risen. Cool slightly, then invert the tart onto a large, warmed serving plate. Serve in slices, with some salad leaves.

Lemon, Thyme and Bean Stuffed Mushrooms

[V]

Portabello mushrooms have a rich flavor and a meaty texture that go well with this fragrant herb-and-lemon stuffing. The garlicky pine nut accompaniment is a traditional Middle Eastern dish with a smooth, creamy consistency similar to that of hummus.

INGREDIENTS

Serves 4–6

7 ounces/1 cup dried or 14 ounces/2 cups
   drained, canned aduki beans
3 tablespoons olive oil, plus extra
   for brushing
1 onion, finely chopped
2 garlic cloves, crushed
2 tablespoons chopped fresh thyme
   or 1 teaspoon dried thyme
8 large portabello mushrooms, stalks
   finely chopped
2 ounces/1 cup fresh whole-wheat
   bread crumbs
juice of 1 lemon
6 1/2 ounces/3/4 cup goat cheese,
   crumbled
salt and ground black pepper

For the pine nut sauce
2 ounces/1/2 cup pine nuts, toasted
2 ounces/1 cup cubed white bread
2 garlic cloves, chopped
7 fluid ounces/scant 1 cup milk
3 tablespoons olive oil
1 tablespoon chopped fresh parsley,
   to garnish (optional)

1 If using dried beans, place them in a bowl, add cold water to cover and soak overnight. Drain and rinse well. Place in a pan, add enough fresh water to cover and bring to the boil. Boil rapidly for 10 minutes, then reduce the heat and cook for about 1 hour, until tender, then drain. If using canned beans, rinse, drain well, then set aside.

2 Preheat the oven to 400°F. Heat the oil in a large, heavy frying pan, add the onion and garlic and cook for 5 minutes, until softened. Add the thyme and the mushroom stalks and cook for a further 3 minutes, stirring occasionally, until tender.

3 Stir in the beans, bread crumbs and lemon juice, season well, then cook for 2 minutes, until heated through. Mash about two-thirds of the beans with a fork or potato masher.

4 Brush an ovenproof dish and the base and sides of the mushrooms with oil, then top each one with a spoonful of the bean mixture. Place the mushrooms in the dish, cover with foil and bake for 20 minutes. Remove the foil. Top each mushroom with some of the goat cheese and bake for a further 15 minutes, or until the cheese is melted and bubbly and the mushrooms are tender.

5 To make the pine nut sauce, place all the ingredients in a food processor or blender and blend until smooth and creamy. Add more milk if the mixture appears too thick. Sprinkle with parsley, if using, and serve with the stuffed mushrooms.

Griddled Tomatoes on Soda Bread

Nothing could be simpler than this delightful appetizer, yet a drizzle of olive oil and balsamic vinegar and shavings of Parmesan cheese transform it into something truly special.

INGREDIENTS

Serves 4

extra virgin olive oil, for brushing
    and drizzling
6 tomatoes, thickly sliced
4 thick slices soda bread
balsamic vinegar, for drizzling
salt and ground black pepper
freshly shaved Parmesan cheese,
    to serve

1 Brush a griddle pan with oil and heat. Add the tomato slices and cook them for 4 minutes, turning once, until softened and slightly blackened. Alternatively, heat the broiler to high and line the rack with foil. Broil the tomato slices for 4–6 minutes, turning once, until softened.

2 Meanwhile, lightly toast the soda bread. Place the tomatoes on top of the toast and drizzle each portion with a little olive oil and balsamic vinegar. Season to taste with salt and pepper and serve immediately with thin shavings of Parmesan cheese.

COOK'S TIP

Using a griddle pan reduces the amount of oil required for cooking the tomatoes which is useful for those watching their weight. It also gives them a delicious barbecue flavor.

Twice-baked Gruyère and Potato Soufflé

This recipe can be prepared in advance and given its second baking just before you serve it up.

INGREDIENTS

Serves 4

8 ounces floury potatoes

2 eggs, separated

6 ounces/1½ cups grated Gruyère cheese

2 ounces/½ cup self-rising flour

2 ounces spinach leaves

butter, for greasing

salt and ground black pepper

salad leaves, to serve

3 Finely chop the spinach and fold into the potato mixture.

4 Whisk the egg whites until they form soft peaks. Fold a little of the egg white into the mixture to slacken it slightly. Using a large spoon, fold the remaining egg white into the mixture.

5 Grease four large ramekins. Pour the mixture into the dishes. Place on a baking sheet and bake for 20 minutes. Remove from the oven and leave to cool.

6 Turn the soufflés out onto a baking sheet and sprinkle with the remaining cheese. Bake for 5 minutes. Serve with salad leaves.

1 Preheat the oven to 400°F. Peel the potatoes and cook in lightly salted boiling water for 20 minutes, until very tender. Drain and mash with the egg yolks.

2 Stir in half of the Gruyère cheese and all of the flour. Season to taste with salt and ground black pepper.

VARIATION
〜

For a different flavoring, try replacing the Gruyère with a crumbled blue cheese, such as Stilton or Shropshire Blue, which have a stronger taste.

Risotto Frittata

Half omelette, half risotto, this makes a delightful and satisfying appetizer. If possible, cook each frittata separately, and preferably in a small, cast-iron pan, so that the eggs cook quickly underneath, but stay moist on top. Or cook in one large pan and serve in wedges.

INGREDIENTS

Serves 4

2–3 tablespoons olive oil

1 small onion, finely chopped

1 garlic clove, crushed

1 large red bell pepper, seeded and cut into thin strips

5 ounces/¾ cup risotto rice

14–16 fluid ounces/1²⁄₃–2 cups simmering Vegetable Stock

1–1½ ounces/2–3 tablespoons butter

6 ounces/2½ cups white mushrooms, thinly sliced

4 tablespoons freshly grated Parmesan cheese

6–8 eggs

salt and ground black pepper

1 Heat 1 tablespoon oil in a large frying pan and cook the onion and garlic over a gentle heat for 2–3 minutes, until the onion begins to soften but does not brown. Add the pepper and cook, stirring, for 4–5 minutes, until soft.

2 Stir in the rice and cook gently for 2–3 minutes, stirring constantly, until the grains are evenly coated with oil.

3 Add a quarter of the vegetable stock and season with salt and pepper. Stir over a low heat until the stock has been absorbed. Continue to add more stock, a little at a time, allowing the rice to absorb the liquid before adding more. Continue cooking in this way for 20–25 minutes, until the rice is *al dente*.

4 In a separate small pan, heat a little of the remaining oil and some of the butter and quickly cook the mushrooms until golden. Transfer to a plate.

5 When the rice is tender, remove the pan from the heat and stir in the cooked mushrooms and the Parmesan cheese.

6 Beat the eggs with 8 teaspoons cold water and season well with salt and pepper. Heat the remaining oil and butter in an omelette pan and add the risotto mixture. Spread the mixture out in the pan, then immediately add the beaten egg mixture, tilting the pan so that it is evenly distributed. Cook the omelette over a moderately high heat for 1–2 minutes, then transfer to a warmed plate and serve.

COOK'S TIP

Don't be impatient while cooking the rice. Adding the stock gradually guarantees a wonderfully creamy consistency.

Leek and Onion Tartlets

V

Baking in individual pans makes for easier serving for an appetizer, and it looks attractive too.

INGREDIENTS

Serves 6

1 ounce/2 tablespoons butter
1 onion, thinly sliced
½ teaspoon dried thyme
1 pound leeks, thinly sliced
2 ounces Gruyère or Emmenthal
   cheese, grated
3 eggs
½ pint/1¼ cups light cream
pinch of freshly grated nutmeg
salt and ground black pepper
mixed salad leaves, to serve

For the pastry

6 ounces/1⅓ cup all-purpose flour
3 ounces/6 tablespoons cold butter
1 egg yolk
2–3 tablespoons cold water
½ teaspoon salt

1 To make the pastry, sift the flour into a bowl and rub in the butter with your fingertips until it resembles bread crumbs. Make a well in the center.

2 Beat the egg yolk with the water and salt, pour into the well and combine the flour and liquid until it begins to stick together. Form into a ball. Wrap and chill for 30 minutes.

3 Butter six 4-inch muffin pans. On a lightly floured surface, roll out the dough until ⅛-inch thick, then using a 5-inch cutter, cut as many rounds as possible. Gently ease the rounds into the pans, pressing the pastry firmly into the base and sides. Re-roll the trimmings and line the remaining pans. Prick the bases all over and chill in the refrigerator for 30 minutes.

4 Preheat the oven to 375°F. Line the pastry shells with foil and fill with baking beans. Place on a baking sheet and bake for 6–8 minutes, until golden at the edges. Remove the foil and beans and bake for a further 2 minutes until the bases appear dry. Transfer to a wire rack to cool. Reduce the oven temperature to 350°F.

5 In a large frying pan, melt the butter over a medium heat, then add the onion and thyme and cook for 3–5 minutes, until the onion is just softened, stirring frequently. Add the leeks and cook for 10–12 minutes, until they are soft and tender, stirring occasionally. Divide the leek mixture among the pastry shells and sprinkle each with cheese, dividing it evenly.

6 In a medium bowl, beat the eggs, cream, nutmeg and salt and pepper. Place the pastry shells on a baking sheet and pour in the egg and cream mixture. Bake for 15–20 minutes, until set and golden. Transfer the tartlets to a wire rack to cool slightly, then remove them from the pans and serve either warm or at room temperature with salad leaves.

Zucchini Fritters with Chile Jam

*Chile jam is hot, sweet and sticky –
rather like a thick chutney. It adds a
delicious piquancy to these light
zucchini fritters, which are always a
popular dish.*

INGREDIENTS

Makes 12 Fritters

1 pound/3½ cups coarsely grated zucchini

50g/2oz/⅔ cup freshly grated
   Parmesan cheese

2 eggs, beaten

4 tablespoons all-purpose flour

vegetable oil, for frying

salt and ground black pepper

For the chile jam

5 tablespoons olive oil

4 large onions, diced

4 garlic cloves, chopped

1–2 fresh green chiles, seeded
   and sliced

2 tablespoons dark brown sugar

1 First make the chile jam. Heat
the oil in a frying pan until
hot, then add the onions and the
garlic. Reduce the heat to low, then
cook for 20 minutes, stirring
frequently, until the onions are
very soft.

COOK'S TIP

Stored in an airtight jar in the
refrigerator, the chile jam will
keep for up to 1 week

2 Leave the onion mixture to
cool, then transfer to a food
processor or blender. Add the
chiles and sugar and blend until
smooth, then return the mixture
to the pan. Cook for a further
10 minutes, stirring frequently,
until the liquid evaporates and the
mixture has the consistency of
jam. Cool slightly.

3 To make the fritters, squeeze
the zucchini in a dish towel to
remove any excess liquid, then
combine with the Parmesan, eggs,
and flour and season to taste with
salt and pepper.

4 Heat enough oil to cover the
base of a large frying pan. Add
2 tablespoons of the mixture for
each fritter and cook three fritters
at a time. Cook for 2–3 minutes on
each side until golden, then keep
warm while you cook the rest of
the fritters. Drain on paper towels
and serve warm with a spoonful of
the chile jam.

v

Son-in-law Eggs

This fascinating name comes from a story about a prospective bridegroom who wanted to impress his future mother-in-law and devised a recipe from the only other dish he knew how to make – boiled eggs. The hard-boiled eggs are deep fried and then drenched with a sweet piquant tamarind sauce.

INGREDIENTS

Serves 4–6

3 ounces/generous ⅓ cup palm sugar

4 tablespoons light soy sauce

7 tablespoons tamarind juice

oil, for frying

6 shallots, thinly sliced

6 garlic cloves, thinly sliced

6 fresh red chiles, seeded and sliced

6 hard-boiled eggs, shelled

fresh cilantro sprigs, to garnish

lettuce, to serve

1 Combine the palm sugar, soy sauce and tamarind juice in a small pan. Bring to the boil, stirring until the sugar dissolves, then simmer the sauce for about 5 minutes.

2 Taste and add more palm sugar, soy sauce or tamarind juice, if necessary. It should be sweet, salty and slightly sour. Transfer the sauce to a bowl and set aside until needed.

3 Heat 2 tablespoons of the oil in a frying pan and cook the shallots, garlic and chiles until golden brown. Transfer the mixture to a bowl and set aside.

4 Deep-fry the eggs in hot oil for 3–5 minutes, until golden brown. Drain on kitchen paper, quarter and arrange on a bed of lettuce. Sprinkle the shallot mixture over, drizzle with the sauce and garnish with cilantro.

Fried Rice Balls Stuffed with Mozzarella

V

These deep-fried balls of risotto go by the name of suppli al telefono – *telephone wires – in their native Italy. Stuffed with mozzarella cheese, they are very popular snacks, which is hardly surprising, since they are quite delicious. They make a wonderful start to any meal.*

INGREDIENTS

Serves 4

1 quantity Risotto alla Milanese, made without the saffron and with vegetable stock

3 eggs

bread crumbs and all-purpose flour, to coat

4 ounces/⅔ cup mozzarella cheese, cut into small cubes

oil, for deep-frying

dressed frisée lettuce and cherry tomatoes, to serve

1 Put the risotto in a bowl and leave it to cool completely. Beat two of the eggs, and stir them into the cooled risotto until well mixed.

2 Use your hands to form the rice mixture into balls the size of a large egg. If the mixture is too moist to hold its shape well, stir in a few spoonfuls of bread crumbs. Poke a hole in the center of each ball with your finger, then fill it with small cubes of mozzarella, and close the hole over again with the rice mixture.

3 Heat the oil for deep-frying until a small piece of bread sizzles as soon as it is dropped in.

4 Spread some flour on a plate. Beat the remaining egg in a shallow bowl. Sprinkle another plate with bread crumbs. Roll the balls in the flour, then in the egg, and, finally, in the bread crumbs.

5 Fry the rice balls, a few at a time, in the hot oil until golden and crisp. Drain on paper towels and keep warm while the remaining balls are being fried. Serve immediately, with a simple salad of dressed frisée lettuce leaves and cherry tomatoes.

COOK'S TIP

These provide the perfect solution for what to do with leftover risotto, since they are best made with a cold mixture, cooked the day before.

V

Greek Eggplant and Spinach Pie

Eggplant layered with spinach, feta cheese and rice make a flavorsome and dramatic filling for a pie. It can be served warm or cold in elegant slices.

Serves 12

13 ounces unsweetened pastry, thawed
   if frozen
3–4 tablespoons olive oil
1 large eggplant, sliced
1 onion, chopped
1 garlic clove, crushed
6 ounces spinach, washed
4 eggs
3 ounces/½ cup crumbled feta cheese
1½ ounces/½ cup freshly grated
   Parmesan cheese
4 tablespoons plain yogurt
6 tablespoons milk
8 ounces/2 cups cooked white or brown
   long grain rice
salt and ground black pepper

2 Heat 2–3 tablespoons of the oil in a frying pan and fry the eggplant slices for 6–8 minutes on each side, until golden. You may need to add a little more oil at first, but this will be released as the flesh softens. Lift out and drain well on paper towels.

3 Add the onion and garlic to the oil remaining in the pan, then cook over a gentle heat for 4–5 minutes, until soft, adding a little extra oil if necessary.

5 Spread the rice in an even layer over the base of the part-baked pastry shell. Reserve a few eggplant slices for the top, and arrange the rest in an even layer over the rice.

6 Spoon the spinach and feta mixture over the eggplant and place the remaining slices on top. Bake for 30–40 minutes until lightly browned. Serve the pie while warm, or leave it to cool completely before transferring to a serving plate.

1 Preheat the oven to 350°F. Roll out the pastry thinly and use to line a 10-inch quiche pan. Prick the base all over and bake for 10–12 minutes, until the pastry is pale golden. (Alternatively, bake blind, having lined the pastry with baking parchment and weighted it with a handful of baking beans.)

4 Chop the spinach finely, by hand or in a food processor. Beat the eggs in a large mixing bowl, then add the spinach, feta, Parmesan, yogurt, milk and the onion mixture. Season well with salt and ground black pepper and stir thoroughly to mix.

COOK'S TIP

Zucchini could be used in place of the eggplant. Cook the sliced zucchini in a little oil for 3–4 minutes, until evenly golden. You will need to use three to four standard zucchini, or choose baby zucchini instead and slice them horizontally.

FISH APPETIZERS

~

Fish is always a popular first course, not least because it is such a versatile ingredient. Recipes here range from elegant pâtés and terrines to crisp croquettes and tasty fish cakes. Dishes that are served cold can be made in advance, so they are ideal for entertaining, freeing you from the kitchen to greet your guests in the knowledge that there are no lingering fishy smells. On the other hand, the appetizing aroma as you cook Deep-fried Whitebait or Seafood Pancakes will make fish-lovers' mouths water with anticipation.

Potted Salmon with Lemon and Dill

This sophisticated dish would be ideal for a dinner party. Preparation is done well in advance, so you can concentrate on the main course, or if you are really well organized, you can enjoy a pre-dinner conversation with your guests. If you cannot find fresh dill use 1 teaspoon dried dill instead.

INGREDIENTS

Serves 6

12 ounces cooked salmon, skinned

5 ounces/⅔ cup butter, softened

rind and juice of 1 large lemon

2 teaspoons chopped fresh dill

salt and ground white pepper

3 ounces/¾ cup sliced almonds,
   coarsely chopped

1 Flake the salmon into a bowl and then place in a food processor together with two-thirds of the butter, the lemon rind and juice, half the dill, and plenty of salt and pepper. Process until the mixture is quite smooth.

2 Mix in the sliced almonds. Check the seasoning and pack the mixture into small ramekins.

3 Sprinkle the remaining dill over the top of each ramekin. Clarify the remaining butter, and pour over each ramekin to make a seal. Chill. Serve with crudités.

Salmon Rillettes

*This is an economical way of serving
a first course of salmon.*

INGREDIENTS

Serves 6

12 ounces salmon fillets

6 ounces/¾ cup butter, softened

1 celery stick, finely chopped

1 leek, white part only, finely chopped

1 bay leaf

¼ pint/⅔ cup dry white wine

4 ounces smoked salmon trimmings

generous pinch of ground mace

4 tablespoons farmer's cheese

salt and ground black pepper

salad leaves, to serve

1 Lightly season the salmon.
Melt 1 ounce/2 tablespoons of
the butter in a medium sauté pan.
Add the celery and leek and cook
for about 5 minutes. Add the
salmon and bay leaf and pour the
white wine over. Cover and cook
for about 15 minutes, until tender.

2 Strain the cooking liquid into a
pan and boil until reduced to
2 tablespoons. Cool. Meanwhile,
melt 2 ounces/4 tablespoons of the
remaining butter and gently cook
the smoked salmon trimmings
until pale pink. Leave to cool.

3 Remove the skin and any
bones from the salmon fillets.
Flake the flesh into a bowl and add
the reduced, cooled cooking liquid.

4 Beat in the remaining butter,
with the ground mace and the
farmer's cheese. Break up the
cooked smoked salmon trimmings
and fold into the fresh salmon
mixture with all the juices from the
pan. Taste and adjust the seasoning.

5 Spoon the salmon mixture
into a dish or terrine and
smooth the top level. Cover with
plastic wrap and chill. The
prepared mixture can be left in the
refrigerator for up to 2 days.

6 To serve the salmon rillettes,
shape the mixture into oval
quenelles using two dessert spoons
and arrange on individual plates
with the salad leaves. Accompany
the rillettes with brown bread,
if you like.

Smoked Salmon Pâté

Making this pâté in individual ramekins wrapped in extra smoked salmon gives a really special presentation. Taste the salmon pâté as you are making it, as some people prefer more lemon juice and salt and pepper.

INGREDIENTS

Serves 4

12 ounces thinly sliced smoked salmon

¼ pint/⅔ cup heavy cream

finely grated rind and juice of 1 lemon

salt and ground black pepper

Melba toast, to serve

1 Line four small ramekin dishes with plastic wrap. Then line the dishes with 4 ounces of the smoked salmon cut into strips long enough to flop a little way over the edges.

2 In a food processor fitted with a metal blade, process the rest of the smoked salmon with the heavy cream, lemon rind and juice and season to taste with salt and plenty of pepper.

3 Pack the lined ramekins with the smoked salmon pâté and wrap over the loose strips of salmon. Cover with plastic wrap and chill for 30 minutes. Invert onto plates and serve with Melba toast.

Brandade of Salt Cod

There are almost as many versions
of this creamy salt cod purée as there
are regions of France. Some contain
mashed potatoes, others truffles.
This fairly light recipe includes
garlic, but you can omit it and serve
the brandade on toasted slices of
French bread rubbed with garlic.

INGREDIENTS

Serves 6

7 ounces salt cod

8 fluid ounces/1 cup extra virgin olive oil

4 garlic cloves, crushed

8 fluid ounces/1 cup whipping or
    heavy cream

ground white pepper

shredded scallions, to garnish

herbed crispbread, to serve

1 Soak the fish in cold water for
24 hours, changing the water
often. Drain. Cut into pieces, place
in a shallow pan and pour in cold
water to cover. Heat the water until
simmering, then poach the fish for
8 minutes, until it is just cooked.
Drain, then remove the skin and
bone the cod carefully.

2 Combine the olive oil and
garlic in a small pan and heat
to just below boiling point. In
another pan, heat the cream until
it starts to simmer.

3 Put the cod into a food
processor, process it briefly,
then gradually add alternate
amounts of the garlic-flavored
olive oil and cream, while keeping
the machine running.

4 Once the mixture has the
consistency of mashed potato,
add white pepper to taste, then
scoop the brandade into a serving
bowl. Garnish with shredded
scallions and serve warm with
herbed crispbread.

COOK'S TIP

You can purée the fish mixture in
a mortar with a pestle. This gives
a better texture, but is
notoriously hard work.

Striped Fish Terrine

Serve this terrine cold or just warm, with a hollandaise sauce if you like.

INGREDIENTS

Serves 8

1 tablespoon sunflower oil
1 pound salmon fillet, skinned
1 pound sole fillets, skinned
3 egg whites
7 tablespoons heavy cream
1 tablespoon finely chopped fresh chives
juice of 1 lemon
4 ounces/scant 1 cup fresh or frozen
    peas, cooked
1 teaspoon chopped fresh mint
salt, ground white pepper and
    grated nutmeg
thinly sliced cucumber, salad cress and
    whole chives, to garnish

1 Grease a 1¾ pint/4 cup loaf pan or terrine pan with the oil. Slice the salmon thinly; cut it and the sole into long strips, 1-inch wide. Preheat the oven to 400°F.

2 Line the terrine pan neatly with alternate slices of salmon and sole, leaving the ends overhanging the edges. You should be left with about a third of the salmon and half the sole.

3 In a grease-free bowl, beat the egg whites with a pinch of salt until they form soft peaks. Process the remaining sole in a food processor. Spoon into a mixing bowl, season, then fold in two-thirds of the egg whites, followed by two-thirds of the cream. Put half the mixture into a second bowl and stir in the chives. Add nutmeg to the first bowl.

4 Process the remaining salmon, scrape it into a bowl and add the lemon juice. Fold in the remaining egg whites, then the remaining cream.

5 Process the peas with the mint. Season the mixture with salt and pepper and spread it over the base of the terrine, smoothing the surface with a spatula. Spoon over the sole with the chives mixture and spread evenly.

6 Add the salmon mixture, then finish with the plain sole mixture. Cover the top with the overhanging fish fillets and make a lid of oiled foil. Stand the terrine in a roasting pan and pour in enough boiling water to come halfway up the sides.

7 Bake for 15–20 minutes, until the top fillets are just cooked and the terrine feels springy. Remove the foil, lay a wire rack over the top of the terrine and invert both rack and terrine onto a lipped baking sheet to catch the cooking juices that drain out. Keep these to make fish stock or soup.

8 Leaving the pan in place, let the terrine stand for about 15 minutes, then turn it over again, invert it onto a serving dish and lift off the pan carefully. Serve warm, or chill in the refrigerator first and serve cold. Garnish with thinly sliced cucumber, salad cress and chives before serving.

Sea Trout Mousse

This deliciously creamy mousse makes a little sea trout go a long way. It is equally good made with salmon if sea trout is unavailable. Serve with crisp Melba toast or toasted pitta bread.

INGREDIENTS

Serves 6

9 ounces sea trout fillet

4 fluid ounces/½ cup Fish Stock

2 gelatine leaves, soaked in cold water, or
  1 tablespoon powdered gelatine,
  softened in water for 5 minutes

juice of ½ lemon

2 tablespoons dry sherry or dry vermouth

2 tablespoons freshly grated Parmesan

½ pint/1¼ cups whipping cream

2 egg whites

1 tablespoon sunflower oil, for greasing

salt and ground white pepper

For the garnish

2-inch piece of cucumber, with peel,
  thinly sliced and halved

fresh dill or chervil

1 Put the sea trout in a shallow pan. Pour in the fish stock and heat to simmering point. Poach the fish for about 3–4 minutes, until it is lightly cooked. Strain the stock into a pitcher and leave the trout to cool slightly.

2 Add the gelatine to the hot stock and dissolve, according to the packet instructions. Set aside until required.

3 When the trout is cool enough to handle, remove the skin and flake the flesh. Pour the stock into a food processor or blender. Process briefly, then gradually add the flaked trout, lemon juice, sherry or vermouth and Parmesan through the feeder tube, continuing to process the mixture until it is smooth. Scrape into a large bowl and leave to cool completely.

4 Lightly whip the cream in a bowl, then fold it into the cold trout mixture. Season to taste, then cover with plastic wrap and chill until the mousse is just starting to set. It should have the consistency of mayonnaise.

5 In a grease-free bowl, beat the egg whites with a pinch of salt until they are softly peaking. Then, using a large metal spoon, stir about one-third of the egg whites into the sea trout mixture to slacken it slightly, then fold in the remainder.

6 Lightly grease six ramekins or similar individual serving dishes. Divide the mousse among the dishes and level the surface. Place in the refrigerator for 2–3 hours, until set. Just before serving, arrange slices of cucumber and a small herb sprig on top of each mousse and sprinkle over a little chopped dill or chervil too.

Ceviche

You can use almost any firm-fleshed fish for this South American dish, provided that it is perfectly fresh. The fish is "cooked" by the action of the acidic lime juice. Adjust the amount of chile according to your taste.

INGREDIENTS

Serves 6

1½ pounds halibut, turbot, sea bass or
    salmon fillets, skinned

juice of 3 limes

1–2 fresh red chiles, seeded and
    very finely chopped

1 tablespoon olive oil

salt

For the garnish

4 large tomatoes, peeled, seeded
    and diced

1 ripe avocado, peeled and diced

1 tablespoon lemon juice

2 tablespoons olive oil

2 tablespoons fresh cilantro leaves

1 Cut the fish into strips measuring about 2 x ½ inches. Lay these in a shallow, non-metallic dish and pour over the lime juice, turning the fish strips to coat them all over in the juice. Cover with plastic wrap and leave for 1 hour.

2 Meanwhile, prepare the garnish. Mix together all the ingredients except the cilantro leaves. Set aside.

3 Season the fish with salt and sprinkle over the chiles. Drizzle with the olive oil. Toss the fish in the mixture, then re-cover. Leave in the refrigerator to marinate for 15–30 minutes more. To serve, divide the garnish among six plates. Arrange the ceviche, then sprinkle with cilantro.

Haddock and Smoked Salmon Terrine

This is a fairly substantial terrine, so serve modest slices, perhaps accompanied by fresh dill mayonnaise or a fresh mango salsa. Follow with a light main course and a fruit-based dessert.

INGREDIENTS

Serves 10–12

1 tablespoon sunflower oil, for greasing
12 ounces oak-smoked salmon
2 pounds haddock fillets, skinned
2 eggs, lightly beaten
7 tablespoons crème fraîche
2 tablespoons drained capers
2 tablespoons drained soft green or pink peppercorns
salt and ground white pepper
crème fraîche, peppercorns and fresh dill sprigs and arugula, to garnish

1 Preheat the oven to 400°F. Grease a 1¾ pint/4 cup loaf pan or terrine pan with the sunflower oil. Use some of the smoked salmon to line the loaf pan or terrine pan, allowing some of the ends to overhang the edges. Reserve the remaining smoked salmon until required.

2 Cut two long slices of haddock the length of the pan and set aside. Cut the remainder of the haddock fillets into small pieces. Season all of the haddock with salt and ground white pepper to taste.

3 Combine the eggs, crème fraîche, capers and green or pink peppercorns in a bowl. Add salt and pepper; stir in the haddock pieces. Spoon the mixture into the mold until it is one-third full. Smooth the surface with a spatula.

4 Wrap the long haddock fillets in the reserved salmon. Lay them on top of the layer of the fish mixture in the pan.

5 Cover with the rest of the fish mixture, smooth the surface and fold the overhanging pieces of salmon over the top. Cover tightly with a double thickness of foil. Tap the terrine to settle the contents.

6 Stand the terrine in a roasting pan and pour in boiling water to come about halfway up the sides. Place in the oven and cook for 45 minutes–1 hour, until the filling is just set.

7 Take the terrine out of the roasting pan, but do not remove the foil cover. Place two or three large heavy cans on the foil to weight it and leave until cold. Chill in the refrigerator for 24 hours.

8 About an hour before serving, remove the terrine from the refrigerator, lift off the weights and remove the foil. Carefully invert onto a serving plate and garnish with crème fraîche, peppercorns and sprigs of dill and arugula leaves.

COOK'S TIP

Use any thick white fish fillets for this terrine; try cod, whiting, hake or hoki.

Smoked Haddock Pâté

Arbroath smokies are small haddock that are beheaded and gutted but not split before being salted and hot-smoked, creating a great flavor.

INGREDIENTS

Serves 6

3 large Arbroath smokies, or smoked
   haddock fillets, about 8 ounces each
10 ounces/1¼ cups medium-fat
   soft cheese
3 eggs, beaten
2–3 tablespoons lemon juice
ground black pepper
fresh chervil sprigs, to garnish
lemon wedges and lettuce leaves,
   to serve

1 Preheat the oven to 325°F. Butter six ramekin dishes.

2 Lay the smokies in a single layer in an ovenproof dish and heat through in the oven for 10 minutes. Carefully remove the skin and bones from the smokies, then flake the flesh into a bowl.

3 Mash the fish with a fork and work in the cheese, then the eggs. Add lemon the juice and season with pepper to taste.

4 Divide the fish mixture among the ramekins and place in a roasting pan. Pour hot water into the roasting pan to come halfway up the dishes. Bake for 30 minutes, until just set.

5 Leave to cool for 2–3 minutes, then run a knife point around the edge of each dish and invert on to a warmed plate. Garnish with chervil sprigs and serve with the lemon wedges and lettuce.

Egg and Salmon Puff Parcels

These crisp elegant parcels conceal a mouth-watering collection of flavors and textures and make a delicious appetizer or lunch dish.

Serves 6

3 ounces/scant ½ cup long grain rice

½ pint/1¼ cups Fish Stock

12 ounces piece salmon tail

juice of ½ lemon

1 tablespoon chopped fresh dill

1 tablespoon chopped fresh parsley

2 teaspoons mild curry powder

6 medium eggs, soft-boiled and cooled

15 ounces flaky pastry, thawed if frozen

1 medium egg, beaten

salt and ground black pepper

1 Cook the rice in boiling fish stock for 15 minutes. Drain and set aside to cool. Preheat the oven to 425°F.

2 Poach the salmon, then remove the bones and skin and flake the fish into the rice. Add the lemon juice, herbs, curry powder and seasoning and mix well. Peel the soft-boiled eggs.

COOK'S TIP

You can also add a spoonful of cooked, chopped fresh or frozen spinach to each parcel.

3 Roll out the pastry and cut into six 5½–6-inch squares. Brush the edges with the beaten egg. Place a spoonful of rice in the middle of each square, push an egg into the middle and top with a little more rice.

4 Pull over the pastry corners to the middle to form a square parcel, squeezing the joins together well to seal. Brush with more egg, place on a baking sheet and bake the puffs for 20 minutes, then reduce the oven temperature to 375°F and cook the puffs for a further 10 minutes, or until golden and crisp underneath.

5 Cool slightly before serving, with a curry flavored mayonnaise or hollandaise sauce, if you like.

Seafood Pancakes

The combination of fresh and smoked haddock imparts a wonderful flavor to the filling.

INGREDIENTS

Serves 6

For the pancakes

4 ounces/1 cup all-purpose flour

pinch of salt

1 egg plus 1 egg yolk

$\frac{1}{2}$ pint/$1\frac{1}{4}$ cups milk

1 tablespoon melted butter, plus extra
for cooking

2–3 ounces/$\frac{1}{2}$–$\frac{3}{4}$ cup grated
Gruyère cheese

frisée lettuce, to serve

For the filling

8 ounces smoked haddock fillet

8 ounces fresh haddock fillet

$\frac{1}{2}$ pint/$1\frac{1}{4}$ cups milk

$\frac{1}{4}$ pint/$\frac{2}{3}$ cup light cream

$1\frac{1}{2}$ oz/3 tablespoons butter

4 tablespoons all-purpose flour

freshly grated nutmeg

2 hard-boiled eggs, peeled and chopped

salt and ground black pepper

1 To make the pancakes, sift the flour and salt into a bowl. Make a well in the center and add the egg and yolk. Whisk the egg, starting to incorporate the flour.

2 Gradually add the milk, whisking constantly until the batter is smooth and has the consistency of thin cream. Stir in the measured melted butter.

3 Heat a small crêpe pan or omelette pan until hot, then rub around the inside of the pan with a pad of paper towels dipped in melted butter.

4 Pour about 2 tablespoons of the batter into the pan, then tip the pan to coat the base evenly. Cook for about 30 seconds, until the underside of the pancake is brown.

5 Flip the pancake over and cook on the other side until it is lightly browned. Repeat to make 12 pancakes, rubbing the pan with melted butter between each pancake. Stack the pancakes as you make them between sheets of waxed paper. Keep warm on a plate set over a pan of simmering water.

6 Put the haddock fillets in a large pan. Add the milk and poach for 6–8 minutes, until just tender. Lift out the fish using a slotted spoon and, when cool enough to handle, remove the skin and any bones. Reserve the milk.

7 Measure the light cream into a measuring cup, then strain enough of the reserved milk into the cream to make up the quantity to $\frac{3}{4}$ pint/scant 2 cups in total.

8 Melt the butter in a pan, stir in the flour and cook gently for 1 minute. Gradually mix in the milk mixture, stirring constantly. Cook for 2–3 minutes, until thickened. Season with salt, black pepper and nutmeg. Coarsely flake the haddock and fold into the sauce with the eggs. Leave to cool.

9 Preheat the oven to 350°F. Divide the filling among the pancakes. Fold the sides of each pancake into the center, then roll them up to enclose the filling completely.

10 Butter six individual ovenproof dishes and then arrange two filled pancakes in each, or butter one large dish for all the pancakes. Brush with melted butter and cook for 15 minutes. Sprinkle over the Gruyère and cook for a further 5 minutes, until warmed through. Serve hot with frisée lettuce leaves.

Three-color Fish Kebabs

Don't leave the fish to marinate for more than an hour. The lemon juice will start to break down the protein fibers of the fish after this time, and it will then be difficult to avoid overcooking it.

INGREDIENTS

Serves 4

4 fluid ounces/½ cup olive oil

finely grated rind and juice of
   1 large lemon

1 teaspoon crushed chili flakes

12 ounces monkfish fillet, cubed

12 ounces swordfish fillet, cubed

12 ounces thick salmon fillet or
   steak, cubed

2 red, yellow or orange bell peppers,
   seeded and cut into squares

2 tablespoons finely chopped fresh flat
   leaf parsley

salt and ground black pepper

For the sweet tomato and chile salsa

8 ounces ripe tomatoes, finely chopped

1 garlic clove, crushed

1 fresh red chile, seeded and chopped

3 tablespoons extra virgin olive oil

1 tablespoon lemon juice

1 tablespoon finely chopped fresh flat
   leaf parsley

pinch of sugar

1 Put the olive oil in a shallow glass or china dish and add the lemon rind and juice, the chili flakes and pepper to taste. Whisk to combine, then add the fish chunks. Turn to coat evenly.

2 Add the bell pepper squares, stir, then cover with plastic wrap and marinate in a cool place for 1 hour, turning the fish chunks occasionally with a slotted spoon.

3 Drain the fish and peppers, reserving the marinade. Thread the fish and peppers onto eight oiled metal skewers. Cook the skewered fish on a barbecue or under a broiler for 5–8 minutes, turning once.

4 Meanwhile, make the salsa by mixing all the ingredients in a bowl, and seasoning to taste with salt and pepper.

5 Heat the reserved marinade in a small pan, remove from the heat and stir in the parsley, then season with salt and pepper to taste. Serve the kebabs hot, with the marinade spooned over and accompanied by the salsa.

COOK'S TIP

Use tuna instead of swordfish, if you like. It has a similar meaty texture and will be equally tasty and successful.

Deep-fried Whitebait

*A spicy coating on these fish gives
this favorite dish a crunchy bite.*

INGREDIENTS

Serves 6

4 ounces/1 cup all-purpose flour

½ teaspoon curry powder

½ teaspoon ground ginger

½ teaspoon cayenne pepper

pinch of salt

2½ pounds whitebait, thawed if frozen

vegetable oil, for deep-frying

lemon wedges, to garnish

1 Mix together the all-purpose
flour, curry powder, ground
ginger, cayenne pepper and a little
salt in a large bowl.

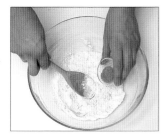

2 Coat the fish in the seasoned
flour, covering them evenly
and shaking off any excess.

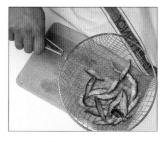

3 Heat the oil in a large, heavy
pan until it reaches a
temperature of 375°F. Deep-fry the
whitebait, in batches, for about
2–3 minutes, until the fish is
golden and crisp.

4 Drain the whitebait well on
paper towels. Keep warm in
a low oven until you have cooked
all the fish. Serve immediately,
garnished with lemon wedges for
squeezing over.

Smoked Salmon and Rice Salad Parcels

Feta, cucumber and tomatoes give a Greek flavor to the salad in these parcels, a combination that goes well with the rice, especially if a little wild rice is added.

INGREDIENTS

Serves 4

6 ounces/scant 1 cup mixed wild rice and
    basmati rice

8 slices smoked salmon, total weight
    about 12 ounces

4-inch piece of cucumber, finely diced

about 8 ounces feta cheese, cubed

8 cherry tomatoes, quartered

2 tablespoons mayonnaise

2 teaspoons fresh lime juice

1 tablespoon chopped fresh chervil

salt and ground black pepper

lime slices and fresh chervil, to garnish

1 Cook the rice according to the instructions on the packet. Drain, tip into a bowl and leave to cool completely.

2 Line four ramekins with plastic wrap, then line each ramekin with two slices of smoked salmon, allowing the ends to overlap the edges of the dishes.

COOK'S TIP
Use smoked sea trout in place of the salmon if you like.

3 Add the cucumber, feta and tomatoes to the rice and stir in the mayonnaise, lime juice and chervil. Mix together well. Season with salt and ground black pepper to taste.

4 Spoon the rice mixture into the salmon-lined ramekins. (Any leftover mixture can be used to make a rice salad.) Then fold over the overlapping ends of salmon so that the rice mixture is completely encased.

5 Place the fish parcels in the refrigerator to chill for 30–60 minutes, then invert each parcel onto a plate, using the plastic wrap to ease them out of the ramekins. Carefully peel off the plastic wrap, then garnish each parcel with slices of lime and a sprig of fresh chervil and serve.

Thai Fish Cakes with Cucumber Relish

These wonderful small fish cakes are very familiar and popular. They are usually accompanied with Thai beer, or you could choose a robust, oaked Chardonnay instead.

INGREDIENTS

Makes about 12

11 ounces white fish fillet, such as cod,
  cut into chunks

2 tablespoons Thai red curry paste

1 egg

2 tablespoons Thai fish sauce

1 teaspoon granulated sugar

2 tablespoons cornstarch

3 kaffir lime leaves, shredded

1 tablespoon chopped fresh cilantro

2 ounces green beans, thinly sliced

vegetable oil, for frying

Chinese mustard cress, to garnish

For the cucumber relish

4 tablespoons Thai coconut or
  rice vinegar

4 tablespoons water

2 ounces sugar

1 bulb pickled garlic

1 cucumber, quartered and sliced

4 shallots, thinly sliced

1 tablespoon chopped fresh root ginger

1 To make the relish, bring the vinegar, water and sugar to the boil. Stir until the sugar dissolves, then set aside to cool.

2 Combine the rest of the relish ingredients together in a bowl and pour the vinegar mixture over.

3 Combine the fish, curry paste and egg in a food processor and process well. Transfer the mixture to a bowl, add the rest of the ingredients, except the oil and garnish, and mix well.

4 Mold and shape the mixture into cakes about 2-inches in diameter and ¼-inch thick.

5 Heat the oil in a wok or deep-fat fryer. Deep-fry the fish cakes, working in small batches, for about 4–5 minutes, or until golden brown. Remove and drain on paper towels. Keep warm in a low oven. Garnish with Chinese mustard cress and serve with a little cucumber relish spooned on the side.

Salmon Cakes with Butter Sauce

Salmon fish cakes make a real treat for the start of a dinner party. They are also economical, as you could use any small tail pieces that are on special offer.

INGREDIENT

Makes 6

8 ounces salmon tail piece, cooked
2 tablespoons chopped fresh parsley
2 scallions, trimmed and chopped
grated rind and juice of ½ lemon
8 ounces mashed potato (not too soft)
1 egg, beaten
2 ounces/1 cup fresh white bread crumbs
3 ounces/6 tablespoons butter, plus extra
    for frying (optional)
vegetable oil, for frying (optional)
salt and ground black pepper
zucchini and carrot slices and fresh
    cilantro sprigs, to garnish

1 Remove all the skin and bones from the fish and mash or flake it well. Add the fresh parsley, scallions and 1 teaspoon of the lemon rind, and season with salt and lots of black pepper.

2 Gently work in the potato and then shape into six round shapes, triangles or croquettes. Chill the salmon cakes for 20 minutes.

3 Preheat the broiler. When chilled, coat the salmon cakes well in beaten egg and then in the bread crumbs. Broil gently for 5 minutes on each side, or until they are golden, or fry in a mixture of butter and oil.

4 To make the butter sauce, melt the butter, whisk in the remaining lemon rind, the lemon juice, 1–2 tablespoons water and seasoning to taste. Simmer for a few minutes and serve with the hot fish cakes, garnished with slices of zucchini and carrot and a sprig of fresh cilantro.

Herbed Plaice Croquettes

Serve these baby croquettes with a tartare sauce if you like. Simply chop some capers and gherkins, and stir into homemade or good-quality store-bought mayonnaise. Season to taste with salt and pepper.

INGREDIENTS

Serves 4

1 pound plaice or flounder fillets

½ pint/1¼ cups milk

1 pound cooked potatoes

1 fennel bulb, finely chopped

3 tablespoons chopped fresh parsley

2 eggs

½ ounce/1 tablespoon sweet butter

9 ounces/2 cups white bread crumbs

1 ounce/2 tablespoons sesame seeds

vegetable oil, for deep-frying

salt and ground black pepper

1 Gently poach the fish fillets in the milk for about 15 minutes, until the flesh flakes easily. Drain and reserve the milk.

2 Peel the skin off the fish and remove any bones. In a food processor fitted with a metal blade, process the fish, potatoes, fennel, parsley, eggs and butter.

3 Add 2 tablespoons of the reserved cooking milk and season with salt and plenty of ground black pepper. Mix well. Chill for 30 minutes, then shape into twenty even-size croquettes with your hands.

4 Mix together the bread crumbs and sesame seeds, then roll the croquettes in this mixture to form a good coating. Heat the oil in a large, heavy pan to 375°F or until it is hot enough to brown a cube of stale bread in 30 seconds. Deep-fry the croquettes, in small batches, for about 4 minutes, until they are golden brown all over. Drain well on paper towels and serve the croquettes hot.

Fish Sausages

This recipe originated in Hungary during the 17th century. It is still popular today.

Serves 4

13 ounces fish fillets, such as perch, pike,
   carp or cod, skinned

1 white bread roll

5 tablespoons milk

1½ tablespoons chopped fresh flat
   leaf parsley

2 eggs, well beaten

2 ounces/½ cup all-purpose flour

2 ounces/1 cup fine fresh white
   bread crumbs

vegetable oil, for shallow frying

salt and ground black pepper

deep-fried fresh parsley sprigs and lemon
   wedges, dusted with paprika, to garnish

1 Grind or process the fish fillets coarsely in a food processor or blender. Soak the roll in the milk for about 10 minutes, then squeeze it out. Mix the fish and bread together before adding the chopped parsley, one of the eggs and plenty of seasoning.

2 Using your fingers, shape the fish mixture into 4-inch long sausages, making them about 1-inch thick.

3 Carefully roll the fish "sausages" in the flour, then in the remaining egg and finally in the bread crumbs.

4 Heat the oil in a pan, then gently cook the "sausages" until golden brown all over. (You may need to work in batches.) Drain well on crumpled paper towels. Garnish with the deep-fried parsley sprigs and lemon wedges dusted with paprika.

Breaded Sole Batons

Goujons of lemon sole are coated in seasoned flour and then in bread crumbs, and fried until deliciously crisp. They are served with piquant tartare sauce.

INGREDIENTS

Serves 4

10 ounces lemon sole fillets, skinned

2 eggs

4 ounces/1½ cups fine fresh bread crumbs

3 ounces/6 tablespoons all-purpose flour

salt and ground black pepper

vegetable oil, for frying

tartare sauce and lemon wedges, to serve

1 Cut the fish fillets into long diagonal strips about ¾-inch wide, using a sharp knife.

2 Break the eggs into a shallow dish and beat well with a fork. Place the bread crumbs in another shallow dish. Put the flour in a large plastic bag and season with salt and plenty of freshly ground black pepper.

3 Dip the fish strips in the egg, turning to coat well. Place on a plate and then, taking a few at a time, shake them in the bag of flour. Dip the fish strips in the egg again, then in the bread crumbs, turning to coat well. Place on a tray in a single layer, not touching. Place in the refrigerator and let the coating set for at least 10 minutes.

4 Heat ½-inch oil in a large frying pan over a medium-high heat. When the oil is hot (a cube of bread will sizzle), fry the fish strips for 2–2½ minutes, in batches, turning once, taking care not to overcrowd the pan. Drain on paper towels and keep warm. Serve the fish with tartare sauce and lemon wedges.

SHELLFISH
APPETIZERS

~

For sheer visual appeal, shellfish appetizers are hard to beat.
There is little more tempting than a plate – or skewer – full
of plump, succulent sizzling shrimp and there is a uniquely
naughty pleasure found in the delightful messiness of peeling
them at the table. For more formal occasions and for those
with more sophisticated table manners, serve creamy crab
meat, delicately flavored scallops or a delicious shellfish
mousse. Even that old favorite, Shrimp Cocktail,
is given a fabulous, new, contemporary treatment.

Shrimp Cocktail

There is no nicer appetizer than a good, fresh shrimp cocktail – and nothing nastier than one in which soggy shrimp swim in a thin, vinegary sauce embedded in limp lettuce. This recipe shows just how good a shrimp cocktail can be.

INGREDIENTS

Serves 6

4 tablespoons heavy cream,
    lightly whipped
4 tablespoons mayonnaise
4 tablespoons tomato ketchup
1–2 teaspoons Worcestershire sauce
juice of 1 lemon
½ cos, romaine or other very crisp lettuce
1 pound/4 cups cooked peeled shrimp
salt, ground black pepper and paprika
6 large whole cooked unpeeled shrimp,
    to garnish (optional)
thinly sliced brown bread and lemon
    wedges, to serve

1 In a bowl, mix together the whipped cream, mayonnaise and tomato ketchup. Stir in Worcestershire sauce to taste, then stir in enough lemon juice to make a very tangy cocktail sauce.

2 Finely shred the lettuce and fill six individual glasses one-third full. Stir the shrimp into the sauce, then check the seasoning. Spoon the shrimp mixture generously over the lettuce.

3 If you like, drape a whole cooked shrimp over the edge of each glass (see Cook's Tip). Sprinkle each of the cocktails with ground black pepper and some paprika. Serve immediately, with thinly sliced brown bread and butter and lemon wedges for squeezing over.

> COOK'S TIP
>
> To prepare the garnish, peel the body shell from the shrimp and leave the tail "fan" for decoration.

Piquant Shrimp Salad

The Thai-inspired dressing, which includes fish sauce and sesame oil, adds a superb flavor to the rice noodles and jumbo shrimp. This delicious salad can be served warm or, alternatively, chilled before serving.

INGREDIENTS

Serves 6

7 ounces rice vermicelli or stir-fry
   rice noodles
8 baby corn cobs, halved
5 ounces snow peas
1 tablespoon sunflower oil
2 garlic cloves, finely chopped
1-inch piece of fresh root ginger,
   finely chopped
1 fresh red or green chile, seeded and
   finely chopped
1 pound raw peeled jumbo shrimp
4 scallions, thinly sliced
1 tablespoon sesame seeds, toasted
1 lemon grass stalk, thinly shredded,
   to garnish

For the dressing
1 tablespoon chopped fresh chives
1 tablespoon Thai fish sauce
1 teaspoon soy sauce
3 tablespoons peanut oil
1 teaspoon sesame oil
2 tablespoons rice vinegar

1 Put the rice vermicelli or noodles in a wide, heatproof bowl, pour over boiling water and leave for 5 minutes. Drain, refresh under cold water and drain again. Tip back into the bowl and set aside until required.

2 Boil or steam the corn cobs and snow peas for about 3 minutes; they should still be crunchy. Refresh under cold water and drain. Now make the dressing. Mix all the ingredients in a screw-top jar, close tightly and shake well to combine.

3 Heat the oil in a large frying pan or wok. Add the garlic, ginger and red or green chile and stir-fry for 1 minute. Add the jumbo shrimp and stir-fry for 3 minutes, until they have just turned pink. Add the scallions, corn cobs, snow peas and sesame seeds, and toss lightly to mix.

4 Tip the contents of the pan or wok over the rice vermicelli or noodles. Pour the dressing on top and toss well. Serve, garnished with lemon grass, or chill for 1 hour before serving.

Jumbo Shrimp with Romesco Sauce

This sauce, originally from the Catalan region of Spain, is served with fish and shellfish. Its main ingredients are sweet pepper, tomatoes, garlic and almonds.

INGREDIENTS

Serves 6–8

24 raw jumbo shrimp
2–3 tablespoons olive oil
flat leaf parsley, to garnish
lemon wedges, to serve

For the sauce

2 well-flavored tomatoes
4 tablespoons olive oil
1 onion, chopped
4 garlic cloves, chopped
1 canned pimiento, chopped
½ teaspoon dried chili flakes or powder
5 tablespoons Fish Stock
2 tablespoons white wine
10 blanched almonds
1 tablespoon red wine vinegar
salt

3 Toast the almonds under the broiler until golden. Leave to cool slightly, then transfer to a blender or food processor and grind coarsely. Add the remaining 2 tablespoons of oil, the vinegar and the remaining garlic clove and process until evenly combined. Add the tomato and pimiento sauce and process until smooth. Season with salt, to taste.

4 Remove the heads from the shrimp leaving them otherwise unpeeled and, with a sharp knife, slit each one down the back and remove the dark vein. Rinse and pat dry on paper towels. Preheat the broiler. Toss the shrimp in olive oil, then spread out in the broiler pan. Broil for about 2–3 minutes on each side, until pink. Arrange on a serving platter with the lemon wedges, and the sauce in a small bowl. Serve immediately, garnished with parsley.

1 To make the sauce, immerse the tomatoes in boiling water for about 30 seconds, then refresh them under cold water. Peel away the skins and coarsely chop the tomato flesh.

2 Heat 2 tablespoons of the oil in a pan, add the onion and 3 of the garlic cloves and cook until soft. Add the pimiento, tomatoes, chili, fish stock and wine, then cover and simmer for 30 minutes.

Italian Shrimp Skewers

*Parsley and lemon are all that is
required to create a lovely jumbo
shrimp dish. Broil them or cook on
a barbecue for an informal al fresco
summer appetizer.*

INGREDIENTS

Serves 4

2 pounds raw jumbo
   shrimp, peeled
4 tablespoons olive oil
3 tablespoons vegetable oil
3 ounces/1¼ cups very fine dry
   bread crumbs
1 garlic clove, crushed
1 tablespoon chopped fresh parsley
salt and ground black pepper
lemon wedges, to serve

1 Slit the shrimp down their
  backs and remove the dark
vein. Rinse in cold water and pat
dry on paper towels.

2 Put the olive oil and vegetable
  oil in a large bowl and add the
shrimp, mixing them to coat
evenly. Add the bread crumbs,
garlic and parsley and season with
salt and pepper. Toss the shrimp
thoroughly, to give them an even
coating of bread crumbs. Cover
and leave to marinate for 1 hour.

3 Thread the jumbo shrimp
  onto four metal or wooden
skewers, curling them up as you
work, so that the tails are skewered
neatly in the middle.

4 Preheat the broiler. Place the
  skewers in the broiler pan and
cook for 2 minutes on each side,
until the coating is golden. Serve
with lemon wedges.

Jumbo Shrimp in Sherry

*This dish just couldn't be simpler.
The sherry brings out the sweetness
of the seafood perfectly.*

INGREDIENTS

Serves 4

12 raw jumbo shrimp, peeled
2 tablespoons olive oil
2 tablespoons medium or dry sherry
few drops of Tabasco sauce
salt and ground black pepper

1 Using a very sharp knife, make
a shallow cut down the back of
each shrimp, then pull out and
discard the dark vein.

2 Heat the oil in a frying pan
and cook the shrimp for about
2–3 minutes, until pink. Pour over
the sherry and season to taste with
Tabasco sauce and salt and pepper.
Turn into a dish and serve the
shrimp immediately.

Sizzling Shrimp

*This dish works especially well with
tiny shrimp that can be eaten whole,
but any type of unpeeled shrimp will
be fine. Choose a small casserole or
frying pan that can be taken to the
table for serving while the garlicky
shrimp are still sizzling.*

INGREDIENTS

Serves 4

2 garlic cloves, halved
1 ounce/2 tablespoons butter
1 small fresh red chile, seeded and sliced
4 ounces/1 cup unpeeled cooked shrimp
sea salt and coarsely ground
   black pepper
lime wedges, to serve

1 Rub the cut surfaces of the
garlic cloves over the base and
sides of a frying pan, then throw
the garlic cloves away. Add the
butter to the pan and melt over a
fairly high heat until it just begins
to turn golden brown.

2 Toss in the sliced red chile
and the shrimp. Stir-fry for
1–2 minutes, until heated through,
then season to taste with sea salt
and plenty of black pepper. Serve
directly from the pan with lime
wedges for squeezing over.

COOK'S TIP

Wear gloves when handling chiles,
or wash your hands thoroughly
afterward, because the juices can
cause severe irritation to sensitive
skin, especially around the eyes,
nose or mouth.

Jumbo Shrimp with Mint, Dill and Lime

A wonderful combination – mint, dill and lime blend together to make a magical concoction to flavor succulent jumbo shrimp that will delight everyone who tries it.

INGREDIENTS

Serves 4

4 large sheets phyllo pastry

3 ounces/⅓ cup butter, melted

16 large cooked peeled jumbo shrimp

1 tablespoon chopped fresh mint, plus extra to garnish

1 tablespoon chopped fresh dill

juice of 1 lime

8 cooked unpeeled jumbo shrimp and lime wedges, to serve

1 Keep the sheets of phyllo pastry covered with a dry, clean cloth to keep them moist. Cut one sheet of phyllo pastry in half widthwise and brush with melted butter. Place one half on top of the other.

2 Preheat the oven to 450°F. Slit each of the jumbo shrimp in half down the back of the shrimp and remove the dark vein.

3 Place four shrimp in the centre of the phyllo pastry and sprinkle a quarter of the mint, dill and lime juice over the top. Fold over the sides, brush with butter and roll up to make a parcel.

4 Once you have filled all the parcels place them, join side down, on a greased baking sheet. Bake for 10 minutes, or until golden. Serve with whole jumbo shrimp, lime wedges and mint.

Scallop-stuffed Roast Peppers with Pesto

Serve these scallop-and-pesto-filled sweet red peppers with Italian bread, such as ciabatta or focaccia, to mop up the garlicky juices.

INGREDIENTS

Serves 4

4 squat red bell peppers

2 large garlic cloves, cut into thin slivers

4 tablespoons olive oil

4 shelled scallops

3 tablespoons pesto

salt and ground black pepper

freshly grated Parmesan cheese, to serve

salad leaves and fresh basil sprigs,
    to garnish

1 Preheat the oven to 350°F. Cut the peppers in half lengthwise, through their stalks. Scrape out and discard the seeds. Wash the pepper shells and pat dry with paper towels.

2 Put the peppers, cut-side up, in an oiled roasting pan. Divide the slivers of garlic equally among them and sprinkle with salt and ground black pepper to taste. Then spoon the oil into the peppers and roast for 40 minutes.

3 Using a sharp knife, carefully cut each of the shelled scallops in half horizontally to make two flat disks each with a piece of coral. When cooked, remove the peppers from the oven and place a scallop half in each pepper half. Then top with the pesto.

4 Return the pan to the oven and roast for 10 minutes more. Transfer the peppers to individual serving plates, sprinkle with grated Parmesan and garnish each plate with a few salad leaves and basil sprigs. Serve warm.

COOK'S TIP

Scallops are available from most supermarkets with a fresh-fish counter. Never cook scallops for longer than the time stated in the recipe, or they will be tough and rubbery.

Shrimp, Egg and Avocado Mousses

A light creamy mousse with lots of texture and a great mix of flavors. Serve chilled on the day you make it.

INGREDIENTS

Serves 6

a little olive oil

4 teaspoons powdered gelatine

juice and rind of 1 lemon

4 tablespoons mayonnaise

4 tablespoons chopped fresh dill

1 teaspoon anchovy paste

1 teaspoon Worcestershire sauce

1 large avocado, ripe but just firm

4 hard-boiled eggs, peeled and chopped

6 ounces/1 cup cooked peeled shrimp,
    coarsely chopped if large

8 fluid ounces/1 cup heavy or whipping
    cream, lightly whipped

2 egg whites, whisked

salt and ground black pepper

fresh dill or parsley sprigs, to garnish

warmed whole-grain bread or toast,
    to serve

1 Prepare six small ramekins. Lightly grease the dishes with olive oil, then wrap a waxed paper collar around the top of each and secure with tape. This makes sure that you can fill the dishes as high as you like and that the extra mixture will be supported while it is setting. The mousses will, therefore, look very impressive when you remove the paper. Alternatively, prepare just one small soufflé dish.

2 Dissolve the gelatine in the lemon juice with 1 tablespoon hot water in a small bowl set over hot water, until clear, stirring occasionally. Allow to cool slightly, then blend in the lemon rind, mayonnaise, dill, anchovy paste and Worcestershire sauce.

3 In a medium bowl mash the avocado flesh. Add the eggs and shrimp. Stir in the gelatine mixture and then fold in the cream, egg whites and seasoning to taste. When evenly blended, spoon into the ramekins or soufflé dish and chill for 3–4 hours. Garnish with the herbs and serve with bread.

COOK'S TIP

Other fish can make a good alternative to shrimp. Try substituting the same quantity of smoked trout or salmon, or cooked crab meat.

Crab and Ricotta Tartlets

Use the meat from a freshly cooked crab, weighing about 1 pound, if you can. Otherwise, look out for frozen brown and white crab meat.

INGREDIENTS

Serves 4

8 ounces/2 cups all-purpose flour

pinch of salt

4 ounces/$\frac{1}{2}$ cup butter, diced

8 ounces/1 cup ricotta cheese

1 tablespoon grated onion

2 tablespoons freshly grated
   Parmesan cheese

$\frac{1}{2}$ teaspoon mustard powder

2 eggs, plus 1 egg yolk

8 ounces crab meat

2 tablespoons chopped fresh parsley

$\frac{1}{2}$ teaspoon anchovy paste

1–2 teaspoon lemon juice

salt and cayenne pepper

salad leaves, to garnish

1 Preheat the oven to 400°F. Sift the flour and salt into a bowl, add the butter and rub it in until the mixture resembles fine bread crumbs. Stir in about 4 tablespoons cold water to make a firm dough.

2 Turn the dough onto a floured surface and knead lightly. Roll out the pastry and use to line four 4-inch muffin pans. Prick the bases with a fork, then chill for 30 minutes.

3 Line the tartlet shells with waxed paper and fill with baking beans. Bake for 10 minutes, then remove the paper and beans. Return to the oven and bake for a further 10 minutes.

4 Place the ricotta, grated onion, Parmesan and mustard powder in a bowl and beat until soft. Gradually beat in the eggs and egg yolk.

5 Gently stir in the crab meat and chopped parsley, then add the anchovy paste, lemon juice, salt and cayenne pepper, to taste.

6 Remove the tartlet shells from the oven and reduce the temperature to 350°F. Spoon the crab meat and ricotta filling into the shells and bake for 20 minutes, until set and golden brown. Serve hot with a garnish of salad leaves.

Garlic Shrimp in Phyllo Tartlets

Tartlets made with crisp layers of phyllo pastry and filled with garlic shrimp make a tempting appetizer.

INGREDIENTS

Serves 4

For the tartlets

2 ounces/4 tablespoons butter, melted
2–3 large sheets phyllo pastry

For the filling

4 ounces/½ cup butter
2–3 garlic cloves, crushed
1 fresh red chile, seeded and chopped
12 ounces/3 cups cooked peeled shrimp
2 tablespoons chopped fresh parsley
salt and ground black pepper

1 Preheat the oven to 400°F. Brush four individual 3-inch quiche pans with melted butter.

2 Cut the phyllo pastry into twelve 4-inch squares and brush with the melted butter.

3 Place three squares inside each tin, overlapping them at slight angles and carefully frilling the edges and points while forming a good hollow in each center. Bake for 10–15 minutes, until crisp and golden. Leave to cool slightly, then remove the tartlet shells from the tins.

4 Meanwhile, make the filling. Melt the butter in a large frying pan, then add the garlic, chile and shrimp and cook quickly for 1–2 minutes to warm through. Stir in the chopped fresh parsley and season with salt and plenty of black pepper.

5 Spoon the shrimp filling into the tartlets and serve immediately, perhaps with some sour cream.

Paella Croquettes

Paella *is probably Spain's most famous dish, and here it is used for a tasty fried tapas. In this recipe, the paella is cooked from scratch, but you could, of course, use leftover paella instead.*

Serves 4

pinch of saffron threads

¼ pint/⅔ cup white wine

2 tablespoons olive oil

1 small onion, finely chopped

1 garlic clove, finely chopped

5 ounces/⅔ cup risotto rice

½ pint/1¼ cups hot Chicken Stock

2 ounces/½ cup cooked peeled shrimp, deveined and coarsely chopped

2 ounces cooked chicken, coarsely chopped

3 ounces/⅔ cup baby peas, thawed if frozen

2 tablespoons freshly grated Parmesan cheese

1 egg, beaten

2 tablespoons milk

3 ounces/1½ cups fresh white bread crumbs

vegetable or olive oil, for shallow frying

salt and ground black pepper

flat leaf parsley, to garnish

1 Stir the saffron into the wine in a small bowl and set aside.

2 Heat the oil in a pan and gently cook the onion and garlic for 5 minutes, until softened. Stir in the risotto rice and cook, stirring constantly, for 1 minute.

3 Keeping the heat fairly high, add the wine-and-saffron mixture to the pan, stirring until it is all absorbed. Gradually add the stock, about 1 ladleful at a time, stirring constantly until all the liquid has been absorbed and the rice is cooked and tender – this should take about 20 minutes.

4 Stir in the shrimp, chicken, baby peas and freshly grated Parmesan. Season to taste with salt and pepper. Leave to cool slightly, then use two tablespoons to shape the mixture into 16 small lozenges.

5 Mix the egg and milk in a shallow bowl. Spread out the bread crumbs on a sheet of foil. Dip the croquettes in the egg mixture, then coat them evenly in the bread crumbs.

6 Heat the oil in a large frying pan. Then shallow-fry the croquettes for 4–5 minutes, until crisp and golden brown. Work in batches. Drain on paper towels and keep hot. Serve garnished with a sprig of flat leaf parsley.

MEAT AND POULTRY APPETIZERS

~

Look no further for appetizers to impress even the most
discerning guest. Salads, pâtés, meaty skewers or crisp-coated
chicken – these really are appetizers to sink your teeth into.
These tempting morsels of succulent meat and chicken have
been inspired by recipes from countries as far apart as France
and India, Poland and Indonesia, and they range from the
hot and spicy to the subtle and aromatic. Set the table,
set the mood and set the taste buds tingling.

Melon and Prosciutto Salad

*Sections of cool fragrant melon
wrapped with slices of air-dried
ham make a delicious appetizer.
If strawberries are in season, serve
with a savory-sweet strawberry
salsa, and watch it disappear.*

INGREDIENTS

Serves 4

1 large melon, cantaloupe, Charentais
   or honeydew
6 ounces prosciutto or Serrano ham,
   thinly sliced

For the salsa

8 ounces/2 cups strawberries
1 teaspoon superfine sugar
2 tablespoons sunflower oil
1 tablespoon orange juice
$\frac{1}{2}$ teaspoon finely grated orange rind
$\frac{1}{2}$ teaspoon finely grated fresh
   root ginger
salt and ground black pepper

1 Halve the melon and scoop the
seeds out with a spoon. Cut
the rind away with a paring knife,
then slice the melon thickly. Chill
until ready to serve.

2 To make the salsa, hull the
strawberries and cut them into
large dice. Place in a small mixing
bowl with the sugar and crush
lightly to release the juices. Add the
oil, orange juice, orange rind and
ginger. Season with salt and plenty
of ground black pepper.

3 Arrange the melon on a
serving plate, lay the ham over
the top and serve with a bowl of
salsa, handed around separately.

Prosciutto Salad with an Avocado Fan

*Avocados are amazingly versatile –
they can serve as edible containers,
be sliced or diced in a salad, or form
the foundation of a delicious soup or
sauce. However, they are at their
most elegant when sliced thinly and
fanned on a plate.*

INGREDIENTS

Serves 4

3 avocados

5 ounces prosciutto

3–4 ounces arugula leaves

24 marinated black olives, drained

For the dressing

1 tablespoon balsamic vinegar

1 teaspoon lemon juice

1 teaspoon prepared English mustard

1 teaspoon sugar

5 tablespoons olive oil

salt and ground black pepper

1 First, make the dressing.
Combine the balsamic
vinegar, lemon juice, mustard and
sugar in a bowl. Whisk in the olive
oil, season to taste with salt and
pepper and set aside.

2 Cut two of the avocados in
half. Remove the pits and
skins, and cut the flesh into
½-inch thick slices. Toss with half
the dressing. Place the prosciutto,
avocado slices and arugula on four
serving plates. Sprinkle the olives
and the remaining dressing over
the top.

3 Halve, pit and peel the
remaining avocado. Slice each
half lengthwise into eighths.
Gently draw a zester across the
quarters at ½-inch intervals to
create regular stripes.

4 Make four cuts lengthwise
down each avocado eighth,
leaving ½ inch intact at the end.
Carefully fan out the slices and
arrange them on the side of
each plate.

Prosciutto with Potato Rémoulade

Rémoulade is a classic piquant dressing based on mayonnaise. The traditional French version is flavored with mustard, gherkins, capers and herbs, but simpler variations are seasoned only with mustard. Lime juice brings a contemporary twist to this recipe for a cream-enriched dressing.

INGREDIENTS

Serves 4

2 potatoes, each weighing about 6 ounces, quartered lengthwise

¼ pint/⅔ cup mayonnaise

¼ pint/⅔ cup heavy cream

1–2 teaspoons Dijon mustard

juice of ½ lime

2 tablespoons olive oil

12 prosciutto slices

1 pound asparagus spears, halved

salt and ground black pepper

1 ounce wild arugula, to garnish

extra virgin olive oil, to serve

1 Put the potatoes in a pan. Add cold water to cover and bring to the boil. Add a pinch of salt, then simmer over a medium-low heat for about 15 minutes, or until the potatoes are tender, but do not let them get too soft. Drain them thoroughly and leave to cool, then cut into long, thin strips.

2 Beat together the mayonnaise, cream, mustard, lime juice and seasoning in a large bowl. Add the potatoes and stir carefully to coat them with the dressing.

3 Heat the oil in a griddle or frying pan and cook the prosciutto, in batches, until crisp and golden. Use a slotted spoon to remove the ham, draining each piece well. Cook the asparagus in the fat remaining in the pan for about 3 minutes, or until tender and golden.

4 Put a generous spoonful of potato rémoulade on each plate and top with several slices of prosciutto. Add the asparagus and garnish with arugula. Serve, offering olive oil to drizzle over.

Thai Beef Salad

All the ingredients for this traditional Thai dish – known as yam nua yang *– are widely available in larger supermarkets.*

INGREDIENTS

Serves 4

1½ pounds fillet or round steak

2 tablespoons olive oil

2 small fresh mild red chiles, seeded and sliced

8 ounces/3¼ cups shiitake mushrooms, sliced

For the dressing

3 scallions, finely chopped

2 garlic cloves, finely chopped

juice of 1 lime

1–2 tablespoons fish or oyster sauce

1 teaspoon soft light brown sugar

2 tablespoons chopped fresh cilantro

To serve

1 cos or romaine lettuce, torn into strips

6 ounces cherry tomatoes, halved

2-inch piece of cucumber, peeled, halved and thinly sliced

3 tablespoons toasted sesame seeds

1 Preheat the broiler until hot, then cook the steak for about 2–4 minutes on each side, depending on how well-done you like steak. (In Thailand, the beef is traditionally served quite rare.) Set the steak aside to cool for at least 15 minutes.

2 Use a very sharp knife to slice the meat as thinly as possible and place the slices in a bowl.

3 Heat the olive oil in a small frying pan. Add the sliced red chiles and the sliced mushrooms and cook for 5 minutes, stirring occasionally. Turn off the heat and add the broiled steak slices to the pan, then stir well to coat the beef slices in the chile and mushroom mixture.

4 Stir all the ingredients for the dressing together, then pour the dressing over the meat mixture and toss gently.

5 Sprinkle over the sesame seeds. Arrange the salad ingredients on a serving plate. Spoon the warm steak mixture in the center and serve immediately.

COOK'S TIP

~

If you can find one, a yellow chile would make a colorful addition to this dish. Substitute one for one of the red chiles.

Chopped Chicken Livers

It is said that remnants of this classic dish were found in sites dating back to AD 1400 and have been eaten in various guises ever since. The French love of liver-enriched pâtés is an inheritance from the Jews of Alsace, Strasbourg and the East, who brought their specialities with to France.

INGREDIENTS

Serves 4–6

9 ounces chicken livers

2–3 onions, chopped, plus ½ onion, finely chopped or grated

4 tablespoons rendered chicken fat or vegetable oil

3–4 scallions, thinly sliced

2–3 hard-boiled eggs, coarsely chopped or diced

2 teaspoons mayonnaise or firm chicken fat (optional)

1–2 teaspoons chopped fresh dill

salt and ground black pepper

chopped fresh dill or parsley, to garnish

lettuce, thin slices of crisp matzos or rye bread and a few slices of dill pickle, to serve

1 Broil the chicken livers lightly to bring the blood out onto the surface and render them kosher. Rinse, place in a pan, cover with cold water and bring to the boil. Reduce the heat, simmer gently for 5–10 minutes, then leave to cool in the water. (The livers should be firm but not dry and brown.)

2 In a large, heavy pan, cook the onions in the fat or oil over a medium heat, sprinkling with salt and pepper, until well browned and beginning to crisp, and caramelized around the edges.

3 To hand-chop the livers, use a round-bladed knife and chop the livers finely. Place in a bowl and mix in the fried onions and oil. If using a food processor, put the livers and fried onions in the bowl of the food processor with just enough oil from the fried onions to process to a thick paste.

4 In a bowl, combine the livers with the finely chopped or grated onion, the scallions, hard-boiled eggs, mayonnaise or chicken fat, if using, and chopped dill. Cover and chill the livers for an hour or so until firm.

5 Mound the chopped livers on plates and garnish with the chopped fresh dill or parsley. Serve with lettuce, matzos or rye bread and dill pickles.

Herbed Liver Pâté Pie

Serve this highly flavored pâté with a glass of Pilsner beer for a change from wine.

Serves 10

1½ pounds ground pork
12 ounces pork liver
12 ounces/2 cups diced cooked ham
1 small onion, finely chopped
2 tablespoons chopped fresh parsley
1 teaspoon German mustard
2 tablespoons kirsch
1 teaspoon salt
beaten egg, for sealing and glazing
1-ounce sachet aspic jelly
8 fluid ounces/1 cup boiling water
ground black pepper
mustard, bread and dill pickles, to serve

For the pastry
1 pound/4 cups all-purpose flour
pinch of salt
10 ounces/1¼ cups butter
2 eggs plus 1 egg yolk
2 tablespoons water

1 Preheat the oven to 400°F. To make the pastry, sift the flour and salt and rub in the butter. Beat the eggs, egg yolk and water, add to the dry ingredients and mix.

2 Knead the dough briefly until smooth. Roll out two-thirds on a lightly floured surface and use to line a 4 x 10-inch hinged loaf pan. Trim off any excess dough.

3 Process half the pork with all of the liver until fairly smooth. Stir in the remaining ground pork, the ham, onion, parsley, mustard, kirsch and seasoning.

4 Spoon the filling into the pan, and level the surface.

5 Roll out the remaining pastry on the lightly floured surface and use it to top the pie, sealing the edges with some of the beaten egg. Decorate with the pastry trimmings and glaze with the remaining beaten egg. Using a fork, make 3 or 4 holes in the top, for the steam to escape.

6 Bake for 40 minutes, then reduce the oven temperature to 350°F and cook for 1 further hour. Cover the pastry with foil if the top begins to brown too much. Remove from the oven and leave the pie to cool in the pan.

7 Make up the aspic jelly, using the boiling water. Stir to dissolve, then leave to cool.

8 Make a small hole near the edge of the pie with a skewer, then pour in the aspic through a waxed paper funnel. Chill for at least 2 hours before serving the pie in slices with mustard, bread and dill pickles.

Beef Satay with a Hot Mango Dip

Strips of tender beef are flavored with a delicious spicy marinade before being broiled, then served with a fruit dip.

INGREDIENTS

Makes 12 skewers
1 pound sirloin steak, trimmed

For the marinade
1 tablespoon coriander seeds
1 teaspoon cumin seeds
2 ounces/¹⁄₃ cup raw cashew nuts
1 tablespoon vegetable oil
2 shallots or 1 small onion,
    finely chopped
¹⁄₂-inch piece fresh root ginger,
    finely chopped
1 garlic clove, crushed
2 tablespoons tamarind sauce
2 tablespoons dark soy sauce
2 teaspoons sugar
1 teaspoon rice or white wine vinegar

For the mango dip
1 ripe mango
1–2 small fresh red chiles, seeded and
    finely chopped
1 tablespoon Thai fish sauce
juice of 1 lime
2 teaspoons sugar
¹⁄₄ teaspoon salt
2 tablespoons chopped fresh cilantro

1 Soak 12 bamboo skewers for 30 minutes. Slice the beef into long narrow strips and thread, zigzag-style, onto the skewers. Lay on a flat plate and set aside.

2 For the marinade, dry-fry the seeds and nuts in a large wok until evenly brown. Transfer to a mortar with a rough surface and crush finely with the pestle. Add the oil, shallots or onion, ginger, garlic, tamarind and soy sauces, sugar and rice or white wine vinegar.

3 Spread this marinade over the beef and leave to marinate for up to 8 hours. Cook the beef under a moderate broiler or over a barbecue for 6–8 minutes, turning to make sure of an even color. Meanwhile, make the mango dip.

4 Cut away the skin and remove the pit from the mango. Process the mango flesh with the red chiles, fish sauce, lime juice, sugar and salt until smooth, then add the cilantro. Serve immediately.

Barbecue-glazed Chicken Skewers

Known as yakitori in Japan, these skewers are popular throughout the country and are often served as an appetizer with drinks.

INGREDIENTS

Makes 12 skewers and 8 wing pieces

8 chicken wings

4 skinless chicken thighs,

4 scallions, blanched and cut into
   short lengths

For the basting sauce

4 tablespoons sake

5 tablespoons/⅓ cup dark soy sauce

2 tablespoons tamari

1 tablespoon mirin, or sweet sherry

1 tablespoon sugar

1 Remove the wing tip of the chicken at the first joint. Chop through the second joint, revealing the two narrow bones. Take hold of the bones with a clean cloth and pull, turning the meat around the bones inside out. Remove the smaller bone and discard. Set the wings aside.

2 Bone the chicken thighs and cut the meat into large dice. Thread the scallions and thigh meat onto 12 skewers.

3 Measure the basting sauce ingredients into a stainless-steel or enamel pan and simmer until reduced by two-thirds. Cool.

4 Heat the broiler to a moderately high temperature. Broil the skewers without applying any oil. When juices begin to emerge from the chicken, baste liberally with the sauce. Allow a further 3 minutes for the chicken on skewers and not more than 5 minutes for the wings.

Lamb Tikka

Creamy yogurt and ground nuts go wonderfully with these spices.

Makes about 20

1 pound lamb fillet
2 scallions, chopped

For the marinade

12 fluid ounces/1½ cups plain yogurt
1 tablespoon ground almonds,
   cashew nuts or peanuts
1 tablespoon vegetable oil
2–3 garlic cloves, finely chopped
juice of 1 lemon
1 teaspoon garam masala or curry powder
½ teaspoon ground cardamom
¼ teaspoon cayenne pepper
1–2 tablespoons chopped fresh mint

1 To prepare the marinade, stir together the marinade ingredients. In a separate small bowl, reserve about 4 fluid ounces/ ½ cup of the mixture to use as a dipping sauce for the meatballs.

2 Cut the lamb into small pieces and put in the bowl of a food processor with the scallions. Process, using the pulse action, until the meat is finely chopped. Add 2–3 tablespoons of the marinade and process again.

3 Test to see if the mixture holds together by pinching a little between your fingertips. Add a little more marinade, if necessary, but do not make the mixture too wet and soft.

4 With moistened palms, form the meat mixture into slightly oval balls, about 1½-inch long, and arrange in a shallow dish. Spoon over the remaining marinade, cover and chill the meatballs in the refrigerator for 8–10 hours or overnight.

5 Preheat the broiler and line a baking sheet with foil. Thread each meatball onto a skewer and arrange on the baking sheet. Broil for 4–5 minutes, turning them occasionally, until crisp and golden on all sides. Serve with the reserved marinade as a dipping sauce.

Pork Satay

Originating in Indonesia, satay are skewers of meat marinated with spices and grilled quickly over charcoal. It's street food at its best, prepared by vendors with portable grills who set up stalls at every road side and market place. It makes a great-tasting appetizer, too. It's not too filling but bursting with flavor. You can make satay with chicken, beef or lamb. Serve with satay sauce, and a cucumber relish if you like.

INGREDIENTS

Makes about 20

1 pound lean pork
1 teaspoon grated fresh root ginger
1 lemon grass stalk, finely chopped
3 garlic cloves, finely chopped
1 tablespoon medium curry paste
1 teaspoon ground cumin
1 teaspoon ground turmeric
4 tablespoons coconut cream
2 tablespoons Thai fish sauce
1 teaspoon granulated sugar
vegetable oil, for brushing
fresh herbs, to garnish

For the satay sauce

8 fluid ounces/1 cup coconut milk
2 tablespoons Thai red curry paste
3 ounces crunchy peanut butter
4 fluid ounces/½ cup Chicken Stock
3 tablespoons brown sugar
2 tablespoons tamarind juice
1 tablespoon Thai fish sauce
½ teaspoon salt

1 Cut the pork thinly into 2-inch strips and place in a shallow dish. Mix together the fresh root ginger, lemon grass, garlic, curry paste, cumin, turmeric, coconut cream, fish sauce and sugar.

2 Pour over the pork and leave to marinate for about 2 hours.

3 Meanwhile, make the sauce. Heat the coconut milk over a medium heat, then add the red curry paste, peanut butter, chicken stock and sugar.

4 Cook, stirring constantly, for about 5–6 minutes, until smooth. Add the tamarind juice, fish sauce and salt to taste.

5 Thread the meat onto skewers. Brush with oil and cook over charcoal or under a hot broiler for 3–4 minutes on each side, turning occasionally, until cooked and golden brown. Serve with the satay sauce garnished with fresh herbs.

Skewered Lamb with Red Onion Salsa

This summery tapas dish is ideal for outdoor eating, although, if the weather fails, the skewers can be cooked in the kitchen. The simple tomato and onion salsa makes a refreshing accompaniment – make sure that you use a mild-flavored red onion that is fresh and crisp, and a ripe tomato that is full of flavor.

INGREDIENTS

Serves 4

8 ounces lean lamb, cubed

½ teaspoon ground cumin

1 teaspoon paprika

1 tablespoon olive oil

salt and ground black pepper

For the salsa

1 red onion, very thinly sliced

1 large tomato, seeded and chopped

1 tablespoon red wine vinegar

3–4 fresh basil or mint leaves,
    coarsely torn

small mint leaves, to garnish

1 Place the lamb in a bowl with the cumin, paprika, olive oil and plenty of salt and pepper. Toss well until the lamb is coated with spices.

2 Cover the bowl with plastic wrap and set aside in a cool place for a few hours, or in the refrigerator overnight, so that the lamb absorbs the flavors.

3 Spear the lamb cubes on four small skewers – if using wooden skewers, soak them first in cold water for 30 minutes to prevent them from burning.

4 To make the salsa, put the sliced onion, tomato, red wine vinegar and basil or mint leaves in a small bowl and stir together until thoroughly blended. Season to taste with salt, garnish with mint, then set aside while you cook the lamb skewers.

5 Cook over the barbecue or under a preheated broiler for 5–10 minutes, turning frequently, until the lamb is well browned all over, but still slightly pink in the center. Serve hot, with the salsa.

Stuffed Garlic Mushrooms with Prosciutto

Portabello mushrooms can vary greatly in size. Choose similar-size specimens with undamaged edges.

INGREDIENTS

Serves 4

1 onion, chopped
3 ounces/6 tablespoons sweet butter
8 portabello mushrooms
½ ounce/¼ cup dried ceps, soaked in
    warm water for 20 minutes
1 garlic clove, crushed
3 ounces/¾ cup fresh bread crumbs
1 egg
5 tablespoons chopped fresh parsley
1 tablespoon chopped fresh thyme
salt and ground black pepper
4 ounces prosciutto di Parma or
    San Daniele, thinly sliced
fresh parsley, to garnish

1 Preheat the oven to 375°F. Cook the onion gently in half the butter for 6–8 minutes, until soft but not colored. Meanwhile, break off the stems of the Portabello mushrooms, setting the caps aside. Drain the dried mushrooms and chop these and the stems of the Portabello mushrooms finely. Add to the onion together with the garlic and cook for a further 2–3 minutes.

2 Transfer the mixture to a bowl, add the bread crumbs, egg, herbs and seasoning. Melt the remaining butter in a small pan and generously brush over the mushroom caps. Arrange the mushrooms on a baking sheet and spoon in the filling. Bake in the oven for 20–25 minutes, until they are well browned.

3 Top each mushroom with a slice of prosciutto, garnish with parsley and serve.

COOK'S TIP

• Garlic mushrooms can be easily prepared in advance, ready to go into the oven.
• Fresh bread crumbs can be made and then frozen. They can be taken from the freezer as they are required and do not need to be thawed first.

Chicken with Lemon and Garlic

Easy to cook and delicious to eat,
serve this tapas dish with aioli.

Serves 4

8 ounces skinless, boneless chicken
    breast portions
2 tablespoons olive oil
1 shallot, finely chopped
4 garlic cloves, finely chopped
1 teaspoon paprika
juice of 1 lemon
2 tablespoons chopped fresh parsley
salt and ground black pepper
flat leaf parsley, to garnish
lemon wedges, to serve

1 Sandwich the chicken between two sheets of plastic wrap or waxed paper. Bat out with a rolling pin or meat mallet until the portions are about ¼-inch thick.

2 Cut the chicken into strips about ½-inch wide. Heat the oil in a large frying pan. Stir-fry the chicken strips with the shallot, garlic and paprika over a high heat for about 3 minutes, until lightly browned and cooked through.

3 Add the lemon juice and parsley and season with salt and pepper to taste. Serve with lemon wedges, garnished with flat leaf parsley.

Smoked Chicken with Peach Mayonnaise Tartlets

These are attractive and, because smoked chicken is sold ready-cooked, they require the minimum of culinary effort. The filling can be prepared a day in advance and chilled, but do not fill the pastry shells until you are ready to serve them, or they will become soggy.

INGREDIENTS

Makes 12

1 ounce/2 tablespoons butter

3 sheets phyllo pastry, each measuring
18 x 11 inches, thawed if frozen

2 skinless, boneless smoked chicken
breast portions, thinly sliced

¼ pint/⅗ cup mayonnaise

grated rind of 1 lime

2 tablespoons lime juice

2 ripe peaches, peeled, pitted
and chopped

salt and ground black pepper

fresh tarragon sprigs,
lime slices and salad leaves,
to garnish

1 Preheat the oven to 400°F.
Melt the butter in a small pan.
Brush 12 small individual muffin pans with a little of the melted butter. Cut each sheet of phyllo pastry into 12 equal rounds large enough to line the pans, allowing enough to stand up above the tops of the pans.

2 Place a round of pastry in each
pan and brush with a little melted butter, then add another round of pastry. Brush each with more melted butter and add a third round of pastry.

3 Bake the tartlets for 5 minutes,
or until the pastry is golden brown. Leave in the pans for a few moments before transferring to a wire rack to cool.

4 Mix the chicken, mayonnaise,
lime rind and juice and peaches and season to taste with salt and pepper. Chill this chicken mixture for at least 30 minutes, or up to 12 hours. When ready to serve, spoon the chicken mixture into the phyllo tartlets and garnish with tarragon sprigs, lime slices and salad leaves.

Pork and Bacon Rillettes with Onion Salad

Rillettes are portions of potted meat, and the most famous type is made in Tours, France, from pork and ham. This version makes a great appetizer or light meal.

INGREDIENTS

Serves 8

4 pound belly of pork, boned and cut into
    cubes (reserve the bones)
1 pound rindless fatty bacon,
    finely chopped
1 teaspoon salt
¼ teaspoon ground black pepper
4 garlic cloves, finely chopped
1 fresh bouquet garni containing parsley,
    bay leaf, thyme and sage
½ pint/1¼ cups water
rustic French bread, to serve

For the onion salad
1 small red onion, halved and
    finely sliced
2 scallions, cut into thin matchsticks
2 celery sticks, cut into thin matchsticks
1 tablespoon freshly squeezed lemon juice
1 tablespoon light olive oil
ground black pepper

1 In a large bowl, mix the pork, bacon and salt. Cover and leave at room temperature for 30 minutes. Preheat the oven to 300°F. Stir the pepper and garlic into the meat. Add the bouquet garni to the meat.

2 Spread the meat mixture in a large roasting pan and pour in the water. Place the bones from the pork on top and cover tightly with foil. Cook for 3½ hours.

3 Discard the bones and herbs, and ladle the meat mixture into a metal sieve set over a large bowl. Allow the liquid to drain. Repeat until all the meat is drained. Reserve the liquid. Use two forks to pull the meat apart into fine shreds.

4 Line a 2½ pint/6¼ cup terrine pan or deep, straight-sided dish with plastic wrap and spoon the shredded meat into it. Strain the reserved liquid through a sieve lined with cheesecloth and pour it over the meat. Leave to cool. Cover and chill in the refrigerator for at least 24 hours, or until set.

5 To make the onion salad, place the sliced onion, scallions and celery in a bowl. Add the lemon juice and olive oil and toss gently. Season with freshly ground black pepper, but do not add any salt as the rillettes is well salted.

6 Serve the rillettes, cut into thick slices, on individual plates with a little onion salad and thick slices of rustic French bread and sweet butter.

Deep-fried Lamb Patties

These patties are a tasty North African speciality – called kibbeh – of minced meat and bulghur wheat. They are sometimes stuffed with additional meat and deep-fried. Moderately spiced, they're good served with yogurt.

INGREDIENTS

Serves 6

1 pound lean lamb or lean ground lamb
   or beef
salt and ground black pepper
vegetable oil, for deep-frying
avocado slices and fresh cilantro sprigs,
   to serve

For the patties

8 ounces/1⅓ cups bulghur wheat
1 fresh red chile, seeded and chopped
1 onion, coarsely chopped

For the stuffing

1 onion, finely chopped
2 ounces/⅔ cup pine nuts
2 tablespoons olive oil
1½ teaspoon ground allspice
4 tablespoons chopped fresh cilantro

1 If necessary, chop the lamb and process in a blender or food processor until minced. Divide into two equal portions.

2 For the patties, soak the bulghur wheat for 15 minutes in cold water. Drain, then process in a blender or a food processor with the chile, onion, half the meat and salt and pepper.

3 For the stuffing, cook the onion and pine nuts in the oil for 5 minutes. Add the allspice and remaining meat and cook gently, breaking up the meat with a wooden spoon, until browned. Stir in the cilantro and seasoning.

4 Turn the patty mixture out onto a work surface and shape into a cake. Cut into 12 wedges.

5 Flatten one piece and spoon some stuffing into the center. Bring the edges of the patty up over the stuffing , making sure that the filling is completely encased.

6 Heat oil to a depth of 2 inches in a large pan until a few patty crumbs sizzle on the surface.

7 Lower half of the filled patties into the oil and deep-fry for about 5 minutes, until golden. Drain on paper towels and keep hot while cooking the remainder. Serve with avocado slices and cilantro sprigs.

Spicy Koftas

These tasty meatballs will have to be cooked in batches.

INGREDIENTS

Makes 20–25

1 pound lean ground beef

2 tablespoons finely ground ginger

2 tablespoons finely chopped garlic

4 fresh green chiles, finely chopped

1 small onion, finely chopped

1 egg

½ teaspoon ground turmeric

1 teaspoon garam masala

2 ounces/2 cups cilantro
    leaves, chopped

4–6 mint leaves, chopped, or
    ½ teaspoon mint sauce

6 ounces raw potato

salt

vegetable oil, for deep-frying

1 Place the beef in a large bowl with the ground ginger, garlic, chiles, onion, egg, turmeric, garam masala and herbs. Grate the potato into the bowl, and season with salt. Knead together to blend well and form a soft dough.

COOK'S TIP

Leftover koftas can be coarsely chopped and packed into pitta bread spread with chutney or relish for a quick and delicious snack.

2 Using your fingers, shape the kofta mixture into portions the size of golf balls. You should be able to make 20–25 koftas. Set the balls aside at room temperature to rest for about 25 minutes.

3 In a wok or frying pan, heat the oil to medium-hot and deep-fry the koftas, in small batches, until they are golden brown in color. Drain well and serve hot.

Chicken Bitki

This is a popular Polish dish and makes an attractive appetizer when offset by deep red beet and vibrant green salad leaves.

INGREDIENTS

Makes 12

¹/₂ ounce/1 tablespoon butter, melted

4 ounces flat mushrooms, finely chopped

2 ounces/1 cup fresh white bread crumbs

12 ounces skinless, boneless chicken
   breast portions or guinea fowl,
   ground or finely chopped

2 eggs, separated

¹/₄ teaspoon grated nutmeg

2 tablespoons all-purpose flour

3 tablespoons vegetable oil

salt and ground black pepper

salad leaves and grated pickled beet,
   to serve

1 Melt the butter in a pan and cook the mushrooms for about 5 minutes, until soft, when the juices have evaporated. Leave to cool.

2 Mix together the mushrooms, bread crumbs, chicken or guinea fowl, egg yolks and nutmeg in a bowl and season to taste with salt and pepper.

3 Whisk the egg whites until stiff. Stir half into the chicken mixture to slacken it, then fold in the remainder.

4 Shape into 12 even-size meatballs, about 3-inches long and 1-inch wide. Roll in the flour to coat.

5 Heat the oil in a large, heavy frying pan and cook the bitki, turning frequently, for about 10 minutes, until evenly golden brown and cooked through. Serve immediately with salad leaves and pickled beet.

Golden Parmesan Chicken

These tasty morsels make a great appetizer for an informal dinner.

INGREDIENTS

Serves 4

4 skinless, boneless chicken
    breast portions
3 ounces/1½ cups fresh white
    bread crumbs
1½ ounces/½ cup finely grated
    Parmesan cheese
2 tablespoons chopped fresh parsley
2 eggs, beaten
4 fluid ounces/½ cup mayonnaise
4 fluid ounces/½ cup farmer's cheese
1–2 garlic cloves, crushed
2 ounces/4 tablespoons butter, melted
salt and ground black pepper

1 Cut each chicken portion into four or five chunks. Combine the bread crumbs, Parmesan, parsley and seasoning in a dish.

2 Dip the chicken pieces in the egg, then into the bread crumb mixture. Place in a single layer on a baking sheet. Chill for 30 minutes.

3 Meanwhile, to make the garlic mayonnaise, mix together the mayonnaise, farmer's cheese and garlic, and season to taste with ground black pepper. Spoon the mayonnaise into a small serving bowl. Cover and chill in the refrigerator until required.

4 Preheat the oven to 350°F. Drizzle the melted butter over the chicken pieces and cook them for about 20 minutes, until crisp and golden. Serve the chicken immediately accompanied by the garlic mayonnaise for dipping.

SALADS

Salads are among the most varied and versatile dishes. When summer weather arrives, cold dishes are a welcome change to the family menu, warm and cold salads make perfect appetizers for more formal occasions and, whether made with crisp green leaves or substantial legumes, they are the perfect accompaniment for all kinds of dishes all year around. This section includes a helpful glossary of ingredients, advice on vegetable and fruit preparation and recipes for popular dressings, plus a collection of truly mouth-watering recipes.

Salad Vegetables

The salad vegetable is any type of vegetable that earns its keep in a salad by virtue of freshness and flavor. Vegetables for a salad can be raw or lightly cooked. If cooked, they are best served at room temperature to bring out their full flavor. Here is a selection of the most commonly used salad vegetables.

Avocado

This has a smooth, buttery flesh when ripe and is an asset to many salads, of which Guacamole is perhaps the best known. Avocados can also be served on their own as an appetizer, with a light vinaigrette dressing or a spoonful of lemon mayonnaise, or even just a squeeze of lemon juice and salt.

Baby corn cobs

Baby corn cobs can be eaten whole, lightly cooked or raw, and should be served warm or at room temperature.

Carrots

These should be young, slender and sweet to taste. Either cooked or raw, they bring flavor and color to a salad.

Celery

A useful salad vegetable, celery is grown all year for its robust, earthy flavor. The crisp stems should be neither stringy nor tough. Celery partners well with cooked ham, apple and walnut in Waldorf Salad and is also used as a crudité.

Cucumbers

A common salad ingredient that turns up, invited or not, in salad bowls everywhere. The quality of this popular vegetable is best appreciated in salads with a strong flavor.

Fennel

The bulb (or Florence) variety has a strong, aniseed flavor and looks like a squat head of celery. Because the flavor can be dominant, it may be blanched in boiling water for 6 minutes before use in a salad.

Garlic

Strong to taste, garlic is essential to the robust cooking of South America, Asia and the Mediterranean. Garlic should be used carefully, as it can mask other flavors, but it is a vital part of salad preparation. To impart a very gentle hint of garlic, rub around the inside of your salad bowl with a cut clove. Another way to moderate the strength of fresh garlic is to store a few crushed cloves in a bottle of olive oil, and use the oil sparingly in dressings.

Green beans

The varieties are too numerous to mention here, but they all have their merits as salad vegetables. To appreciate the sweet flavor of young tender green beans, cook them for 6 minutes and then refresh immediately in cold running water so that the crispness and color are retained. An essential ingredient of Salade Niçoise, green beans are an ideal crudité and also make good partners to a spicy tomato sauce.

Mushrooms

These provide a rich tone to many salads and are eaten both raw and cooked. The oyster mushroom, which grows wild but is also cultivated, has a fine flavor and texture. White mushrooms are widely available and are often used raw, thinly sliced, in a mixed salad. Cremini mushrooms are similar to white mushrooms but have slightly more flavor.

Onions

Several varieties are suited to salads. The strongest is the small, brown onion, which should be chopped finely and used sparingly. Less strong is the large, white Spanish onion, which has a sweeter, milder flavor and may be used coarsely chopped.

Potatoes

These are a staple carbohydrate ingredient to add bulk to a salad or provide a main element.

Scallions

These have a milder flavor than the common onion and give a gentle bite to many popular salads.

Tomatoes

Technically a fruit rather than a vegetable, tomatoes are valued for their flavor and color. Small varieties usually ripen more quickly than large ones and have a better flavor.

Zucchini

These can be bitter to taste and are usually cooked before being combined with other young vegetables. Smooth in texture when cooked, they blend well with tomatoes, eggplant, bell peppers and onions. Use baby zucchini for a sweeter flavor if you want to serve them raw as a crudité.

Salad Fruit

The contents of the fruit bowl offer endless possibilities for sweet and savory salads.

Apples
This versatile fruit offers a unique flavor to both sweet and savory salads.

Apricots
You can use apricots raw, dried or lightly poached.

Bananas
These bring a special richness to fruit salads, although their flavor can often interfere with more delicate fruit.

Blackberries
With a very short season, wild blackberries have more flavor than cultivated.

Blueberries
These tight-skinned berries combine well with the sharpness of fresh oranges.

Cherries
Cherries should be firm and glossy and are a deliciously colorful ingredient in many kinds of fruit salad.

Cranberries
Too sharp to eat raw, but very good for cooking.

Dates
Fresh dates are sweet and juicy, dried ones have a more intense flavor. Both kinds work well in fresh fruit salads.

Figs
Green- or purple-skinned fruit, with sweet, pinkish-red flesh. Eat whole or peeled.

Gooseberries
Dessert types can be eaten raw, but cooking varieties are more widely available.

Grapefruit
These can have yellow, green or pink flesh; the pink-fleshed or ruby varieties are the sweetest.

Grapes
Large Muscat varieties, whose season runs from late summer to autumn, are the most highly prized and also the most expensive.

Kiwi fruit
Available all year around.

Kumquats
Tiny relatives of the orange and can be eaten raw or cooked.

Lemons and limes
Both these indispensable citrus fruits are used for flavor and to prevent fruit from turning brown.

Lychees
A small fruit with a hard pink skin and sweet, juicy flesh.

Mangoes
Tropical fruit with an exotic flavor and golden-orange flesh that is wonderful in sweet or savory salads.

Melons
These grow in abundance from mid- to late summer and provide a resource of freshness and flavor. Melon is at its most delicious served icy cold.

Nectarines
A relative of the peach with a smoother skin.

Oranges
At their best during winter, they can be segmented and added to sweet and savory salads.

Papayas
These fruits of the tropics have a distinctive, sweet flavor. When ripe they are yellow-green.

Peaches
Choose white peaches for the sweetest flavor, and yellow for a more aromatic taste.

Pears
Perfect for savory salads, and with strong blue cheese and toasted pecan nuts.

Physalis
Small, fragrant, pleasantly tart orange berries, wrapped in a paper cape.

Pineapples
Ripe pineapples resist firm pressure in the hand and have a sweet smell.

Plums
There are many dessert and cooking varieties.

Raspberries
Much-coveted soft fruits that partner well with ripe mango, passion fruit and strawberries.

Rhubarb
Technically a vegetable, too tart to eat raw.

Star fruit
When sliced, this makes a pretty shape perfect for garnishes.

Strawberries
A popular summer fruit.

Lettuces and Leaves

One particular aspect of lettuce that sets it apart from any other vegetable is that you can buy it in only one form – fresh.

Lettuce has been cultivated for thousands of years. In Egyptian times it was sacred to the fertility god Min. It was then considered a powerful aphrodisiac, yet for the Greeks and the Romans it was thought to have quite the opposite effect, making one sleepy and generally soporific. Chemists today confirm that lettuce contains a hypnotic similar to opium, and in herbal remedies lettuce is recommended for insomniacs.

There are hundreds of different varieties of lettuce. Today, an increasing choice is available in stores, so that the salad bowl can become a wealth of color, taste and texture with no other ingredient than a selection of leaves.

Butterhead

These are the classic round lettuces. They have a pale heart and floppy, loosely packed leaves. They have a pleasant flavor as long as they are fresh. Choose the lettuce with the best heart by picking it up at the base and gently squeezing to check there is a firm center.

Lollo rosso

Lollo rosso and lollo biondo – similar in shape but a paler green without any purple edges – are both non-hearting lettuces. Although they do not have a lot of flavor, they look superb and are often used to form a nest of leaves on which to place the rest of a salad.

Romaine

The romaine lettuce would have been known in antiquity. It has two names, romaine, used in the United States and France, and cos, derived from the Greek island where it was found. Romaine is considered to have the best flavor and is the correct lettuce for use in Caesar Salad.

Escarole

Escarole is one of the more robust lettuces in terms of flavor and texture. Like the curly-leafed frisée, escarole has a distinct bitter flavor. Served with other leaves and a well-flavored dressing, escarole and frisée will give your salad a pleasant "bite."

Oak leaf lettuce

Oak leaf lettuce, together with lollo rosso and lollo biondo, is another member of the loosehead lettuce group. Oak leaf lettuce has a very subtle flavor. It is a very decorative leaf and makes a beautiful addition to any salad, and a lovely garnish.

Bibb

Looking like a cross between a baby romaine and a furled butterhead lettuce, they have firm hearts. Their tight centers mean that they can be sliced whole and the quarters used for carrying slivers of smoked fish or anchovy as a simple appetizer.

Chinese cabbage

This has pale green, crinkly leaves with long, wide, white ribs. Its shape is a little like a very fat head of celery, which gives rise to another of its names, celery cabbage. It is crunchy, and since it is available all year around, it makes a useful winter salad component.

Radicchio

This is a variety developed from wild Belgian endive. It looks like a lettuce with deep wine-red leaves and cream ribs and owes its splendid foliage to careful shading from the light. If it is grown in the dark, the leaves are marbled pink. Its flavor is quite bitter .

Mâche

Mâche or lamb's lettuce is a popular winter leaf that does not actually belong to the lettuce family but is terrific in salads. Called lamb's lettuce in England, mâche has small, attractive, dark green leaves and grows in pretty little sprigs. Its flavor is mild and nutty.

Watercress

Watercress is perhaps the most robustly flavored of all the salad ingredients, and a handful of watercress is all you need to perk up a dull salad. It has a distinctive "raw" flavor, peppery and slightly pungent, and this, together with its shiny leaves, make it a popular garnish.

Arugula

Arugula has a wonderful peppery flavor and is excellent in a mixed green salad. It was eaten by the Greeks and Romans as an aphrodisiac. Since it has such a striking flavor, a little goes a long way; just a few leaves will transform a green salad and liven up a sandwich.

Herbs

For as long as salads have drawn on the qualities of fresh produce, sweet herbs have played an important part in providing individual character and flavor. When herbs are used in a salad, they should be as full of life as the salad leaves they accompany. Dried herbs are no substitute for fresh ones and should be kept for cooked dishes, such as casseroles. Salad herbs are distinguished by their ability to release flavor without lengthy cooking.

Most salad herbs belong finely chopped in salad dressings and marinades, while the robust flavors of rosemary, thyme and fennel branches can be used on the barbecue to impart a smoky herb flavor. Ideally salad herbs should be picked just before use, but if you cannot use them immediately, keep them in water to retain their freshness. Parsley, mint and cilantro will keep for up to a week in this way if also covered with a plastic bag and placed in the refrigerator.

Basil
Remarkable for its fresh, pungent flavor unlike that of any other herb, basil is widely used in Mediterranean salads, especially Italian recipes. Basil leaves are tender and delicate and should be gently torn or snipped with scissors, rather than chopped with a knife.

Chives
Chives belong to the onion family and have a mild onion flavor. The slender, green stems and soft mauve flowers are both edible. Chives are an indispensable flavoring for potato salads.

Cilantro
The chopped leaves of this pungent, distinctively flavored herb are popular in Middle Eastern and Eastern salads.

Lavender
This soothingly fragrant herb is edible and may be used in both sweet and savory salads, as it combines well with thyme, garlic, honey and orange.

Mint
This much-loved herb is widely used in Greek and Middle Eastern salads, such as Tzatziki and Tabbouleh. It is also a popular addition to fruit salads. Garden mint is the most common variety; others include spearmint and the round-leaf apple mint.

Clockwise from top left: thyme, cilantro, parsley, chives, lavender, rose , mint and basil.

Parsley
Curly and flat leaf parsley are both used for their fresh, green flavor. Flat leaf parsley is said to have a stronger taste. Freshly chopped parsley is used by the handful in salads and dressings.

Rose
Although it is not technically a herb, the sweet-scented rose can be used to flavor fresh fruit salads. It combines well with blackberries and raspberries.

Thyme
An asset to salads featuring rich, earthy flavors, this herb has a penetrating flavor.

Spices

Spices are the aromatic seasonings found in the seed, bark, fruit and sometimes flowers of certain plants and trees. Spices are highly valued for their warm, inviting flavors, and thankfully their price is relatively low. The flavor of a spice is contained in the volatile oils of the seed, bark or fruit; so, like herbs, spices should be used as fresh as possible. Whole spices keep better than ground ones, which tend to lose their freshness in 3–4 months.

Not all spices are suitable for salad-making, although many allow us to explore the flavors of other cultures. The recipes in this book use curry spices in moderation so as not to spoil the delicate salad flavors.

Above: Flavorsome additions to salads include (clockwise from top left) celery salt, caraway seeds, curry paste, saffron threads, peppercorns and cayenne pepper.

Caraway

These savory-sweet-tasting seeds are widely used in German and Austrian cooking and feature strongly in many Jewish dishes. The small ribbed seeds are similar in appearance and taste to cumin. The flavor combines especially well with German mustard in a dressing for frankfurter salad.

Cayenne pepper

Also known as chili powder, this is the dried and finely ground fruit of the hot chile pepper. It is an important seasoning in South American cooking and is often used when seasoning fish and shellfish. Cayenne pepper can be blended with paprika if it is too hot and should be used with care.

Celery salt

A combination of ground celery seed and salt, this spice is used for seasoning vegetables, especially carrots.

Cumin seeds

Often associated with Asian and North African cooking, cumin can be bought ground or as small, slender seeds. It combines well with coriander seeds.

Curry paste

Prepared curry paste consists of a blend of Indian spices preserved in oil. It may be added to dressings, and is particularly useful in this respect for showing off the sweet qualities of fish and shellfish.

Paprika

Made from a variety of sweet red bell pepper, this spice is mild in flavor and adds color.

Pepper

Undoubtedly the most popular spice used in the West, pepper features in the cooking of almost every nation. Pepper-corns can be white, black, green or red and should always be freshly milled rather than bought already ground.

Saffron

The world's most expensive spice, made from the dried stigma of a crocus, real saffron has a tobacco-rich smell and gives a yellow tint to liquids used for cooking. It can be used in creamy dressings and brings out the richness of fish and shellfish dishes. There are many powdered imitations, which provide color without the flavor of the real thing.

Oils, Vinegars and Flavorings

OILS

Oil is the main ingredient of most dressings and provides an important richness to salads. Neutral oils, such as sunflower, safflower or peanut, are ideally used as a background for stronger oils. Sesame, walnut and hazelnut oils are the strongest and should be used sparingly. Olive oil is prized for its clarity of flavor and clean richness. The most significant producers of olive oil are Italy, France, Spain and Greece. These and other countries produce two main grades of olive oil: estate-grown extra virgin olive oil and semi-fine olive oil, which is of a good, basic standard.

Olive oils

French olive oils are subtly flavored and provide a well-balanced lightness to dressings.

Greek olive oils are typically strong in character. They are often green with quite a thick texture and are unsuitable for making mayonnaise.

Italian olive oils are noted for their vigorous Mediterranean flavors. Tuscan oils are noted for their well-rounded, spicy flavor. Sicilian oils tend to be lighter in texture, although they are often stronger in flavor.

Spanish olive oils are typically fruity and often have a nutty quality with a slight bitterness.

Nut oils

Hazelnut and walnut oils are valued for their strong, nutty flavor. Tasting richly of the nuts from which they are pressed, both are usually blended with neutral oils for salad dressings.

Seed Oils

Peanut oil and sunflower oil are valued for their clean, neutral flavor.

SALAD FLAVORINGS

Capers

These are the pickled flower buds of a bush native to the Mediterranean. Their strong, sharp flavor is well suited to richly flavored salads.

Lemon and lime juice

The juice of lemons and limes is used to impart a clean acidity to oil dressings. They should be used in moderation.

Mustard

Mustard has a tendency to bring out the flavor of other ingredients. It also acts as an emulsifier in dressings and allows oil and vinegar to merge for a short period of time. The most popular mustards for use in salads are French, German, English and whole-grain.

Top left to right; Italian virgin olive oil, Spanish olive oil, Italian olive oil, safflower oil, hazelnut oil, walnut oil, peanut oil, French olive oil, Italian olive oil, white wine vinegar. Left to right bottom: lemon, olives, limes, capers and mustard.

Olives

Black and green olives belong in salads with a Mediterranean flavor. As a general rule, black olives are sweeter and juicier than green ones.

VINEGARS

White wine vinegar

This should be used in moderation to balance the richness of an oil. A good-quality white wine vinegar will serve most purposes.

Balsamic vinegar

Sweeter than other vinegars, only a few drops of balsamic vinegar are necessary to enhance a salad or dressing. It is also a good substitute for lemon juice.

Making Herbed Oils and Vinegars

Many herbed oils and vinegars are available commercially, but you can very easily make your own. Pour the oil or vinegar into a sterilized jar and add your flavoring. Leave to steep for 2 weeks, then strain and decant into an attractive bottle that has also been sterilized properly. Add a seal and an identifying label. Flavored vinegars should be used within 3 months, and flavored oils within 10 days. Fresh herbs should be clean and completely dry before you use them.

BASIL AND CHILI OIL

Steep basil and 3 fresh chiles in virgin olive oil, then decant. Add to tomato and mozzarella salads.

DILL AND LEMON OIL

Steep a handful of fresh dill and a large strip of lemon rind in virgin olive oil, then decant. Use for salads containing fish or shellfish.

LEMON AND LIME VINEGAR

Steep strips of lemon and lime rind in white wine vinegar, then decant. Pour into a sterilized, clean bottle and add fresh strips of mixed rind for color.

MEDITERRANEAN HERB OIL

Steep fresh rosemary, thyme and marjoram in extra virgin olive oil, then decant.

RASPBERRY VINEGAR

Pour vinegar into a pan with 1 tablespoon of pickling spices and heat gently for 5 minutes. Pour the hot mixture over the raspberries in a bowl and then add 2 fresh lemon thyme sprigs. Cover and leave the mixture to steep for 2 days in a cool, dark place. Strain the liquid and pour the flavored vinegar into a sterilized bottle and seal.

ROSEMARY VINEGAR

Steep a fresh rosemary sprig in red wine vinegar, then decant. Pour into a sterilized, dry bottle and add a few long stems of fresh rosemary as decoration.

TARRAGON VINEGAR

Steep tarragon in cider vinegar, then decant. Insert 2 or 3 long sprigs of tarragon into the bottle.

WARNING

There is some evidence that oils containing fresh herbs and spices can grow harmful molds, especially once the bottle has been opened and the contents are not fully covered by the oil. To protect against this, it is recommended that the herbs and spices are removed once their flavor has passed into the oil.

Left: Beautiful and delicious, herbal vinegars make exquisite gifts. From left: Tarragon Vinegar, Rosemary Vinegar, Raspberry Vinegar and Lemon and Lime Vinegar.

Vegetable Preparation

SHREDDING CABBAGE

Cabbage features in many salad recipes, such as coleslaw, and this method for shredding can be used for white, green or red varieties.

1 Use a large knife to cut the cabbage into quarters.

2 Cut the hard core from each quarter and discard; this part is not really edible when raw.

3 Slice each quarter to form fine shreds. Shredded cabbage will keep for several hours in the refrigerator, but do not dress it until you are ready to serve.

CHOPPING AN ONION

Chopped onions are used in many recipes and, whether they are finely or coarsely chopped, the method is the same; just vary the gap between cuts to give different-size pieces.

1 Cut off the stalk end of the onion and cut in half through the root, leaving the root intact. Remove the skin and place the halved onion, cut-side down, on the board. Make lengthwise vertical cuts into the onion, taking care not to cut right through to the root.

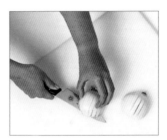

2 Make two or three horizontal cuts from the stalk end through to the root, but without cutting all the way through.

3 Turn the onion onto its side. Cut the onion across from the stalk end to the root. The onion will fall away in small squares. Cut further apart for larger squares.

PREPARING GARLIC

Don't worry if you don't have a garlic press: try this method, which gives wonderful, juicy results.

1 Break off the clove of garlic, place the flat side of a large knife on top and strike with your fist. Remove all the papery outer skin. Begin by finely chopping the clove.

2 Sprinkle over a little table salt and, using the flat side of a large knife blade, work the salt into the garlic, until the clove softens and releases its juices. Use the garlic pulp as required.

PREPARING CHILES

Chiles add a distinct flavor, but remove the fiery-hot seeds.

1 Always protect your hands, as chiles can irritate the skin; wear gloves and never rub your eyes after handling chiles. Halve the chile lengthwise and remove and discard the seeds.

2 Slice, finely chop and use as required. Wash the knife and chopping board thoroughly in hot, soapy water. Always wash your hands thoroughly after preparing chiles and avoid touching your eyes and face.

PEELING TOMATOES

If you have the time, peel tomatoes before adding them to sauces or purées. This avoids rolled-up, tough pieces of tomato skin that don't soften during cooking.

1 Make a cross in each tomato with a sharp knife and place in a bowl.

2 Pour over enough boiling water to cover and leave to stand for 30 seconds. The skins should start to come away. Slightly unripe tomatoes may take a little longer.

3 Drain the tomatoes and peel the skin away with a sharp knife. Don't leave the tomatoes in the boiling water for too long.

CHOPPING HERBS

Chop herbs just before you use them.

1 Remove the leaves and place on a clean, dry board. Use a large, sharp cook's knife.

2 Chop the herbs, as finely or as coarsely as required, by holding the tip of the blade on the board and rocking the handle up and down.

CUTTING JULIENNE STRIPS

Small julienne strips of vegetables make an attractive salad ingredient or garnish. Use this technique for carrots, cucumber and celery.

1 Peel the vegetable and use a large knife to cut it into 2-inch lengths. Cut a thin sliver from one side of the first piece so that it sits flat on the board.

2 Cut each piece into thin slices lengthwise. Stack the slices of vegetable and then cut through them again to make fine strips.

PREPARING SCALLIONS

Scallions make a crisp and tasty addition to salads. They are rather awkward to prepare, but the flavor is worth it.

1 Trim off the root of the scallion with a sharp knife. Peel away any damaged or tough leaves.

2 For an intense flavor and a green color cut the dark green part into thin matchsticks.

3 For a milder flavor just use the white part of the scallion, discard the root and slice thinly on a slight diagonal.

Fruit Preparation

CITRUS FRUIT

1 To peel, cut a slice from the top and from the base. Set the fruit base down on a work surface.

2 Cut off the peel lengthwise in thick strips. Take the colored rind and all the white pith (which has a bitter taste). Cut following the curve of the fruit.

1 To remove the thin, colored rind, use a vegetable peeler to shave off the rind in wide strips, taking none of the white pith. You can use these strips as they are or cut them into fine shreds with a sharp knife.

2 Alternatively, rub the fruit against the fine holes of a metal grater, turning the fruit so that you take just the colored rind and not the white pith. Or use a special tool, called a citrus zester, to take fine threads of rind. Finely chop the threads with a sharp knife for tiny pieces.

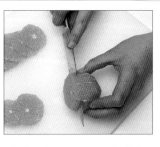

1 For slices, cut across the fruit in slices with a serrated knife.

2 For segments, hold the fruit over a bowl to catch the juice. Working from the side of the fruit to the center, slide the knife down first one side of a separating membrane and then the other. Continue cutting out segments.

FRESH CURRANTS

Pull through the tines of a fork to remove red, black or white currants from the stalks.

APPLES AND PEARS

1 For whole fruit, use an apple corer to stamp out the whole core from stalk end to base.

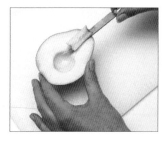

2 For halves, use a melon baller to scoop out the core. Cut out the stalk and base with a sharp knife.

3 For rings, remove the core and seeds. Set the fruit on its side and cut across, as required.

4 For slices, cut the fruit in half and remove the core and seeds. Set one half, cut-side down, and cut it across into neat slices. Repeat with the other half.

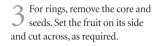

FRESH DATES

Halve the fruit lengthwise and lift out the pit.

PAPAYAS AND MELONS

Halve the fruit. Scoop out the seeds from the central hollow, then scrape away any fibers. For slices, follow the pear technique.

KIWI FRUIT, CARAMBOLA

Cut the fruit across into neat slices; discard the ends.

PINEAPPLES

1 To peel the pineapple, set the pineapple on its base, hold it at the top and cut thick slices of skin from top to bottom. Dig out any eyes that remain with the point of the knife.

2 For chunks, halve the peeled fruit lengthwise and then cut into quarters. Cut each quarter into spears and cut out the core. Cut each spear into chunks.

3 For rings, cut the peeled fruit across into slices and cut out the core.

KEEPING FRESH COLOR

If exposed to the air for long, the cut flesh of fruits, such as apples, bananas and avocados, starts to turn brown. So if cut fruit has to wait before being served, sprinkle the cut surfaces with lemon juice, or immerse hard fruits in water and lemon juice, but do not soak or the fruit may become soggy.

MANGOES

1 Cut lengthwise on either side of the pit. Then cut from the thin ends of the stone.

2 Remove the skin and cut the flesh into slices or cubes.

PEACHES, NECTARINES, APRICOTS AND PLUMS

Cut the fruit in half, cutting around the indentation. Twist the halves apart. Lift out the pit, or lever it out with the tip of a knife. Or cut the unpeeled fruit into wedges, removing the stone. Set each wedge, peel-side down, and slide the knife down to peel.

Salad Dressings

Although the ingredients of a salad are important, the secret of a perfect salad is a good dressing. A French dressing made from the very best olive oil and vinegar can rescue even the dullest selection of lettuce leaves, while a homemade mayonnaise is always impressive. If you are a confident and experienced salad dresser, you might feel able to add oil and vinegar directly to your salad just before serving, but the safest way of creating a perfect dressing is to prepare it in advance. Homemade dressings can be stored in the refrigerator for up to a week and will improve in flavor. Here is a selection of dressings that should be part of every cook's repertoire.

THOUSAND ISLANDS DRESSING

This creamy dressing is great with green salads and grated carrot, hot potato, pasta and rice salads.

INGREDIENTS

Makes about 4 fluid ounces/¹⁄₂ cup

5 tablespoons sunflower oil
1 tablespoon orange juice
1 tablespoon lemon juice
2 teaspoons grated lemon rind
1 tablespoon finely chopped onion
1 teaspoon paprika
1 teaspoon Worcestershire sauce
1 tablespoon finely chopped fresh parsley
salt and ground black pepper

Put all the ingredients into a screw-top jar and season to taste. Replace the lid and shake well.

FRENCH DRESSING

French vinaigrette is the most widely used salad dressing.

INGREDIENTS

Makes about 4 fluid ounces/¹⁄₂ cup

6 tablespoons extra virgin olive oil
1 tablespoon white wine vinegar
1 teaspoon French mustard
pinch of superfine sugar

1 Place the extra virgin olive oil and white wine vinegar in a clean screw-top jar.

2 Add the French mustard and a pinch of sugar.

3 Replace the lid and shake the jar vigorously.

FRENCH HERB DRESSING

The delicate scents and flavors of fresh herbs combine especially well in a French dressing. Use just one herb or a selection. Toss with a simple green salad and serve with good cheese, fresh bread and wine.

INGREDIENTS

Makes about 4 fluid ounces/¹⁄₂ cup

4 tablespoons extra virgin olive oil
2 tablespoons sunflower oil
1 tablespoon lemon juice
4 tablespoons finely chopped fresh herbs (parsley, chives, tarragon and marjoram)
pinch of superfine sugar

1 Place the olive oil and sunflower oil in a clean screw-top jar.

2 Add the lemon juice, chopped fresh herbs and sugar.

3 Replace the lid and shake the jar vigorously.

MAYONNAISE

Mayonnaise is a simple emulsion made with egg yolks and oil. For consistent results, make sure that both egg yolks and oil are at room temperature before combining. Homemade mayonnaise is made with raw egg yolks and may therefore be considered unsuitable for young children, pregnant mothers and the elderly.

Makes about ¹/₂ pint/1¹/₄ cups

2 egg yolks

1 teaspoon French mustard

¹/₄ pint/²/₃ cup extra virgin
    olive oil

¹/₄ pint/²/₃ cup peanut or
    sunflower oil

2 teaspoon white wine vinegar

salt and ground black pepper

1 Place the egg yolks and mustard in a food processor and process until smooth.

2 Add the olive oil, a little at a time, while the processor is running. When the mixture is quite thick, add the peanut or sunflower oil in a slow, steady stream through the feeder tube.

3 Add the vinegar and season to taste with salt and pepper.

YOGURT DRESSING

This is a less rich version of a classic mayonnaise and is much easier to make. It can be used as a low-fat substitute. Change the herbs as you like, or leave them out.

Makes about 7 fluid ounces/scant 1 cup

¹/₄ pint/²/₃ cup plain yogurt

2 tablespoons mayonnaise

2 tablespoons milk

1 tablespoon chopped fresh parsley

1 tablespoon chopped fresh chives

salt and ground black pepper

Put all the ingredients together in a bowl. Season to taste with salt and pepper and mix well.

BLUE CHEESE AND CHIVE DRESSING

Blue cheese dressings have a strong, robust flavor and are well suited to winter salad leaves, such as escarole, Belgian endive and radicchio.

Makes about 12 fluid ounces/1¹/₂ cups

3 ounces blue cheese (Stilton, Bleu
    d'Auvergne or Gorgonzola)

¹/₄ pint/²/₃ cup medium-fat
    plain yogurt

3 tablespoons olive oil

2 tablespoons lemon juice

1 tablespoon chopped fresh chives

ground black pepper

1 Remove the rind from the cheese. Combine the cheese with a third of the yogurt.

2 Add the remainder of the yogurt, the olive oil and the lemon juice.

3 Stir in the chopped chives and season to taste with ground black pepper.

BASIL AND LEMON MAYONNAISE

This luxurious dressing is flavored with lemon juice and two types of basil. Serve with all kinds of leafy salads, crudités or coleslaws. It is also good with baked potatoes or as a delicious dip for French fries. The dressing will keep in an airtight jar for up to a week in the refrigerator.

INGREDIENTS

Makes about ¹/₂ pint/1¹/₄ cups

2 extra large egg yolks
1 tablespoon lemon juice
¹/₄ pint/²/₃ cup extra virgin
    olive oil
¹/₄ pint/²/₃ cup sunflower oil
4 garlic cloves
handful of fresh green basil
handful of fresh opal basil
salt and ground black pepper

1 Place the egg yolks and lemon juice in a blender or food processor and process briefly until lightly blended.

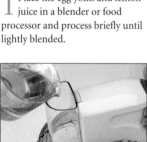

2 In a pitcher, stir together both oils. With the machine running, pour in the oil very slowly, a little at a time.

3 Once half of the oil has been added and the dressing has successfully emulsified, the remaining oil can be incorporated a little more quickly. Continue processing until a thick, creamy mayonnaise has formed.

4 Peel and crush the garlic cloves and add them to the mayonnaise. Alternatively, place the garlic cloves on a chopping board and sprinkle with a little salt, then flatten them with the heel of a heavy-bladed knife and chop the flesh. Flatten the garlic again to make a coarse purée. Add to the mayonnaise.

5 Remove the basil stalks and tear both types of leaves into small pieces. Stir into the mayonnaise.

6 Add salt and pepper to taste, then transfer the mayonnaise to a serving dish. Cover and chill until ready to serve.

Instant Dressings and Dips

If you need an instant dressing or dip, try one of these quick and easy recipes. Most of them use pantry ingredients.

CREAMY BLACK OLIVE DIP

Stir a little black olive paste into a carton of extra-thick heavy cream until smooth and well blended. Add salt, ground black pepper and a squeeze of lemon juice to taste. Serve chilled.

CRÈME FRAÎCHE DRESSING WITH SCALLIONS

Finely chop a bunch of scallions and stir into a carton of crème fraîche. Add a dash of chili sauce, a squeeze of lime juice, salt and ground black pepper.

YOGURT AND MUSTARD DIP

Mix a small carton of creamy, strained plain yogurt with 1–2 teaspoons whole-grain mustard. Serve with crudités.

HERB MAYONNAISE

Liven up ready-made French-style mayonnaise with a handful of chopped fresh herbs – try flat leaf parsley, basil, dill or tarragon.

TOMATO AND HORSERADISH DIP

Bring a little tang to a small carton or bottle of bottled strained tomatoes by adding some horseradish sauce or 1–2 teaspoons creamed horseradish and season with salt and pepper to taste. Serve with a selection of lightly-cooked vegetables.

PESTO DIP

For a simple, speedy, Italian-style dip, stir 1 tablespoon ready-made red or green pesto into a carton of sour cream. Serve with crisp crudités or wedges of oven-roasted Mediterranean vegetables, such as bell peppers, zucchini and onions.

SOFT CHEESE AND CHIVE DIP

Mix a tub of soft cheese with 2–3 tablespoons chopped fresh chives and season to taste with salt and black pepper. If the dip is too thick, stir in a little milk to soften it. Use as a dressing for all kinds of salads, especially winter coleslaws.

Above: Top row: Creamy Black Olive Dip, Crème Fraîche Dressing with Scallions. Second row: Herb Mayonnaise, Sun-dried Tomato Dip. Third row: Greek Yogurt and Mustard Dip, Soft Cheese and Chive Dip, Spiced Yogurt Dressing. Fourth row: Pesto Dip, Tomato and Horseradish Dip.

SPICED YOGURT DRESSING

Stir a little curry paste and chutney into a carton of yogurt.

SUN-DRIED TOMATO DIP

Stir 1–2 tablespoons sun-dried tomato paste into a carton of strained plain yogurt. Season to taste.

INSTANT
SALADS

Made in minutes, these salads are not so much thrown
together as tossed together, and their harmonious
combinations of ingredients and complementary dressings
belie the speed with which they are made. They are ideal for
easy entertaining or speedy midweek meals when you are
too tired, too busy or too hot to spend much time in
the kitchen. They can all be served as appetizers, and many
of them would also work well as a refreshing accompaniment
to fish or meat dishes.

V

Lettuce and Herb Salad

Stores now sell many different types of lettuce leaves all year, so try to use a mixture. Look for pre-packed bags of mixed baby lettuce leaves.

INGREDIENTS

Serves 4

½ cucumber

mixed lettuce leaves

1 bunch of watercress, about 4 ounces

1 Belgian endive head, sliced

3 tablespoons chopped fresh herbs, such as parsley, thyme, tarragon, chives, chervil

For the dressing

1 tablespoon white wine vinegar

1 teaspoon prepared mustard

5 tablespoons olive oil

salt and ground black pepper

3 Either toss the cucumber, lettuce, watercress, endive and herbs together in a bowl, or arrange them in the bowl in layers.

4 Stir the dressing, then pour over the salad and toss lightly to coat the salad vegetables and leaves. Serve immediately.

1 To make the dressing, mix the vinegar and mustard together, then whisk in the oil and seasoning.

2 Peel the cucumber, if you like, then halve it lengthwise and scoop out the seeds. Thinly slice the flesh. Tear the lettuce leaves into bitesize pieces.

Fresh Spinach and Avocado Salad

V

Young, tender spinach leaves make a change from lettuce. They are delicious served with avocado, cherry tomatoes and radishes in an unusual tofu sauce.

INGREDIENTS

Serves 2–3

1 large avocado
juice of 1 lime
8 ounces baby spinach leaves
4 ounces cherry tomatoes
4 scallions, sliced
$\frac{1}{2}$ cucumber
2 ounces radishes, sliced

For the dressing

4 ounces soft silken tofu
3 tablespoons milk
2 teaspoons mustard
$\frac{1}{2}$ teaspoon white wine vinegar
cayenne pepper
salt and ground black pepper
radish roses and fresh herb sprigs,
    to garnish

1 Cut the avocado in half, remove the pit and peel. Cut the flesh into slices. Transfer to a plate, drizzle over the lime juice and set aside.

2 Wash and dry the baby spinach leaves. Put them in a mixing bowl.

3 Cut the larger cherry tomatoes in half and add all the tomatoes to the mixing bowl with the scallions. Cut the cucumber into chunks and add to the bowl with the sliced radishes.

COOK'S TIP
~

Use soft silken tofu rather than the firm block variety. It can be found in most supermarkets in long-life cartons.

---

4 To make the dressing, put the tofu, milk, mustard, vinegar and a pinch of cayenne in a food processor or blender. Add salt and pepper to taste. Process for 30 seconds, until smooth. Scrape the dressing into a bowl and add a little extra milk if you like a thinner dressing. Sprinkle with a little extra cayenne, garnish with radish roses and herb sprigs and serve separately. Place the avocado slices with the spinach salad on a serving dish.

Mixed Green Salad

A good combination of leaves for this salad would be arugula, radicchio, mâche and frisée lettuce, with herbs, such as chervil, basil, parsley and tarragon.

INGREDIENTS

Serves 4–6

1 garlic clove, peeled

2 tablespoons red wine or sherry vinegar

1 teaspoon Dijon mustard (optional)

5–8 tablespoons extra virgin olive oil

7–8 ounces mixed salad leaves and herbs

salt and ground black pepper

1 Rub a large salad bowl with the garlic clove. Leave the garlic clove in the bowl.

2 Add the vinegar, salt and pepper and mustard, if using. Stir to mix the ingredients and dissolve the salt, then gradually whisk in the olive oil.

3 Remove and discard the garlic clove and stir the vinaigrette again to combine.

4 Add the salad leaves to the bowl and toss well. Serve the salad immediately, before it starts to wilt.

VARIATION

A salad like this should always contain some pungent leaves. Try young dandelion leaves when they are in season, but be sure to pick them far away from traffic routes and agricultural crop spraying.

Apple and Celeriac Salad

Celeriac, despite its coarse appearance, has a sweet and subtle flavor. Traditionally parboiled in lemony water, in this salad it is served raw, allowing its unique taste and texture to come through.

INGREDIENTS

Serves 3–4

1½ pounds celeriac, peeled

2–3 teaspoons lemon juice

1 teaspoon walnut oil (optional)

1 apple

3 tablespoons mayonnaise

2 teaspoons Dijon mustard

1 tablespoon chopped fresh parsley

salt and ground black pepper

1 Using a food processor or coarse cheese grater, shred the celeriac. Alternatively, cut it into very thin julienne strips, using a sharp knife.

2 Place the prepared celeriac in a bowl and sprinkle with the lemon juice and the walnut oil, if using. Stir well to mix.

3 Peel the apple if you like. Cut the apple into quarters and remove the core. Slice the apple quarters thinly crosswise and toss together with the celeriac.

4 Mix together the mayonnaise, mustard, parsley and salt and pepper to taste. Add to the celeriac mixture and stir well. Chill for several hours until ready to serve.

v

Green Bean and Sweet Red Pepper Salad

A galaxy of color and texture, with a jolt of heat from the chili, will make this a favorite salad.

INGREDIENTS

Serves 4

12 ounces cooked green beans, quartered

2 red bell peppers, seeded and chopped

2 scallions, both white and green
  parts, chopped

1 or more drained pickled serrano chiles,
  well rinsed, seeded and chopped

1 iceberg lettuce, coarsely shredded, or
  mixed salad leaves

green olives, to garnish

For the dressing

3 tablespoons red wine vinegar

9 tablespoons olive oil

salt and ground black pepper

1 Combine the green beans, bell peppers, scallions and chile(s) in a salad bowl.

2 To make the dressing, pour the red wine vinegar into a bowl or pitcher. Season with salt and black pepper to taste, then gradually whisk in the olive oil until well combined.

3 Pour the dressing over the prepared vegetables and toss lightly together to mix and to coat them thoroughly.

4 Line a large serving platter with the shredded lettuce or mixed salad leaves and arrange the vegetable mixture attractively on top. Garnish with the olives and serve.

Bell Pepper and Cucumber Salad

Generous quantities of fresh herbs transform ordinary ingredients.

INGREDIENTS

Serves 4

1 yellow or red bell pepper

1 large cucumber

4–5 tomatoes

1 bunch of scallions

2 tablespoons fresh parsley

2 tablespoons fresh mint

2 tablespoons fresh cilantro

2 pitta breads, to serve

For the dressing

2 garlic cloves, crushed

5 tablespoons olive oil

juice of 2 lemons

salt and ground black pepper

1 Slice the bell pepper, discard the seeds and core. Coarsely chop the cucumber and tomatoes. Place in a large salad bowl.

2 Trim and slice the scallions. Add to the cucumber, tomatoes and pepper. Finely chop the parsley, mint and cilantro and add to the bowl. If you have plenty of herbs, you can add as much as you like.

3 To make the dressing, blend the garlic with the olive oil and lemon juice in a pitcher, then season to taste with salt and pepper. Pour the dressing over the salad and toss lightly to mix.

4 Toast the pitta breads in a toaster or under a hot broiler until crisp and serve them alongside the salad.

VARIATION

If you like, serve this Middle Eastern salad in the traditional way. After toasting the pitta breads, crush them in your hand and then sprinkle the pieces over the salad before serving.

V

Classic Greek Salad

If you have ever visited Greece, you'll know that this salad accompanied by a chunk of bread makes a delicious first course.

INGREDIENTS

Serves 4

1 romaine lettuce

½ cucumber, halved lengthwise

4 tomatoes

8 scallions, sliced

black olives

4 ounces feta cheese

For the dressing

6 tablespoons white wine vinegar

¼ pint/⅔ cup extra virgin
   olive oil

salt and ground black pepper

1 Tear the lettuce leaves into pieces and place in a large bowl. Slice the cucumber and add to the bowl.

2 Cut the tomatoes into wedges and put them into the bowl.

COOK'S TIP

The salad can be assembled in advance and chilled, but should be dressed only just before serving. Keep the dressing at room temperature as chilling deadens the flavor.

3 Add the scallions to the bowl together with the olives, and toss well.

4 Cut the feta cheese into cubes and add to the salad.

5 Put the vinegar, olive oil and seasoning into a small bowl and whisk well. Pour the dressing over the salad and toss to combine. Serve immediately, with extra olives and chunks of bread.

Tomato and Feta Cheese Salad

Sweet, sun-ripened tomatoes are rarely more delicious than when served with feta cheese and olive oil.

INGREDIENTS

Serves 4

2 pounds tomatoes

7 ouncds feta cheese

4 fluid ounces/$\frac{1}{2}$ cup olive oil

12 black olives

4 fresh basil sprigs

ground black pepper

2 Slice the tomatoes thickly and arrange them attractively in a shallow serving dish.

3 Crumble the feta over the tomatoes, sprinkle with oil, then strew with the olives and basil sprigs. Season to taste with pepper and serve at room temperature.

1 Remove the tough cores from the tomatoes, using a small, sharp knife.

COOK'S TIP

Feta cheese has a strong flavor and can be salty. The least salty variety is imported from Greece and Turkey, and is available from specialist delicatessens.

V

Spinach and Mushroom Salad

This nutritious salad goes well with strongly flavored dishes. If served alone as a light lunch, it could be dressed with a French vinaigrette and served with warm, rustic French bread.

Serves 4

10 baby corn cobs

2 tomatoes

4 ounces/1½ cups mushrooms

1 onion cut into rings

20 small spinach leaves

1 ounce salad cress (optional)

salt and ground black pepper

2 Trim the mushrooms and cut them into thin slices.

3 Arrange all the salad ingredients attractively in a large bowl. Season with salt and pepper to taste and serve.

1 Using a sharp knife, halve the baby corn cobs lengthwise and slice the tomatoes.

Nutty Salad

A delicious salad with a tangy bite to it that can be served as an accompaniment to a main meal, or as an appetizer. For wholesome finger food at a party, serve mini pitta breads stuffed with the salad.

Serves 4

1 onion, cut into 12 rings

4 ounces/¾ cup canned red kidney beans, drained and rinsed

1 green zucchini, sliced

1 yellow zucchini, sliced

2 ounces/½ cup pasta shells, cooked

2 ounces/½ cup cashew nuts

1 ounce/¼ cup peanuts

lime wedges and fresh cilantro sprigs, to garnish

For the dressing

4 fluid ounces/½ cup farmer's cheese

2 tablespoons plain yogurt

1 fresh green chile, seeded and chopped

1 tablespoon chopped fresh cilantro

½ teaspoon crushed black peppercorns

½ teaspoon crushed dried red chili

1 tablespoon lemon juice

½ teaspoon salt

1 Arrange the onion rings, red kidney beans, green and yellow zucchini slices and pasta shells in a salad dish, ready for serving. Sprinkle the cashew nuts and peanuts over the top.

2 In a separate bowl, blend together the farmer's cheese yogurt, green chilli, cilantro and salt and beat well using a fork.

3 Sprinkle the crushed black pepper, red chili and lemon juice over the dressing. Garnish the salad with the lime wedges and cilantro sprigs and serve with the dressing in a separate bowl or poured over the salad.

Carrot and Orange Salad

A fruit and a vegetable that could have been made for each other form the basis of this wonderful, fresh-tasting salad.

INGREDIENTS

Serves 4

1 pound carrots

2 large oranges

1 tablespoon olive oil

2 tablespoons lemon juice

pinch of sugar (optional)

2 tablespoons chopped pistachio nuts or
   toasted pine nuts

salt and ground black pepper

1 Peel the carrots and grate them into a large bowl.

2 Peel the oranges with a sharp knife and cut into segments, catching the juice in a small bowl.

3 Blend together the olive oil, lemon juice and orange juice. Season with a little salt and pepper to taste, and sugar if you like.

4 Toss the orange segments together with the carrots and pour the dressing over. Sprinkle the salad with the pistachio nuts or pine nuts before serving.

Pear and Roquefort Salad

Choose ripe, firm Comice or Anjou pears for this salad.

INGREDIENTS

Serves 4

3 ripe pears

lemon juice, for tossing

about 6 ounces mixed salad leaves

6 ounces Roquefort cheese

2 ounces/½ cup hazelnuts, toasted
and chopped

For the dressing

2 tablespoons hazelnut oil

3 tablespoons olive oil

1 tablespoon cider vinegar

1 teaspoon Dijon mustard

salt and ground black pepper

1 To make the dressing, mix together the oils, vinegar and mustard in a bowl or screw-top jar. Add salt and black pepper to taste. Stir or shake well.

2 Peel, core and slice the pears and toss them in lemon juice.

3 Arrange the salad leaves on serving plates, then place the pears on top. Crumble the cheese and sprinkle it over the salad with the hazelnuts. Spoon over the dressing and serve immediately.

Arugula and Pear Salad

For a sophisticated start to an
elaborate meal, try this simple salad
of honey-rich pears, fresh Parmesan
and aromatic arugula leaves.

INGREDIENTS

Serves 4

3 ripe pears (Anjou or Bartlett)

2 teaspoons lemon juice

3 tablespoons hazelnut or walnut oil

4 ounces arugula leaves

3-ounce piece of Parmesan cheese

ground black pepper

2 Combine the hazelnut or
walnut oil with the pears. Add
the arugula leaves and toss.

3 Turn the salad out onto four
small serving plates and top
with thin shavings of Parmesan
cheese. Season with pepper and
serve immediately.

1 Peel and core the pears and
slice thickly. Moisten with
lemon juice to keep the flesh white.

COOK'S TIP

Parmesan cheese is a delicious
main ingredient in a salad. Buy a
chunk of fresh Parmesan and
shave strips off the side, using a
vegetable peeler. The distinctive
flavor is quite strong. Store the
rest of the Parmesan wrapped in
foil in the refrigerator.

Radish, Mango and Apple Salad

Radish is a year-round vegetable and this salad, with its clean, crisp tastes and mellow flavors, can be served at any time of year. Serve with smoked fish, such as rolls of smoked salmon, or with flavorful ham or salami.

INGREDIENTS

Serves 4

10–15 radishes

1 apple, peeled, cored and thinly sliced

2 celery sticks, thinly sliced

1 small ripe mango

fresh dill sprigs, to garnish

For the dressing

4 fluid ounces/½ cup sour cream

2 teaspoons creamed horseradish

1 tablespoon chopped fresh dill

salt and ground black pepper

1 To prepare the dressing, blend together the sour cream, horseradish and dill in a small bowl and season with a little salt and pepper.

2 Trim the radishes and slice them thinly. Put in a bowl together with the apple and celery.

3 Halve the mango lengthwise, cutting either side of the stone pit. Make even, criss-cross cuts through the flesh of each section and bend it back to separate the cubes. Remove the cubes with a small knife and add to the bowl.

4 Stir the dressing again, then pour it over the vegetables and fruit and stir gently so that all the ingredients are well coated without breaking up the mango. Garnish with dill sprigs and serve.

Egg, Bacon and Avocado Salad

A glorious medley of colors, flavors and textures to delight the eye and the taste buds.

INGREDIENTS

Serves 4

1 large romaine lettuce

8 bacon strips, fried until crisp

2 large avocados, peeled and diced

6 hard-boiled eggs, chopped

2 beefsteak tomatoes, peeled, seeded and chopped

6 ounces blue cheese, crumbled

For the dressing

1 garlic clove, crushed

1 teaspoon sugar

1½ teaspoons lemon juice

1½ tablespoons red wine vinegar

4 fluid ounces/½ cup peanut oil

salt and ground black pepper

1 Slice the lettuce into strips across the leaves. Crumble the fried bacon rashers.

2 To make the dressing, put the garlic, sugar, lemon juice, vinegar and oil in a screw-top jar, add salt and pepper to taste and shake the jar vigorously. On a large, rectangular or oval platter, spread out the strips of lettuce to make a bed.

3 Arrange the avocados, eggs, tomatoes and cheese neatly in rows on top of the lettuce. Sprinkle the bacon on top.

4 Pour the dressing carefully and evenly over the salad just before serving.

Spicy Corn Salad

V

This brilliant, sweet-flavored salad is served warm with a delicious, spicy dressing.

INGREDIENTS

Serves 4

2 tablespoons vegetable oil

1 pound drained canned corn kernels, or frozen corn kernels, thawed

1 green bell pepper, seeded and diced

1 small fresh red chile, seeded and diced

4 scallions, sliced

3 tablespoons chopped fresh parsley

8 ounces cherry tomatoes, halved

salt and ground black pepper

For the dressing

½ teaspoon sugar

2 tablespoons white wine vinegar

½ teaspoon Dijon mustard

1 tablespoon chopped fresh basil

1 tablespoon mayonnaise

¼ teaspoon chili sauce

1 Heat the vegetable oil in a frying pan. Add the corn, green bell pepper, chile and scallions. Cook over a medium heat, stirring frequently, for about 5 minutes, until softened.

2 Transfer the vegetables to a salad bowl. Stir in the parsley and the cherry tomatoes.

3 To make the dressing, combine all the ingredients in a small bowl and whisk together until thoroughly combined.

4 Pour the dressing over the corn mixture. Season to taste with salt and pepper. Toss well to combine, then serve immediately, while the salad is still warm.

WARM SALADS

~

A relatively recent food fashion that is destined to last, warm
salads offer the best of both worlds. Colorful salad leaves
and crisp vegetables may be served with a topping of freshly
pan-fried meat or a rich warm dressing or, alternatively,
just-cooked vegetables or pasta can be tossed with salad
ingredients and cold dressings. The result is not only a
delicious combination of flavors and textures, but also
a stimulating and appetizing contrast of temperatures.

Warm Fava Bean and Feta Salad

V

This medley of fresh-tasting salad ingredients is lovely served warm or cold as an appetizer or makes a good accompaniment to a main course.

INGREDIENTS

Serves 4–6

2 pounds fava beans, shelled, or
    12 ounces shelled frozen beans
4 tablespoons olive oil
6 ounces fresh plum tomatoes, halved,
    or quartered if large
4 garlic cloves, crushed
4 ounces firm feta cheese, cut
    into chunks
3 tablespoons chopped fresh dill
12 black olives
salt and ground black pepper
chopped fresh dill, to garnish

1 Cook the fava beans in salted, boiling water until just tender. Drain and set aside.

2 Meanwhile, heat the olive oil in a heavy frying pan and add the tomatoes and garlic. Cook until the tomatoes are beginning to change color.

3 Add the feta to the pan and toss the ingredients together for 1 minute. Mix with the drained beans, dill and olives and season to taste with salt and pepper. Serve garnished with chopped dill.

COOK'S TIP
∽

Plum tomatoes are now widely available in supermarkets fresh as well as canned. Their deep red, oval shape is very attractive in salads and they have a sweet, rich flavor.

Halloumi and Grape Salad

V

In this recipe, firm, salty halloumi cheese is fried and then tossed with sweet, juicy grapes which really complement its distinctive flavor.

INGREDIENTS

Serves 4

5 ounces mixed green salad leaves
3 ounces seedless green grapes
3 ounces seedless black grapes
9 ounces halloumi cheese
3 tablespoons olive oil
fresh young thyme leaves or fresh dill,
    to garnish

For the dressing

4 tablespoons olive oil
1 tablespoon lemon juice
1/2 teaspoon superfine sugar
1 tablespoon chopped fresh thyme or dill
salt and ground black pepper

1 To make the dressing, mix together the olive oil, lemon juice and sugar. Season with salt and pepper. Stir in the chopped thyme or dill and set aside.

2 Toss together the salad leaves and the green and black grapes, then transfer to a large serving plate.

3 Thinly slice the cheese. Heat the oil in a large frying pan. Add the cheese and fry briefly until golden on the underside. Turn the cheese with a metal spatula and cook the other side.

4 Arrange the cheese over the salad. Pour over the dressing and garnish with sprigs of fresh thyme or dill.

V

Green Bean Salad

*Green beans are delicious served
with a simple vinaigrette dressing,
but this dish is a little more elaborate.*

INGREDIENTS

Serves 4

1 pound green beans
1 tablespoon olive oil
1 ounce/2 tablespoons butter
1/2 garlic clove, crushed
2 ounces/1 cup fresh white bread crumbs
1 tablespoon chopped fresh parsley
1 hard-boiled egg, finely chopped

For the dressing

2 tablespoons olive oil
2 tablespoons sunflower oil
2 teaspoons white wine vinegar
1/2 garlic clove, crushed
1/4 teaspoon Dijon mustard
pinch of sugar
pinch of salt

1 Cook the green beans in salted
boiling water for 5–6 minutes,
until tender. Drain, refresh under
cold running water and place in a
serving bowl.

2 To make the dressing, mix all
the ingredients thoroughly
together. Pour the dressing over
the beans and toss.

3 Heat the oil and butter in a
heavy frying pan and cook
the garlic for 1 minute. Stir in the
bread crumbs and cook over a
medium heat for 3–4 minutes, until
golden brown, stirring frequently.

4 Remove the pan from the heat
and stir in the parsley and
then the chopped egg. Sprinkle the
bread crumb mixture over the
green beans. Serve warm or at
room temperature.

Lentil and Cabbage Salad

A warm, crunchy salad that makes a satisfying meal if served with rustic French bread or fresh rolls.

INGREDIENTS

Serves 4–6

8 ounces/1 cup Puy lentils

3 garlic cloves

1 bay leaf

1 small onion, peeled and studded with
   2 cloves

1 tablespoon olive oil

1 red onion, thinly sliced

1 tablespoon fresh thyme leaves

12 ounces cabbage, finely shredded

finely grated rind and juice of 1 lemon

1 tablespoon raspberry vinegar

salt and ground black pepper

1 Rinse the lentils in cold water and place in a large pan with 2½ pints/6¼ cups cold water, 1 of the garlic cloves, the bay leaf and clove-studded onion. Bring to the boil and cook for 10 minutes. Reduce the heat, cover and simmer gently for about 15–20 minutes. Drain and discard the onion, garlic and bay leaf.

2 Crush the remaining garlic cloves. Heat the oil in a large pan. Add the red onion, crushed garlic and thyme and cook over a medium heat, stirring occasionally, for 5 minutes, until softened.

3 Add the cabbage and cook for 3–5 minutes, until just cooked but still crunchy.

4 Stir in the cooked lentils, lemon rind and juice and the raspberry vinegar. Season to taste with salt and pepper and serve immediately while still warm.

V

Sweet Potato and Carrot Salad

This warm salad has a sweet-and-sour taste, and several unusual ingredients. It is garnished with whole walnuts, golden raisins and onion rings.

INGREDIENTS

Serves 4

1 sweet potato
2 carrots, cut into thick diagonal slices
3 tomatoes
8–10 iceberg lettuce leaves
3 ounces/¹/₂ cup canned chickpeas, drained

For the dressing

1 tablespoon clear honey
6 tablespoons plain yogurt
¹/₂ teaspoon salt
1 teaspoon ground black pepper

For the garnish

1 tablespoon walnuts
1 tablespoon golden raisins
1 small onion, cut into rings

1 Peel the sweet potato and cut coarsely into cubes. Boil it until it is soft but not mushy, then cover the pan and set aside.

2 Boil the carrots for just a few minutes, making sure that they remain crunchy. Add the carrots to the sweet potato.

3 Drain the water from the sweet potato and carrots and place them together in a bowl.

4 Slice the tops off the tomatoes, then scoop out the seeds with a spoon and discard. Coarsely chop the flesh. Slice the lettuce into strips across the leaves.

5 Line a salad bowl with the shredded lettuce leaves. Mix together the sweet potato, carrots, chickpeas and tomatoes and place the mixture in the center.

6 To make the dressing, mix together all the ingredients and beat well, using a fork.

7 Garnish the salad with the walnuts, golden raisins and onion rings. Pour the dressing over the top just before serving, or serve it in a separate bowl.

COOK'S TIP

This salad makes an excellent main course for lunch or a family supper. Serve it with a sweet mango chutney and warm naan bread.

Chicken Liver, Bacon and Tomato Salad

Warm salads are especially welcome during the autumn months when the days are growing shorter and cooler. This rich salad includes sweet spinach and the bitter leaves of frisée lettuce.

INGREDIENTS

Serves 4

8 ounces young spinach, stems removed

1 frisée lettuce

7 tablespoons sunflower oil

6 ounces rindless unsmoked bacon, cut into thin strips

3 ounces day-old bread, crusts removed and cut into short fingers

1 pound chicken livers

4 ounces cherry tomatoes

salt and ground black pepper

1 Place the spinach and lettuce leaves in a salad bowl. Heat 4 tablespoons of the oil in a large frying pan, add the bacon and cook for 3–4 minutes, or until crisp and brown. Remove the bacon with a slotted spoon and drain on paper towels.

2 To make croûtons, fry the bread in the bacon-flavored oil, tossing until crisp and golden. Drain on paper towels.

3 Heat the remaining 3 tablespoons oil in the frying pan, add the chicken livers and cook briskly for 2–3 minutes. Turn the chicken livers out over the salad leaves and add the bacon, croûtons and tomatoes. Season, toss and serve warm.

VARIATION

If you can't find any baby spinach leaves you can use mâche. Watercress would make a deliciously peppery substitute, but you should use less of it and bulk the salad out with a milder leaf so that the watercress doesn't overwhelm the other flavors.

Warm Pasta Salad with Asparagus

This warm salad is served with ham, eggs and Parmesan. A mustard dressing made from the thick part of the asparagus stalks provides a rich accompaniment.

INGREDIENTS

Serves 4

1 pound asparagus

1 pound dried tagliatelle

8 ounces cooked ham, sliced ¼-inch thick, and cut into fingers

2 eggs, hard-boiled and sliced

2 ounces piece Parmesan cheese

For the dressing

2 ounces cooked potato

5 tablespoons olive oil

1 tablespoon lemon juice

2 teaspoons Dijon mustard

4 fluid ounces/½ cup Vegetable Stock

salt and ground black pepper

1 Bring a pan of salted water to the boil. Trim and discard the tough, woody part of the asparagus stalks. Cut the asparagus in half and boil the thicker halves for 12 minutes, adding the asparagus tips after 6 minutes. Refresh under cold water until warm, then drain.

2 Finely chop 5 ounces of the thicker asparagus pieces. Place in a food processor together with the dressing ingredients and process until smooth. Season the dressing to taste.

3 Boil the pasta in a large pan of salted water until *al dente*. Refresh under cold water.

4 Dress with the asparagus sauce and turn out into four pasta bowls. Top each pile of pasta with some of the ham, eggs and asparagus tips. Using a vegetable peeler, make thin shavings of Parmesan cheese to garnish the salad and serve warm.

Gado Gado

This classic Indonesian vegetable salad is served with a delicious hot peanut sauce.

INGREDIENTS

Serves 4–6

2 potatoes
6 ounces green beans, trimmed
6 ounces Chinese cabbage, shredded
1 iceberg lettuce
6 ounces beansprouts
½ cucumber, cut into fingers
5 ounces daikon, shredded
3 scallions
8 ounces tofu, cut into large slices
3 hard-boiled eggs, shelled
    and quartered
1 small bunch of fresh cilantro
shrimp crackers, to serve

For the peanut sauce

5 ounces/1¼ cups raw peanuts
1 tablespoon vegetable oil
2 shallots or 1 small onion, finely chopped
1 garlic clove, crushed
1–2 small fresh chiles, seeded and
    finely chopped
½-inch square shrimp paste or
    1 tablespoon Thai fish sauce (optional)
2 tablespoons tamarind sauce
4 fluid ounces/½ cup canned
    coconut milk
1 tablespoon clear honey

1 Peel the potatoes. Bring to the boil in salted water and simmer for about 15 minutes, or until tender. Cook the green beans for 3–4 minutes. Drain the potatoes and beans and refresh under cold running water.

2 To make the peanut sauce, dry-fry the peanuts in a wok, or place under a moderate broiler, tossing them all the time to prevent them from burning.

3 Turn the peanuts onto a clean cloth and rub them vigorously with your hands to remove the papery skins. Place the peanuts in a food processor and blend for 2 minutes, until finely crushed.

4 Heat the vegetable oil in a wok and cook the shallots or onion, garlic and chiles without letting them color. Add the shrimp paste or fish sauce, if using, together with the tamarind sauce, coconut milk and honey.

5 Simmer briefly, add to the blended peanuts and process to form a thick sauce. Transfer to a small serving bowl and keep hot.

6 Arrange the potatoes, green beans and all the other salad ingredients on a large serving platter. Serve with the bowl of peanut sauce and shrimp crackers.

Chicken Liver Salad

This delicious salad may be served as a main course for a summer lunch party, or as a tasty first course served on individual plates. The richness of the chicken livers is complemented perfectly by the sweet tangy whole-grain mustard dressing. Serve with warm rustic bread to mop up the dressing.

INGREDIENTS

Serves 4

mixed salad leaves such as frisée, oak leaf
   lettuce, radicchio
1 avocado, diced
2 tablespoons lemon juice
2 pink grapefruit
12 ounces chicken livers
2 tablespoons olive oil
1 garlic clove, crushed
salt and ground black pepper
whole fresh chives, to garnish

For the dressing
2 tablespoons lemon juice
4 tablespoons olive oil
½ teaspoon whole-grain mustard
½ teaspoon clear honey
1 tablespoon chopped fresh chives
salt and ground black pepper

1 To make the dressing, put the lemon juice, olive oil, mustard, honey and chopped fresh chives into a screw-top jar, and shake vigorously. Season to taste with salt and freshly ground black pepper.

2 Arrange the previously washed and well-drained mixed salad leaves attractively on a large serving plate.

3 Peel and dice the avocado and mix with the lemon juice to prevent browning. Add to the plate of mixed leaves.

4 Peel the grapefruit, removing as much of the white pith as possible. Split into segments and arrange with the leaves and avocado on the serving plate.

5 Dry the chicken livers on paper towels and remove any unwanted pieces.

6 Using a sharp knife, cut the larger chicken livers in half. Leave the smaller ones whole.

7 Heat the oil in a large frying pan. Stir-fry the chicken livers and garlic briskly until the livers are brown all over (they should be slightly pink inside).

8 Season the chicken livers to taste with salt and black pepper, remove from the pan and drain on paper towels.

9 Place the chicken livers, while still warm, onto the salad leaves and spoon over the dressing. Garnish with the whole chives and serve immediately.

VEGETARIAN
SALADS
~

This exciting collection of salads features an array of
cheeses, boiled and poached eggs, and nuts combined with
a breathtaking mixture of vegetables and fruit. Serve them as
tempting hors d'oeuvres before any kind of main course,
as a lovely, light vegetarian lunch – perhaps with rustic
bread or fresh rolls – or, in many instances, as a refreshing
accompaniment. Whether based on fresh mushrooms,
asparagus or summer herbs, these are gourmet salads for
the discerning palate.

Caesar Salad

V

This is a well-known and much enjoyed salad, invented in the 1920s by Caesar Cardini. Be sure to use romaine lettuce and add the very soft eggs at the last minute.

INGREDIENTS

Serves 6

6 fluid ounces/³⁄₄ cup salad oil, preferably
    olive oil

4 ounces French or Italian bread, cut in
    1-inch cubes

1 large garlic clove, crushed with the flat
    side of a knife

1 romaine lettuce

2 eggs, boiled for 1 minute

4 fluid ounces/¹⁄₂ cup lemon juice

2 ounces/²⁄₃ cup freshly grated
    Parmesan cheese

salt and ground black pepper

1 Heat 2 fluid ounces/¹⁄₄ cup of the oil in a large, heavy frying pan. Add the bread cubes and garlic. Cook over a medium heat, stirring and turning constantly, until the cubes are golden brown all over. Remove with a slotted spoon and drain well on paper towels. Discard the garlic.

2 Tear large lettuce leaves into smaller pieces. Then put all the lettuce in a bowl.

3 Add the remaining oil to the lettuce and season with salt and plenty of ground black pepper. Toss well to coat the leaves.

4 Break the eggs on top. Sprinkle with the lemon juice. Toss well again to combine.

5 Add the Parmesan cheese and toss gently to mix.

6 Sprinkle the fried bread cubes over the top and serve the salad immediately.

COOK'S TIP

To make a tangier dressing mix 2 tablespoons white wine vinegar, 1 tablespoon Worcestershire sauce, ¹⁄₂ teaspoon mustard powder, 1 teaspoon sugar, salt and pepper in a screw-top jar, then add the oil and shake well.

Tricolor Salad

A popular salad, this dish depends for its success on the quality of its ingredients. Mozzarella di bufala is the best cheese to serve uncooked. Whole ripe plum tomatoes give up their juice to blend with extra virgin olive oil for a natural dressing.

INGREDIENTS

Serves 2–3

5 ounces mozzarella di bufala cheese, thinly sliced

4 large plum tomatoes, sliced

1 large avocado

about 12 basil leaves or a small handful of flat leaf parsley leaves

3–4 tablespoons extra virgin olive oil

sea salt flakes and ground black pepper

ciabatta, to serve

1 Arrange the sliced mozzarella cheese and tomatoes randomly on two salad plates. Crush over a few good pinches of sea salt flakes. This will help to draw out some of the juices from the plum tomatoes. Cover and set aside in a cool place and leave to marinate for about 30 minutes.

2 Just before serving, cut the avocado in half using a large sharp knife and twist the halves to separate. Lift out the pit and remove the peel.

3 Carefully slice the avocado flesh crosswise into half moons, or cut it into large chunks if that is easier.

4 Place the avocado on the salad, then sprinkle with the basil or parsley. Drizzle over the olive oil, add a little more salt, if you like, and some black pepper. Serve at room temperature, with chunks of rustic Italian ciabatta for mopping up the dressing.

V

Goat Cheese and Fig Salad

Fresh figs and walnuts are perfect partners for goat cheese and toasted buckwheat. The olive and nut oil dressing contains no vinegar, depending instead on the acidity of the goat cheese.

INGREDIENTS

Serves 4

6 ounces/1 cup couscous

2 tablespoons toasted buckwheat

1 egg, hard-boiled

2 tablespoons chopped fresh parsley

4 tablespoons olive oil

3 tablespoons walnut oil

4 ounces arugula leaves

1/2 frisée lettuce

6 ounces crumbly white goat cheese

2 ounces/1/2 cup broken walnuts, toasted

4 ripe figs, trimmed and almost cut into
   four (leave the pieces joined at the base)

1 Place the couscous and toasted buckwheat in a bowl, cover with boiling water and leave to soak for 15 minutes. Place in a sieve to drain off any remaining water, then spread out on a metal tray and leave to cool.

2 Shell the hard-boiled egg and grate finely.

3 Toss the grated egg, parsley, couscous and buckwheat together in a bowl. Combine the olive and walnut oils, using half to moisten the couscous mixture.

4 Toss the salad leaves in the remaining oil and distribute among four large serving plates.

5 Pile the couscous mixture in the center of each plate and crumble the goat cheese over the top. Sprinkle with toasted walnuts, place a fig in the centre of each plate and serve.

COOK'S TIP

Goat cheeses vary in strength from the youngest, which are soft and mild, to strongly flavored, mature cheeses, which have a firm and crumbly texture. The crumbly varieties are best suited to salads.

Spinach and Roast Garlic Salad

V

Don't worry about the amount of garlic in this salad. During roasting, the garlic becomes sweet and subtle and loses its pungent taste.

INGREDIENTS

Serves 4

12 garlic cloves, unpeeled

4 tablespoons extra virgin olive oil

1 pound baby spinach leaves

2 ounces/½ cup pine nuts,
  lightly toasted

juice of ½ lemon

salt and ground black pepper

1 Preheat the oven to 375°F. Place the garlic in a small roasting pan, add 2 tablespoons of the olive oil, tossing well to coat all over, and roast for about 15 minutes, until the garlic cloves are softened and slightly charred around the edges.

2 While still warm, tip the garlic into a salad bowl. Add the spinach, pine nuts, lemon juice, remaining olive oil and a little salt. Toss well and add black pepper to taste. Serve immediately, inviting guests to squeeze the softened garlic purée out of the skin to eat.

Marinated Cucumber Salad

A wonderfully cooling salad for the summer, with the distinctive flavor of fresh dill.

INGREDIENTS

Serves 4–6

2 medium cucumbers
1 tablespoon salt
3½ ounces/½ cup granulated sugar
6 fluid ounces/¾ cup hard cider
1 tablespoon cider vinegar
3 tablespoons chopped fresh dill
ground black pepper

1 Slice the cucumbers thinly and place them in a colander, sprinkling salt between each layer. Put the colander over a bowl and leave to drain for 1 hour.

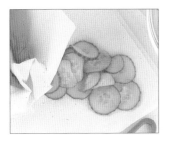

2 Thoroughly rinse the cucumber under cold running water to remove excess salt, then pat dry with paper towels.

3 Gently heat the sugar, cider and vinegar in a pan until the sugar has dissolved. Remove from the heat and leave to cool. Put the cucumber slices in a bowl, pour over the cider mixture and leave to marinate for 2 hours.

4 Drain the cucumber and sprinkle with the dill and pepper to taste. Mix well and transfer to a serving dish. Chill until ready to serve.

COOK'S TIP

The salad would be a perfect accompaniment for fresh salmon.

V

Flower Garden Salad

*Dress a colorful mixture of salad
leaves with good olive oil and lemon
juice, then top it with crisp croûtons.*

INGREDIENTS

Serves 4–6

3 thick slices day-old bread, such
    as ciabatta

4 fluid ounces/¹/₂ cup extra virgin
    olive oil

1 garlic clove, halved

¹/₂ small romaine lettuce

¹/₂ small oak leaf lettuce

1 ounce arugula leaves or salad cress

1 ounce fresh flat leaf parsley

a small handful of young dandelion leaves

juice of 1 lemon

a few nasturtium leaves and flowers

pansy and pot marigold flowers

sea salt flakes and ground black pepper

1 Cut the slices of bread into
¹/₂-inch cubes.

2 Heat half the oil gently in a
frying pan and cook the bread
cubes in it, tossing them until they
are well coated and lightly
browned. Remove and cool.

3 Rub the inside of a large salad
bowl with the cut sides of the
garlic clove, then discard. Pour
the remaining oil into the base of
the bowl.

4 Tear all the salad leaves into
bitesize pieces and pile them
into the bowl with the oil. Season
with salt and pepper. Cover and
keep chilled until you are ready to
serve the salad.

5 To serve, toss the leaves in the
oil at the base of the bowl,
then sprinkle with the lemon juice
and toss again. Sprinkle the
croûtons and the flowers over the
top and serve immediately.

Panzanella Salad

If sliced juicy tomatoes layered with day-old bread sounds strange for a salad, don't be deceived – it's quite delicious. A popular Italian salad, this dish is ideal for serving as an appetizer. Use full-flavored tomatoes for the best result.

INGREDIENTS

Serves 4–6

4 thick slices day-old bread, white, brown or rye

1 small red onion, thinly sliced

1 pound ripe tomatoes, thinly sliced

4 ounces mozzarella cheese, thinly sliced

1 tablespoon fresh basil, shredded, or fresh marjoram

4 fluid ounces/½ cup extra virgin olive oil

3 tablespoons balsamic vinegar

juice of 1 small lemon

salt and ground black pepper

pitted and sliced black olives or salted capers, to garnish

1 Dip the bread briefly in cold water, then carefully squeeze out the excess water. Arrange the bread in the base of a shallow salad bowl.

2 Soak the onion slices in cold water for about 10 minutes while you prepare the other ingredients. Drain and reserve.

3 Layer the tomatoes, cheese, onion, basil or marjoram in the bowl, seasoning well with salt and pepper in between each layer. Sprinkle with oil, vinegar and lemon juice.

4 Top the salad with the olives or capers, cover with plastic wrap and chill in the refrigerator for at least 2 hours or overnight, if possible.

Poached Egg Salad with Croûtons

V

Soft poached eggs, hot garlic croûtons and cool, crisp salad leaves make a great combination.

INGREDIENTS

Serves 2

½ small loaf white bread
5 tablespoons/⅓ cup extra virgin olive oil
2 eggs
4 ounces mixed salad leaves
2 garlic cloves, crushed
½ tablespoons white wine vinegar
1-ounce piece Parmesan cheese
ground black pepper

3 Meanwhile, bring a pan of water to the boil. Carefully slide in the eggs, one at a time. Gently poach the eggs for 4 minutes until lightly cooked.

4 Divide the salad leaves between two plates. Remove the croûtons from the frying pan and arrange them over the leaves. Wipe the frying pan clean with paper towels.

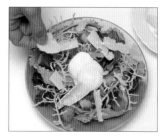

6 Place a poached egg on each plate of salad. Sprinkle with shavings of Parmesan and a little black pepper and serve.

COOK'S TIP

Add a dash of vinegar to the water before poaching the eggs. This helps to keep the whites together.

To make sure that a poached egg has a good shape, swirl the water with a spoon, whirlpool-fashion, before sliding in the egg.

Before serving, trim the edges of the egg for a neat finish.

1 Remove the crust from the loaf of bread. Cut the bread into 1-inch cubes.

5 Heat the remaining oil in the pan, add the garlic and vinegar and cook over a high heat for 1 minute. Pour the warm dressing over each salad.

2 Heat 2 tablespoons of the oil in a frying pan. Cook the bread for about 5 minutes, tossing the cubes occasionally, until they are golden brown.

| V |

Fresh Cèpes Salad

To capture the just-picked flavor of a cèpe, this delicious salad is enriched with an egg yolk and walnut oil dressing. Choose small cèpes that will have a firm texture and the very best flavor.

INGREDIENTS

Serves 4

12 ounces fresh cèpes

6 ounces mixed salad leaves, including
   young spinach and frisée

2 ounces/½ cup broken walnut
   pieces, toasted

2-ounce piece Parmesan cheese

salt and ground black pepper

For the dressing

2 egg yolks

½ teaspoon French mustard

5 tablespoons peanut oil

3 tablespoons walnut oil

2 tablespoons lemon juice

2 tablespoons chopped fresh parsley

pinch of superfine sugar

1 To make the dressing, place the egg yolks in a screw-top jar with the mustard, peanut and walnut oils, lemon juice, parsley and sugar. Shake well.

2 Trim the cèpes and cut them into thin slices.

3 Place the cèpes in a large salad bowl and combine with the dressing. Leave for 10–15 minutes for the flavors to mingle.

4 Wash and dry the salad leaves, then toss them together with the cèpes.

5 Turn the salad out onto four large serving plates. Season well, sprinkle with the toasted walnuts and shavings of Parmesan cheese, then serve.

Bean Sprout and Daikon Salad

Thin slices of crisp vegetables mixed with bean sprouts make the perfect foil for an unusual Asian dressing.

INGREDIENTS

Serves 4

8 ounces/1 cup bean sprouts

1 cucumber

2 carrots

1 small daikon

1 small red onion, thinly sliced

1-inch piece of fresh root ginger, cut into
    thin matchsticks

1 small fresh red chile, seeded and sliced

handful of fresh cilantro or mint leaves

For the dressing

1 tablespoon rice wine vinegar

1 tablespoon light soy sauce

1 tablespoon Thai fish sauce

1 garlic clove, finely chopped

1 tablespoon sesame oil

3 tablespoons peanut oil

2 tablespoons sesame seeds,
    lightly toasted

1 First make the dressing. Place all the dressing ingredients in a bottle or screw-top jar and shake well. The dressing may be made in advance and will keep well for a couple of days if stored in the refrigerator or a cool place.

2 Wash the bean sprouts and drain thoroughly in a colander.

3 Peel the cucumber, cut in half lengthwise and scoop out the seeds. Peel the cucumber flesh into long ribbon strips using a vegetable peeler or mandoline.

4 Peel the carrots and daikon into long strips in the same way as for the cucumber.

5 Place the carrots, daikon and cucumber in a large, shallow serving dish, add the red onion, ginger matchsticks, chile and cilantro or mint leaves and toss to mix. Pour the dressing over just before serving.

V

Asparagus and Orange Salad

A slightly unusual combination of ingredients with a simple dressing based on good-quality olive oil.

INGREDIENTS

Serves 4

8 ounces asparagus, trimmed and cut into
   2-inch lengths

2 large oranges

2 well-flavored tomatoes, cut
   into eighths

2 ounces romaine lettuce leaves

2 tablespoons extra virgin olive oil

$\frac{1}{2}$ teaspoon sherry vinegar

salt and ground black pepper

1 Cook the asparagus in salted, boiling water for 3–4 minutes, until just tender. The cooking time may vary according to the size of the asparagus stems. Drain and refresh under cold water, then leave to cool.

2 Grate the rind from half an orange and reserve. Peel both the oranges and cut into segments over a bowl to catch any juice. Squeeze the juice from the membrane into the bowl and reserve for the dressing.

3 Put the asparagus, orange segments, tomatoes and lettuce into a salad bowl.

orange juice and 1 teaspoon of the grated orange rind. Season to taste with salt and pepper. Just before serving, pour the dressing over the salad and mix gently to coat all the ingredients.

4 Mix together the olive oil and sherry vinegar, and add 1 tablespoon of the reserved

Coronation Salad

The famous salad dressing used in this dish was created especially for the coronation dinner of Queen Elizabeth II of Great Britain. It is a wonderful accompaniment to hard-boiled eggs and vegetables.

INGREDIENTS

Serves 6

1 pound new potatoes
3 tablespoons French Dressing
3 scallions, chopped
6 eggs, hard-boiled and halved
frisée lettuce leaves
¼ cucumber, cut into thin strips
6 large radishes, sliced
1 carton salad cress
salt and ground black pepper

For the coronation dressing
2 tablespoons olive oil
1 small onion, chopped
1 tablespoon mild curry powder or korma
    spice mix
2 teaspoons tomato paste
2 tablespoons lemon juice
2 tablespoons sherry
½ pint/1¼ cups mayonnaise
¼ pint/⅔ cup plain yogurt

1 Boil the potatoes in salted water until tender. Drain them, transfer to a large bowl and toss in the French dressing.

2 Stir in the scallions and salt and pepper to taste and leave to cool thoroughly.

3 Meanwhile, make the coronation dressing. Heat the oil in a small pan and cook the onion for 3 minutes, until soft. Stir in the curry powder or spice mix and cook for 1 further minute. Remove from the heat and mix in all the other dressing ingredients.

4 Stir the dressing into the potatoes, add the eggs, then chill. Line a serving platter with lettuce leaves and pile the salad in the center. Sprinkle over the cucumber, radishes and cress.

Potato Salad with Curry Plant Mayonnaise

Potato salad can be made well in advance and is therefore a useful dish for serving as an unusual appetizer at a party. Its popularity means that there are very rarely any leftovers to be cleared away at the end of the day.

INGREDIENTS

Serves 6

2¼ pounds new potatoes, in skins

½ pint/1¼ cups mayonnaise

6 curry plant leaves,
    coarsely chopped

salt and ground black pepper

mixed lettuce leaves or other salad leaves,
    to serve

1 Place the unpeeled potatoes in a large pan of lightly salted water, bring to the boil and cook over a low heat for 15 minutes, or until tender. Drain well in a colander, place in a large bowl and leave to cool slightly.

2 Mix the mayonnaise with the curry plant leaves and black pepper. Stir this mixture into the potatoes while they are still warm. Leave to cool completely, then serve on a bed of mixed lettuce leaves or other salad leaves.

Pear and Pecan Nut Salad

Toasted pecan nuts have a special affinity with crisp white pears. Their robust flavors combine well with a rich Blue Cheese and Chive dressing to make this a salad to remember.

INGREDIENTS

Serves 4

3 ounces/$\frac{1}{2}$ cup shelled pecan nuts,
   coarsely chopped

3 crisp pears

6 ounces young spinach, stems removed

1 escarole or butterhead lettuce

1 radicchio

2 tablespoons Blue Cheese and
   Chive Dressing

salt and ground black pepper

rustic bread, to serve

1 Toast the pecan nuts under a moderate broiler to bring out their flavor.

COOK'S TIP

The pecan nuts will burn very quickly under the broiler, so keep constant watch over them and remove them as soon as they change color.

2 Cut the pears into even slices, leaving the skins intact but discarding the cores.

3 Place the spinach, lettuce and radicchio leaves in a large bowl. Add the pears and toasted pecans, pour over the Blue Cheese and Chive Dressing and toss well. Distribute among four large serving plates and season to taste with salt and pepper. Serve the salad with warm rustic bread.

v

Black and Orange Salad

This dramatically colorful salad, with its spicy dressing, is very unusual. It is a feast for the eyes as well as for the taste buds.

INGREDIENTS

Serves 4

3 oranges

4 ounces/1 cup pitted black olives

1 tablespoon chopped fresh cilantro

1 tablespoon chopped fresh parsley

For the dressing

2 tablespoons olive oil

1 tablespoon lemon juice

½ teaspoon paprika

½ teaspoon ground cumin

1 With a sharp knife, cut away the peel and pith from the oranges and divide the fruit into segments.

2 Place the oranges in a salad bowl and add the black olives, cilantro and parsley.

3 Blend together the olive oil, lemon juice, paprika and cumin. Pour the dressing over the salad and toss gently. Cover with plastic wrap and chill for about 30 minutes, then serve.

v

Arugula and Cilantro Salad

Arugula leaves have a wonderful, peppery flavor. However, unless you have a plentiful supply of arugula, you may well have to use extra spinach or another green leaf to pad out this salad.

INGREDIENTS

Serves 4

4 ounces or more arugula leaves

4 ounces young spinach leaves

1 large bunch fresh cilantro, about 1 ounce

2–3 fresh parsley sprigs

For the dressing

1 garlic clove, crushed

3 tablespoons olive oil

2 teaspoons white wine vinegar

pinch of paprika

cayenne pepper

salt

1 Place the arugula and spinach leaves in a salad bowl. Chop the cilantro and parsley and sprinkle them over the top.

2 In a small pitcher, blend together the garlic, olive oil, vinegar, paprika, cayenne pepper and salt.

3 Pour the dressing over the salad and serve immediately.

V

Orange and Water Chestnut Salad

*Crunchy water chestnuts combine
with radicchio or red lettuce and
oranges in this unusual salad.*

INGREDIENTS

Serves 4

1 red onion, thinly sliced
    into rings
2 oranges, peeled and cut into segments
1 can drained water chestnuts, peeled and
    cut into strips
2 radicchio heads, cored, or 1 red-leaf
    lettuce, leaves separated
3 tablespoons chopped fresh parsley
3 tablespoons chopped fresh basil
1 tablespoon white wine vinegar
2 fluid ounces/¼ cup walnut oil
salt and ground black pepper
1 fresh basil sprig, to garnish

1 Put the onion in a colander
and sprinkle with 1 teaspoon
salt. Leave to drain for 15 minutes.

2 In a large mixing bowl
combine the oranges and
water chestnuts.

3 Spread out the radicchio or
red-leaf lettuce leaves in a
large, shallow bowl or on a
serving platter.

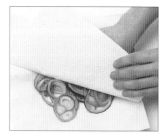

4 Rinse the onion to remove
excess salt and dry on paper
towels. Toss it with the water
chestnuts and oranges.

5 Arrange the water chestnut,
orange and onion mixture on
top of the radicchio or lettuce
leaves. Sprinkle with the chopped
parsley and basil.

6 Put the vinegar, oil and salt
and pepper to taste in a screw-
top jar and shake well to combine.
Pour the dressing over the salad
and serve immediately, garnished
with a sprig of basil.

Plantain and Green Banana Salad

Cook the plantains and bananas in their skins to retain their soft texture. They will then absorb all the flavor of the dressing.

INGREDIENTS

Serves 4

2 firm yellow plantains

3 green bananas

1 garlic clove, crushed

1 red onion

1–2 tablespoons chopped
    fresh cilantro

3 tablespoons sunflower oil

1½ tablespoons malt vinegar

salt and ground black pepper

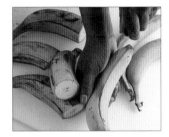

1 Slit the plantains and bananas lengthwise along their natural ridges, then cut in half and place in a large pan.

2 Cover the plantains and bananas with water, add a little salt and bring to the boil. Boil gently for 20 minutes, until tender, then remove from the water. When they are cool enough to handle, peel and cut into medium-size slices.

3 Put the plantain and banana slices into a bowl and add the garlic, turning them with a wooden spoon to distribute the garlic evenly.

4 Halve the onion and slice thinly. Add to the bowl with the cilantro, oil and vinegar and season with salt and pepper to taste. Toss together to mix, then transfer to a serving bowl.

PASTA,
NOODLE
AND LEGUME
SALADS

These are substantial salads with plenty of texture. They
make good main-course dishes but are equally
delicious served in smaller quantities, as appetizers and
accompaniments. Great family favorites, pasta salads are
especially popular with children if you use interesting shapes.
Noodle salads, particularly with exotic dressings, ring a
welcome change at mealtimes, while salads made with legumes
are the perfect choice in the winter, when the more usual
green vegetables are not in season.

V

Pasta, Avocado, Tomato and Cheese Salad

This popular salad is made from ingredients representing the colors of the Italian flag – a sunny, cheerful dish! The addition of pasta turns it into a main-course meal for a light summer lunch.

INGREDIENTS

Serves 4

6 ounces pasta bows (farfalle)
6 ripe red tomatoes
8 ounces mozzarella cheese
1 large ripe avocado
2 tablespoons chopped fresh basil
2 tablespoons pine nuts, toasted
fresh basil sprig, to garnish

For the dressing

6 tablespoons olive oil
2 tablespoons wine vinegar
1 teaspoon balsamic vinegar (optional)
1 teaspoon whole-grain mustard
pinch of sugar
salt and ground black pepper

1 Cook the pasta bows in in a large pan of lightly salted, boiling water until *al dente*.

2 Slice the tomatoes and mozzarella cheese into thin round shapes.

3 Halve the avocado, remove the pit and peel off the skin. Slice the flesh lengthwise.

4 To make the dressing, whisk the oil, vinegars, mustard and sugar in a small bowl and season to taste with salt and pepper.

5 Arrange the tomato, mozzarella and avocado slices in overlapping slices around the edge of a flat serving plate.

6 Toss the pasta with half of the dressing and the chopped basil. Pile into the center of the plate. Pour over the remaining dressing, sprinkle over the pine nuts and garnish with a sprig of fresh basil. Serve immediately.

COOK'S TIP

The pale green flesh of the avocado quickly discolors once it is cut. Prepare it at the last minute and place immediately in dressing. If you do have to prepare it ahead, squeeze lemon juice over the cut side and cover with plastic wrap.

Pasta, Olive and Avocado Salad

The ingredients of this salad are united by a wonderful sun-dried tomato and fresh basil dressing.

INGREDIENTS

Serves 6

8 ounces pasta spirals (fusilli) or other
    small pasta shapes
4 ounces can corn, drained, or frozen
    corn, thawed
½ red bell pepper, seeded and diced
8 black olives, pitted and sliced
3 scallions, finely chopped
2 medium avocados

For the dressing

2 sun-dried tomato halves, loose-packed
    (not preserved in oil)
1½ tablespoons balsamic or white
    wine vinegar
1½ tablespoons red wine vinegar
½ garlic clove, crushed
½ teaspoon salt
5 tablespoons olive oil
1 tablespoon chopped fresh basil

1 To make the dressing, drop the sun-dried tomatoes into a small pan containing 1-inch boiling water and simmer for about 3 minutes, until tender. Drain and chop finely.

2 Process the sun-dried tomatoes, both types of vinegar, garlic and salt in a food processor. With the machine running, add the olive oil in a stream. Stir in the basil.

3 Cook the pasta in a large pan of lightly salted, boiling water until *al dente*. Drain well. In a large bowl, combine the pasta, corn, red pepper, black olives and scallions. Add the dressing and toss well to mix.

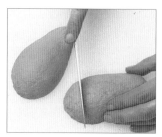

4 Just before serving, peel and pit the avocados and cut the flesh into cubes. Gently stir the cubes into the pasta mixture, then transfer the salad to a large serving dish. Serve immediately at room temperature.

Pasta, Asparagus and Potato Salad

V

Made with whole-wheat pasta, this delicious salad is a real treat, especially when made with fresh asparagus just in season.

INGREDIENTS

Serves 4

8 ounces whole-wheat pasta shapes

4 tablespoons extra virgin olive oil

12 ounces baby new potatoes

8 ounces asparagus

4 ounces piece Parmesan cheese

salt and ground black pepper

1 Cook the pasta in lightly salted, boiling water until *al dente*.

2 Drain well and toss with the olive oil while the pasta is still warm. Season with salt and ground black pepper.

3 Scrub the potatoes and cook in salted, boiling water for about 15 minutes, or until tender. Drain the potatoes and toss together with the pasta.

4 Trim any woody ends off the asparagus and halve the stalks if very long. Blanch in salted, boiling water for 6 minutes, until bright green and still crunchy. Drain. Plunge into cold water to stop the asparagus from cooking and leave to cool. Drain and dry on paper towels.

5 Toss the asparagus with the potatoes and pasta, adjust the seasoning to taste and transfer to a shallow serving bowl. Using a vegetable peeler, thinly shave the Parmesan over the salad.

V

Roquefort and Walnut Pasta Salad

This is a simple, earthy salad, relying totally on the quality of the ingredients. There is no real substitute for the Roquefort – a blue-veined ewe's-milk cheese from southwestern France.

INGREDIENTS

Serves 4

8 ounces pasta shapes
selection of salad leaves such as
    arugula, frisée lettuce, mâche,
    baby spinach, radicchio
2 tablespoons walnut oil
4 tablespoons sunflower oil
2 tablespoons red wine vinegar or
    sherry vinegar
8 ounces Roquefort cheese,
    coarsely crumbled
4 ounces/1 cup walnut halves
salt and ground black pepper

3 Pile the pasta in the center of the salad leaves, sprinkle over the crumbled Roquefort and pour over the dressing.

4 Sprinkle the walnuts over the top. Toss the salad just before serving at room temperature.

1 Cook the pasta in plenty of salted, boiling water until *al dente*. Drain well and cool. Place the salad leaves in a bowl.

2 Whisk together the walnut oil, sunflower oil and vinegar. Season with salt and pepper to taste.

COOK'S TIP

Toast the walnuts under the broiler to add extra flavor.

Roast Bell Pepper and Mushroom Pasta Salad

V

A combination of grilled bell peppers and two different kinds of mushroom makes this salad colorful as well as nutritious.

INGREDIENTS

Serves 6

1 red bell pepper, halved
1 yellow bell pepper, halved
1 green bell pepper, halved
12 ounces whole-wheat pasta shells
2 tablespoons olive oil
3 tablespoons balsamic vinegar
5 tablespoons tomato juice
2 tablespoons chopped fresh basil
1 tablespoon chopped fresh thyme
6 ounces/2¼ cups shiitake
    mushrooms, diced
6 ounces/2¼ cups oyster
    mushrooms, sliced
14-ounce can black-eyed peas,
    drained and rinsed
4 ounces/¾ cup golden raisins
2 bunches of scallions,
    finely chopped
salt and ground black pepper

1 Preheat the broiler to hot. Put the peppers cut-side down on a broiler-pan rack and place under the broiler for 10–15 minutes, until the skins are charred. Cover the peppers with a clean, damp dish towel and set aside to cool.

2 Meanwhile, cook the pasta shells in a large pan of lightly salted, boiling water until *al dente*, then drain thoroughly.

3 Mix together the oil, vinegar, tomato juice, basil and thyme, add to the warm pasta and toss.

4 Remove and discard the skins from the peppers. Seed and slice and add to the pasta.

5 Add the mushrooms, beans, golden raisins, scallions and seasoning. Toss the ingredients to mix and serve immediately. Alternatively, cover with plastic wrap and chill in the refrigerator before serving.

Mediterranean Pasta Salad

A type of Salade Niçoise with pasta, conjuring up all the sunny flavors of the Mediterranean.

INGREDIENTS

Serves 4

8 ounces chunky pasta shapes
6 ounces fine green beans
2 large ripe tomatoes
2 ounces fresh basil leaves
7 ounces can tuna in oil, drained
2 hard-boiled eggs, shelled and sliced
   or quartered
2 ounces can anchovy fillets, drained
capers and black olives, to taste

For the dressing
90ml/6 tablespoons extra virgin olive oil
2 tablespoons white wine vinegar or
   lemon juice
2 garlic cloves, crushed
2.5ml/½ teaspoon Dijon mustard
2 tablespoons chopped fresh basil
salt and ground black pepper

1 To make the dressing, whisk all the ingredients together in a small bowl. Leave to steep while you prepare the salad.

> ### COOK'S TIP
>
> Don't be tempted to chill this salad – the flavor will be dulled.

2 Cook the pasta in plenty of salted, boiling water until *al dente*. Drain well and cool.

3 Trim the green beans and blanch in lightly salted, boiling water for 3 minutes. Drain and refresh in cold water.

4 Slice the tomatoes and arrange on the base of a serving bowl. Moisten with a little dressing and cover with a quarter of the basil leaves. Then cover with the beans. Moisten with a little more dressing and cover with a third of the remaining basil.

5 Cover the vegetables with the pasta tossed in a little more dressing, half the remaining basil and the coarsely flaked tuna.

6 Arrange the eggs on top, then finally sprinkle over the anchovy fillets, capers and olives. Spoon over the remaining dressing and garnish with the remaining basil. Serve immediately.

Smoked Bacon and Green Bean Pasta Salad

A tasty pasta salad, subtly flavored
with smoked bacon.

INGREDIENTS

Serves 4

12 ounces whole-wheat pasta twists
8 ounces green beans
8 strips smoked bacon
2 bunches of scallions
12 ounces cherry tomatoes, halved
14 ounces can chickpeas, drained

For the dressing

6 tablespoons tomato juice
2 tablespoons balsamic vinegar
1 teaspoon ground cumin
1 teaspoon ground coriander
2 tablespoons chopped fresh cilantro
salt and ground black pepper

2 Preheat the broiler and cook
the bacon for 2–3 minutes
on each side. Dice and add to
the beans.

3 Chop the scallions and put
them in a large bowl with the
tomatoes and chickpeas. In a small
bowl, mix together the tomato
juice, vinegar, spices, fresh cilantro
and seasoning.

4 Pour the dressing into the
large bowl. Drain the cooked
pasta thoroughly and add to the
tomato mixture with the green
beans and bacon. Toss all the
ingredients together to mix
thoroughly. Serve warm or cold.

1 Cook the pasta in a large pan of
lightly salted, boiling water until
al dente. Meanwhile, trim and halve
the green beans and cook them in
boiling water for about 5 minutes,
until tender. Drain thoroughly and
keep warm.

COOK'S TIP

Always rinse canned beans and
pulses well before using, to
remove as much of the brine
(salt water) as possible.

Deviled Ham and Pineapple Salad

This tasty salad, with a crunchy topping of toasted almonds, can be quickly prepared. It is delicious served with rustic bread.

INGREDIENTS

Serves 4

8 ounces whole-wheat penne

¼ pint/⅔ cup plain yogurt

1 tablespoon cider vinegar

1 teaspoon whole-grain mustard

large pinch of superfine sugar

2 tablespoons hot mango chutney

4 ounces cooked lean ham, cubed

7-ounce can pineapple chunks, drained

2 celery sticks, chopped

½ green bell pepper, seeded and diced

1 tablespoon toasted sliced almonds,
    coarsely chopped

salt and ground black pepper

1 Cook the pasta in a large pan of salted boiling water until *al dente*. Drain and rinse thoroughly. Leave to cool.

2 To make the dressing, mix the yogurt, vinegar, mustard, sugar and mango chutney together. Season with salt and pepper. Add the pasta and toss lightly together.

3 Transfer the pasta to a serving dish. Add the ham, pineapple, celery and green bell pepper.

4 Sprinkle the toasted almonds over the top of the salad to garnish. Serve immediately.

Spicy Pasta and Chicken Salad

Marinate the chicken in advance for this tasty salad, which is otherwise quick to prepare.

INGREDIENTS

Serves 6

1 teaspoon ground cumin seeds
1 teaspoon paprika
1 teaspoon ground turmeric
1–2 garlic cloves, crushed
2 tablespoons lime juice
4 skinless, boneless chicken breast portions
8 ounces rigatoni
1 red bell pepper, seeded and chopped
2 celery sticks, thinly sliced
1 shallot or small onion, finely chopped
1 ounce/¼ cup stuffed green
   olives, halved
2 tablespoons clear honey
1 tablespoon whole-grain mustard
1–2 tablespoons lime juice
mixed salad leaves
salt and ground black pepper

1 Mix the cumin, paprika, turmeric, garlic and lime juice in a bowl. Season with salt and pepper. Rub this mixture over the chicken portions. Lay these in a shallow dish, cover with plastic wrap and leave in a cool place for 3 hours or overnight.

2 Preheat the oven to 400°F. Put the chicken on a broiler rack and bake for 20 minutes. (Alternatively broil for 8–10 minutes on each side.)

3 Cook the rigatoni pasta in a large pan of lightly salted, boiling water until *al dente*. Drain and rinse under cold water. Leave to drain thoroughly.

4 Put the red bell pepper, celery, shallot or small onion and olives into a large bowl with the pasta. Mix together.

5 Mix the honey, mustard and lime juice together in a small bowl and pour over the pasta mixture. Toss to coat.

6 Cut the chicken into bitesize pieces. Arrange the mixed salad leaves on a serving dish, spoon the pasta mixture into the center and top with the spicy chicken pieces.

Smoked Trout Pasta Salad

The little pasta shells catch the trout creating tasty mouthfuls.

INGREDIENTS

Serves 8

½ ounce/1 tablespoon butter

6 ounces/1 cup minced bulb fennel

6 scallions, 2 minced and the rest
thinly sliced

8 ounces skinless smoked trout
fillets, flaked

3 tablespoons chopped fresh dill

4 fluid ounces/½ cup mayonnaise

2 teaspoons fresh lemon juice

2 tablespoons whipping cream

1 pound/4 cups small pasta shapes

salt and ground black pepper

fresh dill sprigs, to garnish

1 Melt the butter in a small pan. Cook the minced fennel and scallions for 3–5 minutes. Transfer to a large bowl and cool slightly.

2 Add the sliced scallions, trout, dill, mayonnaise, lemon juice and cream. Season with salt and pepper and mix.

3 Bring a large pan of lightly salted water to the boil and add the pasta. Cook according to the instructions on the packet until just *al dente*. Drain thoroughly and leave to cool.

4 Add the pasta to the vegetable and trout mixture and toss to coat evenly. Taste for seasoning. Serve the salad lightly chilled or at room temperature, garnished with sprigs of dill.

Smoked Trout and Noodle Salad

It is important to use ripe, juicy tomatoes for this fresh-tasting salad. For a special occasion you could use smoked salmon.

Serves 4

8 ounces somen noodles

2 smoked trout, skinned and boned

2 hard-boiled eggs, coarsely chopped

2 tablespoons chopped fresh chives

lime halves, to serve (optional)

For the dressing

6 ripe plum tomatoes

2 shallots, finely chopped

2 tablespoons tiny capers, rinsed

2 tablespoons chopped fresh tarragon

finely grated rind and juice of ¹/₂ orange

4 tablespoons extra virgin olive oil

salt and ground black pepper

1 To make the dressing, cut the tomatoes in half, remove the cores and cut the flesh into chunks.

2 Place in a bowl with the shallots, capers, tarragon, orange rind and juice and olive oil. Season with salt and pepper and mix well. Leave to marinate at room temperature for 1–2 hours.

3 Cook the noodles in a large pan of boiling water, following the directions on the packet, until just tender. Drain and rinse under cold running water. Drain well.

4 Toss the noodles with the dressing, then adjust the seasoning to taste. Arrange the noodles on a large serving platter or individual plates.

5 Flake the smoked trout over the noodles, then sprinkle the eggs and chives over the top. Serve, with lime halves on the side of the plate, if you like.

Noodles with Pineapple, Ginger and Chiles

A coconut, lime and fish sauce dressing is the perfect partner to this fruity and spicy salad.

Serves 4

10 ounces dried udon noodles

½ pineapple, peeled, cored and sliced into 1½-inch rings

3 tablespoons soft light brown sugar

4 tablespoons lime juice

4 tablespoons coconut milk

2 tablespoons Thai fish sauce

2 tablespoons grated fresh root ginger

2 garlic cloves, finely chopped

1 ripe mango or 2 peaches peeled, pitted and finely diced

ground black pepper

2 scallions, finely sliced, 2 fresh red chiles, seeded and finely shredded, and fresh mint leaves, to garnish

1 Cook the noodles in a large pan of boiling water until tender, following the directions on the packet. Drain, refresh under cold water and drain again.

2 Place the pineapple rings in a flameproof dish, sprinkle with 2 tablespoons of the sugar and broil for about 5 minutes, or until golden. Cool slightly and cut into small dice.

3 Mix the lime juice, coconut milk and fish sauce in a salad bowl. Add the remaining brown sugar with the ginger, garlic and black pepper and whisk well. Add the noodles and pineapple.

4 Add the mango or peaches and toss. Sprinkle over the scallions, chiles and mint leaves before serving.

Buckwheat Noodles with Smoked Salmon

Young pea sprouts are available for only a short time. You can substitute watercress, salad cress, young leeks or your favorite green vegetable or herb in this dish.

Serves 4

8 ounces buckwheat or soba noodles

1 tablespoon oyster sauce

juice of ½ lemon

2–3 tablespoons light olive oil

4 ounces smoked salmon, cut into fine strips

4 ounces young pea sprouts

2 ripe tomatoes, peeled, seeded and cut into strips

1 tablespoon chopped chives

ground black pepper

1 Cook the buckwheat or soba noodles in a large pan of boiling water until tender, following the directions on the packet. Drain, then rinse under cold running water and drain well.

2 Tip the noodles into a large bowl. Add the oyster sauce and lemon juice and season with pepper to taste. Moisten the noodles with the olive oil.

3 Add the smoked salmon, pea sprouts, tomatoes and chives. Mix well and serve immediately.

V

Thai Noodle Salad

The addition of coconut milk and sesame oil gives an unusual nutty flavor to the dressing for this colorful noodle salad.

INGREDIENTS

Serves 4–6

12 ounces somen noodles

1 large carrot, cut into thin strips

1 bunch of asparagus, trimmed and cut
   into 1½-inch lengths

1 red bell pepper, seeded and cut into
   fine strips

4 ounces snow peas, trimmed and halved

4 ounces baby corn cobs,
   halved lengthwise

4 ounces beansprouts

4 ounces can water chestnuts, drained and
   thinly sliced

lime wedges, 2 ounces/½ cup roasted
   peanuts, coarsely chopped, and fresh
   cilantro leaves, to garnish

For the dressing

3 tablespoons coarsely torn fresh basil

5 tablespoons coarsely chopped
   fresh mint

8 fluid ounces/1 cup coconut milk

2 tablespoons dark sesame oil

1 tablespoon grated fresh root ginger

2 garlic cloves, finely chopped

juice of 1 lime

2 scallions, finely chopped

salt and cayenne pepper

1 To make the dressing, combine
   all the ingredients in a bowl
and mix well. Season to taste with
salt and cayenne pepper.

2 Cook the noodles in a pan of
   boiling water, following the
directions on the packet, until just
tender. Drain, rinse under cold
running water and drain again.

3 Cook all the vegetables, except
   the water chestnuts, in
separate pans of boiling, lightly
salted water until they are tender,
but still crisp. Drain, plunge them
immediately into cold water and
drain again.

4 Toss the noodles, vegetables,
   water chestnuts and dressing
together. Arrange on individual
serving plates and garnish with the
lime wedges, chopped peanuts and
cilantro leaves.

Shrimp Noodle Salad with Fragrant Herbs

A light, refreshing salad with all the tangy flavor of the sea. Instead of shrimp, you can also use squid, scallops, mussels or crab.

INGREDIENTS

Serves 4

4 ounces cellophane noodles, soaked in
   hot water until soft
1 small green bell pepper, seeded and cut
   into strips
½ cucumber, cut into strips
1 tomato, cut into strips
2 shallots, thinly sliced
16 cooked peeled shrimp
salt and ground black pepper
fresh cilantro leaves, to garnish

For the dressing
1 tablespoon rice wine vinegar
2 tablespoons Thai fish sauce
2 tablespoons lime juice
½ teaspoon grated fresh root ginger
1 lemon grass stalk, finely chopped
1 fresh red chile, seeded and finely sliced
2 tablespoons coarsely chopped
   fresh mint
few tarragon,sprigs coarsely chopped
1 tablespoon chopped fresh chives

1 To make the dressing, combine all the ingredients in a small bowl or pitcher and whisk.

2 Drain the noodles, then plunge them into a pan of boiling water for 1 minute. Drain, rinse under cold running water and drain again well.

3 In a large bowl, combine the noodles with the green bell pepper, cucumber, tomato and shallots. Lightly season with salt and pepper, then toss with the dressing.

COOK'S TIP

Shrimp are available ready-cooked and often peeled. To cook shrimp, boil them for 5 minutes. Leave them to cool in the cooking liquid, then gently pull off the tail shell and twist off the head.

4 Spoon the noodles onto individual serving plates, arranging the shrimp on top. Garnish with a few cilantro leaves and serve immediately.

Egg Noodle Salad with Sesame Chicken

Quickly stir-fried chicken is served warm in a nest of noodles.

INGREDIENTS

Serves 4–6

14 ounces fresh thin egg noodles
1 carrot, cut into long fine strips
2 ounces snow peas, cut into fine strips
    and blanched
4 ounces/½ cup beansprouts, blanched
2 tablespoons olive oil
8 ounces skinless, boneless chicken breast
    portions, thinly sliced
2 tablespoons sesame seeds, toasted
2 scallions, finely sliced diagonally,
    and fresh cilantro leaves,
    to garnish

For the dressing
3 tablespoons sherry vinegar
5 tablespoons soy sauce
4 tablespoons sesame oil
6 tablespoons light olive oil
1 garlic clove, finely chopped
1 teaspoon grated fresh root ginger
salt and ground black pepper

1 To make the dressing, whisk together all the ingredients in a small bowl. Season to taste.

2 Cook the noodles in a large pan of boiling water. Stir them occasionally to separate. They will take only a few minutes to cook; be careful not to overcook them. Drain the noodles, rinse under cold running water and drain well. Tip into a bowl.

3 Add the carrot, snow peas and bean sprouts to the noodles. Pour in about half the dressing, then toss the mixture well and adjust the seasoning according to taste.

4 Heat the oil in a large frying pan. Add the chicken and stir-fry for 3 minutes, or until cooked and golden. Remove from the heat. Add the sesame seeds and drizzle in some of the remaining dressing.

5 Arrange the noodle mixture on individual serving plates, making a nest on each plate. Spoon the chicken on top. Sprinkle with the scallions and cilantro leaves and serve any remaining dressing separately.

Sesame Duck and Noodle Salad

This salad is complete in itself and makes a lovely summer lunch. The marinade is a marvelous blend of Asian flavors.

Serves 4

2 boneless duck breasts
1 tablespoon oil
5 ounces sugar snap peas
2 carrots, cut into 3-inch sticks
8 ounces medium egg noodles
6 scallions, sliced
salt
2 tablespoons fresh cilantro leaves,
    to garnish

For the marinade
1 tablespoon sesame oil
1 teaspoon ground coriander
1 teaspoon Chinese five-spice powder

For the dressing
1 tablespoon rice wine vinegar
1 teaspoon soft light brown sugar
1 teaspoon soy sauce
1 garlic clove, crushed
1 tablespoon sesame seeds, toasted
3 tablespoons sunflower oil
2 tablespoons sesame oil
ground black pepper

1 Slice the duck breasts thinly across and place in a shallow dish. Mix together the ingredients for the marinade, pour over the duck and turn well to coat thoroughly. Cover with plastic wrap and leave in a cool place for 30 minutes.

2 Heat the oil in a frying pan, add the slices of duck breast and stir-fry for 3–4 minutes, until cooked. Set aside.

3 Bring a pan of lightly salted water to the boil. Place the sugar snap peas and carrots in a steamer that will fit on top of the pan. When the water boils, add the noodles. Place the steamer on top and steam the vegetables while cooking the noodles.

4 Set the steamed vegetables aside. Drain the noodles, refresh under cold running water and drain again. Place them in a large serving bowl.

5 To make the dressing, mix the vinegar, sugar, soy sauce, garlic and sesame seeds in a bowl. Add a generous grinding of pepper, then whisk in the oils.

6 Pour the dressing over the noodles and mix well. Add the peas, carrots, scallions and duck slices and toss to mix. Sprinkle the cilantro leaves over the top and serve immediately.

V

Peppery Bean Salad

This pretty salad uses canned beans for speed and convenience.

INGREDIENTS

Serves 4–6

15-ounce can red kidney beans
15-ounce can black-eyed peas
15-ounce can chickpeas
¼ red bell pepper
¼ green bell pepper
6 radishes
2 scallions, chopped

For the dressing
1 teaspoon ground cumin
1 tablespoon tomato ketchup
2 tablespoons olive oil
1 tablespoon white wine vinegar
1 garlic clove, crushed
½ teaspoon hot pepper sauce

1 Drain the canned red kidney beans, black-eyed peas and chickpeas and rinse well under cold running water. Shake off the excess water and tip them into a large bowl.

2 Core, seed and chop the red and green bell peppers. Trim the radishes and slice thinly. Add the bell peppers, radishes and scallions to the beans.

3 Mix together the cumin, tomato ketchup, oil, vinegar and garlic in a small bowl. Add a little salt and hot pepper sauce to taste and stir again thoroughly.

4 Pour the dressing over the salad and mix. Chill the salad for at least 1 hour before serving, garnished with extra slices of scallion.

Green Green Salad

You could make this dish any time of the year with frozen vegetables and still get a pretty salad.

INGREDIENTS

Serves 4

6 ounces shelled fava beans

4 ounces green beans, quartered

4 ounces snow peas

8–10 small fresh mint leaves

3 scallions, chopped

For the dressing

4 tablespoons green olive oil

1 tablespoon cider vinegar

1 tablespoon chopped fresh mint

1 garlic clove, crushed

salt and ground black pepper

1 Plunge the fava beans into a pan of boiling water and bring back to the boil. Remove from the heat immediately and plunge into cold water. Drain. Repeat with the green beans.

COOK'S TIP

Frozen fava beans are a good stand-by, but for this salad it is worth shelling fresh beans for the extra flavor.

2 In a large bowl, mix the blanched fava beans and green beans with the raw snow peas, mint leaves and scallions.

3 In another bowl, mix together the olive oil, vinegar, chopped or dried mint, garlic and salt and pepper. Pour over the salad and toss well. Chill until ready to serve.

V

White Bean and Celery Salad

This simple bean salad is a delicious
alternative to the potato salad that
seems to appear on every salad
menu. If you do not have time to
soak and cook dried beans, you can
use canned ones.

INGREDIENTS

Serves 4

1 pound dried white beans (navy,
    cannellini or lima beans) or
    3 x 14-ounce cans white beans
1¾ pints/4 cups Vegetable Stock
3 celery sticks, cut into 1cm/½in strips
4 fluid ounces/½ cup French Dressing
3 tablespoons chopped fresh parsley
salt and ground black pepper

3 Place the cooked beans in a
large pan. Add the vegetable
stock and celery, bring to the boil,
cover and simmer for 15 minutes.
Drain thoroughly. Moisten the
beans with the French dressing and
leave to cool.

4 Add the chopped parsley and
mix. Season to taste with salt
and pepper, transfer to a salad
bowl and serve.

1 If you are using dried beans,
cover them with plenty of cold
water and soak for at least 4 hours.
Discard the soaking water, then
place the beans in a heavy pan.
Cover with water.

2 Bring to the boil and simmer
without a lid for 1½ hours, or
until the skins are broken. Cooked
beans will squash readily between
a thumb and forefinger. Drain the
beans. If using canned beans, drain
and rinse.

Smoked Ham and Bean Salad

A fairly substantial salad that should be served in small quantities if intended as an accompaniment.

Serves 8

6 ounces black-eyed peas

1 onion

1 carrot

8 ounces smoked ham, diced

3 tomatoes, peeled, seeded and diced

salt and ground black pepper

For the dressing

2 garlic cloves, crushed

3 tablespoons olive oil

3 tablespoons red wine vinegar

2 tablespoons vegetable oil

1 tablespoon lemon juice

1 tablespoon chopped fresh or 1 teaspoon dried basil

1 tablespoon whole-grain mustard

1 teaspoon soy sauce

1/2 teaspoon dried oregano

1/2 teaspoon superfine sugar

1/4 teaspoon Worcestershire sauce

1/2 teaspoon chili sauce

1 Soak the beans in cold water to cover overnight. Drain.

2 Put the beans in a large pan and add the onion and carrot. Cover with fresh cold water and bring to the boil. Lower the heat and simmer for about 1 hour, until the beans are tender.

3 Drain the beans, reserving the onion and carrot. Transfer the beans to a salad bowl.

4 Finely chop the onion and carrot. Toss with the beans. Stir in the ham and tomatoes.

5 For the dressing, combine all the ingredients in a small bowl and whisk to mix.

6 Pour the dressing over the ham and beans. Season with salt and pepper. Toss to combine, then serve.

FISH, MEAT AND POULTRY SALADS

If you ever doubted that salads could be considered culinary
masterpieces, the recipes here will certainly convince you of
their true splendor. Fish and shellfish, steak and chicken,
ham and bacon are combined with tropical fruit, tender
vegetables or crisp salad leaves, then served with a "designer"
dressing to complement them perfectly. Whether classic salads
or imaginative innovations, these are dishes for a special
occasion and a cause for celebration in themselves.

Thai Scented Fish Salad

For a tropical taste of the Far East, try this delicious fish salad scented with coconut, exotic fruits and warm Thai spices.

INGREDIENTS

Serves 4

12 ounces red mullet or snapper fillets
1 romaine lettuce
½ lollo biondo lettuce
1 papaya or mango, peeled and sliced
1 pithaya, peeled and sliced
1 large ripe tomato, cut into wedges
½ cucumber, peeled and cut
   into strips
3 scallions, sliced

For the marinade
1 teaspoon coriander seeds
1 teaspoon fennel seeds
½ teaspoon cumin seeds
1 teaspoon superfine sugar
½ teaspoon hot chili sauce
2 tablespoons garlic oil
salt

For the dressing
4 tablespoons coconut cream
4 tablespoons safflower oil
finely grated rind and juice of
   1 lime
1 fresh red chile, seeded and chopped
1 teaspoon sugar
3 tablespoons chopped fresh cilantro

1 Cut the fish into even strips and place them on a plate or in a shallow bowl.

2 To make the marinade, crush the coriander, fennel and cumin seeds together with the sugar. Add the chili sauce, garlic oil and salt and combine.

3 Spread the marinade over the fish, cover with plastic wrap and leave to stand in a cool place for at least 20 minutes.

4 To make the dressing, place the coconut cream, safflower oil, lime rind and juice, chopped red chile, sugar and chopped cilantro in a screw-top jar. Screw on the lid, shake the jar well to combine the ingredients, then set aside.

5 Combine the lettuce leaves with the papaya or mango, pithaya, tomato, cucumber and scallions. Toss with the dressing, then distribute among four large serving plates.

6 Heat a large non-stick frying-pan, add the fish and cook for 5 minutes, turning once. Place the cooked fish over the salad and serve immediately.

COOK'S TIPS

If planning ahead, you can leave the fish in the marinade for up to 8 hours. The dressing can also be made in advance, minus the fresh cilantro. Store at room temperature and add the cilantro when you are ready to assemble the salad.
Pithaya is also known as dragon fruit. If unavailable, you can replace it with an extra slice of melon.

Shrimp and Artichoke Salad

The mild flavors of shrimp and artichoke hearts are complemented by a zingy herb dressing.

INGREDIENTS

Serves 4

1 garlic clove

2 teaspoons Dijon mustard

4 tablespoons red wine vinegar

¼ pint/⅔ cup olive oil

3 tablespoons shredded fresh basil leaves
    or 2 tablespoons finely chopped
    fresh parsley

1 red onion, very finely sliced

12 ounces cooked peeled shrimp

14-ounce can artichoke hearts

½ iceberg lettuce

salt and ground black pepper

1 Chop the garlic, then crush it to a pulp with 1 teaspoon salt, using the flat edge of a heavy knife blade. Mix the garlic and mustard to a paste in a small bowl.

2 Beat in the vinegar and, finally, the olive oil, beating hard to make a thick, creamy dressing. Season with black pepper and, if necessary, additional salt.

3 Stir the basil or parsley into the dressing, followed by the sliced onion. Leave the mixture to stand for 30 minutes at room temperature, then stir in the shrimp and chill for 1 hour, or until ready to serve.

4 Drain the artichoke hearts and halve each one. Shred the lettuce finely.

5 Make a bed of lettuce on a serving platter or on four individual salad plates and spread the artichoke hearts over it.

6 Immediately before serving, pour the shrimp and their marinade over the top of the salad.

Salade Niçoise

Made with the freshest ingredients, this classic Provençal salad makes a simple yet unbeatable summer dish. Serve with country-style bread and chilled white wine for a substantial appetizer.

INGREDIENTS

Serves 4–6

4 ounces green beans

1 tuna steak, about 6 ounces

olive oil, for brushing

4 ounces mixed salad leaves

½ small cucumber, thinly sliced

4 ripe tomatoes, quartered

2-ounce can anchovies, drained and
 halved lengthwise

4 hard-boiled eggs, quartered

½ bunch radishes, trimmed

2 ounces/½ cup small black olives

salt and ground black pepper

flat leaf parsley, to garnish

For the dressing

6 tablespoons virgin olive oil

2 garlic cloves, crushed

1 tablespoon white wine vinegar

salt and ground black pepper

1 Whisk together the oil, garlic and vinegar, then season to taste with salt and pepper.

2 Preheat the broiler. Brush the tuna steak with olive oil and season with salt and black pepper. Broil for 3–4 minutes on each side until cooked through. Set aside to cool.

3 Trim and halve the green beans. Cook them in a pan of boiling water for 2 minutes, until only just tender, then drain, refresh and leave to cool.

4 Mix together the salad leaves, sliced cucumber, tomatoes and green beans in a large, shallow bowl. Flake the tuna steak with your fingers or two forks.

5 Sprinkle the tuna, anchovies, eggs, radishes and olives over the salad. Pour over the dressing and toss together lightly. Serve garnished with parsley.

San Francisco Salad

California is a salad-maker's paradise and is renowned for the healthiness of its produce. San Francisco has become the salad capital of California, although this recipe is, in fact, based on a salad served at the Chez Panisse restaurant in Berkeley.

INGREDIENTS

Serves 4

2 pounds langoustines or
   jumbo shrimp
2 ounces bulb fennel, sliced
2 ripe medium tomatoes, quartered, and
   4 small tomatoes
2 tablespoons olive oil, plus extra for
   moistening the salad leaves
4 tablespoons brandy
¼ pint/⅔ cup dry white wine
7 fluid ounces can lobster or crab bisque
2 tablespoons chopped fresh tarragon
3 tablespoons heavy cream
8 ounces green beans, trimmed
2 oranges
6 ounces mâche
4 ounces arugula leaves
½ frisée lettuce
salt and cayenne pepper

1 Bring a large pan of salted water to the boil, add the langoustines or jumbo shrimp and simmer for 10 minutes. Refresh under cold running water.

2 Pre-heat the oven to 425°F. Twist off the tails from all but four of the langoustines or jumbo shrimp – reserve these to garnish the dish. Peel the outer shell from the tail meat. Put the tail peelings, carapace and claws, if using langoustines, in a heavy roasting pan with the fennel and medium tomatoes. Toss with the olive oil and roast near the top of the oven for 20 minutes.

3 Remove the roasting pan from the oven and place it over a medium heat on top of the stove. Add the brandy and ignite to release the flavor of the alcohol. Add the wine and simmer briefly.

4 Transfer the contents of the roasting pan to a food processor and process to a coarse purée: this will take 10–15 seconds. Rub the purée through a fine nylon sieve into a bowl. Add the lobster or crab bisque, tarragon and cream. Season to taste with salt and a little cayenne pepper.

5 Bring a pan of salted water to the boil and cook the beans for 6 minutes. Drain and cool under running water. To segment the oranges, cut the peel from the top and bottom, and then from the sides, with a serrated knife. Loosen the segments by cutting between the membranes and the flesh with a small knife.

6 Moisten the salad leaves with olive oil and distribute among four serving plates. Fold the langoustine or jumbo shrimp tails into the dressing and distribute among the plates. Add the beans, orange segments and small tomatoes. Garnish each plate with a whole langoustine or shrimp and serve the salad warm.

Hot Coconut, Shrimp and Papaya Salad

Transport yourself to the Far East with this wonderful dish of juicy papaya and succulent shrimp tails.

INGREDIENTS

Serves 4–6

8 ounces raw or cooked shrimp tails,
    peeled and deveined

2 ripe papayas

8 ounces romaine or iceberg lettuce
    leaves, Chinese cabbage and young
    spinach leaves

1 firm tomato, peeled, seeded and
    coarsely chopped

3 scallions, shredded

1 small bunch fresh cilantro, shredded,
    and 1 large fresh chile, sliced,
    to garnish

For the dressing

3 tablespoons coconut cream

6 tablespoons vegetable oil

juice of 1 lime

½ teaspoon hot chili sauce

2 teaspoons Thai fish sauce (optional)

1 teaspoon sugar

2 If using raw shrimp tails, cover with cold water in a pan, bring to the boil and simmer for no longer than 2 minutes. Drain well and set aside.

3 Cut the papayas in half from top to bottom and remove the black seeds. Peel away the skin and cut the flesh into equal-size pieces.

4 Place the salad leaves in a bowl. Add the shrimp tails, papayas, tomato and scallions. Pour over the dressing, garnish with the cilantro and chile and serve.

1 To make the dressing, place the coconut cream, vegetable oil, lime juice, chili sauce, Thai fish sauce and sugar in a screw-top jar. Screw on the lid, shake the jar well to combine the ingredients, then set aside. Do not chill.

Russian Salad

Russian salad became fashionable in the hotel dining rooms of the 1920s and 1930s. Originally it consisted of lightly-cooked vegetables, egg, shellfish and mayonnaise. Today we find it diced in plastic pots in supermarkets. This version recalls better days and plays on the theme of the Fabergé egg.

INGREDIENTS

Serves 4

4 ounces large white mushrooms
4 fluid ounces/½ cup mayonnaise
1 tablespoon lemon juice
12 ounces cooked peeled shrimp
1 large gherkin, chopped, or
   2 tablespoons capers
4 ounces fava beans (shelled weight)
4 ounces small new potatoes, scrubbed
   or scraped
4 ounces young carrots, trimmed
   and peeled
4 ounces baby corn cobs
4 ounces baby turnips, trimmed
1 tablespoon olive oil
4 eggs, hard-boiled and shelled
1-ounce canned anchovy fillets, drained
   and cut into fine strips
ground paprika
salt, and ground black pepper

1 Slice the mushrooms thinly, then cut into thin matchsticks. Combine the mayonnaise and lemon juice. Fold the mayonnaise into the mushrooms, then add the shrimp, gherkin or capers, and seasoning to taste.

2 Bring a large pan of lightly salted water to the boil, add the fava beans and cook for 3 minutes. Drain and cool under running water, then pinch the beans between thumb and forefinger to release them from their tough skins.

3 Boil the potatoes for about 15 minutes, and the remaining vegetables for 6 minutes. Drain and cool under running water. Moisten the vegetables with oil and divide among four shallow bowls.

4 Spoon on the shrimp mixture and place a hard-boiled egg in the center. Decorate the egg with strips of anchovy, sprinkle with paprika and serve.

Shrimp and Mint Salad

Fresh, uncooked shrimp make all the difference to this salad, as cooking them in butter adds to the piquant flavor. Garnish with shavings of fresh coconut for a tropical topping, if you like.

INGREDIENTS

Serves 4

12 large fresh, raw shrimp
1 tablespoon sweet butter
1 tablespoon Thai fish sauce
juice of 1 lime
3 tablespoons thin coconut milk
1 teaspoon superfine sugar
1 garlic clove, crushed
1-inch piece of fresh root
    ginger, grated
2 red fresh chiles, seeded and chopped
2 tablespoons fresh mint leaves
8 ounces light green lettuce leaves
ground black pepper

1 Carefully peel the raw shrimp, removing and discarding the heads and outer shells, but leaving the tails intact.

2 Using a sharp knife, carefully remove the dark-colored vein that runs along the back of each shrimp.

3 Melt the butter in a large frying pan. When the melted butter is foaming add the shrimp and toss over a high heat until they turn pink. Remove the pan from the heat; it is important not to cook them for too long so that their tenderness is retained.

4 In a small bowl mix the fish sauce, lime juice, coconut milk, sugar, garlic, ginger and chiles together. Season to taste with freshly ground black pepper.

5 Toss the warm shrimp into the sauce with the mint leaves. Arrange the lettuce leaves on a serving plate and place the shrimp and mint mixture in the center.

VARIATION

Instead of shrimp, this dish also works very well with lobster tails if you are feeling very extravagant.

COOK'S TIP

If you can't find any fresh, raw prawns, you could use frozen ones. To make the most of their flavor, toss very quickly in the hot butter when they are completely thawed.

Genoese Squid Salad

This is a good salad for summer, when green beans and new potatoes are at their best. Serve it for a first course or light lunch.

Serves 4–6

1 pound prepared squid, cut into rings
4 garlic cloves, coarsely chopped
½ pint/1¼ cups Italian red wine
1 pound waxy new potatoes, scrubbed
8 ounces green beans, trimmed and cut into short lengths
2–3 sun-dried tomatoes in oil, drained and thinly sliced lengthwise
4 tablespoons extra virgin olive oil
1 tablespoon red wine vinegar
salt and ground black pepper

1 Preheat the oven to 350°F. Put the squid rings in an earthenware dish with half the garlic, the wine and pepper to taste. Cover and cook for 45 minutes, or until the squid is tender.

2 Put the potatoes in a pan, cover with cold water and add a good pinch of salt. Bring to the boil, cover and simmer for about 15 minutes, until tender. Using a slotted spoon, lift out the potatoes and set aside. Add the beans to the boiling water and cook for 3 minutes. Drain.

3 When the potatoes are cool enough to handle, slice them thickly on the diagonal and place them in a bowl with the warm beans and sun-dried tomatoes. Whisk the oil, vinegar and the remaining garlic in a pitcher and add salt and pepper to taste. Pour over the potato mixture.

4 Drain the squid and discard the liquid. Add the squid to the potato mixture and mix very gently. Arrange on individual plates and season liberally with pepper.

COOK'S TIP

The French potato called Charlotte is perfect for this salad because it retains its shape when boiled. Prepared squid can be bought from supermarkets with fresh fish counters.

Tuscan Tuna and Bean Salad

A great pantry dish that can be put together in very little time. Served with rustic bread, this salad makes a meal in itself.

INGREDIENTS

Serves 4

1 red onion

2 tablespoons smooth French mustard

1/2 pint/1 1/4 cups olive oil

4 tablespoons white wine vinegar

2 tablespoons chopped fresh parsley

2 tablespoons chopped fresh chives

2 tablespoons chopped fresh tarragon
   or chervil

14-ounce can navy beans

14-ounce can kidney beans

8 ounces canned tuna in oil, drained and
   lightly flaked

fresh chives and tarragon sprigs,
   to garnish

1 Chop the red onion finely, using a sharp knife.

2 To make the dressing, whisk together the mustard, oil, vinegar, parsley, chives and tarragon or chervil.

3 Drain the navy and kidney beans in a colander, then rinse well in fresh water.

4 Mix the chopped onion, beans and dressing together thoroughly, then carefully fold in the tuna. Garnish with chives and tarragon sprigs and serve.

Mixed Seafood Salad

Use fresh seafood that is in season, or you can use a combination of fresh and frozen seafood.

INGREDIENTS

Serves 6–8

12 ounces small squid
1 small onion, cut into quarters
1 bay leaf
7 ounces raw shrimp, in their shells
1¹/₂ pounds fresh mussels, in
   their shells
1 pound fresh small clams
6 fluid ounces/³/₄ cup white wine
1 fennel bulb

For the dressing

5 tablespoons extra virgin olive oil
3 tablespoons lemon juice
1 garlic clove, finely chopped
salt and ground black pepper

1 Working near the sink, clean the squid by first peeling off the thin skin from the body section. Rinse well.

2 Pull the head and tentacles away from the sac section. Remove and discard the translucent quill and any remaining insides from the sac. Sever the tentacles and head.

3 Discard the head and intestines. Remove the small, hard beak from the base of the tentacles. Rinse the tentacles and sac under cold water. Drain.

4 Bring a large pan of water to the boil. Add the onion and bay leaf. Drop in the squid and cook for about 10 minutes, until tender. Remove with a slotted spoon and leave to cool before slicing into rings ¹/₂-inch wide. Cut each tentacle section into two pieces. Set aside.

5 Drop the shrimp into the same boiling water and cook for about 2 minutes, until they turn pink. Remove with a slotted spoon. Shell and devein. (The cooking liquid may be strained and kept for soup.)

6 Cut the "beards" from the mussels. Scrub and rinse the mussels and clams well in several changes of cold water. Any that are open should close if given a sharp tap; if they fail to do so, discard. Place in a large pan with the wine. Cover and steam until all the shells have opened. (Discard any that do not open.) Lift the clams and mussels out of the pan.

7 Remove all the clams from their shells with a small spoon. Place in a large serving bowl. Remove all but eight of the mussels from their shells and add them to the clams in the bowl. Leave the remaining mussels in their half-shells, and set aside.

8 Cut the green, fronds of the fennel away from the bulb. Chop finely and set aside. Chop the bulb into bitesize pieces and add it to the serving bowl together with the squid and shrimp.

9 To make the dressing, combine the oil, lemon juice and garlic in a bowl. Add the reserved chopped fennel fronds and salt and pepper to taste. Pour over the salad, and toss well. Decorate with the remaining mussels in their half-shells. Serve the salad at room temperature or lightly chilled.

"*Poor Boy*" *Steak Salad*

"Poor Boy" started life in New Orleans when the poor survived on sandwiches filled with left-over scraps. Times have improved since then, and today the "Poor Boy" sandwich is commonly filled with tender beef steak and other goodies. This is a salad version of "Poor Boy".

INGREDIENTS

Serves 4

4 sirloin or round steaks, each about
   6 ounces
1 escarole lettuce
1 bunch of watercress
4 tomatoes, quartered
4 large gherkins, sliced
4 scallions, sliced
4 canned artichoke hearts, halved
6 ounces white mushrooms, sliced
12 green olives
4 fluid ounces/$\frac{1}{2}$ cup French Dressing
salt and ground black pepper

1 Season the steaks with black pepper. Cook under a medium broiler for 6–8 minutes, turning once, until they are medium-rare. Cover and leave to rest in a warm place.

2 Combine the lettuce and watercress leaves with the tomatoes, gherkins, scallions, artichoke hearts, mushrooms and olives and toss with the French Dressing.

3 Divide the salad among four serving plates. Slice each steak diagonally and arrange over the salad. Season to taste with salt and serve immediately.

Mushroom Salad with Prosciutto

Pancake ribbons create a lovely light texture to this salad. Use whatever edible wild mushrooms you can find, or substitute interesting cultivated varieties if you need to.

INGREDIENTS

Serves 4

1½ ounces/3 tablespoons sweet butter
1 pound assorted wild and cultivated
    mushrooms, such as chanterelles, ceps,
    oyster and portabello mushrooms,
    trimmed and sliced
4 tablespoons Madeira or sherry
juice of ½ lemon
½ oak leaf lettuce
½ frisée lettuce
2 tablespoons walnut oil
salt and ground black pepper

For the pancake and ham ribbons
1 ounce/3 tablespoons all-purpose flour
5 tablespoons milk
1 egg
4 tablespoons freshly grated
    Parmesan cheese
4 tablespoons chopped fresh herbs, such
    as parsley, thyme, marjoram or chives
salt and pepper
butter, for frying
6 ounces prosciutto, thickly sliced

1 To make the pancakes, blend the flour and the milk. Beat in the egg, cheese, herbs and some seasoning. Heat the butter in a frying pan and pour enough of the mixture to coat the base. When the batter has set, turn the pancake over and cook until firm.

2 Turn out and cool. Roll up the pancake and slice to make ½-inch ribbons. Cook the remaining batter the same way and cut the prosciutto into similar size ribbons. Toss with the pancake ribbons. Set aside.

3 Gently soften the mushrooms in the butter for 6–8 minutes until the moisture has evaporated. Add the Madeira or sherry and lemon juice and season.

4 Toss the salad leaves in the oil and arrange on four plates. Place the prosciutto and pancake ribbons in the center, spoon on the mushrooms and serve.

Wilted Spinach and Bacon Salad

The hot dressing wilts the spinach and provides a taste sensation.

Serves 6

1 pound fresh young spinach leaves

8 ounces fatty bacon strips

1 1/2 tablespoons vegetable oil

4 tablespoons red wine vinegar

4 tablespoons water

4 teaspoon superfine sugar

1 teaspoon dry mustard

8 scallions, thinly sliced

6 radishes, thinly sliced

2 hard-boiled eggs, coarsely grated

salt and ground black pepper

1 Pull any coarse stalks from the spinach leaves and rinse well and pat dry with paper towels. Put the leaves in a large salad bowl.

2 Fry the bacon strips in the oil until crisp and brown. Remove with tongs and drain on paper towels. Reserve the cooking fat in the pan. Chop the bacon and set aside until needed.

3 Combine the vinegar, water, sugar, mustard, and salt and ground black pepper in a bowl and stir until smoothly blended. Add to the fat in the frying pan and stir to mix. Bring the dressing to the boil, stirring constantly.

4 Pour the hot dressing over the spinach leaves. Sprinkle the bacon, scallions, radishes and eggs over and toss, then serve.